Qliphoth

The Complete Series

The Awakening
Flesh Totems & Bone Masks
Infernal Essence
The Draconian Flames
The Black Arts

Arranged by
EDGAR KERVAL
Edited by
TIMOTHY
✦ **BECOME A LIVING GOD**

ORDERS

View a complete catalog at: BecomeALivingGod.com.

DISCLAIMER

Consider this adult knowledge, and not legal or medical advice. Become A Living God is not responsible for consequences of actions. This book is for readers of age 18 or older.

CREDITS

Authors: Edgar Kerval, Dante Miel, Sean Woodward, S. Ben Qayin, Nicholaj De Mattos Frisvold, Black Lotus Kult, Orryelle Defenestrate Bascule, Frater Malus II/XVI, Alexander Dray, Kyle Fite, Ljossál Loðursson, Andi Moon, Sarah Price, Daemon Barzai, Andrew Dixon, R.N. Lant, Angela Edwards, Alexei Dzyuba, Claudio Cesar de Carvalho, Carlos Montenegro, Lukasz Grochocki, Louie Martinié, Tau Palamas, Aion 131, Cort Williams, Chaos Therion, Nemirion 71, Asenath Mason, Kabultiloa Zamradiel, S. Connolly, Brian Dempsey, Anuki Gabual, N:A:O, Typhon Draconis, Matthew Wightman, Necro Magickal, Bo Headlan, Leonard Dewar, Asbjörn Torvol, J.A. Perez

Illustrators: Therion Teth Trismegistos, Hagen Von Tulien, Dolorosa De La Cruz, Orryelle Bascule, Edgar Kerval, Sean Woodward, Andi Moon, Comes Dietrich, Lucas Pandolfelli & Kyle Fite

Co-editors: Edgar Kerval & Timothy Donaghue

Publisher: Become A Living God ✶

𝔗ablet of 𝔐agick

✦

𝔗he 𝒜wakening

Flesh Totems & Bone Masks

Infernal Essence

Draconian Flames

The Black Arts

Qliphoth

The Awakening

QLIPOTH stands as a gateway of *manifestation and no manifestation*, the apotheosis of matter representing the *yoni-phallic* and *solar-lunar* spirituality, the subconscious zones veiled by formulas of sorcery and etheric manifestations. This esoteric journal possesses a sacred elixir formulated in a black atavism of enlightenment and power, hidden behind the scales of the Black Serpent.

EDGAR KERVAL
Colombia ✶

Transcendental Shadow Magic

Dante Miel

T RANSCENDENTAL Shadow Magic is a process the initiate of the Black Arts goes through in order to achieve an awakening of their own shadow self. The shadow can be viewed in Jungian psychological terms, or in meta-magical ways. The basic principal remains the same either way. It is the arduous process of coming to know one's own darker self. Darkness and the shadow are the sources of self-creation.

Darkness exists beyond the realm of the living, on the periphery of ordinary human conscious expression. The shadow is our own personal internal black flame mirror image of this great creative magical force known as darkness. It is more than just a reflection or image of our self, cast outwards beyond our self. It has substance. This substance is a sort of essence of Being. It needs to be charged, consecrated, and empowered. Over the course of time and with much effort on the magician's part, this shadow self can be imbued with consciousness and self-expression.

It is in a very literal sense the double, or doppelganger. It is the source of such legendary things as bio-location, anthropomorphism, and vampirism. The shadow can continue to live on beyond the physical death of the body. However, it is at this point that the double needs to be brought into the self. If the self and the double remain separate, then drastic results can take effect.

The magician must master the self-first and then master the shadow so that the shadow is under the full conscious control of the self as an aspect of that self.

This shadow we speak of also harbors memories and experiences that help to develop the psychological functions of the human mind and intellect. This is the Jungian aspect of it and how it relates to Jungian psychology. It should be obvious to the experienced sorcerer at this point why it is so important to have mastery of the self to pursue this form of magical practice.

This isn't just something to dabble with. Doors can be opened which there after cannot be closed. This is a re-occurring theme in the teachings of the black arts, and rightly so.

By consciously working with the dark art of shadow magic, the magician can manifest changes that may perhaps be unintended. Messing around with spatial forms of magic, the magician can enable unwanted outcomes to slip into manifestation.

This shouldn't be taken as a threatening warning as much as a blessing for positive change, that will by its very nature also involve a lot of very terrifying experiences. However, at the same time, it is a sort of warning to just simply be careful and to be fully aware of what one is dealing with, and the results then can manifest that lie at the periphery of one's understanding. We carry in our hearts the black flame of magical power.

It is the source of all the creativity in us that leads to self- evolution and the manifestation of our magical will power. It is through us that the dark chaotic cosmic void flows through us allowing us to awaken ourselves to our own internal and external self-created divine spark of dark inter-dimensional creative magical force. We are the harbingers of the next lever of dark manifestation in this world. This darkness is not related to juvenile acts of random or premeditated manslaughter or murder.

Nor is it related in any way to physical violence. It is a self- created force. Just as the universe we live in is born out of darkness. So are we. Darkness composes the mass majority of the universe. However, there is not just one universe (uni = one; verse = an interplay of various components making up a whole unit; one whole unit), but rather an entire multi-verse. We are each and every one of us a universe unto ourselves, if not a multi-verse unto ourselves.

Getting familiar with and coming to know one's own shadow allows the individual to work with the deeper levels of Transcendental Shadow Magic. We can work with our shadow in ways unimaginable to the average human being, let alone the average magician.

Especially those caught up in the trap of Right Hand Path dogma, or Western Left Hand Path indoctrination. The human consciousness is key in these workings. There are parallels with shadow and the doppelganger.

The black magician immerses their consciousness into their shadow and exists as one with it. This can be done during sleep in the form of lucid dream magic or while awake. In a waking state the magician casts their consciously imbued shadow out into the nether regions of existence.

This is what most people would refer to as astral projection or out of body experiences. The key difference being that the black magician projects their will power out along with their shadow and guides it with focus and intent.

Most astral travelers just go along with the flow and experience whatever is thrown before them. The black magician deliberately uses their inherent magical force to guide their shadow, or doppelganger, out on journeys to gain knowledge of other dimensions and to empower the self. When the shadow returns to the physical body of the black magician, all of its experiences are brought into the conscious sphere of that person's forefront of knowledge and knowing. ✦

Sean Woodward, *Sorcerer ov the Insect Loa*

The Shadow

Queen of Sirius

Sean Woodward

THE town of Blackmouth lay close to the sea's edge and seemed with the passing of each year to come closer to it. To outsiders it was a quiet, almost sleepy place with little in the way of attractions. It had none of the oriental glamour of Brighton, nor the history of Hastings. It lay close to the borders of Cornwall and for many that alone placed it at the edge of the known world.

Its stretch of beach lay beneath high dark cliffs and offered nothing in the way of harbor or sanctuary to any of the boats that fished this stretch of the coast. It was a town that was lost to the modern age, its scatter of shops still bore hand-painted family names and buses only stopped in the nearby village of Understone. The population was a mix of retired local dignitaries and the occasional university student engaged on a fruitless survey.

The young headed for the cities as quickly as they could and the early morning beach remained empty save for the occasional jogger or fossil hunter.

It would have remained in a fog of obscurity if not for the many stories and legends of strange creatures spotted close to the water's edge that had been told over the years. Other parts of the country had their mysterious big cats, their panthers and leopards. Blackmouth had its sea-folk.

These were a mix of mermaid and mermen stories. Darker in nature to the sirens of the Caribbean, these were like the warrior-mermaid of Warsaw, potent forces of retribution. Descriptions varied but all seemed to possess small horrific details.

It was said that only a few of the hardened old fishermen would travel the cliff path after dark, such was the dread with which the stories filled the locals. There were some who spoke of turning the tales to the town's advantage, of creating a tourist trail down to the cliffs.

Every time this was raised at the town hall it was quickly dismissed. This was something that could never be treated so lightly. Prayers were regularly said for the poor souls who had witnessed such things for none of them would travel far from their homes.

Fortunately for those scarred by what they had seen, the Church of the Magdalene stood close to the town. It too was surrounded by many of its own legends, but these were considered to be far more positive than those of the shoreline. The church was said to have been built under the direction of Sir James Sinclair after he had returned from the first crusades. Together with a nearby preceptory of the order accounted for the majority of land ownership during the 13th century. At the height of its power it collected taxes from the whole county.

With this money he established a library and scriptorium and engaged monks from the nearby abbey to help with the copying of books that Sir James had brought back from the east.

Some of these were said to even contain the script of the Moors. So rare did Sir James consider them that they were encased in metal covers and chained to the walls of the library.

The later custodians of the library had managed to keep a low profile throughout history.

All save for the rector Thomas Absalom, who in the 1920s had added a number of medieval grimoires including the Sixth Book of King Solomon which contained a number of interesting magic squares. To the untrained eye these were nothing more than planetary talismans but to the educated mind of Thomas Absalom they were three-dimensional puzzles that spoke of complex physics. To this collection he had added a number of sub-Saharan anthropological studies regarding different forms of divination and the talismanic structures of tribal dwellings. Thus it became an eclectic collection of works, which unknown to many, held the remaining copies of certain books. I knew of a number of people for whom these would be unbelievable treasures.

Once they would have also interested me. The days when the hermetic corpus of the west was attractive were now long gone. I had no time for the quasi-masonic rituals, the recitation of pages of oaths or even the study of Solomon's planetary talismans. I had been exposed to the raw and direct power of the Loa. It was akin to the link that great Solomonic scholar Mac-Gregor Mathers had made with the secret chiefs of the Golden Dawn or Aleister Crowley in his communion with the masters of the third order. Now these western magicks were like toys, playthings that no longer held my attention.

Increasingly it was a far more African, more primitive form of the esoteric that intrigued me, that walked in my dreams and directed my actions.

It was in a market in Haiti that I had first experienced the touch of the Loa. The man I had thought to be nothing more than an artisan, displaying his artworks made of human skulls and motorcycle parts was much more. He conferred on me the secrets of his bizango society and wrapping a drapo flag around my shoulders, the title of Hougan. He had shown me the simplicity of his work, of the Hoo Queen and the Doo King and how to summon them. Shipping the artwork home was actually more difficult. Soon after the earthquake swallowed the market, taking his works with it. So much changed. It was my final break with years of hermetic tradition, that exposure to a different, simple and more brilliantly illuminated path.

It was my search for the manifestations of the Hoo Queen which led me to the library of the church of the Magdalene originally, for amongst its books it was documented by the Knights of Malta that there existed a secret journal of Sir James. Within its pages was a history of his time in Acre.

There existed pages that he had copied from a manuscript taken from the library of Alexandria. It was one of the few surviving examples of a work that Arab traders had brought from the heart of Africa. For many years I had heard tales of this book and of a statue venerated by its keepers. I had known of Sir James' time in the crusader state and the friendships he had made, but not of his return to England and patronage of Blackmouth's church. Many of the chronicles stated that he had died at the siege of Acre, fighting valiantly at the walled city's breach.

When I first visited Blackmouth, having learned of its library, it was clear that the church had clearly fallen upon hard times in subsequent centuries and although its books had mostly been forgotten, its collection of statues had not.

Much of the exterior stonework was covered in moss and old granite coffins lay scattered at propped up against it. The walls were plain with high, brightly-colored stained glass windows and an ornately carved entrance porch. The low wooden gate was often unlocked and sheltered from the elements by the ancient yew tree to its side.

I had opened the creaking gate carefully and used the deacon's two keys to unlock the main, heavily studded door. Immediately on entering the church the mass of statues imposed themselves upon you, a number bearing the likeness of Sir James' comrades, their Templar banners wrought in marble.

Of all of these, there was one wooden statue that had become legend itself, said to have been carved by one of the original Grand Masters of the order. It was this statue that had originally drawn me to the salt-aired town. It was of the Madonna with child but her skin was the color of night. To me she was a manifestation of the Hoo Queen and it was to her that I was now drawn.

As I had made more frequent trips to Blackmouth, spending many hours in the Red Lion pub, I slowly became aware of a local group of people who held the church and the statue in high regard. It was said by some that the deacon himself was party to this and that at certain times of the year lights could be seen in the chapel in the middle of the night and strange chanting heard.

No matter who I spoke to though, nobody would reveal any more to the story than this. Twice I had been warned off, told nothing good would come of my questions. No doubt my status as an outsider was too great to permit me entrance to their circle. I was also a little suspicious that my primary mode of transport, a Ducati 996 motorbike also contributed to their icy welcome. The first time I had walked into the Red Lion, lunch was no longer being served, the pool table was broken and there was a strict dress code. This initial air of hostility slowly began to fade and gradually the lore of the place began to unfold before me.

I had heard many of these tales before, having researched the history of the town the previous year. It was the statue that had drawn me here, not the strange shoreline stories. I had visited others like it across the world and with each there seemed to be something more to them than simple Christian iconography. After years of study and practice I had awoken my own visionary powers and heard the calling of the Loa.

The associations of Sir James' diary and Africa were intriguing. I knew it would take time to uncover the truths here, to enable me to undertake the rite of the Hoo Queen. For I knew within my bones that it was her who was at the heart of this mystery. It would be easy to source the materials I needed for the rite - a few candles, some flour and solitude. The location had been the hardest part. It had taken a few phone calls, the calling of a few favors, the removal of some old debts. I was never at ease having to deal with the clergy or their minions but at least I still had some acquaintances who could facilitate that. It was never easy in England, but once you had discovered a person's weakness, be it money, vice or pride, it didn't matter what their religious persuasion. And so events were set in motion. And so everything has its time of gestation, of simmering in the cauldron of possibility. I had always known that the ebony Hoo Queen of the Loa had waited patiently below the spirit waves in the sea-forest, rising with the high tide, crossing the waters to the Caribbean, sliding down the tree-poles and taking the form of her human worshipers. I had heard her call in Port-au-Prince, in Havana and in London.

It was fitting that this church should be so close to the sea's edge, so close to the rumors and histories of strange events. For it was in the deep that this Queen of the Loa had first slept, her dark skin covered in heavy fathoms.

Drafts coming from beneath the church's old oak door broke my reverie and had threatened to overwhelm my flour pattern three times already, delicately drawn as it was across the stone floor. The candle at its centre had fared no better, three times had I re-lit it, invoking the name of Legba each time and spilling whiskey in his name. The rite was simple, but drawn out over the hours as it now was, my mind was beginning to become numb, as I fought to concentrate on her image as much as I could.

She stares back at me from her alcove above, the same way she has stared at the faithful for centuries. I could feel the cold brass key in my pocket. By requesting access to the library the deacon had also inadvertently given me access to the knave and the reliquary.

The majesty of my references had blinded him to this and any other objections. It was not often that he had seen the Archbishop's seal and it was not something he would question. So here I am, alone in the church before sunrise, the famous statue staring down at me.

As I speak the last words of the rite, the Queen has crossed the ocean to the delta home of the Yoruba, hovered across the desert plains to the edge of

Europe and descended through the basilica domes of ancient churches and monasteries.

She sits there now, her form contracted into the ebony faced wooden statue above me, its eyes pulsing with scarlet in my second-vision. With that sight I can see the fine web of energies that surround her, that vibrate with the trans-Yuggothian soniks.

I had often wondered how her ways and graces could be felt this far from her home, often wondered why it would take hours of drumming and whiskey before she appeared. As I rose on my second-body from the basilica floor to the lip of its dome and gazed back down at the darkened space below I realized that the Ebony Spirit-Queen had hidden herself in plain sight for all these centuries. It made perfect sense given the way that her transported followers had adopted Catholic masks for the Lwa, but for a long time her true nature had been hidden.

Her black-faced King is the Master of Doo Words, as she is the Mistress of Hoo Signs, keeper of the veves and sigils that call her forth from the depths, that impress upon reality the gateways of the spirits. She takes many forms, with my second- sight I see her body of snakeskin and frog-skin, the shimmer of underwater ways, the faint cloud of air bubbles that envelop her form. As I watch her spirit-body rise from the wooden statue below me, I see it flicker between forms. For a moment she is Kuan Yin, for another she becomes Gai, once again the ebony faced Mary and then finally, her oldest, sea-form. As the bubbles dance around her she whispers in the old blood- language, speaks the words of her King that call him forth to my form. Afar in the second-hearing he gallops across the dunes of North Africa, his neck-gills opening and closing in syncopated rhythm. As he discards his mount, the young boy runs back into the crowded kasbah of Cassablanca, dazed by the journey he has taken, whilst the King steps across the water into Europe, drawing ever closer to this church, riding body after body as each collapses in exhaustion.

I did not know the moment he arrived, such was the speed and complete-ness of his ownership. I simply ceased to be. My last memory was of a cacoph-ony of voices, of slow sounds and backwards words, of layers upon layers of speech, turning in a maelstrom storm of grinding, creaking sounds.

I could not watch objectively from the sidelines, could not hear myself speak with the Queen or know of any of the actions for which my body was used. Like the Moroccan boy, I simply came to my senses once more upon the dark checkered floor of the church, once more the glass cased statue of the Black Madonna before me, the exposed hand shining from the touches of the faithful. Soon other pilgrims would be arriving with the dawn, but for now I had a little time before the vast oak doors were unlocked.

Steadying myself against one of the pews and pulling myself along them, I retrieved my bag and made ready to leave. The lock was open and the cover of my notebook all battered. I opened it carefully and turned to freshly penned pages towards the back, covered in diagrams and veves. I read the words slowly.

She is the Shadow Queen of Sirius, the home of the Loa before they journeyed to the trans-Yugghothian worlds, before they settled in the great forested land of pale bone temples that came to be known as Atlantis. Its lands now drowned it resembles the environment of her childhood home on Sirius-B, a world with ocean moons, a world full of the tunes of dull drums.

Her people had mastered the very forces which bound the stars in space, the planets to their paths amongst the stellar dust. In their obsidian mirrors her priests opened the tangents and trapezoids between times and watched the fate of whole worlds. In the distant world-land that they called Dahom they watched the advent of man, the destruction he wrought upon the planet and the extinction he would very nearly not survive.

They saw their own intervention, the arrival of their Sirian Soniks to the world of Dahom, their Templargram engines that would power man's future time-ships and the snippets of wisdom that would pass down the ages in a pack of cards. They also saw the coming cataclysms for their own world, held so delicately in the pull of stars. Very soon the time would come when they would have to leave, journey to the world of Dahom and complete the prophecies that they foresaw. With each passing cycle of Sirius-A they gathered together the ark of their knowledge, fired their lasers towards distant constellations, giving notice to their kin across the stars. On scarlet beams they wrapped neutrino messages, packets of tri-dimensional data to be encoded into crystals on their arrival at Dahom. Whole cities were stripped back to their bone-frames and folded into Qube constructs. Glittering arrays of information crystals were slotted into computational Qubes the size of small buildings.

High above, abyss monitoring stations hanging on the edge of their atmosphere were turned towards deep space, their radiation lattices unfurled and then left to drift, each containing the duplicated memories and seed-gens of their race. Day by day their most fantastic technologies were sent ahead through trapezoid-traps, their decaying power-sources dragged to high orbit and set to fast-burn, enabling the slow-velocity planetary escape trajectories needed to conjunct with the galaxy arms where the planet of Dahom lay. As they made ready to leave their dying watery world they saw its beauty for the first time, suddenly aware of their loss.

Never in their history had so many nations of the Loa come together.

Even the children of Guede walked in daylight, bringing their bone treasures to the archivists. As the great council convened for the last time, their seers and dreamers gathered together all the signs of opening that would reveal the quick-paths and hot-roads through the cosmos.

The face of the statue changed to that of the Hoo Queen as she looked at me, her eyes close to tears. "We had considered ourselves the greatest race in the galaxy and now we were nomads about to embark into the unknown". My notebook pages were covered with diagrams that looked like star charts of the journey from Sirius-B to Earth.

As I looked at them, I saw the shape of ancient pictographs, of Dogon letters and signs. Against each one was the name of a Loa, for in each of their constellation homes, that now circle our pole star, the laser-light messages had been retrieved, their own ships made ready to join the Loa armada as it continued on towards Dahom, our Earth. I could hear their names chanted in the dark nights of the desert, from the time when humans had first seen their great ships arrive.

I had hoped to learn something of the experience of possession, of the nature of the Hoo Queen, but the images of the Loa and their vast night-ships crossing the great expanses of space burned in my mind's eye like a dream that would not fade. There were fleeting snippets of memory, of gazing down at the watery blue ball of the Earth, of the unfolding of the bone-city in the middle of a vast ocean, of the shining towers of crystal that contained the dancing information neutrinos.

I saw the council of the Loa gathering as that city too began to fail as they looked to the futures shown in the vast obsidian mirrors in its central plaza. Soon they would travel again, to the shores of Africa and South America, to the icy wastes of Antarctica, to their trans-Yuggothian empire, to the places between worlds.

I shut the notebook and pushed it deep into the backpack. The flour lines I had drawn in the early evening were gone now, the statue returned to its silent state, the church eerily quiet. In the place where the veve and candle had been was just a trace of white wax, like a scar on the floor. On top of it lay a 3 inch piece of crystal, illuminated from within like the great information stores of the Loa. I placed it carefully in the inside pocket of my jacket, feeling a heat emanate from it.

As I shut the church door behind me I could see locals beginning to walk towards the path the led up to the old building. I circled around the back, past the old braces and flying buttress which had been added over the ages. Following the old railings, I quickly found the spot where I'd left the Ducati and unlocking my helmet, fired the ignition, riding down to the shore and the rising sun. ✶

The Vortex of the Primigenian Sun

Edgar Kerval

This is the solitude of Mage, the inner marriage of flesh,
spirit and mind

Cycles of Kaos manifested in nameless Eons

Self-procreative madness masked in many shadows
but one incarnated mirror

A black hole in my mind, converging and devouring me,
myself for eternity

Decadent in nature, self-erotic transmutation of senses

Incarnating beyond Primigenian Sun, is myself,
in a neither - neither sphere

Unlimited nature converging in self-illuminative process

Ecstasy and agony in parallel universes in
non-dualistic Transcendence

Oh inner light, Oh sun, Oh phallus devour me

Makes me one with your Primigenian Light,
with your forbidden wisdom! ✦

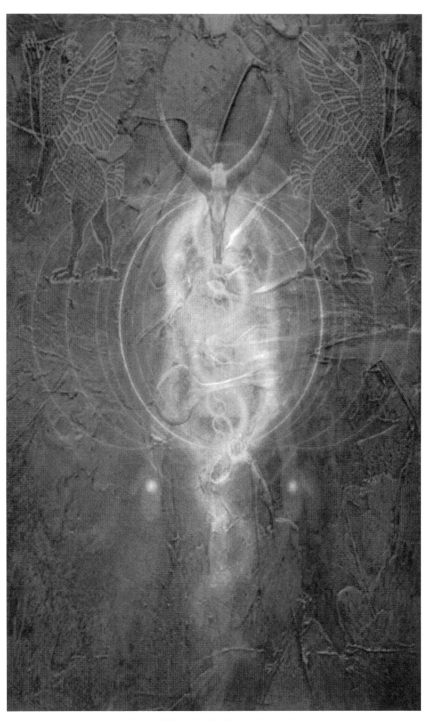

Edgar Kerval, *Aetheric Ascension*

The Science of Magic

S. Ben Qayin

It is for the philosophic student to trace the train of thought which underlies the magician's practice; to draw out the few simple threads of which the tangled skein is composed; to disengage the abstract principles from their concrete applications; in short, to discern the spurious science behind the bastard art.

—Frazer, *The Golden Bough*

FOR aeons sympathetic magic has been utilized to work countless rites in witchcraft and sorcery throughout the world, and has proved to be one of the most effective and influential means to obtain a magical desired end, encompassing everything from love to death, in cultural practices universally. These practices have been viewed in large by the majority of the scientific community as primitive and quite useless.

It is only now that advanced science is producing the same effects that magic has been producing all the while. The same exact results and principals are being pondered and put to use, that have been in use for ages. This is a turning point in man's history, a revelation to be had, illumination to be basked in, for man has so much potential, if only he could embrace the possibilities of 'otherness'.

The concept of Sympathetic Magic has been around since there has been magic, which is essentially since there has been man. However, Sir James George Frazer first categorized this system of magic into two distinct groups so that they may be more readily understood and scientifically analyzed. The first of the groups he titled 'Similarity,' and the second group 'Contact or Contagion,' he writes:

If we analyze the principles of thought on which magic is based, they will probably be found to resolve themselves into two: first, that like produces like, or that an effect resembles its cause; and, second, that things which have once been in contact with each other continue to act on each other at a distance after the physical once in contact, whether it formed part of his body or not.

— The Golden Bough

Frazer did not believe in the system of magic, in fact found it ridiculous: If my analysis of the magician's logic is correct, its two great principles turn out to be merely two different misapplications of the association of ideas. Homoeopathic magic is founded on the association of ideas by similarity: contagious magic is founded on the association of ideas by contiguity. Homoeopathic magic commits the mistake of assuming that things which resemble each other are the same: contagious magic commits the mistake of assuming that things which have once been in contact with each other are always in contact. But in practice the two branches are often combined; or, to be more exact, while homoeopathic or imitative magic may be practiced by itself, contagious magic will generally be found to involve an application of the homoeopathic or imitative principle. Thus generally stated the two things may be a little difficult to grasp, but they will readily become intelligible when they are illustrated by particular examples. Both trains of thought are in fact extremely simple and elementary. It could hardly be otherwise, since they are familiar in the concrete, though certainly not in the abstract, to the crude intelligence not only of the savage, but of ignorant and dull-witted people everywhere. Both branches of magic, the homoeopathic and the contagious, may conveniently be comprehended under the general name of Sympathetic Magic, since both assume that things act on each other at a distance through a secret sympathy, the impulse being transmitted from one to the other by means of what we may conceive as a kind of invisible ether, not unlike that which is postulated by modern science for a precisely similar purpose, namely, to explain how things can physically affect each other through a space which appears to be empty.

Ironically the definition of 'Entanglement' used in quantum physics states exactly what Frazer claims as idiotic and is believed by magicians that are of a, "...crude intelligence not only of the savage, but of ignorant and dull-witted..." The definition of 'Quantum Entanglement' is thus:

Quantum entanglement is a physical resource, like energy, associated with the peculiar non-classical correlations that are possible between separated quantum systems. Entanglement can be measured, transformed, and purified. A pair of quantum systems in an entangled state can be used as a quantum A pair of quantum systems in an entangled state can be used as a quantum information channel to perform computational and cryptographic tasks that are impossible for classical systems. The general study of the information-processing capabilities of quantum systems is the subject of quantum information theory.

—Stanford Encyclopedia of Philosophy

Sympathetic magic works, it has always worked. Ironically, science is finally catching up with magic, and not vice versa as was always predicted by the scientific community.

And so now we enter an age where science is ever moving closer to what we have termed as 'Magic' all those many moons ago. Teleportation is very closely related to 'Entanglement.' It is a process created in a scientific lab where a particle is teleported across the room from point: A, to point: B. H.P. Lovecraft speaks of teleportation:

...What made the students shake their heads was his sober theory that a man might—given mathematical knowledge admittedly beyond all likelihood of human acquirement—step deliberately from the earth to any other celestial body which might lie at one of an infinity of specific points in the cosmic pattern. Such a step, he said, would require only two stages; first, a passage out of the three-dimensional sphere we know, and second, a passage back to the three-dimensional sphere at another point, perhaps one of infinite remoteness.

That this could be accomplished without loss of life was in many cases conceivable. Any being from any part of three- dimensional space could probably survive in the fourth upon what alien part of three-dimensional space it might select for its re-entry. Denizens of some planets might be able to live on certain others—even planets belonging to other galaxies, or to similar dimensional phases of other space-time continua - though of course there must be vast numbers of mutually uninhabitable even though mathematically juxtaposed bodies or zones of space.

It was also possible that the inhabitants of a given dimensional realm could survive entry to many unknown and incomprehensible realms of additional or indefinitely multiplied dimensions—be they within or outside the given space-time continuum—and that the converse would be likewise true. This was a matter for speculation, though one could be fairly certain that the type of mutation involved in a passage from any given dimensional plane to the next higher one would not be destructive of biological integrity as we understand it... Professor Upham especially liked his demonstration of the kinship of higher mathematics to certain phases of magical lore transmitted down the ages from an ineffable antiquity—human or pre-human—whose knowledge of the cosmos and its laws was greater than ours.

—H.P. Lovecraft, *Dreams in the Witch House*

Lovecraft has ever infused our idea of interdimensional travel with angles. Angles beyond reason, "an angle which was acute, but behaved as if it were obtuse..." as he describes in "The Call of Cthulhu". Angles are the key to unlocking the dimensions, the key to traveling 'in-between' just as Keziah Mason used them to escape her prison cell in, *The Dreams in the Witch House*:

...not even Cotton Mather could explain the curves and angles smeared on the grey stone walls with some red, sticky fluid.

She had told Judge Hathorne of lines and curves that could be made to point out directions leading through the walls of space to other spaces beyond, and had implied that such lines and curves were frequently used at certain midnight meetings in the dark valley of the white stone beyond Meadow Hill and on the unpeopled island in the river.

One could only draw the natural conclusion that within angles, there is power. And within the 'correct' angles, doorways between realms can, will, and have opened.

If the correct angles are utilized in conjunction with the correct vocal vibrations, such as in the evocation of Yog~Sothoth given in "Volubilis Ex Chaosium", doors to other dimensions reveal themselves, and are unlocked for travel, both to and from the 'other point'. At this juncture between dimensions often lie guardians or guides that one must either master or follow, such as Choronzon, Papa Legba, Nyarlathotep, etc., depending on which system of magic is being utilized.

Though angles may be the 'key' to opening portals to the 'in- between,' embracing the 'otherness' does not come without its wear on the human psyche, and is often associated with obsession:

'As time wore along, his absorption in the irregular wall and ceiling of his room increased; for he began to read into the odd angles a mathematical significance...' For some time, apparently, the curious angles of Gilman's room had been having a strange, almost hypnotic effect on him; and as the bleak winter advanced he had found himself staring more and more intently at the corner where the down-slanting ceiling met the inward-slanting wall.

H.P. Lovecraft, *The Dreams in the Witch House*

This is a reoccurring theme when using Lovecraftian based magical paradigms. In *The Pseudonomicon*, Phil Hine states in the disclaimer of the book:

It is generally agreed by experienced magicians that working with the Cthulhu Mythos is dangerous due to the high risk of obsession, personality disintegration or infestation by parasitic shells...

—Phil Hine

And to quote from *Volubilis Ex Chaosium*:

It is advised that one working this system should already be familiar with ceremonial magic and its various traditions and foundations. Also be aware that this series of workings can be dangerous both physically and psychologically, the entities that are to be called forth are among the most feared in Chaos Magic, and conventional magical laws are not always applicable to, or observed by, these beings.

—S. Ben Qayin

These entities are real, they are powerful and can be very devastating to work with. They are raw primal Chaos itself, in its most basic of forms. Lovecraft as well as Macgregor Mathers both suffered greatly physically and mentally when working with the Old Ones as described in *Volubilis Ex Chaosium*.

Pete Carroll adds his own warning as well from his online blog:

Lovecraft's 'Elder Gods' have dangerous Promethean and Luciferian types of knowledge, knowledge with which we could easily destroy ourselves:

Direct power over the mind and the brain itself, power over the core processes of biology, the power of creating life and physical immortality, the understanding of the strange and secret geometries of the universe at both the cosmic and quantum levels, and the power to manipulate them, the powers of chaos and of creation itself.

Science is just now accepting and recognizing that many of the 'old myths' hold great truth in being literal rather than metaphorical in nature.

These 'stories' whether they be carved into the side of an ancient temple wall, or printed in a pulp fiction magazine, hold very real truths that can unlock our shrouded past if viewed in the right context, that of course being open mind-edness.

For the Universe holds more secrets than one can ever imagine or unravel. And though we have 'scientific' laws and systems in place that are said to govern our 'reality', they are constantly being revised and replaced with new more advanced thought and practice that an older way of thinking has long embraced in its occult traditions. Breathe in new concepts, ideas and change, for that is the very essence of the Left Hand Path, for the path of Chaos has no one form... Change must always occur... ✦

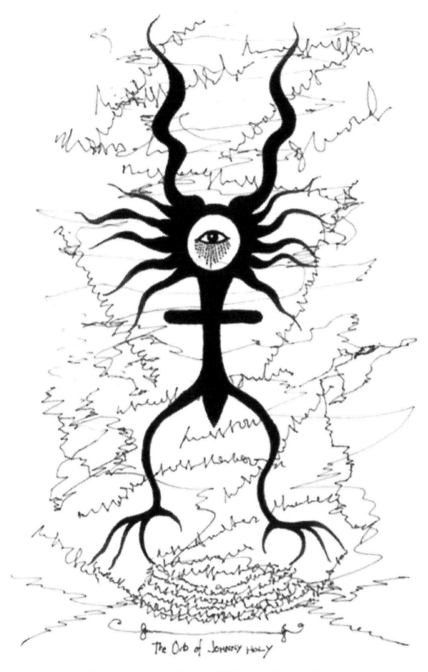

The Orb of Jeremy Holy

Dolorosa de La Cruz, *Poems for the Children of the Black Sun*

Antinomian Sorcery

& Perfect Nature

Nicholaj De Mattos Frisvold

Magic is but one's natural ability to attract without asking.

—Austin O. Spare

THE Modern magical condition appears to be composed of two streams of thought that at first might seem contrary to each other, the antinomian and the traditional. We see the modern magical revival searching back in time and find echoes of itself in the African heritage in the Diaspora. At the same time the intense exchange and availability of all kinds of information also lead to an antinomian attitude towards magic where the cornucopia of information is seen as something to be freely taken and used. In both cases there is a restless spirit at play. This restless spirit drives those inclined towards tradition towards root and beginning of wisdom and it moves those motivated by the antinomian spirit to exalt themselves in the world by whatever means that resonates or 'feels right'. It is the path of mind and the path of passion that flows crookedly through the world and claims its own. There is a dynamic in these two perspectives – a dance between memory and the present where the search for Self is the common compass. The compass is however utilized differently.

I myself am rooted in the traditionalist stream, which means that I obey order and hierarchy and give much importance to the lineage and succession of a faith or cult to possess the powers that support the work done. In a traditional approach towards magic and sorcery we find the circle squared as it were and a foundation is made. This foundation rests upon eternal principles as it stretches its canvas with the fabric of cosmos and creation.

It is about understanding ones celestial constitution as a man or woman of earth – because in this understanding rests wisdom – and wisdom is the key to the secrets of being. The traditional perspective sees the world of matter as a mirror of the celestial and takes the hermetic axiom, `as above, so below` as a constant truth in all matters and as the divide between doing magic and living a profane life is wiped out, the journeyman becomes magic.

In becoming magic we also becomes the axis mundi, rooted in source as we move forward horizontally and turn into the perpetual crossroad of Self in all its transmutations. I believe this is the field of Lucifer. The constant realization of truth, as in flashes and rushes is the truth of the Luciferian impulse as it is constantly ignited by flashes of inspiration and insight. The Luciferian touch is like a lightening than cracks open rivers of Truth in the matter of seconds – and it is always too much to take in for anyone. It is up to the one experiencing it to take the light and insight further. In this way, Lucifer is the messenger of Truth, but he is also the torch each and every one holds uniquely at their own crossroad of Self, because truth hides itself in shades of possibility and assumptions; hence the Luciferian inspiration can inform traditional truths as much as subjective truths – and from these flashes light and truth bleed out in the world and...

...into our world, this marketplace of wild dances and unholy trades where the illusion of freedom moves mankind into accepting the Hell, we know as democracy, as the summit of evolved society. In reality democracy is just another form of slavery that worships the illusion of freedom while all is controlled by a sheep herd called the majority. It is servitude of common man.

I find several modern magical perceptions to be moved by this same democratic idea. Typical for these perceptions are the tendencies of giving supreme importance to the world of matter and to bend ones will in conformity with one's passions and temporal interests. This in turn is informed by a theosophy that do not allow us to go beyond the fantasies of our inner world and the world of fantasy and desire changes hands with the world of ideas and true imagination. That the world of matter is more real than anything is the greatest of illusions because it bars us from perusing the source of conditions. It also bars us from merging with source in a constant realization of Self along the starry pole of all worlds that reveal each and every one as legion. The world is a marketplace and we make the good and bad deal.

We meet truth and falsity and we meet masters and misguides, friends and foes are made as we walk the world. In this journey we are constantly flooded with ideas, impulses and all forms of manipulations, we get so saturated with the world of matter that Self gets veiled in cloud upon cloud of frustration.

With this intensity our search for essence and truth becomes erratic and wild we unleash the beast within. The rebellion against the world is instigated and the hunt for Self is sought within the host upon host of secular identities and in the saturation we kick back and leap forth! It is an attempt of making the world to stop so we can realize where we are and how our landscape really is.

The silence is available only for short intervals and we need more, want more of this silence of Self and we agitate against the voices of repression in the depth of our own psyche and in the texture of social moral and law. It is the ur-screech of freedom that sets out to ravish the world. We read up on our Chaos theory and embrace sorcerous techniques of repute as we embrace Austin Osman Spare as a saint of liberation we he says: "the law of the great Id? To trespass all laws", - like this is enough to find our core. In reality we have uncovered a reservoir of energy that well directed can blow all illusions and bring on the silence of Self that holds all, but is neither.

What I find often saddening in the modern occult condition is that the rebellion is so often rooted in a shallow idea of what 'do your will' really means. I believe rebellion is important, but it must be strategic and informed by wisdom in order to have an effect that generates the crossroad where the truth from source moves us onwards closer towards Self. If this is the prime goal, we can on the road towards this effectuate changes in the world and in our life.

At times the antinomian path is understood to be sorcerous — but all sorcery arises from an understanding of how the creation works — only in this way can we manipulate the world in a wise way. A sorcerer is not someone who elects a practice appearing to be powerful, uninterested or unaware of its foundation, and apply this rite in self-serving ways upon the world.

A Sorcerer is in fact the Nigromancer par excellence, someone who knows the art of riding the worlds because he or she holds this particular knowledge that enables effective manipulation by rite or personal power to manipulate the world.

Spiritual rebellion is not something new. Most traditional faiths and cults hold an idea, it be metaphysical or in the form of legends, that motion was accomplished by rebellion — some antinomian action. It is just to go to our own Christian mythology to see the potential for movement and transformation in the acts of the apostate angels, the first murder and Nimrods' Tower of Babel. The Bauls of Bengal, several Skanda cults and the Nath Siddhas as well as Bektashi Sufism and the libertine Sufism of the Qalandariyyas have all been judged as antinomian—in the sense of being against the sacred and written law.

In Buddhism and Hinduism, the Vama Marg paths have been judged as antinomian because of the ways they challenged the priestly dogmas and broke religious taboos. The purpose for all of these were liberation, by breaking taboos the dogma supporting it fell and made it possible to connect with source directly.

There is also the idea of several shayyks and saddhus that breaking taboos is like shaking the attention of the soul of the world and in this act a portal is opened.

The word 'antinomian' was actually coined by Martin Luther in reference to a certain sect that rejected the Holy Scripture in favour of the importance of faith alone. It is important to observe in this that the rebellion happened in the same plane, sacred faith challenged sacred write doctrine challenged dogma. The metaphysical effect of this is that the rebellion ensures fluidity in the doctrine and becomes a constant threat for the solidification of doctrine into dogma. What happens often today is that the rebellion stretches the planes and a sacred vision leads to attack on secular rules and laws. In this we are in the field of psychology where it merges with sorcery and tradition, we are actually in the world of Austin Osman Spare.

Austin Osman Spare inspired Chaos magic and also had a great impact upon modern western magic and sorcery, often this impact is based on a face value of the idea of 'self-pleasure' in ways that discard the whole reasoning Spare held of this concept. I do admit that Spare can, as any genius working in axioms, images and metaphors, be read from a variety of angels all of them holding a truth, but it is here in the shades of truth we find the essence of Spare's sorcery. Spare was solidly lodged within a traditional mindset. For him the world was enchanted and the divine artist was he who marked the world with the abysmal nothingness of beginning. For Spare, it was crucial to disbelief in order to arrive at the core.

Dolorosa De La Cruz, *Medusa*

Love for Self had as its goal to replicate the erotic pulse itself, a state of pleasure where there was no duality but rather a transgression of unity into bliss. Spare elected the language of Jasper and Freud in his attempts of painting with ink and words the condition of a sorcerer standing on sacred foundation in a profane world. In this he set psychology straight as a logia or knowledge of the psyche.

Spares' The Book of Pleasure' is actually constructed in a scholastic way and is aping or echoing Thomas Aquinas in its way of argument and counter-argument. In The Book of Pleasure this dialogue is between body (Zos) and the shades of Self and Ego (Kia).

This paradoxical dialogue between arguments leads to the formulae known as the death posture where the powers of Thanatos (death) are invoked upon the flesh to free the Self in a flash of Eros and pleasure equated with freedom and the idea of neither-neither. It is a moment of ecstatic silence, a moment of being in pleasure unqualified. Spare tells in the beginning of The Book of Pleasure the following about belief and Self:

"What is there to believe, but in Self? And Self is the negation of completeness as reality. No man has seen self at any time. We are what we believe and what it implies by a process of time in the conception; creation is caused by this bondage to formula."

Going ahead in the text we find the following observation:

You disbelieve in Ghosts and God-because you have not seen them? What! You have never seen the mocking ghosts of your beliefs? the Laughing Bedlam of your humility or Mammon your grotesque Ideas of "Self"? Yea, your very faculties and your most courageous Lies are Gods! Who is the slayer of your Gods-but a God!

There is something here that brings the mind to Advaita Vedanta, as passed down in the Upanishades, the philosophical orientation underlying antinomian sects like the Nath Siddhas. Advaita would agree in the importance of how negation upon negation would reveal that the greatest illusion is our Manas, or mind/consciousness. The explanation of what something is by constant reference to its negation is easily applied on Spare's concept 'neither-neither' but in this even the point and focus is dissolved into pure being or bliss. In this lies the constant pleasure unmoved. It is almost like the mind, the consciousness; the intellect itself is the door, closed or open for the becoming and annihilation of the crossroad of Self all possibility not – not...

It is about a process of constant slaying of illusion a sorcerous work on the imagination itself to make it truthful in its nakedness where qualities and directions are declared void and our center being one with source, what the Advaita philosophers understood to be unqualified monism.

There is a resonance here with the Fa Rune a´ in the Armanen runes that see the first rune, the Fa Rune, as the flash of spirit which is remarkably similar to how the 1st degree of Aries is viewed in classical hermetic texts about astrology. This is also found in the first lunar mansion, Al Sharatain, which starts

from the 0 degree of Aries ! and is seen as the horns of Aries equated with the nous or divine mind and the flash of fire in change and transmutation. The talismanic image of Al Sharatain is of a lance bearing warrior, black of hue that smells of storax and aloes wood. This mansion is also favorable for beginnings, especially of love. It is the mansion and degree for self-love and Spare summarizes self-love as follows in the Book of Pleasure:

> The center of belief is love for one's self, projecting environment for fulfillment but allowing its distortion to simulate denial, an ambition to become ulterior to self-desire, but you cannot get further than the center, so one multiplies (believes) in order to be more unaware of the fundamental... Now self-love is explained. It is the completion of belief. The "self" is the "Neither-Neither," nothing omitted, indissoluble, beyond pre possession; dissociation of conception by its own invincible love is the only true, safe, and free. The desire, will, and belief ceasing to exist as separate. Attraction, repulsion, and control self-contained, they become the original unity, inert in pleasure. There is no duality. There is no desire for unity.

From this it is evident for me that Spare can be viewed as a meeting point between traditional doctrine as reflected in Advaita unqualified monism and sorcery. I believe this fusion is caused by Spare's initiation by the witch mother 'Mrs. Patterson' at the age of fourteen that quickened his blood and set on fire the witch within him and in this a merging with Self occurred as moved by his invisible Daimons.

My experience is that life as well as magic and sorcery benefits from being worked on a well-made traditional foundation. With this I mean, there is a certain metaphysic at the root of it all that informs with solid knowledge how the architecture of the world is. This knowledge gives us understanding and as we experience the world we grow wise. The tools might be the same as for any eclectic sorcerer, but he sorcerer on a traditional foundation will possess an uncanny cunning of how to use the sorcerous arsenal, mostly because he or she is always closer to Self by virtue of the foundation made.

The phrase 'Know Thyself' that was inscribed on the arch at the entrance of the temple of Apollo in Delphi is well known as it was in Western magic used as integral with the Great Work. This knowledge is at the root of Spare's sorcery and it lies as a foundation in hermetic magic and sorcery. I have here in mind Picatrix and the importance this grammar of Art gives to traditional metaphysics and cosmogonies. Picatrix is having at its core talismanic and celestial magic – but within this fabric we do find formulas and procedures of manipulation that we would deem sorcerous.

In the Third book and sixth Chapter of Picatrix we find a ritual described and explained that is about making a connection to Self, in this particular chapter it is spoken of as the Perfect Nature understood to be our daimon and planetary intelligences.

The connection with our perfect nature enables us to establish the axis mundi within our very being so we can move on in the world enflamed in Self but the moment of merging, the instant when the crossroad flashes forth is both of light and silence marking a moment of abysmal bliss bound in pure love that seeks nothing but Self. We can read in this chapter:

"Nothing in this science can be perfected, unless the virtue and disposition of the planets are inclined toward it by their own nature. This is what Aristotle writes in the Book of Antimaquis (an Arabic 11th Century hermetic text dealing with talismanic magic), where he says:

Perfect Nature fortifies those who seeks wisdom, and strengthens their intellect and wisdom, ensuring a quick route towards fulfillment and success in all works."

In order to conjure the spirits of Perfect Nature it was necessary to call upon the aid of four spirits, Meegius (east), Betzahuech (west), Vacdez (south) and Nufeneguediz (north), which appears to be royal powers ascribed to the four elements, revealing themselves in winds, as support for the summoning of Perfect Nature.

Picatrix advices further: "When I wanted to understand and draw the secrets of the work of the world and of its qualities, I place myself above a deep and dark well, out of which comes a violent wind; I am unable to see there because of its darkness. And when I bring there a burning candle, soon the wind extinguishes it. And a handsome man, of imperious authority, appeared to me in dreaming..."

The dream counsels consisted in taking a candle and place it into a glass lantern and take it to a well. At this well you will make the talismanic image and dig it down in the center and lower the candle upon it. These being done the four corners are dug out and offerings of oil and incense are given here to the four royal guardians of the Perfect Nature. The dreamer ask the spirit what its name is and it responds that it is Perfect Nature and its name is the name of the four powers combined – Perfect nature being the sum of these, defining itself as the origin of all things. The dreamer is also given another ritual.

This ritual must be done when the moon is in the first degree of Aries and can be done by day as well as night. Here a table is erected in the east and at the four corners of the table is placed four jugs, one with melted bovine butter/ghee (east) and the others with walnut oil (west), sesame seed oil (north) and almond oil (south). You will then take more four jugs, smaller and fill with red wine.

You will then at the center of the table present a mixture of walnut oil, butter, honey, sugar and flour and add to this some of the contents from all eight vessels and make from this a cake. Bake the cake and replace it with a beeswax candle and cense the altar with frankincense, mastic and aloes wood. The cake will then be brought to the shrine and everything censed again. You will then summon the four royal elemental spirits by name seven times each whilst facing the east and then recite the following invocation:

"I invoke you, Oh mighty spirits, powerful, and lofty, because it is from you that proceed the knowledge of the wise and the intellect of those who understand, and it is by your virtue that the requests of philosophers are manifested, so that you may answer me, that you may be with me, that you may link me to yourself by your powers and virtues, that you may strengthen me in your knowledge, so that I may understand what I do not understand, that I may know that of which I am ignorant, that I may see that which I see not; set far from me blindness, indignity, forgetfulness, and weakness; make me to climb to the degree of the wise ones of old - those who had a heart full of knowledge, wisdom, intellect, and savvy - fasten that in my heart in such a manner similar to the heart of the wise ones of old."

This being done the Perfect Nature would make itself known and the wines, oils and cake should be subject for joyous feast, preferably with friends and lovers. Picatrix tells that sages and kings performed this ritual once a year in order to ensure that the doors of perception, intellect and wisdom were constantly open and that it led to all kinds of success in study, work and love. Socrates understood Perfect Nature to be the Sun of the wise and the root of light. He understood Perfect Nature to be the power that bound the wise one to the planet/daimon that guarded him or her. It is the teacher within that enables understanding.

Towards the end of the chapter we can read:

"It is thusly that the perfect nature properly works by its virtue and its influence in disposing the intellect of the philosopher according to his natural inclination. it is impossible to arrive at his science without a natural inclination for it as much by its proper virtue as by the disposition of the dominant planet within his horoscope."

It should be evident that the ritual itself connects you with the spirits and Daimons that watched over us at birth and they can be placated either on the very day and moment of the celebration of our birth or when the Moon is in the first degree of Aries.

As we see, the Perfect Nature is first and foremost a black well, a circle of abysmal possibility and it is this which is our true Self, the names of the four royal elements gives Perfect Nature presence – but it has no name – but is the state of pleasure. It resonates with what Spare said in Focus of Life that shall close this article:

Thought is the negation of knowledge. Be thy busyness with action only. Purge thyself of belief: live like a tree walking! Take no thought of good or evil. Become self-active causality by Unity of thine, I and Self. ✶

Holy Mother &
Id Ego Superego

Ariock Van De Voorde
& Kindle Black Lotus Kult

Holy Mother

Kneel before my hallowed altar

and bath in blood from holy slaughter

My sacrament is like no other

Virgin, Crone and Holy Mother

I am the Goddess of War

I am the Sacred Whore

I am the best you ever wish you had

I slay the Temple Priest

and slit the throat of your Beast

I am the space between your "good" and "bad"

Id Ego Superego

I'm living inside you

Watching the world behind your eyes

Seeing your fears and making you cry I'm breathing inside you

Each time you move I steal a breath

Bringing you one day closer to death I'm dreaming inside you

Running the nightmares through your head

Feeding the monsters under your bed I'm screaming inside you

Never relenting endless pain

Dragging my nails across your brain ✦

Hagen Von Tulien, *Black Lotus Kult Sigil*

I'm dying inside you

Taking you with me as I die

Voice in your head becomes a lie

I

Am

The Sacrament ov the Red Serpent

Edgar Kerval

Part 1

My Flesh is the Flesh of the Rising Serpent

My Eyes, the Eyes of a Thousand Moons Bleeding
My Voice, the Primigenian, Call from Eons to Eons
My Womb, a Black Hole in the Cosmos,

A Portal of Inner Wisdom

My Mouth, the Venom of A Thousand Serpents
My Arms, the Tentacles of Whispering Typhoons

My Presence, the Infinite Void, Devouring Humanity!

I am The Red Serpent, whose name is

BABALON, BABALON

Edgar Kerval, *Babalon Serpent*

Part 2

Io Crowned Serpent, with Many Eyes and Poisonous Kisses

Drain my Life and Make Me One with You...
Thou Crowned Scarlet Goddess,
I Invoke You under the Stars
Your Smell, is the Smell of a Thousand Chalices

Filled with Blood.

So Let Me Drink from your Sacred Elixirs!

Oh my Red Goddess

Be One with Me, One more Time,

And Together We Will Explore Infinite

Realms of Ecstasy and Pain!

Oh My Lustful Goddess

Take My Blood, Take My Sacred Seed

And Make me Immortal for Aeons and Aeons!

Oh my Red Serpent

IO BABALON! ✦

Nightside Notes 2

Orryelle Defenestrate-Bascule

Astral explorations of the Tunnels of Set (reflexes on the Nightside of the Tree of the dayside Tarot paths), employing the Sigils from Crowley's Liber CCXXXI and Linda Falorio's, Shadow Tarot

THIS is my second progressive exploration of all the Tunnels, about a decade since the first. My purpose this time was to find more imagery and concepts for a large picture on black paper which I have been drawing.

What I'm finding interesting about my current explorations is how the imagery from the different tunnels is linking together into a big picture which also includes the all-connecting tree (roots) itself and also the Nightside Sephiroth.

The angles of it all are quite strange, certainly a contrast from the smooth harmonic geometries of the Golden Mean I explored in Coagula (the Gold Book of the Tela Quadrivium).

Aptly non-linear, the tunnels are presented here not in numerical sequence but in the order in which I performed the operations...

MALKUNOFAT

Hanged Man 'the right way up' but still in 1-legged position. Hanged Man's ejaculation creating white flecks on fly agaric mushrooms in Baratchial tunnel 'below'. Head immersed in Well.

GARGOPHIAS

Priestess turned 'inside-out'. Black tree-body, path crossing Daath. Daath as Priestess's yoni, seen from the Nightside as glowing white within- portal to dayside.

URIENS

Pasifae bound and fucked by a bull to conceive the Minotaur. Rather than the intelligence and wisdom of the dayside Heirophant, brute force and raw primal power.

The sigil is the 7 infernal sephiroth. The Hierophant should be a channel between the supernals and the lower tree, but here there is no communication.

Eventually breaking through this second time, I find a tunnel littered with corpses and mangled bodies in the dark. This is Apocalypse, the shadow side of the Aeon in the collective unconsciousness. Judgement in the worst fundamental Christian sense. Unsurprising as the Hecatochirons or hundred-handed giants who blocked the tunnel were mythically bound to Tartarus, this tunnel seems to connect directly (yet on an obscure angle) to:

SHALICU

Gnosis: Sexual energy raised up with extensive pranayama.

Hundreds of hands fill the tunnel, obstructing entrance: A tactile Chthonic barrier. The sigil for this tunnel says 'Do not pass' in Latin, and this was my second attempt to penetrate its mysteries -the first I drew a blank then drifted off to sleep.

NIANTIEL

Nightside reflex of the Death card: The Alchymic Siamese Twins in the Chemical Bath as coffin, rotting and semi skeletal. His eye is missing (Horus-Odin mythic symbolism), carried away by the Ravens of Dispersion, Qlippoth of Nightside Netzach which the tunnel leads to. Another raven carries away Her missing head (Medusa-Chinnamasta mythic symbolism).

Ravens of Dispersion, Qlippoth of Nightside Netzach which the tunnel leads to. Another raven carries away Her missing head (Medusa-Chinnamasta mythic symbolism).

Branches from the Tree and winding ivy grow around and through the bodies- death as compost.

Unexpected continuation from journey in Shalicu. Also seems to be diagonally connected to Zamradiel in which these Lovers/Siamese-Twins are severed from each other.

Raflifu

Black Flame from the Nigri Solis of Nightside Tiphereth dances down this tunnel. It becomes molten, like black lava. At the other end of the tunnel it is jettisoning like ink from a phallic squid.

Hemethterith

Nightsky. Sensation/visual of the stars melting upwards.

Parfaxitas & Saksalim

Journeyed Saksalim (sigil) and experienced Parfaxitas also unsurprising as the crossing of these two paths on the dayside has been a major nexus for me, and the method of gnosis used seemed also to relate to both tunnels:

Non-ejaculatory orgasm to Parfaxitas as an implosive rather than explosive phallic force. This was combined with smoking a mild dose of Changa/Dreamtime (DMT-infused herbs) -an alchemical concoction for nightside Art/Temperance. Visions were minimal but the powerful sensation was of Inner lightning, within rather than without the towers of the phallus and the spine.

Thantifaxat

Gnosis: Changa/Dreamtime DMT-infused herbs, smoked (larger dose).

A simultaneous sense of otherness and here-ness. Presence, clarity, visual enhancement and distortion but very much within the physical reality of my temple. Rather than springing off into other dimensions like the tortoise in the sigil as expected from other Changa experiences, the sigil crystalized, became hyper real but very static. This effect then spread over my body and the room. Nightside Universe/World as contraction rather than expansion, the density and power of the microcosm.

Characith

Gnosis: Mantra, Bloodletting (fragnum lignum muscle under tongue)

Every last drop into the Cup of Babalon -visions of swirling blood and semen. Vampirism as the nature of life and death, as ecstatic when surrendered too. ✦

Dolorosa De La Cruz, *La Inquieta*

Deific Masks & Luciferian Flame

Frater Malus II/XVI

I PRESENT here my personal morning ritual, which I do right before my morning meditation. The reason I'm sharing this is because it gave me some good results, as I did it for a period of weeks.

Now, as a Luciferian it is the symbolic which plays the most important part in this ritual. In this ritual it's clear to me, and easy to take in and reap the fruits they give me, but for those not familiar with the Luciferian tradition, I'll give a little insight into the meaning of those symbols and thus you can achieve the same results I get from this, the same feeling of accomplishment.

The reason I mentioned the word symbolism a few times, is that this ritual consists of symbolically doing things from various scriptures (including The Bible), which I as an anti- theistic Luciferian see as fairytales, but useful metaphors, when used in a way like I do in this ritual. Use them as metaphors. Every God, Goddess, Demon, and Spirit is human made so they can manifest only through us, You are the only God(-dess) there is, we use them as Deific Masks. (They don't appear in front of anyone in any anthropomorphic physical form whatsoever) They represent certain characteristics in each of us, we just have to dive deep into the ocean of Leviathan (the sub-consciousness) to get them rise within us, to manifest. And when they manifest in your flesh, you are the judge how and why they manifest the way they do, since you are the one summoning them.

See, to me Theistic-Satanism is that one believes that Satan is a real guy or whatever, an anthropomorphic deity and it basically boils down to this,

They have chosen a side in Christianity's "Holy Book," the Devil and decided to worship him/her, well, to me theistic satanism is exactly the same as being Jehovah worshiping Christian with a difference that they choose a different side than the Christians and that is just something I Don't want anything to do with, because I don't believe in Santa Claus anymore, and believing , really believing in God and Satan falls to same category as unicorns and Santa Claus.

If someone isn't familiar whit the Deific Mask principal, ill clarify it with an example; I know I'm gonna have to fight tomorrow, and I'm a bit uncertain of my fighting spirit, so I evoke Asmodeus, the Demon of violence, of bloody mace to get the killer-spirit in me.

I summon the Demon by using Luciferian Goetia`s methods, knowing that the only way to really see the demon is to be insane or to take LSD or something. I call the Demon with his sigil, the basic evocation stuff. After I got the Gnosis going on and feel I have summoned the spirit of Asmodeus (in reality that is characteristic of mine within me that Asmodeus represents; Violent killer.) I symbolically absorb the Asmodeus as a part of me, one could say i use the Demon like an armor/sword which fits that fight, or as a DEIFIC MASK, I became him. Just like all the Luciferians goal is to become Lucifer (Lilith) themselves, Lucifer's a great role model: After you have been struck down, you will rise and shine ever brighter. So next day i go to that inevitable fight and put on the Deific Mask of Asmodeus and beat the shit out of the fucker, probably holding the Asmodeus sigil in my pocket and burn it after i have finished whit that one i was fighting. That's Black Magick, Luciferian Witchcraft.

OK, so to the actual point, or did I lose it? Hmmm... no!

You can use Magickal tools for this or choose not to. I sometimes even put on my robe, but usually I go naked in front of my altar in front of some expression of Leviathan Clay figure, Baphomet, a poster) Lilith, a Statue of a naked sinister woman and Samael, a Statue. And I have a Dagger and a Bone where I have painted the sigil of Kain/Cain with paint, and my blood too. It's a big bone, I could imagine one could crush a brother's skull with it. And that's it, it's go-time. First little about Luciferian tradition about this ritual's subject: I first crush Abel's skull because Abel (or Kain) is not real, they are metaphorical, see to Luciferians Abel represents the ignorance, stupidity, blind faith, un-initiation, a sheep and then again Kain represents a Luciferian in he's initiations beginning, want to learn, to initiate him/herself to Luciferianism, to sacrifice the everyday personality, in one word: *antinomian*. Kain is more to us more complex, but I want to make this simple, in a nutshell, Leviathan then is the circle in where Samael and Lilith has mated to beget Kain and also where this soon coming transformation can happen (Leviathan=sub-consciousness), transformation from Kain to Baphomet to The Beast which is all of them manifested in you after you`ve traveled like Kain (Luciferian initiation) and gone through the hardship to finally get together with his Father (Samael/Satan), his Mother (Lilith) and transformed to Baphomet in the Ocean of Leviathan (Sub-consciousness): So you see it's a metaphorical journey to my whole initiation; it can be yours too.

I feel I have completed that journey, so I can really relate to this ritual, and I understand all of it, but even if you are a beginner Luciferian, do this ritual frequently, and after some time of Luciferian initiation, you'll get it, and you are the Antichrist/Satan/Lucifer, the Beast in flesh in your left hand you need to have what you think Cain used to brake Abel's scull and in right hand Dagger/Athame (I use Cain's weapon my huge bone whit my blood and sigil of Kain).

See, in Luciferian tradition Abel represents un-initiated ignorant and sheepish minds.

1. Prepare the place by your style the surroundings I recommend 1 black candle, incense stick, and the statue or alike to represent Luciferian mirror image of you. And in case you want to burn wish parchment take Will Burn bucket.

2. Do Luciferian Cross. Touch forehead, exclaim "LUCIFER." Touch chest, declare "SATAN," Touch genitalia-area, say "BELIAL." Spread your arms and be in a posture like a letter "X" and exclaim "LEVIATHAN."

3. Take to your left hand, Abel's skull-crusher, and in the right hand dagger.

4. Strike whit sudden movement Abel's scull broken, "I stroke Abel's scull open, because it represents ignorance, weak will, stupidity of mind, that's why I had to kill Abel: I AM KAIN."

5. Now strike forward with the dagger, impale the invisible.

I have impaled illusion with my dagger, which is my
Will that sees through illusions. My Will
changes that what is and will be.

Now feel your will's great power.

6. Spread your hands with those objects in your hands like a sundering Adept of Darkness!

> *My Father Samael and my Mother Lilith unite and*
> *fornicate in me I AM BAPHOMET!*

(Understand this is what is now happening)

7. Point with the object in your hands towards and make a circle around you anti clockwise:

> *Leviathan makes a circle around me whit His body, inside his circle hap-*
> *pens the transformation and change opens inside*
> *the circle of Leviathan the change opens.*
> *My Will reflects from Leviathans scales.*

8. Spread your hands and announce:

> *My Name is (Magickal Name) and my Will changes*
> *what Is and bend's reality.*

> *So it is Done, Hail The Luciferian model of me and my Will: My will is*
> *the Fiery eye which changes what it*
> *and bends the reality.*

Note: If you are vampire, you can do every morning by draining and devouring the Forces we just get to know Samael, Lilith, Cain, etc.

Now you are ready to take on the day ahead of you, with an awesome feeling. If you do morning yoga and meditate do it after this. Or combine this ritual with your meditation and thus you don't need anything other than well-practiced visualization skills, which are paramount to every Luciferian/Satanist/Black Magick practitioner.

I hope I did my good deed of this day by sharing these thoughts with you. May Light of Lucifer Guide You All. ✶

Lucas Pandolfelli, *Untitled*

The Shift Below

FORMULA 89 & THE PRACTICE OF KAREZZA WITHIN LEFT HAND PATH SEXUAL SORCERY

Alexander Dray

OUT of all the particular branches of magic there has never been one that is so utterly convoluted and bloated with the over use of obscure terminology and half-witted wishful thinking. Sex magic itself is a term thrown about with abandon and with little care for its origins or proper usage. For the black magician, sex magic is a vital tool that can be easily employed to dramatically alter perception and reality itself within the sorcerer's sphere of influence. As with all things magical, when I focus and magnify a specific sorcery topic I like to ask myself why so little is known about the area in question. Many times, the topic has a long tradition of being well hidden from outsiders as is the case of some Afro-shamanic systems. In others it is simply because a would-be magician made up the system in its entirety in an effort to gain favor, fame or wealth through the sale of fancy "grimoires."

In many cases these systems prove to be legitimate totalities unto themselves and suffice as paths to the unknown and in some cases these sorceries legitimize themselves through use over many years; Wicca being a prime example of this phenomenon. The primary reason that I find in depth information often lacking is the simple fact that no one really knows anything about it, and when an alleged expert is approached you can be sure that they shall lead you down halls of smoking mirrors and on the wildest chases imaginable.

I remember some years ago that there were many books being published on the subject of sex magic, some good, some decent enough and some absolutely useless. From my perusal of these works, I gathered that most of the authors of sex magic occult related material blended together what they could find out concerning tantric sex yoga, other yoga like practices and western style ceremonial magick. This was generally the theme many of these books seemed to carry during that brief era in magical publications. There was much deep breathing during intercourse, much visualization of the chakras and much circulation of energy. This is all fine and well, even from the self-centered, "I" driven perspective of the Black School because within these rudimentary practices one would most certainly develop a core of discipline which in turn will of course consolidate one's magical will even further. We shall not dismiss practical and sound sorcery practice regardless of its unsavory origin if in the end it helps to produce a black magician of high standards, achievement, skill and caliber.

But where do we go from having mastered the fundamentals? The ancient sorcerers of Mexico and South America understood sexual energy to be a real, tangible substance that one either had in abundance or lacked. When we speak of energy of a substance it is done as a kind of prop. Dealing with an energetic reality forces us to make certain exception with how we choose to interact with that world and we are caught in apposition where we can either name a thing or not be capable of having a reference point with which to refer. Talking about energy in terms of a physical substance that can be stored like nuts for the winter is one of these exceptions and it is done to aid us in directing this energy in the direction we desire. For the ancient ones, sexual energy was a fixed personal attribute and one either had an abundance of it or one needed to store it due to a deficiency. There are of course those rare individuals who we could say fall right in the middle, displaying perfectly balanced sexual energy.

This being their sexual energetic world schemata, the ancient ones advised those with a normal amount of sexual energy or a deficiency to store it for acts of sorcery rather than wasting it on sexual intercourse without the result of human conception. This is the simplified version of these sorcery tenets passed down to us through the works of Carlos Castaneda and other Toltec sorcery writers and practitioners and as will all things acquired, we of the black school take that which we have found works and leave the rest to rest.

From a Left Hand Path perspective, we can clearly see the most optimal way in which to regard sexual energy.

As a young magician I was for some years under the tutelage of a more experienced sorcerer who told me that he understood that the retention and redeployment of sexual energy by the adept was essentially the magical sexual formula of the Black School of magic in that its aim was to prevent the sexual energy of the sorcerer from being unintentionally absorbed back into the "universal" energy matrix at large. He said that the white magician seeks total release and Dionysian gnosis through sexual union and complete identification with a sexual partner (and thus the "god" or "goddess") while the black adept strives to accumulate unimaginable levels of energy for purposes of dramatic perceptual alteration, acts of dreaming, re-manifestation, physical longevity and many other diabolical, "selfish" pursuits.

As the years went on I continually tested this basic assertion, developing over much time a very clear understanding of the practice called karezza. The magical conception of the universe is symbolic of greater realities and energetic themes that expand and run through all of existence. My one time teacher tried to simplify these ideas for me saying that white sex magic relies on a buildup and final release while Left Hand Path sex magic is based around the buildup, retention and redirection of the accumulated energy with no sexual release; the release being substituted by the pragmatic goals of the dark sorcerer.

This is a simplification of an entire realm of sex magic discipline and my intention is to provide the Left Hand Path adept with a rare and unusual introduction into the sex magic practices of the black school.

The practice of Karezza is the foundation of Left Hand Path sex magic, or the sexual sorcery of the black school. As a foundation it represents our primary philosophy in its core understandings, but the sexual magic of our orientation branches off into many varied actual practices other than the basic act of karezza. We are interested in results that strengthen the black magician in all their individual pursuits. We do not seek to unify our consciousness with the remnants of some forgotten egregore that has not been properly worshipped in thousands of years. We want repeatable, practical yet abstract sorceries that have a definite purpose. Mental masturbation is for the armchair magician; the path worker delicately sipping tea of damiana whilst poorly visualizing the attributes of the paths and spheres and their imagined grand adventures therein.

Black magic is for the scientifically minded, yet also for those who are imaginative and energetic. It is for those who see the world and all in it for what it really is and so turn to a calling to excel and be more than they ever thought possible. If we dark sorcerers have a reputation for snobbery and intolerance, it is not without some cause as we resent even those features of our very own selves that would hold us back from the mysteries of creation and from acquiring the power of the predator that is the birthright of every still thinking human organism.

While magic is for many nothing more than a way to momentarily expand the consciousness and feel a part of something immense and mysterious, it is for those of the black sister and brotherhood an evolutionary imperative that is embraced with respect and dignity. Black magic is honest in its objectives and highly intricate in its abstract implications. It is a tool and a philosophy that nature has selectively lead a few to its use, and the sexual sorcery of the left hand path can be a continually recharging power cell, giving our diabolical apparatus continual life so that we may ever seek to pursue our "great work," the strengthening of our individual psyche and body, the passionate exploration of the multiverse, mastery over awareness itself and the arts of pleasure and self-gratification.

Coitus reservatus is generally considered to be the action of engaging in some form of sexual activity, remaining at the pre-orgasmic stage and then withdrawing from the sexual activity without having achieved orgasm or having released orgasmic fluids. It is engaged in by both sexes and used to increase the duration of sexual intercourse and as a form of birth control. Karezza is the utilization of coitus reservatus to increase the duration of sexual pleasure so that sexual energy may be built up within the respective bodies of the sorcerer until a peak level has been reached. This energy can then be willfully projected in any direction desirable by the mind of the black magician. It is similar in theory to the raising of the witch's "cone of power," but with the ultimate objective of mastery and control over the powerful subtle energies of the self.

The magical formula of the sexual sorcery known as karezza equates to the formula 89 of the Black School as it directly reflects the retaining, cycling, increase and manipulation of the magician's vital energy. Formula 89 is the fundamental magical formula of the Black School and this is reflected by its cabalistic reference to the Hebrew gematria /vg which is to be shut or closed up. The essence of the magical formula of the Black School is the willful shutting of one's self up against the continuous natural entropy and all those forces associated with this which occur in the universe and act to dissolve individual human awareness. For a more in depth essay on the philosophy of the Black School and its relation to the other primary schools of magic please refer to my essay entitled The Formula of Dispersion. The complete essay can be found in Pandora's Mansion Volume One, Dark Harvest Occult Publishers. Suffice it to say that the Black Magician's methods concern utilizing the natural sexual energy that flows through the power zones of the human body in a way that strictly enables the sorcerer to accumulate more power in the material as well as energetic sense, and to channel this power in specific ways which are always aimed at enhancing and preserving the sorcerer's basic interests.

The practice of Karezza is intense and can be dangerous if the proper procedures are not followed. When the Black magician begins this form of sorcery, they must understand that if they are very young in years, they will experience intense pain even if the body's vital energy is properly circulated throughout the power centers. I began this practice around the age of 23 and due to my already high level of pranic sexual energy I would often experience pain in certain areas of my body. This is caused by either a failure to properly circulate the buildup of energy throughout the physical body, or because the individual practitioner already has too much accumulated energy and it is in an imbalanced state. If this is the case, karezza will throw one's entire energetic system into a feverish state of which pain and mild mental imbalance can result. Visualization is both a discipline and an art. It is necessary for the sorcerer to constantly and continually seek to develop this talent.

To visualize well is to intend intent itself into acts of sublime creation of will. When we visualize properly we are effectively moving energy in a particular direction and this is why the practice of visualization is so heavily emphasized in almost every basic magical text of any theoretical orientation whatsoever. If you cannot visualize or find that you are having difficulty with it, I suggest unremitting practice until you find that it has become easier. These difficulties on the Left Hand Path are of the kind that are most welcome, and the Black Masters smile to themselves when they see a new initiate experience apparently insurmountable obstacles. These obstacles themselves truly indicate where the adept will eventually find their greatest strengths and talents. These temporary hindrances are what shape us and give us the chance of attaining dominion.

The late Kenneth Grant is one of the few occult scholars who offers his readers sound information concerning karezza as a sorcery technique. In The

Magical Revival (1972) Grant touches on the practice and gives us a some-what elusive, yet sound place for the Black Magician to start their explorations.

Objurations against masturbation, onanism, coitus interruptus, karezza and other apparently sterile methods of using sexual energy, follow logically upon awareness (however consciously unacknowledged this awareness may be) of the sacramental nature of the generative act. Erroneous conclusions drawn from incomplete apprehension of the factors involved led in the past to the "fire and brimstone" admonitions directed against "abuses", which at one time were thought to lead to degeneration of the nervous system, blindness, paralysis and insanity. In actual fact, none of the actual energy is lost, though it fails to fins a field of operation in the matrix which nature has provided for it. It breeds, instead of physical offspring, phantoms composed of tenuous matter. Through the deliberate and persistent practice of such "abuses", Qliphothic entities are engendered; they prey upon the mind and feed upon the nervous fluid. As Crowley notes: "The ancient Jewish Rabbis knew this, and taught that before Eve was given to Adam the demon Lilith was conceived by the spilt of his dreams, so that the hybrid races satyrs, elves, and the like began to populate those secret places of the earth which are not sensible by the organs of the normal man.

Generally speaking, the view that sexual practices which do not result in the production of physical human offspring are "abuses" of energy is close to correct. Sorcerers are beings who tamper with the natural flow of things, so if we define the word abuse as the improper use, misuse or maltreatment of a thing, then it follows logically that any deviation from one's biological reproductive imperative would be seen from the perspective of the mundane as a perversion or abuse. The idea that all forms of Left Hand Path sexual sorcery lead to the creation of malignant phantasmal and etheric beings is an oversimplification and reeks of old world superstition. The sexual energy built up by the Black magician through the practice of karezza certainly is willfully directed and does in fact find a "field of operation" in the matrix which the dark sorcerer has intentionally created for it. The Left Hand Path view of this "field of nature" is that it is formed of the black magician's intent through long periods of development over time. The sorcerer does not regard the etheric as a passive field of activity as does our right hand path counter-parts, but instead understands it to be akin to the sorcerer's second field or night side which has been intentionally identified, constructed and built up over time through the forces of will and intent. Black magicians exist within this field or matrix of their own construction and all acts of magic that take place therein are purposeful and directed. Black magicians above all others are hoarders of energy.

We are misers with our precious resources and would simply not tolerate the unintentional creation of entities who would wreak havoc in our lives. The idea that the spilt seed breeds these creatures if it does not find a home in the womb of a woman is simply primitive and animistic in its metaphysics.

Grant defines karezza as "a method of sexual magic advocated in the West by Thomas Lake Harris (1823-1906) who adapted the formula from certain Tantric practices of building up magical energy by erotic stimulation and by suppressing its expression on the physical plane in order to create astral entities or magical manikins on the astral plane." While this type of operation is highly feasible, so are many others and it only makes sense that if the sorcerer is capable of building up magical energy through sexual stimulation and of suppressing its ordinary expression in favor of utilizing it for sorcery ends, then they should be able to direct this energy in a variety of ways. The use of karezza in sigil magic is a well-known application and essentially represents, in basic form the method whereby any other magical operation using this method would be structured. In sigil sorcery, the magician sexually stimulates themselves while focusing on a self-created sigil designed to embody some particular desire or objective. The sorcerer then attains orgasmic release while gazing at or visualizing the sigil and then promptly put the sigil away, forgetting about the operation in order to let the unconscious mind do its work. Variations on this type of sorcery include anointing the sigil with the sexual fluids and or carrying the sigil on one's person until the specified objective has been made manifest.

Some also choose to destroy the sigil in a ceremonial manner. While this can be a very effective sorcery practice, it is not properly karezza, as there is a release of the energy in orgasm. Properly performed, karezza is the sexual stimulation repeatedly brought to the pre-orgasmic stage and then held off while the sorcerer's intent is focused on their primary objective. No orgasm is attained in this operation and the climax of the sorcery, instead of being a physical orgasm is the release of the magician's will into the void of their creative intent. A specific ceremonial climax may be designed to represent the attainment of the goal, or the sorcerer may simply choose to slowly return to an ordinary state of consciousness, letting the process resemble more of an intense and willful meditation. As we shall soon see, the sexual energies built up within the body through karezza may also be physically moved to chosen power zones within and without the body, corresponding to the Adept's Left Hand Path initiation and the power zones on the Tree of Night.

In the Sorceries of Zos from Cults of the Shadow, Grant elaborates on his personal adaptation of karezza for a system of dream control.

"The mechanics of dream control are in many ways similar to those which effect conscious astral projection. My own system of dream control derives from two sources: the formula of Eroto-Comatose

Lucidity discovered by Ida Nellidoff and adapted by Crowley to his sexmagical techniques, and Spare's system of Sentient Sigils explained below. Sleep should be preceded by some form of Karezza during which a specially chosen sigil symbolizing the desired object is vividly visualized. In this manner the libido is baulked of its natural fantasies and seeks satisfaction in the dream world. When the knack is acquired the dream will be extremely intense and dominated by a succubae or shadow-woman, with whom sexual intercourse occurs spontaneously. If the dreamer has acquired even a moderate degree of proficiency in this technique, he will be aware of the continued presence of the sigil. This he should bind upon the form of the succubae in a place that is within range of his vision during copulation, e.g., as a pendant suspended from her neck; as ear-drops; or as the diadem in a circlet about her brow. Its locus should be determined by the magician with respect to the position he adopts during coitus. The act will then assume all the characteristics of a Ninth Degree Working, because the presence of the Shadow-Woman will be experienced with a vivid intensity of sensation and clarity of vision."

Admittedly, this is a highly personal and developed method of applying the method of Karezza to the development of the energy body and subsequently of attaining expertise in the arts of dreaming. As advanced as this technique is I can understand how Grant came to rely on it, yet I would always tend to recommend basic dreaming practices as a solid foundation for the sorcerer. The basics are those techniques which develop the Black Magician's will to a peak of sharpness, allowing them to leap forward into new and more complicated sorcery abstractions. Utilizing the sorcery dreaming practices associated with the first two Gates of Dreaming will only bolster more advanced dream control such as the one provided by grant. A powerful variant on this technique could be to ensure that the "specially chosen sigil" to which Grant refers is constructed with the sole intent of accomplishing greater control in dreaming. In this way the sexual sorcery of Karezza will be both directed at the act of dreaming while the specially constructed sigil will become a living battery of dreaming energy and a vital portal into powerful dream lucidity. What I am essentially doing here is simply elaborating on Grant's technique by illustrating that the sigilized object of desire should be formulated around the primary desire to dream lucidly and not simply representing any random desire or sorcery goal.

Most Black Magicians who are committed to becoming expert dreamers have enough drive and desire to energize and work with a sigil in this way.

This is not to say that the technique will not work with a sigil representing another objective, but I will venture to say that the resulting dream states may be more difficult to control and dominated by the naturally inherent properties of the sigil used. I would recommend trying multiple variations of the basic formula which Grant goes on to provide.

Briefly, the formula has three stages:

1. Karezza, or unculminating sexual activity, with visualization of the Sigil until sleep supervenes.
2. Sexual congress in the dream-state with the Shadow-woman evoked by Stage I. The Sigil should appear automatically at this second stage; if it does not, the practice must be repeated at another time. If it does, then the desired result will reify in Stage.
3. After awakening (i.e. in the mundane world of everyday phenomena).

A word of explanation is, perhaps, necessary concerning the term Karezza as used in the present context.

Retention of semen is a concept of central importance in certain Tantric practices, the idea being that the bindu (seed) then breeds astrally, not physically. In other words, an entity of some sort is brought to birth at astral levels of consciousness. This, and analogous techniques, have given rise to the impression -- quite erroneous -- that celibacy is a sine qua non of magical success; but such celibacy is of a purely local character and confined to the physical plane, or waking state, alone. Celibacy, as commonly understood, is therefore a meaningless parody or travesty of the true formula."

It seems that in this particular operation, Grant emphasizes the role of the Shadow-woman, or succubae. My natural conclusion regarding this is that the initial energetic charge built up by the practice of Karezza and then transferred to the sigil gives excitation and vitality to the sorcerer's dreaming emissary, who then proceeds to energetically seek to establish a stronger dreaming connection with the sorcerer as was originally intended in the creation of the sigil. The sexual congress with this inorganic being is in all actuality an energetic bonding of the Black Magician's dream double with the dark energy that emanates from the shadow's world and eventually through practice and regular intercourse, one will only need visualize the dreaming sigil before falling into sleep in order to illicit immediate congress with the emissary. I will reiterate here that this operation as it relates to Karezza is really not a necessary consideration for the female sorcerer engaging in dreaming practices. Dreaming in itself is a completely separate discipline for the female and they almost always tend to not need the "props" that we males need to rely on for any degree of progress. The perceptual sex of the succubae is irrelevant and will of course be determined by one's sexual leanings.

Following Grant's short outline of this system for dream control he goes on to a vital explanation of the differences between the magical practice of Karezza, the retention of physical semen in the body of the male sorcerer and the act of celibacy. He states that celibacy as understood in the profane sense is meaningless in relation to the true magical formula. Here, what is meant is that the act of sexual celibacy as a permanent feature of the Black Magician's sorcery practice is unnecessary in order for magical progress and attainment to occur, however I must add that there are truly few drawbacks in the choice of celibacy for any practitioner whose interests and activities reside outside the realms of sex sorcery. For the Black magician, celibacy is not seen as a blasphemy as it is by many a Thelemite. Instead it is viewed as a severe and demanding path chosen by the very few who can truly benefit from the rare gifts it can bestow to its adherents. For the Black Magician, utilizing the sorcery practices of Karezza while also walking the path of sexual celibacy inevitably results in the attainment of power at a level difficult to describe and a state of existence that could be quite undesirable to some. Also, we must consider what the sorcerer Don Juan had to say to Carlos Castaneda regarding celibacy as the optimum way to acquire and store enough personal energy to successfully engage in dreaming. Personally, I believe that Castaneda was "handled" by his teacher in a very specific way catering to his own personal strengths and weaknesses, and that one's level of sexual energy as it relates to dreaming is not an all or nothing affair (see Dreaming the Labyrinth of Penumbra). I have personally maintained extremely long periods of celibacy, devoting all my energy towards dream sorcery only to finally achieve me desired results after giving in and indulging myself in sexual relations. This is a perfect example of etheric tensions being built up through my concentrated will and intent to eventually become energized by the culmination of a sexual act the forgetting of the original goal.

The retention of semen as the physical inevitability of the practice of Karezza can be handled in primarily two ways. It may be retained indefinitely and naturally released by the body through non-sexual processes such as regular urination, or it may be ritually consumed during sexual sorcery practices or utilized to anoint sigilized talismans or energetically feed servitors. The expenditure of physical semen during a naturally occurring nocturnal emission should not be considered a loss of energy or power, but simply as the body's natural reaction to a practice that essentially interferes with the body's routine functioning. The most important thing to keep in mind is that semen should not be expended carelessly during the ongoing course of magical operations. How long semen is retained and in what manner it is finally released will of course be determined by the nature of the operation in question. I should also here briefly mention the magical properties and potential use of the pre-ejaculatory fluid that will accumulate during the utilization of Karezza and in states of high sexual arousal. From a Black Magical perspective this substance is a very desirable result of the energy built up during intense sexual agitation.

It should be used in dream sorcery to anoint the Ajna energy center as well as any other chakra point on the physical body corresponding to the nature of the sorcery operation engaged in. This clear substance is the true elixir vitae of sexual shadow sorcery and due to its energetic potency it can be most effectively used in works of vampiric domination where the Black Magician anoints their chosen sexual partner on certain points over their body before engaging in vampiric sexual intercourse. This will essentially "pin" down the victim and make the resulting energy transfer easier to achieve. Of course, in this technique, the sorcerer will copulate with the victim until they have been exhausted of all the available pranic force. After the operation the sorcerer must then retreat to a quiet place in order to properly circulate and effectively store the energetic gains they have made. The consumption of this fluid by the sorcerer in conjunction with a proper diet and regular physical activity will have a tendency to harden and keep the body young while also sharpening the senses.

Over time the practice of Karezza will have the over-arching effect of encapsulating the Black Magician within a bio-energetic field initiated by their own non-human intent. This self-created shell develops a sustaining force that becomes impregnable by random and unwanted influences stemming from the entropic forces of ordinary consensual reality. The metaphysical formula of Left Hand Path sex magic directly coincides with the formula 89 of the Black School of Magic. It is a turning away from the distorted evolutionary path of the modern human being in favor of the assertion of the individual sorcerer's own creative will in the cosmos. The Black magician takes those major elements of their implied predestination as physical human beings on this planet and masters each one on a path leading away from their absorption and destruction. This is the true and sublime meaning of the inverted pentagram as the primary and dominant seal of the way of the Black Adept.

This way of inversion sometimes termed "the Backwards Way," is the beginning of the transmogrification of the total consciousness and energy shape of the individual. Accumulated sexual energy should be circulated throughout the physical body by means of breathing and visualization. Our essential energies reside in those places within us where we have placed some kind of emphasis, and energetic imbalances will almost always manifest as physical imperfections and disease of mind and body. But, as the sorcerer knows through experience, there is the wider field that we must consider in the experiential existence of the sorcerer's energy body typically described as the luminous egg like structure which envelopes us and extends outward a few feet from the physical self. Energy can neither be created nor destroyed, but as all sorcerers know it can indeed be transferred and transformed.

The initial boost in one's overall energy through the buildup or sexual energy during karezza will act as a catalyst and cause an immediate shift in the assemblage point. This shift will then typically be accompanied by an increase in magical ability, enhanced sensory perception and greater capability in the realms of dreaming and vampiric energy gathering techniques. The one consistent ability I have noticed increase is that of basic visualization. This seems to be true no matter where I have decided to direct an increase in energy, as if the buildup of sexual energy derived from Karezza overflows the power zones of the body and amplifies their natural functioning. In the chakra zone of Ajna, enhanced visualization seems to be the result. I recommend keeping a sorcery journal specifically devoted to the practice of this form of sexual magic, placing particular emphasis on these greater and subtler changes as one's energy increases.

Let the aspirant experiment and create, but also let there always be the unbending and primary intent needed to stabilize the force of this practice. Without the sobriety of a true Black magician energetic imbalances will inevitably occur and the sorcerer will believe themselves to have "achieved" their goal purely as a result of the residual powers. As a kind of magical base line, one should choose to emphasize their basic physical self and their physical health thereby devising the most optimum ways to channel this refined sexual energy throughout the body and effectively slowing down and eventually reversing the entropy of physical ageing. Once again, without health and longevity, the Black Magician will not become capable of permanently fortifying themselves in opposition to the deleterious effects of objective existence and the material plane.

Celibacy in conjunction with the practice of Karezza is a fundamental formula for success in all black magical endeavors and it is also an excellent way for the beginner in black sex magic to introduce themselves to the eventual complexities of Left Hand Path sexual sorcery. It offers a stable platform to leap into other practices and is subsequently just as stable on the return journey. The key to the regular application of Karezza is to turn away from sexual interest immediately after its practice and begin to engage in other non-sexually related activities. If Karezza begins to engender sexual obsessions that lead to compulsive behavior of any kind, then it should be ended. This is not to say that the sorcerer should not be as creative as they wish when engaging in its practice. As long as the practice itself does not become its own addiction one may explore as many avenues of black magical perversity as they see fit, understanding that true titillation and arousal is a veritable art and to achieve this yet deny one's self the immediate reward of physical ecstasy in favor of abstract goals is something only the very few will accomplish. ✦

Kyle Fite, *Gran Bois*

Becoming Hoodoo

PART 1

Kyle Fite

THE opening lessons of the Voudon-Gnostic Workbook comprise the "Folk Grimoire" known as Lucky Hoodoo. Although relatively short and simple, it is an enigmatic text. On one hand, it speaks in terms which are very straightforward, offering uncomplicated exercises for the student to explore. On the other, we find that the more one "sticks with it," regarding the lessons as actual doorways into Gnostic Spaces, the more it is seen to be an operating manual for a Living Machine, the applications of which are nearly limitless.

The first chapter of Lucky Hoodoo ends with the statement:

Be sure of good luck, for you are becoming a Hoodoo.

By the end of the second chapter, it is declared that the student is, in fact, a "Hoodoo." Lesson three continues the pattern with its closing suggestion that You can become a big Lucky Hoodoo.

The first impression here is of a series of grades or stages, corresponding with initiations-or at least the growth of power and ability in the field of magic known as "Hoodoo." We are instructed in how we may speak the language of the spirits, cut deals with them and be lucky or prosperous in the things of this world. It may all seem a tad superstitious and "low magic." This was certainly my first impression of the text.

I would, however, like to reexamine some elements in this text whereby we find ourselves being guided into a deep Theosis, defined by Michael Bertiaux as "the power and mysteries...sufficient for perfection and divinization" (VGW p. 196) and "Union with the Gods" (VGW p. 204).

To begin, Lucky Hoodoo is very inclusive. It offers encouragement and empowerment to anyone who will take an interest in it. There is a direct acknowledgement of the things we struggle with in life, the aspiration to knowledge of a higher and more refined realm behind our material existence and the reality of primal, or elemental, impulses hardwired into our brains and bodies. Lucky Hoodoo, therefore, opens up with an embrace of the immediate concerns and realities with which the average human being must contend.

As we start to find solutions to our practical problems by entering a communion with the Spirits (who begin to show themselves as present behind the veil of our seemingly mundane and day to day affairs), our perspective becomes more "magical." Without fanfare and in the midst of modern life, we become increasingly "shamanic" in our interface with the demands and challenges of human existence.

If we have traveled down the road this far, we will now observe the path extending further outward, further inward. We are faced with the questions: How far does it stretch?

Where does it lead? And how deep into the portal before me am I willing to venture?

Have we really become a Hoodoo?

Lucky Hoodoo, I believe, cannot be read as a common text. Its language is more vivid and organic than the merely didactic. It evokes paradoxes to lock up the gears of intellect and allow the Soul-Self to move deeper into the hidden halls of the Holy House.

An example of this may be found in the very first lesson. With two candles, blue and black, we sit in shadow and call upon the Spirits of Deep Sea, whence no light shines. We call upon the Spirits of the Dead who reside in the darkness of the earth. As these entities come forth, we declare that we are Children of the Light and that there is no Darkness in the Powers of the Dead. By the time we have established our Hoodoo altar with its five candles in place, we intone:

O LIGHT THERE IS NO DARKNESS.
O LIGHT WE ARE
IN THE PRESENCE OF ENDLESS LIGHT.

When I initially began experimentation with this work, this simple set up felt a bit sinister to my modern mind. I grew up in the American Mid-West and my views regarding Vudu were certainly colored by comic-books and cinematic sensationalism. Performing the actual ceremony, however, quickly gives way to a deep feeling of devotion and awareness of sacred space. This is not a rite to instill fear or indulge in fixation on morbid curiosities. If you call the Hoodoo and your inner self matches the outwards gestures, they most assuredly will arrive. You will FEEL their presence and begin to SEE a vast life-stream moving through realms previously invisible. The darkness has been an occluding shroud which we are now pulling to the side. The Dead will reveal the Mystery of the Resurrection, the raising of the corruptible form into incorruptible life. Instead of fear, we may find a feeling of deep love and gratitude rising as our minds touch this larger and more unified spectrum of life.

Now we enter further into paradox. The Hoodoo Spirits are presented as effective servants who will gladly do our bidding if we pay them off with the goods they like. We're here to "make a deal" as magicians. The Goetic approach comes to mind, calling up a useful "demon" and sending it off "on assignment." As Causes which can bring about Effects, the traditional admonition is to handle these critters with care. There are the established rules of constraining, compelling, binding and exorcizing. One must never let the demon get the upper hand, for in the end, we're "boss" and our command and control will determine the success of the operation.

From this medieval mindset, Hoodoo looks appallingly dangerous, if not suicidal:

I DEDICATE MYSELF TO THE
SERVICE OF THE SPIRITS.

I OFFER MYSELF TO THE SERVICE OF
THE GREAT KING OF THE DEAD.

These words conclude with an affirmation to work with these Spirits NOW AND FOREVER.

Repeatedly, we approach the Hoodoo with the words I AM HERE TO SERVE YOU.

Clearly, something other than employing some "lowly elementals" is going on here! We wanted help with a new job, a relationship, some financial woes...and here we are pledging to serve the Hoodoo NOW AND FOREVER.

What are we getting ourselves into?

At this point, I wish to quote at length from the Voudon Gnostic Workbook's chapter on Atlantean Mystery School Readings: The Temple of Esoteric Readings. This is an amazingly powerful passage and truly written from the viewpoint of Gnostic Vision:

The law of esoteric communion is more than the sacramental rite of self-unfoldment, it is the place and power of being a spirit oneself. This means that we are spirits and we must always act and be as if we were perfectly aware of our spiritual powers and Vudu energies. We are Vudu, but we do not yet exercise all of the powers. When we leave the Temple of Esoteric Readings, we have a better understanding of the fact that we do possess these powers of being. They are right within us and we know it now. Thus, we see ourselves as part of their spiritual world or spiritist communion, because we are spirits and we are in the world of mysticism. I look outside and see myself as I used to be and wonder as to how I could ever have thought that I was only in the material world. I am primarily in the world and work of spirits.

This passage puts a rather different spin on the statement that we are "becoming a Hoodoo!"

I once heard report of an individual involved with this and related practices who felt that he had become a Loa and was to be regarded as such, with deference and devotion. Lucky Hoodoo in no way tends towards this sort of megalomania. Our BECOMING might also be called a revealing of the simple fact:

"We are Vudu, but we do not exercise all of the powers."

As we continue to walk this Path, revealing what exists from the vantage point of Eternity, we can focus so much on how we are perceiving things that we disregard how others are experiencing the same phenomena. Our philosophy is not solipsistic. It is spiritist, acknowledging a vast diversity of intelligence permeating the universe, far beyond our immediate and individualized assessment of the situation.

When lighting our candles, intoning our prayers and forging the link between ourselves and the Hoodoo, we may sometimes strain towards a perception of that "other world." New students are especially fond of anything tending towards a table-tapping. We'd like some confirmation that our endeavor is more than wishful thinking or submission to fantasy. We want candles blown out, visions of cadaverous forms emerging from the crypt, the scent of saltwater inexplicably wafting in the window. I have had disappointment expressed to me from students working with this course, feeling that their rite was a "dud" due to such lack. Very swiftly they doubt its most basic claims and abandon the work.

I have no doubt that persistence in this work will, indeed, open the "inner vision" to unearthly sights and sounds. As Michael reminds us:

The spirits want to meet you and they want to get into your life... they are more willing to help you than often you are ready to have them.

We may, however, be so focused on how to open ourselves to the Hoodoo Realm that we don't consider how we, ourselves, appear to the Hoodoo. This is important because we are not trying to bind the Hoodoo like some Medieval Conjurer nor are we treating them as if they were simply elements of our own mind, dressed up in a colorful mythic guise and playing a role in our self-created psychodrama. We are approaching a different level of being, the gulf between us bridged by the dynamics of communion. In our human affairs, we certainly give some consideration to how another person perceives or feels about us. We recognize that they have some equality with us as fellow humans and our interchange is a two-way street.

The Hoodoo are no different in this regard. We would not treat a fellow human as if they were a Goetic demon and try to bind and bully them into doing our bidding (Well, we might-but that typically is not the foundation for a relationship of value. Certainly not a friendship!).

As we consider the elemental nature of the Hoo & Doo, we may be tempted to see them as belonging to a lower order of things. The opposite is really true, however. The Hoo were once Atlantean sages who were able to consciously migrate into a more refined form upon impending disaster. The Doo include our Ancestors, those who once wore bone, blood and skin-and have gone forward into the "Mysterious Country."

It has been said that the skull in the Masonic Lodgeroom not only indicates mortality-but immortality, as well-for it is that portion of the physical form which "remains" and has a type of permanence. When the Doo appear in forms grotesque to the modern mind, they are also demonstrating the life which continues despite dissolution of physical form.

We are not concerned with "earthbound ghosts," "troubling spirits" and the like. The Hoodoo are unified under Papa Nibbho and Maitre. They are understood in context of the "Legbha Physics" whereby the Cosmic Machine, or Body of God, operates towards its transcendental ends.

Returning to the VGW Chapter on The Temple of Esoteric Readings, we find this remarkable statement:

"We hold... that each student contains in his soul the history of the universe of being, because that student is now in being and is a photograph of the mysteries of the universe from its beginnings...the student is the universe in its learning aspect."

Thus we may regard our experiences as tending towards initiations, which occur at "power points" on an ever moving cosmic grid, such points marking a shift from the previous directional denominator. Carlos Castaneda would call this "displacement of the assemblage point." We may see this place of shifting energy as the point where strands of spider-webbing meet, for the Spider Loa are also the Lords of Esoteric Geometry, through which we not only are guided in magical map-making (researching new spaces in the esoteric realms) but called to cooperate in the work which is transpiring there, also.

These Spider Loa are of the Ghuedhe Familie-and the Ghuedhe are over-shadowed by Papa Nibbho. We can see here that the "Hoodoo Man" is not only a mortal who deals with the Spirits from this perspective-but one of the "Familie" Himself. His body is the meat or Zombie and he regards it as such, for he has "become Hoodoo" in this Gnosis and knows himself as a spiritual entity in which is contained the Universe as a whole. For him to be both a singular entity and the sum of all entities is to understand that this truth must likewise apply to all entities differentiated from himself. This fundamental union allows the lightning swift transmission of thought beyond the constraints of time and space. This is the basis for our ability to form the contacts we do with such nonhuman creatures.

Differentiation and Unity need not be at odds. These become perspectives whereby experience is directed beyond limitations and into further areas of Soul-Growth, on both the individual and cosmic level.

My understanding of this arose spontaneously as I was called by the Spirits to perform a certain work in service to them. I did not feel adequate to the task nor qualified for its demands. And yet the same Powers which asked me to go a particular route for definite ends also showed me how I appeared to them. They were not hung up on how I saw my abilities or qualifications. From their view, I was possessed of particular capabilities which would be of use. For me to assess myself as "not up to snuff" was not humility but spiritual pride. I was projecting a false image of an imagined ideal onto the organic fluctuations of reality. This was not an issue of how I regarded myself but how open to cooperation I was. "A House divided against itself shall not stand" and the House in consideration here was the Holy House.

The Hoodoo were not attempting to put me in a triangle and crank down the thumbscrews until I ran off on their errand. They do not work that way. Everyone has a place, a purpose, a job to do, a basic nature which may find fulfillment in the larger scheme of the Great Work. I could understand the different divisions of the Hoodoo pantheon. "Work Loa" weren't slaves... they were energized beings whose nature was fulfilled in the type of work they engaged with. I was also one of these Spirits, guided into my own sphere of activity and infused with the energies necessary to the task.

Kyle Fite, *Nibbho-Ghuedhe*

My feelings turned towards gratitude and deep sense of inspiration. Not the hot flare of sudden enthusiasm which may come and go but an inner conviction as to the continuity of consciousness which runs through all the changes we enter-and the goodness of the creative mind in which are alive and move.

I had called myself "Hoodoo Pilot" when I began my work with Lucky Hoodoo some time ago. My vision was of one navigating the shifting terrain of Inner Space, a turbo-powered astral explorer. Now the title seems even more appropriate. I am "Hoodoo Pilot" as I have become Hoodoo and navigate even the material universe as such. I serve the spirits of lucky Hoodoo not as an inferior but in a Fraternal Spirit. Just as we rise up to a sense of humanity with regards to our fellows, the vision extends and expands...we are in a Brotherhood with more than our species, more than our Orders and collectives. We are all of us pilots who came into s zone through a Lethe-Field. We forgot our origins and our Deep Self was overshadowed and overridden by the vehicles required for movement on the dense plane. This was our "Fall."

Christianity teaches that the plan for Man's Salvation through Christ was foreordained from the beginning of time. Thus, the Old Testament is embraced as presaging the Spirit of Christ and containing its Essence. Jesus comes not to "destroy the law" but to "fulfill it." Our entry into the "Fallen World" is not a curse but a choice. The Salvific Power which releases the Lumen from Darkness is already within us. We don't escape the "Evil World" to somehow "ascend to the Higher Spheres." Instead, we perform the work which accomplishes the New Earth of Revelation 21:1-3

And I saw a new heaven and a new earth: for the first heaven and the first earth were passed away; and there was no more sea. And I John saw the holy city, new Jerusalem, coming down from God out of heaven, prepared as a bride adorned for her husband. And I heard a great voice out of heaven saying, Behold, the tabernacle of God is with men, and he will dwell with them, and they shall be his people, and God himself shall be with them, and be their God.

To entertain the idea that we are Spirits, that we are, in fact, Hoodoo Spirits, is not enough. We are to upgrade our consciousness to a higher and deeper state. We are not looking for a novel experience of seeing things from an altered point of view. Instead, we are going to unlock a portion of the Salvific Power as an empowerment which, once downloaded into our system, will feed in energy from the Hoodoo level of awareness. Not only does this clear away resistance within our system to the influx of "Luck," it allows us to become transmitters of Luck into the Environment. This is a genuine power-and it begets change. The "Hot Points" which have ignited within us may now redirect undulations on the World Web.

In our work with the Hoodoo, we enter into a realm of form and hierarchy. One contact leads to another and we observe the relationship between different patterns of energy as they form connections in the dynamics of our own lives. As we go further into this work, we find definite patterns of relevance to our present state of being on the "grid." This will mark out the different potencies playing their part in our initiatory voyage and herein we find ourselves coming into a direct experiential understanding of the variety of powers we call by the names of Hoodoo, Loa and Les Vudu.

Of the Loa and Les Vudu, Michael writes in VGW on page 181:

While the work with the Loa can be understood as concerning general initiation, esoteric work with the Vudu-Spirits, or Les Vudu is concerned with personal development and esoteric consciousness.

Where, then do the Hoodoo fit into this scheme?

From a hierarchical viewpoint, the Hoodoo would be "below" the Loa. We might envision a threefold structure, some Vudu Ziggurat comprising 3 "Degrees" or "Levels" of Being. We may see in this a correlative to the 3 Degrees of Freemasonry or, perhaps, the 3 Grades described in Crowley's Book Of The Law. . The problem with this is that these are often seen as sequential phases whereby we reach the "top" of some initiatic pyramid. One might feel that after some luck with the Hoodoo, we can then move onto the Loa and Les Vudu, having become more "advanced." If this were the case, we need to ask why the vast compendium of the VGW instructs us to pledge our loyalty and devotion to the Hoodoo "NOW AND FOREVER."

Once we set the hand to the plow, we never loosen our grip. We do not "go beyond" the Hoodoo. We go in. Deeper. The Leaders of Hoo and Doo are Loa themselves and the continuance in this work increasingly moves us into the World of Les Vudu. Our "personal development" is also the development of the Cosmic Being inasmuch as we are the universe of being "in its learning aspect." We are told that we already are "Les Vudu" and simply need to come into this awareness. By doing so, we also become Hoodoo and know ourselves as spirit. This is why the Hoodoo Science teaches "Mind Development." Mind Development feeds and nurtures "esoteric conscious-ness." We begin to see that the Loa, the Vudu, the Ultimate Powers on the periphery of our experience are ALL involved in this work-at the same time.

Magic begets magic. Lucky Hoodoo is a Grimoire whose pages flutter up into an etheric wind and collapse into a Key. This Key finds its keyhole within your mind. With a click and turn, the sealed doorway swings open and new Grimoires rise in the influx of the incoming current.

These Grimoires are yours. You will write them with your own hand. You will speak their mysteries with your own tongue. And like their "parent," they also are procreative and possessed of power. They are links in a chain, stars in a constellation, constellations in the infinite heavens, the infinite heavens in majestic motion, whole galaxies revolving around secret centers and hidden hearts of godlike flame!

Hoodoo brings all of this right into the thick of the moment. It transforms YOU into IT. Burnished and clean, you come out of the furnace with the knowledge that the New Creation is the Eternal Life which always "was, is and is to come." ✦

Rafal Kosela, *Mystery ov Mysteries*

Comes Dietrich, *Azaloke: Black Sun of the Chaos*

Loki & Azatoth
Lords of Fire & Chaos
Ljossál Loðursson

WE, the Walkers of the Left Hand Path, align our consciousness with the gods or deities who have faced the Creator or the Creation. Within the Nordic culture this defier is known as the Þursar Loki. The Eldrþurs or Fire Giant Loki is the Dark Lord of the Flame and Chaos. He is the source of malice, deceit and destruction. Because of these features that aren't considered as positive in the academic religious or moral contexts he has been labeled as a demon or as the antithesis of any divine quality.

During my process in the exploration of the Black Flame I aligned my consciousness with this Giant and inspired by the Sagas, mythological descriptions about Yggdrasil and Heldrasil, I performed numerous invocations and Seiðr practices using Ayahuasca. I was able to blur the essence of this frightful giant inside my being.

I performed my first invocation to Loki at the age of 22 years and as a result several internal changes occurred within me. The main changes were related to the confrontation of my emotional attachments and my fears. Loki urged me to get in trouble in an impulsive manner and due to these stupid decisions the Þurs took many of my friends and loved ones away. He also made me more aware of the consequences of my actions, one year after I unexpectedly had my first child born and none of this was clearly unfounded. Every game and every destruction brought a powerful teaching. He helped me to transmute my pain into joy and laughter, my fear into value, my attachment into free love and my stupidity and arrogance into wisdom and will.

This is the parameter of the Tantric traditions, learning to transmute poison into medicine.

The Chaos emanations are not mere archetypes pigeonholed within academic, theological or mythological concepts. Initially in my spiritual journey I had learned some whispers of the goddess Eris, it was expressed by the runic knowledge taught by "ThoughtMaster Xy" regarding their Discordian Futhark which served as a base ground for future knowledge, in some ways I have considered a certain relationship between Eris and Gullveig. Gods like Loki carry within the mystery of Ater Ignis, Black Flame that burns and destroys Creation and opens the doors for Black Sun and reach the essence of the Unmanifest.

The Gods or Giants of Chaos are not mere archetypes pigeonholed inside academic, theological or mythological concepts. Beings like Loki carry within the mystery of Ignis Ater, the Black Flame that burns and destroys the creation and opens the doors of the Black Sun in order to reach the essence of the Unmanifest.

Acausal expressions such as this Þurs have connected with humanity to teach them how to go beyond anything Cosmic-Finite towards experiencing what is Chaotic-Infinity. Under my personal perception of Dark Alchemy Loki possesses a symbolic level that gives practical knowledge and expertise on all types of Azoth.

Loki is the father of Jǫrmungandr, he is the Father of the Serpent and the Dragon. In the Dragon we find the arcane mysteries of Draconian Energy and Sexual Alchemy, the birth of the Red Azoth.

Loki is the father of Fenrir, the Father of the Wolf. Fenrir is a Ronin, he has no herd and in the process of isolation has learned to confront his anger, fear, anguish and pain, this is the foundation of the Black Azoth.

Loki is the father of Hel, the Father of the Gýgr or Gigantess of two faces. Half of Hel's face is human and shows the essence of life, the other half is blue and violet and shows death as it is rotten. Hel is the Goddess of Heldrasil, the Acausal or Anti-Cosmic Tree, she is the Lady of the 9 underworlds, this is the Purple Azoth.

Finally, Loki is the receptacle of knowledge of Gullveig's heart, Mother of the Nordic Shamanism, of the Seiðr. Through this mystery Loki has traveled all the branches of Yggdrasil and understood the mystery of the Tree, this is the root of the Green Azoth.

Thus, this Lord of the Black Ooze holds within itself all the qualities of the Magickal Quintessence. Under his inspiration and guide he showed me how to deal with the Black Arts and break all my limitations allowing me to see Gnosis Nigreda. When making the first invocation addressed to his spirit he unveiled a specific Rune which could be seen as its essence whenever I needed him. I have seen other works related or dedicated to this Múspellmegir, magnanimous treatises on Pan and Loki, it is clear that the Fire Lord whispers the secrets of his name in different parts of the land of Miðgarð. What follows is part of the knowledge that he whispered to me over the years.

This Bandrúnir or bindrune receives the name of Lokekvisa or Loki's whisper. With it I built a Rune Talisman and carried it with me for several years in each Invocatory process or calling of the Fire Giant. Testing this Rune allowed me to channel its energy without receiving any damage. I remembered that Loki does not destroy without foundation, he rips from our lives all obstacles that prevent us of finding our own internal axis and God.

Lokekvisa

Working with the Loki Rune can bring powerful creative experiences, a lot of Alchemic Salt will manifest in you, the artistic or crafty aspects of yourself will be strongly developed. Anamnesis experiences may also occur where the user "downloads data". In his aspect as a traveler Loki knows all the Yggdrasil, he took me along the various branches of the Tree by their different worlds he allowed me to further develop the experiences of lucid dreaming and astral projection. Finally, I helped to weave some Niðstang or Bane Staffs against my enemies which were defeated one by one.

If the Lokekvisa is used as Talisman it should not be carried or worn all the time, the chaotic essence it holds is quite powerful. To create one, the user performs Evocations or Shamanic Callings to condense the power of the Fire Lord inside. At the time of any invocation make sure you have the Talisman close to your skin so that it receives the Azoth of the Lord of Chaos.

When Loki ate Gullveig's heart, the Lady of the Seiðr, the governess of Black Magic in the Giants and teacher of the Dark Runes, a part of the knowledge and power of the Gullveig was transferred to Loki. The various processes of Invocation, Astral Projection and Lucid Dreaming made to contact with the Lord of Fire and Chaos start to reveal the Dark Runes you can use to your advantage with each of the capabilities they possess. Initially some of them were revealed shortly after their transmission but I kept the others cautiously hidden until the moment my Gnosis Nigreda process had already borne fruit in the Garden of Shadows. These are the Runes of the Heart or Loki's Hjarta Rúnar. Use them at their discretion and their own inspiration, discover the hidden power that lies within them.

Here I will give some basic features but the reader should work on the hidden capabilities of the Runes that Loki gave to mankind.

HJARTA RÚNAR—THE FIERY RUNES OF LOKI

The Heart Runes or Loki's Runes allowed me to internalize the fact that he represents the Acausal or Obverse process. He is one of the manifestations of the Black Sun in the Nordic Tradition. His seemingly erratic and insane qualities lead us to the wisdom that Umbra or the Shadow can lend us, therefore working with the primal instinct is not a distant or foreign event but rather a close and familiar experience. In my experience I perceived that the "madness" or erratic qualities that the Múspellmegir shows are similar (if not identical) to the ones that Azatoth, the Solar God of Lovecraftian fiction, can give us.

Azathoth is known as the antithesis of Creation, as the Sultan of Demons and the Chaos Engine. All these epithets refer to their Anti-Cosmic and Acausal nature- He induces madness through the sound of his flute.

This flute is jagged and this produces a raucous sound. Whenever the Azatoth Flute is played the strength of the shadow or umbra burns with great power within man and this causes the erratic nature to be revealed. Only those who have gone and internalized the dark side of their being can hear the real music that the flute of Madness produces.

Azatoth remains upon the Obsidian Throne, the Green and Black throne that stands above the passage of the Aeons and their destruction thereof. The significance of this symbol is important since it refers to the Gnosis given by the Pleroma, Knowledge and Wisdom without time and space, unlimited in all its forms, beyond Creation and Destruction.

The sound produced by the Azatoth flute brings the awakening of the Nigreda Gnosis inside the Sinister Alchemist as he is the only one longing to hear the notes of this instrument, each of the Runes of the Heart of Loki is one of the notes that this flute can play.

Black Rune	Name	Attributes
		Aett of Creation
	Frud	**Creation.** Increases or develops creativity and artistic inspiration. Fertility and Growth.
	Ipoh	**Laughter.** Positive mood change. Banish negative or adverse energy.
	Nerap	**Shapeshifting.** Allows one to take the form of the Totem, change the astral body or develop atavistic connections.
	Imareh	**Lust.** Generates or cancels the desire of one person over another.
	Jugen	**Deceit.** It makes a lie believable by those who hear it.
		Aett of Destruction
	Soroh	**Discordia.** Separation and conflict occurs between two persons, groups or communities.
	Rah	**Confusion.** Generates or cancels any kind of disorientation, helps or hinders finding important answers.
	Lust	**Attachment.** Generates or destroys the attachment that a person can experience at any aspect, be it a person, habit or vice.
	Gored	**Separation.** End any process that is ongoing. Breaks all enemy defenses.
		Aett of Chaos
	Ophmia	**Dominance.** Grants or suspend control over a situation, skill, title or person.
	Aghar	**Reversion.** Revert any pattern or established current.

He who goes inside the perception of this sound can discern that Loki and Azatoth have the same essence and inner quality, each is the Black Sun of their tradition or personal paradigm.

Together they generate the momentum that leads to the process of awakening and liberation, these two gods are merged into a Alchemical-Chaotic Symbiote which results in the transcendence of the Kingdom of all creation.

Azaloke is the formula and the name by which the union of the Lords of Fire and Dark Sun weave hordes of demons that unceasingly consume humanity and the flock who sleeps in the Kingdom of the Senses.

The sound of the Azaloke flute distorts the walls of Reality weakening each layer of Ego and Cosmic Self in man. Only those who carry the symbol of Chaos and blazon the arms of Death can hear the melody without being destroyed in that moment.

The frequent sound of the flute during the alchemical State of Nigredo - Melanosis can be addictive and in the process can lead to self-destruction. Only those who have reached Albedo or Rubedo can hear the dark notes of the dark instrument without losing their Reason.

Finally, the Azaloke complex can be rationalized as the complementary opposite of Consciousness-Energy similar to Shiva-Shakti, except that in this complex either one can play the role of Consciousness or Energy and its strength is unlimited, timeless and spaceless. ✶

A Malkunofat Working

Andi Moon & Sarah Price

"Then the holy one appeared in the great water of the North; as a golden dawn did he appear, bring benediction to the fallen universe.
— Liber CCXXXI

The Preparation

Immersion. This was the method decided upon in the exploration of the Tunnel of Set under the aegis of Malkunofat. Many years after first reading Kenneth Grant's Nightside of Eden I had found that for me at least using a limited pattern of techniques or even setting a timescale to my workings was/is constraining and self-defeating. Therefore, each Tunnel has been approached in different ways, from simply carrying a charged sigil of the Qliphoth of certain Tunnels, to full blown ritual.

In the case of Malkunofat, immersion and saturation over the period of several weeks prior to the beginning of the rituals and meditations were deemed to be the methods suitable for this venture. A representation of Malkunofat using the sigil from Liber CCXXXI was manifested in a painting which was intended both for use as a focus during the working as to be added to as a record both during and after.

Using this, the symbolism of the deep ocean and the entities therein as a Daathian Gate to cross over into the chthonic abyss of Universe B.

In preparation, as well as the aforementioned painting, various objects were collected to provide ambience in the temple space. Seawater, squid ink, beak, eye lens and tentacle hooks, starfish, crab shell and claws, seashells from a variety of species, all would be used. The squid ink was used on the day of the first ritual to embellish the sigil of Malkunofat.

Books, articles, papers and artwork from a variety of sources were read and studied. Occult, fictional and scientific; from diverse sources any and all included, contrary perspectives, anecdotes, poems. Nothing excluded, everything allowed.

The Temple Space

The sigilized painting of Malkunofat is placed at the centre of the altar, to its left a giant starfish and before it a smaller star made from grey stone. Three shells, one empty, one containing seawater, the other squid ink are also on the altar along with two blue candles, an iron incense burner, the claw bell which will open and close the ceremony and an effigy of Cthulhu to represent the otherworldliness of the Deep Ones.

About the room other objects are positioned, a libation of (Kraken) rum, crab shells and claws, statues and figurines seafaring and seaborne cultures, an obsidian mirror and a singing bowl containing seawater.

The Ritual – The Priestess

Malkunofat Working.

Fifth day of menstruation.

The ritual began with the ringing of a bell.

A breeze blew through the prepared space, but as our chants began and the seawater-filled bowl started to sing a pressure seemed to grow within our temple space. My head was buzzing from the swelling hum of the bowl and I found myself swaying in a tight but slow circle as I called the name Malkunofat over and over. Deep but slow breaths, lungs filling with heavy air. Even the candlelight struggled to penetrate.

The triangle containing the sigil held my gaze and began to pulsate, languorous shapes appearing then changing again. It was fluid like oil; several times an eye peered out, blinking. The top-right corner of the triangle lightened gradually from deep blue-green to purer green and a nautilus spiral took form.

I could feel a presence with us near the scrying mirror, tension growing inside me as the chanting and vibration continued.

We raised a glass then drank a sip of rum, smooth on the tongue, but warming as it slipped down the throat. I lay back and the Priest began the XI° Working upon me as I continued my chanting of the name Malkunofat.

It freed my mind, let it absorb the darkness and the scintillations, the growing pressure and presence. The bowl still sang.

Minutes stretched, measured by my chanting. My pulse was hard against my ribs.

The climax came sound and quick; I still chanted breathlessly, but there was a sparking in my brain. A sigil burned brightly for an instant, the persistence of vision leaching from yellow to algae green and blue over the space of seconds.

Later I had vivid dreams, full of the pressure and airlessness typical of 'feverish' dreams. A man's naked body tumbled across foaming blue and red water. Theme coiled with theme and vanished with the daylight; only a pervading sense of dark eroticism remained.

The Ritual – The Priest

Candles and incense are lit and the claw bell is rung five times: the open of the ritual. The singing bowl containing seawater is vibrated throughout, rum is imbibed. The Priest and Priestess chant the name of Malkunofat into the aether, repeating, joining and mingling with the tones from the bowl, absorbed and released until the sounds are indistinguishable. The air becomes thick and viscous with the vibrations and although the room is lit by only two candles the green and blue sigil of Malkunofat is clearly visible, seeming to pulsate and shimmer with the calls, the sound of the seawater reverberating in the bowl subtly altered.

No robes are worn for this Working and the Priestess lays back and continues to chant as the Priest begins to use his mouth upon her in the XI° Operation of the Moon (both tongues performing a sacrament, both a calling), the salt taste of her focusing the current in him and he pictures the sigil while she sings the name of the sentinel.

Throughout the performance of the ritual the bowl is vibrated and the feeling of a presence in the room is immense, a feeling of pressure not just from above but from all directions. As the Priestess orgasms there is a release, the pressure vanishes and, although the area is in near darkness, light seems to drain away.

The dreams that follow are filled with undulating lengths of iridescence in darkness, spirals and the opening of an enormous triangular maw, fanged at each apex with a single tooth. Sigils are seen and vanish, some return and are recorded, others flit by too swiftly in the depths and are lost for now. Future rituals, meditations and dreams may reveal them again. This is the first night in the Tunnel of Malkunofat; we have much further to go in our journey. ✶

Sigils & Symbols

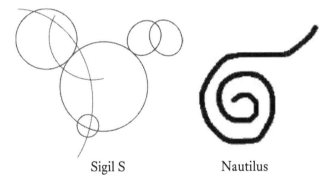

Sigil S   Nautilus

Bibliography

Bertiaux, Michael. *The Voudon Gnostic Workbook*, Magickal Childe, 1988.

Coughlin, John J. *Liber Yog-Sothoth*, Waning Moon, 2007.

Falorio, Linda. *The Shadow Tarot*, Aeon, 2004. Frequency 435: The New Gods and the Exploration of the Nightside, Lulu.

Grant, Kenneth: *Nightside of Eden*, 1977 and Outside the Circles of Time, Muller, 1980

Hay, George (Editor). *The Necronomicon, The Book of Dead Names*, Neville Spearman, 1978. Lovecraft, H.P.: The Call of Cthulhu, 1917.

————. Dagon, 1926.

————. The Colour out of Space, 1927.

————. The Shadow over Innsmouth, 1931. Various Editions.

Miéville, China: *Kraken*, Pan Macmillan, 2010.

Qayin, S. Ben. *Volubilis Ex Chaosium*, Dark Harvest, 2012.

Sennitt, Stephen. The Infernal Texts: Nox and Liber Koth, Original Falcon, 2004.

Venger Satanis. Cthulhu Cult, Waning Moon, 2007.

Verne, Jules. 20,000 Leagues Under the Sea, 1870.

V.S.G: Atua. *The Guardian of the Threshold by Hagen von Tulien*, Fulgur, 2011.

Williams, Wendy. *Kraken*, Abrams Image, 2011.

Gamaliel & the Trip to the Kingdoms of the Lunar Goddesses

Daemon Barzai

GAMALIEL is the dark side of the moon and has an intimate relationship with the dark dream, sexuality, witchcraft and with the dark side of the moon. Here the mage/witch encounters many allies in her/him initiation process. The ritual below is for those who want to discover some of realms of the Dark Goddess Witches. This ritual was design to be conducted in a complete lunar cycle, in other words 28 days. Every invocation and meditation will be conducted in each moon.

We will begin with the Lunar Goddess Naamah (waxing moon), then the invocation of Lilith (full moon), then the invocation of Hecate (waning moon) and the last, the invocation of Tiamat (new moon).

Decorate your temple with red candles, light suitable incense and put some according music.

Invocation of Naamah

(Waxing Moon)

> *Lepaca Naamah!*
> *Lepaca Kiffoth!*

Lepaca Naamah Ama Ruach Maskim Rosaran!
Naamah, princess of darkness, open my eyes and my heart to see the
truth.
Allow me join your kingdom!
Lead me to the other side and be my guide in this journey.
O Naamah Acab Harombrub
Naamah Bacaron Lilith
O Naamah Pachid Labisi
Come to my temple and spread your black winds of darkness.
Tear the veil to see what is hidden before my eyes.
Naamah destroy the lies that take as true and bless me.
Lepaca Naamah Ruach Theli!
Ho Drakon Ho Megas!

Meditation

Imagine that you are at the foot of a very high mountain. You look up; the only thing that you can see is the clouds that cover the peak of the mountain. The atmosphere is cold and wild. You can notice that there is not sings of civilization on the place.

You see a way that conducts you upwards. The way is narrow and steep. Began to rise, while you do, start to darken and the cold is more and more intense, but this is not an obstacle to go on.

The darkness rules over the place. It is really difficult could see where you are going. You look up and see the entry of a cave. The cave seems to be lit up by crimson light. It is there where you have to go.

When you arrived, a weird mist red covers the entry. A voice in your mind tells you that you have to take off your clothes. You do that and go in.

The cave is lit up by the weird red light, you continue go ahead and see a beautiful woman with blond hair and blue eyes. She is naked and she is sitting in luxurious throne.

She welcomes you and stands up and led you to a big mirror. The mirror has inscription carving in it. The mirror is black as night. She touched the crystal and you notice that it is a door to the other side. She stretches out her hand and together cross the portal. Now is when the trip began. Let the vision arises and let that Naamah be your guide in her kingdom.

Invocation of Lilith

(Full Moon)

Lepaca Lilith Ruach Badad Arioth Samolo Sched!
Oh glorious, lady of bloody moon, come to summoning in this dark rite.
Open you womb and let get in your powerful
kingdom of darkness and shadows.
Queen of harlots!
Consort of Samael!
You, who have the fruit of forbidden knowledge, bless me in this
journey with your unholy presence.
Show yourself before me.
Oh mother of the night, show me the mysteries of your kingdom.
You are the empress of Sitra Ahra.
Go with me in this journey and let me found in your kingdom the
occult knowledge that I am looking for.
Show me you hidden face.
Lil-Ka-Litu! Lilith Malkah! Ha'Shadim!
Ho Drakon Ho Megas!

Meditation

You are naked swimming in the sea. It is night and you can see a beautiful full moon that lit the place. Far you can see an island. You go to this place. As you approached, the moon began to change. The white moon becomes red. From the moon began to drop blood and the water becomes thick and red.

You continued swimming in this red, bloody sea.

You go to the island. When you arrived to the firm land, your body is bathed in blood. You walk for this land and you found a big, old, and leafy tree. At the foot of the tree, you can see a little hole. You bend to see more close and an invisible force sucks in.

You began to fall into the darkness. You cross the roots that seem not end. The hole seems endless. Meanwhile you fall; you can hear near of you a great flapping. You feel how the wind hits you naked body, drying the blood in your body.

Opposite you appeared Lilith. Her body is naked but it is difficult see her face. Her hairs are red as fire. She spreads her beautiful black wings. She is flying around you meanwhile you fall into the darkness.

You notice that she has a little bottle in her hands. The bottle has violet liquid. She gives you and tells you "drink it". When you do, you start to feel how your body changes. From you back come out wings.

She invites you to follow her. You do and the journey begins.

Invocation of Hecate

(Waning Moon)

Ave Abnukta Hecate!
Ave Nocticula Hecate!
Ave Trivia Hecate!
Queen of magic, queen of night, I invoke thee in this dark night.
Come Hecate.
Come to this summoning and illuminate my paths with the fire of your torch.
You, who govern in the crossroads, you who are the lady of ghosts and death, I ask you be my guide in yours magical and dark kingdoms.
Provide me your power and give straight to my charm for open the door that leads to the planes beyond the kingdoms of light and darkness.
Old and powerful goddess, queen of witchcraft, guides me to the underworld and let Cerberus allows me cross the threshold that separate the terrible kingdom of elders and the pleasant word of the human.
Salve Hecate!

Meditation

It is night. The sky is starry and the moon is waning. You are in the entry of an old ruin cemetery. The place is huge. There is a big and it is surrounding by a lot of cypresses.

You go in. You can see dilapidate temple; perhaps it is an abandon church. The atmosphere of the place is unholy. You can see black shadows around the coffins. You can hear the laments of the lost souls that could not found the way to the spiritual kingdom.

You come close to the temple/church. Far and near to the trees you hear the howls of dog or wolfs. The sky becomes dark and big electric torment begins. The clouds are dark and a lightning hits the crossroad which is alongside the temple.

Come a dark mist and go out three black dogs that to be with a woman that wearing a black dress, she has a crown with jewels. His presence commands respect.

You come close to her, she raises her hands and an earthquake broke the floor in the middle of the crossroad. She invites you to follow her. You come close and you see ladder that goes down. The ladder is very steep. Go down with her and let her to be your guide in her chthonic world.

Invocation of Tiamat

(New Moon)

IN NOMINE DRACONIS!
SALAMU TAMMABUKKU ELU MUSH
MUSH ELU NEKELMU INA
SALAMU KISHPU INA MUSH ELU MUMMU TIAMAT ELU
Dragon-Goddess of the chaos unmanifest where everything has come
Come from the salad waters and manifest your power over me.
Through my veins runs your blood.
I am your dark progeny.
Lead me to your kingdom of primal darkness.
Open my mind and touch my soul because I want to see the jewels that are
hidden in vacuum and in the remote parts of the universe.
Open the doors of your kingdom and let me honorable of
receiving your knowledge and your glory.
Ho Drakon Ho Megas!

Meditation

Visualize yourself in your temple. Watch each detail. When you are ready, visualize a bubble of energy that began to cover you. The bubble begins to go up. It crosses the roof and you arrived to the middle of the space. The bubble bursts.

Now you are flying in the space. You cannot see anything because it is too dark. Far you see a spark of red and violet light. The spark is closer to you. When the spark is before you, the spark blows and you can see clear the Goddess Dragon Tiamat.

With her fire breaths, she opens a vortex of energy that almost blinds you. It is very powerful; you can feel the power and the energy.

Tiamat invites you to cross together the vortex. Cross it and let the visions flows. ✳

Qliphoth

Flesh Totems & Bone Masks

Sands of Time

Though the sands of time,
And evocation primal forces,
Rises from hidden portals,
A gnosis showing us the path.
It enlightens us with ineffable light,
And brings transcendence with its primigenian wisdom.

The scales of the Black Serpent are open,
To show forbidden, poisonous dreams.
Drink this sacred elixir,
Travel beyond time and space.

We are all and none.
We are all the void,
That resides in Qliphothic energies.
Through flesh totems and mask bones,
We rise.

EDGAR KERVAL
Colombia ✦

Ralifu

The Magician As Vampire

Andrew Dixon

HE magician, in the guise of shaman, witch, magus or siddha, is a mover or manipulator of the energies used in many forms to perform acts of magick, either by integrating herself to channels of force in order to focus or direct this energy onto the arena of hir will. Raising power through the use of ritual in ceremonial magic, calling on the forces of nature as a witch. In lodges and covens or as a lone practitioners using pranayama, tantric or kundalini yogic techniques – directing thought-forms and familiars, spirits, daemons and elementals to perform acts on hir behalf. By altering hir own mental state (using meditative or chemical means) energy is used and released. It being the application or rather the focus/deployment of the kundalini/prana/ki/orgone energy which is essential to the workings of the magical operation.

Throughout the world various Religio-magical cultures use or have used practices which could be considered vampiric. Aztecs, Babylonians and Greeks used blood sacrifice to attract the attention of the gods and daemons, the belief being that from the emanations of the blood, discarnate entities could take on form to make themselves visible or even material on the human plane of existence. The Catholics consumption of the wafer and the wine, the body and the blood of Christ.

The Thelemites Liber XLIV, the Mass of the Phoenix (although in this case the consumption is more than symbolic). The Jivaro Indians of Ecuador who after killing their enemies, take the heads and following an established ritual, remove the skull and shrink the head-skin to the size of a fist.

These shrunken-heads (tsantsa) are used in a variety of magical rites or "Alternatively, pure power can be drawn from the tsantsa using a form of vampirism in which the muisak [the avenging, second soul in the Jivaro belief system] can be made to re-enter the tsantsa in order for it to draw in itska-karma; [power] this is said to increase fertility. Interestingly, the vampire bat is an image of the muisak, connecting the concept of power accumulation with blood and death."1 These as many other, magical systems are generally available for the cost of a paperback book. This essay is directed towards the use of various practices by the vampire- magician in the acquisition of energies for the use in ritual using methods typically frowned upon as vampiric in nature. The vampire being a creature who steals or charms the blood/energy from another for hir own use. The moral ambiguities of these acts are, of course, left to the individual practitioner.

Etheric Feeding

The fact of psychic vampirism is well known in most systems of magic, the vampire being a person who unknowingly or intentionally draws from the life-force of those around hir – either to sustain themselves or, in some instances, to subjugate them, to have them submit to their will. It is this auric energy or life-force which these individuals siphon off from their victims, causing lethargy and/or reducing their natural resistance (both physical and spiritual). Any competent magician who is proficient in the visualization and directing of energies can use this if desired to perform acts of vampirism. Drawing in of ki from others is possible by the positive perception and manipulation of one's own energy field to assess and retain these forces. The proximity of person/s of outgoing natures with high energy levels for this form of absorption is obviously required, these should be people who will easily

Restore their own energy without undue physical or mental stress, of which a little will be said at a later point. While drawing the auric energy of others can empower one providing extra power for the individual it is the subtler emanations that are of more use to the vampire magician to replenish hir own extended or added to hir own to empower ritual. Sexual techniques used by many magical groups or individuals are no longer "occult" in the true sense of the word and the use of these by a magician would forgo the need of any so called vampiric method as it is the creation/exchange of the vibrations originated by these acts which are used to vitalize the ritual enacted. The following techniques are the sole province of the vampire-magician who working alone wishes to access these energies for hir own use.

Astral Rape – Succubi & Incubi

The earliest known representation of a vampire shows her in the act of copulation with a man and we have just observed that Weyer regards the Hebrew Lilith as queen of the succubi.

Sexual energies are some of the most potent forms extant – the nature of the sexual act, as much of the intention, determining the tone of the vibrations released – those being used to access the levels required to execute varying rituals and operations. The magician can make use of a VIII° (masturbatory) working hirself to obtain the sexual energies of another to empower a ritual with the required vitality.

Using whichever forms of sigilization, solipsism or sympathetic magic endemic to the magician's belief system, a link to the object of hirs attentions and the specifics of the type of working should be fabricated as required. Then while at the point of exhaustion or sleep s/he should fixate on the sigil or link while at the same time stimulate hirself to the point of orgasm, stopping as near as possible before the point of climax is reached.

This form of karezza should be continued, without release, until sleep occurs. At this point the subconscious (form) of the practitioner will seek release and directed by whatever link is being used will focus on the object of desire on the astral to enact the form of congress specified in the ritual in the form of an incubi or succubi assault on the vampire-magician's victim. The energy or vibrations released can then be used to perform the chosen working or returned to the magician for absorption by hirself or into the prepared sigil which can then be used as the focus for a later working. This can be of particular use to those needing access to the lunar energies discharged during the dark phase of the moon cycle, which, due to the nature can be problematic to secure.

Any form of sexual release will in many instances attract other entities, some of which by the nature of the act will be vampiric. Care then should be taken to protect the incubi/succubi form of the magician. One of the most potent defenses available is the assumption of the god-from Hoor-Parr-Kraat

(Harpocrates) in the shape of "an egg of vivid blue light flocked with gold; like a stainless summer sky shot through with beams of sunlight. Sexual vampires, seeing this radiant wall of light are drawn precipitately towards it and dash themselves to pieces."3

This (and many others) is a construct which will both protect the vampire's astral form and act as a vessel to contain the relevant Odic vibrations. The reader should realize that approaching anyone using magical forms as described or wards to block or deflect attacks should be avoided, any form of duel or combat on these levels will result in a loss of energies on both sides leaving each participant open to further assault while weakened. It is for the same reasons that one should consider carefully the choice of target in any

Vampiric attack. Someone who naturally has a high level of whichever form of energy desired will be able to replenish themselves easily given a sufficient interval. Constant assaults on any individual will create a deficiency in that person making them unsuitable as a donor not only due to their low levels of energy but also that due to their situation the victim will seek to, even unconsciously, restore that which has been taken from them. Latching onto the assailant or even onto others around them, thus creating another psychic vampire who without the control of the vampire-magician will continue to feed unchecked and uncontrolled.

It is in the form of unfulfilled sexual obsessions that many unintentional vampires, succubi and incubi and engendered. Books containing examples of such entities abound, the works dealing with the Magus Daskalos provide several contemporary examples. One of these describes the shade of a young man who dies of tuberculosis after having been engaged for four years without having intercourse with his fiancée. "He died with this unfulfilled craving. This overwhelming yearning for her kept him floating in the etheric world from where he began harassing her. The girl was going mad.

Each night before she would go to bed he would semi-hypnotize her and induce her to keep the window of her room open. He would then enter inside as a bat and would come to her. The bat would wedge on her neck and draw blood and etheric."4

Familiars

The use of a familiar or servitor by a vampire-magician is fundamentally the same as that used by any other magical practitioner and can be an effective technique in either providing sustenance from the absorption of life-force or auric energy or the specific essences taken from drinking of the chakra lotuses. A familiar (whether natural, called forth or created) to be used by the magician as a stealer of energies should be by its nature a predatory creature. If for nothing more than the sake of tradition bats, wolves and cats are ideal choices. The entity or form of said creatures predisposes it to its task, that of being sent on the behest of its creator to pilfer energies to be returned for absorption by the magician. The advantage of the use of a familiar in this way means that its owner can, if having given the familiar a degree of autonomy let it continue to seek out and replenish its master with energy until it is stopped or is recalled to perform other tasks.

The individuals own input in the conception and use of these entities as well as the care taken in their maintenance is that which will determine the effectiveness of the use of such familiars. Unfortunately, they will of course lack the innate sensibilities and awareness of the sender, so special care should be taken in both the instructing of the familiar in the task, as well as the harvesting of such energies that are obtained in this fashion. Otherwise the magician could find hirself poisoned by the very nourishment s/he has sought.

Chakra Drinking

Other than the natural auric energy given off by people and the vibrations released by various methods of sexual magic, specific vibrations/powers are also intimately linked to the chakra points of the body. These sites are the subject of much study and many books have been written on the methods of empowering and accessing the chakras.

They should be studied in detail before embarking on any process involving raising or raiding the perfumes of these flowers either individually or in sequence as in the arousing of the Kundalini Serpent. The study of these centres will indicate to the adherent the dangers which are involved in any assault of this persuasion as the unbalancing of these vortices can result in the disruption or even degeneration of the psyche in both the vampire and the victim.

Those who are aware of the hazards associated with attempting to vampirically procure such energies can use either hir familiars directed by hir will or by projecting hirself astrally using whatever methods their magical paradigm involves. Otherwise direct contact would be required and necessitate a potentially willing participant in the vampire-magician's rites where the bringing forth of diverse energies can be accomplished by the laying on of hands, drawing in via breath or through the eyes dependent on the facility of the individual.

While as mentioned, assiduous study of all the chakras is essential it is perhaps worth referring briefly to the chakra which is located at the most beloved point to all vampires, the throat. The locus being known variously as the Visuddha-chakra, Akasa and Daath. Many authorities have written concerning the development and use of the vibrations emanating from this point, Sir John Woodroffe states, referring to the Visuddha-chakra "He sees the three periods,* [*Past, present and future – Note by J.W.] and becomes the benefactor of all, free from disease and sorrow and long-lived." 5 While from Kenneth Grant "The symbolism of the serpent drinking fluid which flows from the higher lotuses, especially in the region of the Visuddha (throat) chakra could easily be misinterpreted as a formula of vampirism, and the

Origin of the vampire legend may well have its roots in this tantric-yogic process. The nectar of Immortality is the soma, or Moon Juice."6 Being the locale of Daath (death) this point is the entrance to Universe-B or the Tunnels of Set in Kenneth Grant's "Nightside of Eden", the plane of the qliphoth, some of whom it is said are merely shells of once living persons, ghouls, revenants and elementals who exist only by vampirizing the living of their vitality. It is for this reason that magicians are warned against having commerce with such entities and why the vampire- magician does. For in venturing into the arena of vampirism one is positioning oneself at a very definite point in the magical food chain. Any other vampiric entity therefore can be defined as your hunter, competition or food.

Vampiric Entities

As has been described in this discourse there are a variety of entities that are vampiric in nature. From unintentionally or consciously created thought-forms to shades of the dead and the human psychic vampire all can pose a degree of threat (dependent on their own skills and abilities) to the vampire-magician, but also open up new realms of possibilities.

A psychic-vampire will already be drawing energy from others and consequently will make an ideal quarry, their energy system also being inclined to the flow of vitality making the draining of life-force more accessible. The normal bias of the psychic vampire's system is to the absorption of energy, care therefore is called for so as not to enter into a "tug-of-war" engagement. Safeguarding one's own position by assuming god forms or performing the Rose Cross Ritual for self-enclosure and protection of the astral body.

Spirits and/or shades can be invoked using ceremonial techniques and then bound to the magician's will as a familiar, using a potentially riskier approach involving shamanistic, dervish or voodoo practices, the shade can be allowed to possess the devotee in order to impart its vitality or pass on knowledge or abilities to the adept.

The major risk being that if the entity is stronger than the magician rather than assimilating the creature as intended, s/he will then become the victim. Alternatively, "spirit traps" can be fashioned from especially prepared crystals, boxes or even rooms can be contrived to ensnare thought-forms or creatures on the astral. Once captured these can be restrained and dealt with at the magician's leisure in whatever manner s/he deems suitable or requires.

Another approach to acquiring vampiric endowments involves the accessing of the 18th Tunnel of Set, ascribed to The Chariot on the Tree of Life and tarot, this tunnels sentinel is Characinth. From Aleister Crowley's comments on this path in Liber CCXXXI "He rideth upon the chariot of eternity." The forms of energy (kalas) associated with this tunnel yield the ability to cast enchantments, the capability to assuage ones needs and attain magical immortality. The danger being the addiction to those same energies which will then destroy the magician from depletion through hir relentless pursuit of the substances, that s/he believes will sustain hir, to the exclusion of everything else.

Other tunnels which may be of particular interest to the vampire- magician include that of Niantiel, the 24th tunnel (Death in the dayside tarot) whose Plutonian energies revel in transformations. Parfaxitas, the 27th tunnel beneath the Tower, the sexual formula of which (VIII°+) deals with the assuming of animal forms on the astral. Or even the 29th tunnel of Qulielfi. This tunnel, being the dark side of The Moon holds the keys to dealing with energies on many subtle levels and existing as it does in twilight, the in-between areas of life/death, sleep and waking make it a sublime arena for the workings of any magick.

While only giving an overview of several concepts on the use of magical vampiric techniques rather than detailed descriptions of rituals and practices (any of which can be developed or deduced by any able practitioner) it is hoped that the reader will realize that this short treatise is not a guide or recommendation on magical practice. The descriptions and examples of some of these acts providing sufficient warning of the dangers likely to afflict the follower of such a system and hir victims. ✦

Bibliography

1. Stephen Sennitt: *Monstrous Cults*, p 36-37.
2. Montague Summers: *The Vampire His Kith and Kin*, p. 228-9.
3. Kenneth Grant: *Cult of the Shadow*, p. 178-179.
4. Kyriacos C. Markides: *The Magus of Strovolos*, p. 161.
5. Sir John Woodroffe: *The Serpent Power*, p. 390.
6. Kenneth Grant, *The Magical Revival*, p.148.
7. Aleister Crowley: *Gems from the Equinox*, p. 667.

The Tellvm Scorpionis

R.N. Lant

One Magic

Understood that our Earth exist due to balance only. Our planet turns on its own axis. If the balance vanishes, the earth will collapse and disappear.
I understood its similarity with us. We need balance or we will collapse and disappear as well. The balance factor is to stay realistic...

O believe in the hidden world, the truth other than the one which was imposed became something more allowable for the persons gifted with time, secret, reliable relations and clear tolerance (categorized as intolerance by the common fool in most of the cases). After all, it is not one of the first steps towards wisdom there is to realize that perhaps one can overtakes possibilities on the « not possible.

In a comprehensible vision of occultism, one must remain humble in front of the universal knowledge and the studies of the left hand path & the right hand path, as one can't possibly go without the other if one wants to achieve greatness within the dark arts. The magick. There is no magic reserved for this or that culture, religion or cult, many essences, many different names but one single magick. The fundamental aspect of its practices is simply universal; a single force, a single magic, a whole - one who governs, under the veil, the natural equilibrium of things. As logic teaches us, without hate there is not love, without sadness there is no step in joy, and the essences of these Ying-Yang's are reaching another level of power when achieved side by side with their opposite pairs.

The same principle takes there in relation as regards this logical suite: without the invisible, there is just no visible. Perhaps a sentence which might bring some confusion within minds but all shall be clear and limpid as clear spring water in its own time but by looking at it well, is it so unlikely? Forces or power is therefore a universal thing, through the visible as by the invisible. As every culture aimed to develop certain, dark branches of arts in these different doctrines, others were bare exclusively by the Mesopotamians by example. The Middle East has always been exposed in a powerful sphere, where energies cross and where the people evolved in a more advanced manner than others, but still is accessible to any magus of a certain respected level or wisdom.

Gnostic Dualism: Ingressus Scorpionis

Traditionally the Scorpion has been associated with male sexuality, destruction, the occult, the mystical, illumination, healing and resurrection. Centuries ago, the Scorpion was the agent of divine vengeance. The Scorpion in this context was regarded as the instrument of divine vengeance in itself.

In Babylon, Orion, the Hunter is the heavenly representation of the earthly Nimrod, known for his might within the art of hunting down his enemies and the tower of Babel. The name of a Scorpion in Chaldee (ancient Semitic people who ruled in Babylonia) is Akrab, but Ak-rab, thus divided, signifies 'The Great Oppressor' and this is the hidden meaning of the Scorpion as represented in the Zodiac. That sign typifies him who cut off the Babylonian god, and suppressed the rules and system which were putted in place. Also, in Egypt, it was while the Sun was in the House of Scorpio that Osiris 'disappeared' and great lamentations were made for his disappearance, thus making him an agent of the Red Lord Set.

The Scorpio is as well the symbolic of the occult initiation to the darkest arts, the one who leads to knowledge and embraces Darkness in its whole. A powerful symbolic which advocates equilibrium in all matters, and which is considered as one of the fundamental philosophies of Traditional Satanism and from the ancient philosophies of the cult of Seth (Some of these can still be seen today within the tomb of the Pharaoh Setnakhte (20th Dynasty) in the Valley of the Kings. You understand there that once again, may you take a side or the other, may you be an adept of the Left Hand Path or its counterpart, the two opposites are inexorably attracted, and sometimes unite to and towards each other, one cannot survive without the other. Seth as the sworn enemy of his brother Osiris, still join his force to maintain a certain equilibrium within the darkness and vice-versa, same goes for the other side, and it is as such that only powerful studies and practices of the Occult are possible, one cannot learn mighty skills without knowing how the other side works as well! It is in this form of thoughts that Gnosticism was born; out of the darkness.

Gnosticism (a synthesis of occultism and Jewish Christianism) was a brutal heretic philosophy which started in Alexandria, Egypt and constituted a great threat to the early Holy Church. During the Middle Ages, the Inquisition was directed largely at Gnostic sects such as the Templars, Cathars, Albigenses, Bogomils and the Donatists. Although these groups were eradicated by the Church of Rome, the secret doctrine which they represented was carried forward by a myriad of secret societies spawned by the Invisible College of the Order of the Rosy Cross during the 17th century Rosicrucian Enlightenment. In the middle ages, The Inquisition realized that Gnostic covens were constituted mainly of people who belonged to prestigious orders such as the Templars, Katharian warlords, Albigeans, Bogomils and Donatists. Even if those groups were eradicated by the Vatican, their secret doctrines were reported and passed through generations after generations, some kept in safety and away from the most dedicated followers of the Left Hand Path by l' Ordre de la Croix Rosy in the 17th century which is better known these days under the name of the Rosicrucian Order.

This battle against the Christian Doctrine is actually based upon facts and logics based upon universal dualism: two forces opposing each other on an equal level on a continual struggle to believe on one side that there is a almighty divine figure who created the Universe and its opposite Demiurge, which is a true emanation of a pure essence who created the physical earth which is in itself an Infernal dwelling place. Whilst dualistic Gnostics believe that matter is evil and Spirit is good, monistic Gnostics regard matter not as evil, but as an illusion.

"To believe in God, you need faith, to believe in the devil, you just have to open your Eyes..." Something to think about! My speech might sound chaotic and maybe a bit monotonous to some for now, but one is to be teach how to read in between the lines if he wants to achieve greatness within the Dark Arts and learn to see what lies on the other side of his own face. All shall be cleared to the ones who find the keys and unlock their own sight!

Regarding Blavatsky, the fall of the astral being Adam Kadmon (primal man) led to a drastic transformation within the spiritual belief of the ancient world and made obsolete its actual material situation. The cataclysm related to the first fall was taken in consideration by the followers of the Right Hand Path by an alteration within the sign of Virgo–Scorpio:

Virgo the pure is separated, and from the decreasing of generations, or decreasing of cycles, becomes Scorpio symbol of Sin and matter."(209:502 s.) Scorpio, however, states Fred Getting in The Secret Zodiac, still retains a dual image—the eagle and scorpion—a duality which represents the two natures of man:

Apparently because of its primordial role as the consort of Virgo, the Great Mother Goddess and archetype before Isis, the astrological sign of Scorpio will preside over the restoration of mankind to its previous spiritual state. In reason of her primordial role as the consort of Virgo, the Great Divine Mother Isis, the sign of Scorpio will prevail and will preside at the unanimous symbolic of the restoration of humanity in its original and instinctive state of Spirituality, the agent of men's true nature in this matter, far from the blind folds and brain washings the world knows today since the 19th century.

Worldwide occult sources agree on the point that a transformation a step back on the matter through the «whole world» will occur within the house of the Scorpio.

From early scrolls and tablets to our contemporary discoveries in the matter (and I am not talking here about your usual kind of "Occultism for Dummies" books and other unreliable works of this kind) this has been a proved factor by the people of experience within the practices of the dark Arts and Secret Knowledge. Think about it, after all it is just pure logic... One cannot reach the Angelic Realm, may it be with his fists or his behind, without knowing the corridors leading to the "Pearly Gates of Heaven". It is always the one who spreads the greatest light who cast the darkest shadow upon the unenlightened and is therefore considered as the bringer of darkness...

Oordo ab Chao

I absolutely not pretend to be the agent of THE truth, there are many truths to be seen and understood, as the ones who confine themselves within their own vision without expending the inadmissible, dwell within a hollow world. Fact is that the light of darkness has proven time and time again that its light shines brighter than the supposedly righteous path engendered by Yahweh and his cohorts. No need here to quote again this or that as we all know that this is just facts and therefore shall be used to reach the ascent every practitioner is in reach of. Now it is up to the adept to forge his own weapons, build his own path and walk his way upon the path of the worth or fall on his face that very time too much and be swiped aside as he cannot learn his lesson.

The path of darkness is a dangerous road but oh so beautiful for the ones who walk their journey through with humbleness and wisdom, through the Qliphoth and across the bridge of Da'at and Bar Shasketh. These being just listed as example of course (always better to clarify for those stupid enough to even try or think they can try reaching these before reaching a minimum of understanding), no order comes without chaos and no understanding without confusion, the secret Knowledge has been kept this way for centuries and for very good reasons and since the last years there is a recrudescence of interests within the matter compared to the last two centuries... is it due to some awakening? Hollywood?

The occult Black Metal scene or something else? The only thing that is important is that we don't care, we shouldn't care as only our own path is what matters, are we going to deal with it with haste or with wisdom and balance? Are you gonna be the dove, the vulture or the scorpion? Confusion has always been the key to understanding, the root of all knowledge and the treasure chest waiting to be open by the one, unique key.

This article may seem insignificant or even boring to some but how do you think of those keys were kept away from the eyes of the unworthy during the last millennia? ✦

SMASHAN ULTRA
by kazim

The Arte of Blood

S. Ben Qayin

BLOOD... glorious elixir of life, that which brings light to the darkened eyes of lone night shades, giving breath again to those who dwell in shadow light. It is the fiery essence of magic run course through your burning veins, and the strength of the consuming spirits that drink in its power, whoever wander the halls of endless mists. Blood has an energy to it that many react to; there is something inherently 'forbidden', or sacred that we feel when experiencing it. It is our essence, the spirit liquefied and warm...it is Alchemical, as both a material and a spiritual essence combined into one ever changing beautiful form which gives life and possess power... it is existence.

Much has been written of blood in connection with the spiritual. It has drawn our attention as a race, and been woven into our sacred and holy rites throughout history, imbedded within both philosophic and theological thought, as well as in ritual praxis as central religious applications and symbology. In the Christian bible their god is quoted as saying if one drinks of it, they shall be 'cut off' from heaven and salvation:

> For it is the life of all flesh; the blood of it is for the life thereof: therefore, I said to the children of Israel, You shall eat the blood of no manner of flesh: for the life of all flesh is the blood thereof: whoever eats it shall be cut off.
> —Leviticus 17:14, American King James Version

And yet within their very own rites of Eucharist, they drink wine which is magically/alchemically transformed into the blood of their savior, which makes for an interesting contradiction to the previous passage considering Jesus' own words, Regardless, it is seen by Christians as something sacred

> He who eats My flesh and drinks My blood has eternal life, and I will raise him up on the last day. For My flesh is true food, and My blood

is true drink. He who eats my flesh, and drinks my blood, dwells in me, and I in him.

—John 6:54, King James Version

That either belongs only to their god, or that can only be consumed by followers from the veins of the son of their God, Jesus Christ. Holy blood is also a reoccurring theme in the phenomena known as 'Stigmata', which occurs to believers of Christ who wish to feel his sacrifice and pain. Often the supernatural scene is filled with sacred blood.

All of a sudden there was a dazzling light. It was as though the heavens were exploding and splashing forth all their glory in millions of waterfalls of colors and stars. And in the center of that bright whirlpool was a core of blinding light that flashed down from the depths of the sky with terrifying speed until suddenly it stopped, motionless and sacred, above a pointed rock in front of Francis. It was a fiery figure with wings, nailed to a cross of fire. Two flaming wings rose straight upward, two others opened out horizontally, and two more covered the figure. And the wounds in the hands and feet and heart were blazing rays of blood. The sparkling features of the Being wore an expression of supernatural beauty and grief. It was the face of Jesus, and Jesus spoke. Then suddenly streams of fire and blood shot from His wounds and pierced the hands and feet of Francis with nails and his heart with the stab of a lance. As Francis uttered a mighty shout of joy and pain, the fiery image impressed itself into his body, as into a mirrored reflection of itself, with all its love, its beauty, and its grief. And it vanished within him. Another cry pierced the air. Then, with nails and wounds through his body, and with his soul and spirit aflame, Francis sank down, unconscious, in his blood.

—From A Treasury of Catholic Reading, ed. John Chapin (Farrar, Straus & Cudahy, 1957)

Not only is blood seen and utilized as a path that leads to enlightenment, but pain as well. One sect of the Dervishes in Arabia known as the Rufai, or 'Howling Dervishes' also use blood and pain to elevate their minds to a state of heightened spiritual awareness called 'Melboos'. Another well-known Sufi sect is the 'Swirling Dervishes' who spin round until a trance is laid upon them and they find union with 'God' which they view as life itself and interestingly, that they themselves are 'God' as well. Unlike the Swirling Dervishes, the Rufai are known to inflict physical pain upon themselves in place of 'swirling', to enter into melboos so that they may commune with 'God', or the self in a heightened spiritual trance state.

...The Rufai, or Howling Dervishes who slash their bodies with knives and burn themselves with red-hot irons... In Not only is blood seen and utilized as a path that leads to enlightenment, but pain as well. One sect of the Dervishes in Arabia known as the Rufai, or 'Howling Dervishes' also use blood and pain to elevate their minds to a state of heightened spiritual awareness called 'Melboos'. Another well-known Sufi sect is the 'Swirling Dervishes' who spin round until a trance is laid upon them and they find union with 'God' which they view as life itself and interestingly, that they themselves are 'God' as well. Unlike the Swirling Dervishes, the Rufai are known to inflict physical pain upon themselves in place of 'swirling', to enter into melboos so that they may commune with 'God', or the self in a heightened spiritual trance state.

...The Rufai, or Howling Dervishes who slash their bodies with knives and burn themselves with red-hot irons... In front of them was a brazier, with a glowing bed of charcoal, from which emerged the handles of knives, long iron pins, like spits, with wooden handles, and iron pokers with no handles at all.

—W.B. Seabrook, 'Adventures In Arabia', 1927

This scene is also described by Seabrook further:

Suddenly one of the Dervishes leaped to his feet, threw off his cloak, leaped again into the air, naked to the waist. The Rufai sheik leaped up at the same time, seized a long, red-hot spit by its wooden handle from the brazier, and began waving it wildly in the air...the other Dervish circled, leaping around the sheik and howling, then backed, with his head pressed sideways against the wooden pillar, with his mouth gaping open, and stood rigid, motionless. The sheik inserted the spit at an angle into his mouth, and with a solid blow of his fist drove it through the man's cheek and pinned him to the pillar."

I have personally experienced a very similar ritual where I rose above the pain that was inflicted, and became 'one' with the Universe. I was fortunate to be in a circle of friends who were suspension artists, and one night I was given the rare opportunity to partake in one of their sacred rites. I was pierced with two six gauge, four-foot-long crisscrossing spears through my back and one six gauge, two foot long spear through both cheeks with my mouth open, (very much like the Dervish as described) as well as two more smaller 10 gauge needles pierced through my lower lip. I now intimately relate to this particular kind of unique experience in the quest for finding oneself, or 'God'.

When in such a state, reality is suspended and in place of feeling pain, one rises above it and 'rides' it. The intense pain thrusts the mind and spirit into a state of excitement where ones extra sensory mode is activated and one not only feels life around him, but 'sees' life around him. The energy that resonates off a person while experiencing this transcendent state is quite amazing, it's as if they are 'cracked' open and the energy that lies beneath their material 'shell' radiates out as a star burning its brightest and hottest before it goes out, as the rituals usually don't last more than an hour. It is something I find difficult to describe, as it is such a personal experience, and differs from one individual to another. Though, one thing that is always universally experienced among practitioners is the spiritual feeling of freedom, being alive and connected to all, in a moment frozen in time.

These are just a few examples of the use of blood and pain within different cultures and religious movements of the world. There are many, many more examples, as blood is seen as symbolic for a great multitude of religions and spiritual reasons ranging from life and death, to being purified to unclean. Of course, Pagans and Magicians also view blood as a spiritual essence, though it is seen as something more personal that does not belong to a God, but to them. It is embraced as life, but also serves as a reminder of death, being seen as magical, having unique properties that can be utilized in many different ways concerning ritual and as an agent in contacting spiritual entities. This is age old tradition still being put to use by many modern practitioners and occult orders, especially in the rapidly growing LHP movement along with the new interest in the Afro-Brazilian religious traditions, such as Quimbanda, Palo Mayombe and Voudon.

Personally, I use blood in many rituals and workings, I always have. It is something very sacred to me. In my eyes, it serves as a sign of devotion as well as sacrifice. Within my spiritual beliefs, I kneel before no God, though offer them my essence out of respect and to empower the rite. I see most entities as being equal, some have been here longer than me and have more knowledge and experience, but that does not make them superior to me, only more learned. And, as more learned, they should know this and have the same respect for me, as I do them, equally. Else, why would I commune with them as spiritual brothers? I offer them sacrifice, not out of fear, but honor and re-spect. I beg no entity or God to change things in my life, I ask them to help me as a brother, who walks the same crooked path as they do, and if I can help them in turn, then I gladly do.

My first use of blood in magic was when I was in my teenage years; (buy-ing what I could of magic books that were to be found at the bookstore in the mall) no system that I had found then really resonated with me, so I created my own from elements I did resonate with, from within various systems. I didn't realize at the time that I had just taken my first step on the path to becoming a Chaos Magician. I came to understand that the one dominate re-occurring magical factor in my life was the moon, I was drawn unnaturally (or supernaturally) to the moon. Not only that, but huge life changing events would occur on the first three nights of the waxing crescent moon, to the point that the connection could not be ignored, even by the most skeptical. Therefore, I began honoring it as a sentient being, and quickly found that my life was infused with incredible luck and magic, as if all life's doors were sud-denly open, and I could walk through whichever ones I chose at my leisure with ease.

I would take a wooden box that served as my alter, that I had painted with various symbols (some known, and others my own) along with my ritual sup-plies, up to the top of a large wooded hill that overlooked the city. It was quite beautiful and I would often encounter deer and other wildlife on my journey upward. Once there I would lie out my alter and tools, light the alter candle and meditate on my current position in life, what was important and that which I desired to change. I then would cut my left arm with a clean razor-blade three times, deep enough to let blood flow just a trickle (there is always such a spiritual release that I experience when this occurs, it is no different for me now then it was for me then) and spread a good amount of blood on a dead leaf that I had procured on the trip up the mountain. Once done, I would burn the leaf so that my essence would entwine with the energy of the night as the smoke would rise to caress the moon. At that point in the ritual I would partake of the blood myself, enjoying tasting the raw energy of life itself dance upon my tongue...As said, I had tremendous positive results with this, and still do when practiced, though the ritual has grown to encompass much more meaning and depth.

Of course, now that I am older and have experienced more than what the new age books of the mall had to offer, I work with blood in a more complex way. I have found that spiritual activity is greatly increased when blood is used in ritual. I find this because the energy that is being released by the magician acts as a beacon in the spiritual world, attracting many different curious entities. It is such a personal offering that the magician can fully immerse himself in ritual and the spiritual world, so contact with an entity is stronger and a bond formed.

Naturally, blood is also used in a lot of sigil work I undertake. I believe blood helps to bring 'Life' to a sigil if created with it. This of course again connects the magician with the spiritual entity that is being called forth, creating a pact of sorts as it is the essence of the magician (blood), conjoined with the essence of the spirit (sigil). I see ritual as something very private that takes place between myself and the spirits, something that others should not see. It is a time when my earthly skin is shed, and my spiritual being can fully breathe in the night and embrace the spirits on their ground. It is something sacred and beautiful, and should be respected and seen as such. When one works with blood, spirits, and the night, an amazing collage of magic is painted upon the canvas of reality, immersing the magician in a state of non-reality where the miraculous is able to be brought forth into the magician's plane of awareness.

This twilight of the in-between is where magic is performed, it is where time and space cease to exist and action occurs.

In my book, 'Volubilis Ex Chaosium', blood is used to draw the Old Ones close:

> Throughout the history of magic, blood has been used as a means to attract spirits and to be used as an energy source for them to materialize into visible appearance before the magician. Blood is used in these workings as an energy source for the Old Ones to be drawn to the Trinity of Triangles so that interaction may occur, in whatever form it may take. Blood is the eternal energy and essence of all life. It is the most sacred and personal offering that one can make to the Gods. There are many examples of the use of blood sacrifice in 'Yog~Sothothery', and is definitely a reoccurring theme when evocation of a said entity is to be called forth. Therefore, staying true to Lovecraft's visions, it has been employed in this magical system.

I have found the spiritual interaction within V.E.C., very powerful and effective, as it deals with the very 'edge' or outer realms of the magical Universe in experimental realms such as the 'Tunnels of Set' also known as the

'Vaults of Zin', or what may be called the 'Nagual' (drawing from Don Juan's terminology), though it still utilizes traditional ritual elements within its structure. And, within this system, blood and pain are used, as in the 'Nyarlathotep Initiation Ceremony', as a way to both heighten and excite the spiritual mind of the magician to a level of awareness that is needed for communion with the Old Ones.

There are also a great many who hold the belief that ingesting blood infuses one with spiritual strength or 'energy', resulting in vampiric qualities including heightened senses both spiritually and physically, as well as immortality of either the physical or ethereal body. There have been many throughout history who have been known to utilize blood as an element for the rejuvenation of life. One of the most famous; Elizabeth Bathory, was known to have bathed in, and drank, the blood of over 650 young women in efforts to remain young and live forever. There are reports stating that her desired end result of youth was somewhat achieved, until she was jailed of course.

Though, through the ages a division has been made manifest between the material and the spiritual aspects of blood. There are now recognized vampires who only consume the 'Life Force', or 'Prana' of a person that is carried by the blood throughout the body, rather than ingesting the blood itself, this is well known as psychic vampirism. 'The Temple Of The Vampire' is one such religion which recognizes this praxis as a core pillar in their religious construct.

They hold the belief that they are evolved humans who drink in the personal energy of lesser humans and store it. When enough energy is collected, they enter into a ritual they call 'Communion' where they freely release all their stored energy to the 'Undead Gods' in return for the Undead Gods to release their Vampiric energy upon them. With each transfusion of life-force, they become less human, taking on the qualities of their ascended masters.

The Vampiric Condition is, therefore, a condition of evolution actualized by the exchange of Life-force energy with
Those Who Have Risen (The Undead Gods) above the restriction of a physical body.

—T.O.T.V., 'Revelations', 2006

However, within their Temple, blood drinking is looked down upon:
Drinking physical blood is a socially unacceptable behavior and reveals a deep misunderstanding of our religion.

T.O.T.V., 'Website', 2012

Although this view is not always agreed upon between Vampires and the personal beliefs they hold, and therefore the practice of blood drinking as an energy source is still utilized by many underground societies as well as in individual solitary praxis:

"The grand fantasy that many would be vampires have in these modern times is that the physical consumption of blood is wholly unnecessary for the vampire's maintenance of immortal existence. This is a basic fallacy stemming from the most recent

resurgence in the occult movement of the 1990's...'The simple truth of the matter is that the vampire must, in conjunction with vital energy manipulation, (which begins with techniques of visualization) consume large quantities of food that contains exceedingly high amounts of life-force, prana, etc'...'Now, the truth of the matter is that human blood, being the substance of life for the most highly cognitive and evolved species on this planet, contains the most concentrated degree of life-force available." ~ A.W. Dray, 'Nox Infernus', 2011

The spectrum for the uses of blood in the areas of religion and magic is vast. Another area of interest is the use of blood as a medium for divination. The specific name or names for this are 'Hematomancy' or 'Haematomancy', which breaks down to, Haimat = Blood, and Manteia = Prophecy. Dririmancy is specifically divination by observing dripping blood and the patterns it creates upon whatever surface is being utilized in the ritual. One similar method of spiritual contact that can be utilized, is the use of blood in conjunction with mirrors to open gateways. This is seen in an anonymous rite that was included in Scarlet Imprint's, "Diabolical". The practitioner adorns a full length mirror with demonic sigils drawn of their own blood, especially where the infernalist's face and heart will appear in the reflection. Once done, the Demon is evoked/invoked into the reflection of the magician. This is a very effective operation, as it again relates to connecting the magician to the spirit being called forth through the mirror, by the use of sigils and blood. As stated, this type of bond formed with a spiritual entity is amazingly strong and cannot be easily broken.

Blood...We instinctively know its strength, we feel its seductive rhythm pounding through the world as the drums of destiny pushing us ever forward into the 'Night of Times', pounding as our hearts beat within our own chests, breathing life within our flesh and making 'Alive', that which would not be. For it is the blood of 'God'...of 'Self'...of 'Being' that courses through our veins and bestows upon us the very fragile and easily extinguished flame we call existence. Drink in its essence, feel it flow through you, for this is magic in its purest and strongest form, a magic that ever changes as the raging force of untamed Chaos itself. ✦

Becoming Hoodoo
PART TWO
Kyle Fite

The action of the Paraclete...will extend to the principle of generation. The divine life will sanctify the organs which henceforth procreate only elect creatures, exempt from original sin, creatures whom it will not be necessary to test in the fires of humiliation, as the Holy Bible says. This was the doctrine of Vintras...the doctrine has been continued and amplified, since Vintras's death, by his successor, Dr. Johannes."

> —The Astrologer Gevingey in discourse with Durtal and Des
> Hermies from J.K. Huysmans' *La Bas*

1

THOSE familiar with the biographical details surrounding the writing of Huysmans' La Bas will know that its author was personally acquainted with the Abbe Joseph-Antoine Boullan, who was represented within that tale as the character Dr. Johannes. This is an important fact for us to bear in mind as Boullan's detractors painted him as a grotesque blasphemer immersed in the most perverse practices of a sexual and satanic nature. These detractors included several proponents of "white magic," such as Oswald Wirth who, along with Stanislas de Guaita, disingenuously sought tutelage from Boullan in order to infiltrate his Sanctum Sanctorum at the highest level and thereby discover the truth of his allegedly wicked work.

That Boullan was concerned with those energies infusing "the principle of generation" is not in question. The nature of his practice, however, has not only been maligned by his enemies, it has been embraced in its tabloid misrepresentations by misguided persons seeking to emulate the shadow of a "Satanist" who never existed. We find Huysmans to be a much more accurate representative of the eminent "Dr. Johannes" than those who, reacting to his insight into the sexual nature of divine magic, condemned him as being in league with the devil, setting off a chain reaction of lurid gossip and speculation which has all but shrouded the mission of this almost forgotten priest.

Boullan was a proponent of a philosophy-and rite-which he called "The Union of Life." This outlook saw all Being participating in the Growth and Action of One Being. The One Being referred to is God and therefore All Life is regarded as part of the Body of God. In addressing the problems of mortal manifestation, we are challenged to understand and act in accord with the proper relationship between these parts whereby the whole is most freely expressed in Time. This forms a link between Time and Eternity which finds expression in the figure of Jesus Christ, the "God- Man."

The conceit of man (actively encouraged to this day by aberrant theologies) is put into check by this philosophy. As "Boullanists," we do not see ourselves as sanctioned by some divine decree to trample over all creation as Christic consumers. With the Holy Scriptures declaring that all things were put on earth for man's use, we have seen the rise of a twisted religious justification for abuse of all creation. With the proclamation that the righteous will one day judge the angels, we observe the establishment of a demented superiority complex. Human beings have made of themselves little suns around whom the universe revolves. While thinking we glow with glory, we have actually become enchained in a state of stunted growth, behaving as infants when the same scriptures we quote (to adorn our ignorance) also tell us to put away childish things, moving from the "milk" to "meat" of wisdom.

The Union of Life is a sexual philosophy wherein we relate to all forms of life within the Continuum of Reality. We become a vehicle of the Lord of the Crossroads as we form a living link in the connective chain between the "lower" and the "higher." This is a volitional position. Our contact with the "inferior" is meant to raise that life-condition to the level of our own just as our contact with the "superior" is meant to raise our own life-condition. Contact alone does not facilitate this process. As alluded to above, we can abuse those powers we think of as beneath us. We may, likewise, form imbalanced and destructive relationships with those powers we conceive of as "transcendental." Major world religions have grown and been sustained within this psychosis. In Boullan's teachings, effective relationships between Life-Levels are based in an awareness of necessary interconnectedness as well as the matrix in which that interconnectedness functions.

Within the Lucky Hoodoo Cult aligned with the Boullan Academy of Spiritual Service (itself a body aligned with the occult activities of OTOA-LCN), the Union of Life forms the central teaching whereby Hoodoo Science is directed towards Inner Plane Communion with the Ancestral and Atlantean Spirits. We are Masonic in understanding how the True Temple of Sol-Om-On is fashioned from Living Stones. Through the Gnosis of this Metaphor, we go beyond simply thinking that we are lifting up the Lower while being exalted within the Higher. We literally become the vehicle whereby the Higher communicates with the Lower. This is Christian in the Esoteric sense of the word where a Christian is understood to be "Little Christ" in the World. One must live out the Christ-Drama in his or her life as a Hoodoo. This is not some linear sequence of events traced through Biblical narrative but a superstructure into which we project our karmas for an adjustment that also adjusts the World.

2

It is a difficult thing to express a Cosmic Sexuality to one who understands Sexuality solely in terms of the animal body. It is even more difficult when one regards the animal condition as a blight on the spiritual path. Thus it was that Boullan's teachings concerning the Union of Life were slandered by "critics" who suggested that he was providing justification for all manner of evil, including bestiality. Such is the outlook left for those who can only understand sex in terms of the mammalian man's corporeal body. Our view is not one that eschews this-but it must be noted that human bio-sexuality is only one of myriad expressions of Cosmic Sexuality. Even within our flesh, Sexuality takes on an infinitude of forms. In fact, we will not be amiss to honor this primordial force in EVERY aspect of human existence. The mingling of one thought with another and the new thought arising from this union...this is also sexuality!

Within our Hoodoo Shadowverse, our thought-life does not simply interact with itself. It extends outward and connects into a vast sea of intelligence around us. The Atlantean Awareness residing within each and all of us seeks empowerment through the sacramental technology of the Union of Life whereby its continuous copulation with all phenomena may be both sanctified and fruitful. This gives insight into why the sex magic operations

known within the Crowleyan system as the 8th, 9th and 11th

Degrees are preceded by the 7th in which sexual energy is related to ere it is directed into expression.

The Key is to enter into a full body-mind awareness of the sex- force beyond its particular expression via the human bio-organism. When this is achieved, one's bodily actions may be imbued with the Gnostic influx which is universally radiant. Many curious and intrepid magicians desire to "learn the secrets" of these so-called "upper grades." Hoodoo Science holds the Key whereby these "Operations" reveal themselves. One does not need an Order to explain this magic nor does one who has entered these Mysteries require a human affirmation of attainment. The Monastery of the Seven Rays serves its students on

the Path towards the 7th Degree which, after a manner, is the Highest Degree one may enter in human form. If one has formed a conception of the Qabalistic Grades based on linear consciousness, this statement will sound like admittance to partial knowledge. Let me say this: the Abyss will destroy linear consciousness along with all other modes of consciousness. Entry therein may prove to be a Gateway to insanity-or Supersanity. Despite its dangers, we don't feel that this "Crossing" need be some dread event. It is the natural and inevitable trajectory of the Soul. The Abyss may also be regarded as the Atlantean Deep. This is more than mere metaphor. We are diving the depths of our most extreme karmic past that we may realize our most vital future through magical acceleration in the present.

3

HOODOO LOG

Longing for more than the occlusion of modern materialistic consciousness, I strike a match, light a colored candle and begin my voyage.

Many who begin work with the coursework of Michael Bertiaux's Lucky Hoodoo Grimoire have expressed to me frustration when they don't immediately experience the "bells and whistles" they were hoping for. This is not an issue of failure but a simple need for adjustment in consciousness.

I do not shove expectation onto the Hoodoo any more than I would my earthly friends. I have called up my faith and feel tremendous gratitude for the ability to do so. I simply know that the Spirits are present and my Love eclipses any need for performance on their part. We join in the Field of Love. I open to the Presence of Hoodoo and my Soul is thereby opened to the Presence of God. God is not obligated to manifest in some expected or longed for guise. God has never been unmanifest and therefore I simply open my Being to God. That flame flickering on the candle's wick is God manifest. Do I require more? I am seeing the Salamander in physical manifestation and it silently chants praise to the Lord.

The wax-feeding flame dance is no more a manifestation of God than the thought-life I identify as being "in my head." There is some vague and hazy notion of a scaly form sweeping by me in an oily black space. My rational mind springs forward to target and dispel the form. It is "just imagination," it declares. But it is wrong. This imaginative form is a type of body-a vehicle-through which the Hoodoo are moving. The Rational Mind may as well tell me that my body is "just a body" and, being subject to perpetual change and dissolution without any substantial existence, should be disregarded, along with all its reports. But its reports are all that sustains the Rational Mind and knowing this, the RM retreats to a corner to gnaw its knuckles. Soon it will meet the Gravewalker Without Hands.

Meanwhile, I am taken down into darkness so thick, I cannot determine if there is water or air about me. I cannot tell if I yet live or have died. The darkness gives way to flashings (electrical storm between these two elements) and I enter a world of terrors with a strange detachment. Were I wholly in my bodily soul, I would surely recoil. Instead I drift forward, through carnage and carnality. What I behold doesn't require description. Suffice to say that it is sufficient to punch holes through fears I never knew I had. This is no horror movie. It is a custom-tailored vision quest in which all my walls come tumbling down. What is ugly for me may be a cake-walk for you, dear reader. And vice versa, certainly. It's enough to say that I'm stabbed where I bleed. There will be no tribal scars to tribute my manhood. The blood flow is like a thread being pulled to unravel my entire Self concept. The Tibetans call this the

Bardo. Padmasambhava's revelations were beamed in from Bon Po Time Travelers. And the Bon Po? They were Tibet's Hoodoo Technicians.

4

Let's talk Skulls. One of my earliest childhood memories was being at a grocery store and looking at the small toy selection by the magazine rack. One of these toys was Ghost Rider. It may have been the first time I saw Ghost Rider. I knew nothing of the comic book saga and was simply seeing a little plastic man on a motorcycle with a flaming skull for a head. I was duly impressed. This was one of the coolest things I had seen in my young life.

The Skull is chic. I have one tattooed on my arm. Those empty eyes, that toothy grin. Somehow sinister and humorous at the same time, the Skull is both badass and gothic groovy. Traditional forms of the Great Baron arise and I find myself thinking "Alright, now we're talking!"

The Tibetans are the Biker Gang of the Spirit-World. Their leather jackets are Thangkas. Malas are a chain in the fist. It was, in fact, Mahakala who called me to Buddhism, announcing the existence of religion in which the flaming skull was a Mystery. I dove into the Book of the Dead and thence to Zazen. But it was a vat of hydrochloric-and not lysergic-acid that I would find myself sitting in. I was a fish lunging for the worm on a hook. I was also the fisherman. And I was caught.

When I enter the Graveyard below the worlds, the Baron knows better than to hand me some Halloween mask. What he reveals freezes the blood in my veins. This is not some Hollywood thrill- trip. I meet my loved ones and watch as the ignominy of death drapes itself over those I cherish most. The lovely scent of skin turns sour and the soul flees, leaving me with dull and unresponsive clay. Eyes that once met mine in a darting flash now stare, fish-like, idiot and blind. I am not afraid of the quickly rotting flesh. Grieving overrides horror. I am more than alive even as my heart is collapsing in my chest. The Baron has touched me and my blood has turned black.

I look into his face, draped in the worm-eaten flesh of innocence. I become a dog, snarling spittle at the puppet-people who jerk about on strings and think themselves daringly dancing at some sexy party for esoteric extremists. I am eating my own heart pressed into the form of a broken body, a vessel which once emanated Light. I try to find a glimmer in its inmost warmth and instead crack ice-cubes against my teeth.

I crash through some Tran-spatial membrane and see a Haitian woman wailing with her half-a-boy cradled in trembling arms. Earthquake. It tends to break a body. And broken bodies tend to break a heart.

America bays for the entertainment of torture porn and yet a single tear from this nameless mother's eye rips through the silver screen, announcing a wound that will never heal. I cannot smell the stink of putrefaction as such loss is measured against love.

Histories evaporate beneath cruel suns. Love pulls nails up through hands not yet cruciform. I am father to Herod's victim. My best friends die the stupidest of deaths. The hateful foe takes his place alongside blood clots, wrong turns and chicken bones. I vomit up unspoken words and am bound in chains of remorse.

Each tooth in the Baron's head tells a thousand tales at once. He reveals his great power to heal and preserve as he continuously patches me up to withstand the next round of bullets to the gut.

He retreats now-and yet his face remains. I am holding a mirror. Somewhere, someone is cutting a deal for sex, for money. Someone is praising the ancient ones for a fresh box of vanity delivered Fed-Ex. Might as well credit Jesus for the business merger, the vote, the touchdown.

Me? I am Becoming HOODOO.

As the Atlantean Adepts returned from the Great Deluge, so the Dead shall rise again in the Resurrection wherein Universe Z(ombi) is known in our Gnosis as Universe Z(othyria).

5

We tend to think of our bodies as the dense, tangible and gross portion of what we are. Our "souls" are conceived of as something more light, ethereal and refined. I would encourage the interested reader to take an afternoon and enjoy C.S. Lewis' story The Great Divorce. In this powerful fantasy, Lewis, as narrator and protagonist, arrives in Heaven to find himself, still imperfect and underdeveloped, to be as a ghost compared to the astounding SOLID-NESS of the spiritual world around him. It takes time to adjust to the vibratory level of Heaven and grow into its reality. By the same token, our Hoodoo

Life is not some shadowy corner of the mind called up as an accoutrement to our baseline self. It IS the baseline self.

There are many techniques to come into this awareness. The important thing is to get there. Entry into this zone is a True Initiation which will enable us to engage with our magical work as a critical component of our innermost being. One literally "wakes up" and crawls out of the coffin. Time zones connect within the flesh and there is no question concerning destiny. Awareness and Action supplant speculation. You are no longer a human being seeking contact with entities who may or may not be "real." You ARE an entity.

Wearing a skull in place of a face, your space-spanning sight is no longer occluded by the vegetative vision of twin flesh orbs. Emerging into the Gnosis of the Union of Life, you find creatures and intelligences petitioning YOU in the same way you sought spirit-contact with candles and incense. As you respond, you see how those otherworldly ones who once bent your reality tunnel are, likewise, turning towards their "Elders" for direction on the Path. This vision then buckles and dimensionalizes . No being can be a dot on a line. The continually morphing matrices of Being evoke a multitude of relations. That "inferior" we are lifting up is now seen as our Most Holy Guru, well-disguised and raising us through the actions of service and compassion. This same Guru is being lifted into Awareness beyond our comprehension by virtue of this interaction with US. Outside of time, we are Guru to the Guru and the Universe is Chela to Itself.

6

HOODOO LOG

Watched the E. J. Gold video on Youtube discussing the "Body Of Habits" last night and was struck by the words in the echo- chamber at the end. That first and important question: "Am I alive...or am I dead?" This morning I'm driving to work and, like a ball bounced down into my mind-strata, those words come back. "Am I alive...or am I dead?" Well, how am going to determine this? I check my breathing. Yep, still going. But here's the thing: when the thought occurred to me to observe my breathing, I WASN'T BREATH-ING. It was almost as if my lungs were suddenly springing to life and sucking down a chest load of air IN RESPONSE to my unspoken inquiry. I repeated the same experiment later on in the day. Same thing.

What does this tell me?

It tells me that there is no breathing going on when I am not paying attention to it. I can tell myself it must be so-and then accept my own persuasive words. Of course, I must be right, right? Why, all the people around me would vouchsafe my reason and we all know that popular opinion is to be relied on in all matters of life and death. After all, the majority mind has such wonderful and certain convictions re: God, the Universe and what is Right and Wrong. And look at the way they've surmounted all world problems with this wisdom. If it weren't for them, we'd still be struggling with class division, poverty, crime and all the petty shit that once spread itself all over a Day In The Life Of A Human.

But there remains something inside of me which is perennially perturbed. Call me a malcontent. But the same crew has assured me since I was a boy that I hasten towards a fate where worms will burrow into my brain and my lifeless arms stand no chance of doing a coffin crawl back to the wake world. Despite the overwhelming success in manifesting Heaven On Earth-and answering all ontological inquiries with satisfying reply-I smell a rat. I clawed at the walls and ripped through all the drywall in the house to get its maddening screeching to stop. Alas, the rat had made its home elsewhere. I finally cut it out of my head using some basic kitchen utensils. If anything, I ask you to be impressed with this. It was NOT easy and I lost an eye in the process.

Of course, it would turn out that the eye was my end of a bargain. A raven carried it off as I flailed around on my front lawn clutching my face like some loser in a slasher flick.

So, where was I? Oh yeah. I had a towel stuffed into my orbital socket and was blowing blood bubbles from my nose. And the rat was dead.

And then I was in my car, heading to work and thinking of Mr. Gold's video. My lungs were more than happy to oblige my attention. In truth, everything was. The grass turned green as I looked at it. Cars painted themselves different colors as they passed me by. My office assembled itself into a mass of moving people and it all looked so...natural.

Just like that well-painted corpse in the coffin. God, we never saw her look better.

And like me, she wasn't even breathing.

So, it only takes a few minutes on the internet and my morning routine to turn me into a solipsist. But being the unsatisfied bastard that I am, I now eye that philosophy with suspicion. It's another rat in the house. At least it won't be looking to make a nasty nest in my head. Even rodents have to be wary of what's left above my shoulders.

AM I ALIVE OR AM I DEAD?

Would I even KNOW? And if so, how? You see this is the piss- poor logic of the pedestrian: If I'm aware of myself having some sort of existence, then I must be alive. Who reasons like this? Apparently, the human race. The same gang who must, assuredly, have had occasion to reason, by contrast, that they have been dead, also. Such convincing arguments for this.

Then again, I have played around a little with magic. A ritual here or there. I even did one where I opened my being to the "Hoodoo

Spirits" and entered a binding contract with them for all eternity. Call me impetuous. If the Devil ever wants to buy my soul, I'll be skipping off like the guy who scored a ten spot for the Brooklyn Bridge.

Who are the Hoodoo? Well, if we start with Baca Bacalou's Grimoire- transmitted through that eminent Chicago medium, the Reverend Michael Bertiaux, we'll know they are the Super-Team composed of the transmi- grated Atlantean Magi and our Necro- friends from the Zombi Realm. No, it's really not any stranger than the idea that we are animated flesh-husks composed of "Atoms" who hop about on a whirling marble which repeatedly encircles an incomprehensibly large gas-ball. We've all got our own Mythos. The question is: where is it getting us?

Eventually, for the Big Lucky Hoodoo, this gang takes up residence in the body. Lucky for them, I've evicted the vermin. I don't mind being the Land- lord. I provide space and they ALWAYS pay rent on time. We also have great conversations down at the office.

7

Kyle: So, Dead Dudes, is it really possible that... I'm one of you?

DD: Humans are infants in the Great Cosmic Nursery. Look at how they turn the Soul inside out and embrace their inverted vision with ferocity. We've witnessed their racist idealism with alternating dis- gust and amusement. Not one of them could pick out their chosen "pure-blood" in a room where we've plucked the feathers from the chickens.

K: Plucked the feathers from the chickens?

DD: Flayed them all.

K: So, um, how does this answer my question?

DD: We flay more than flesh. In fact, we show those with eyes to see how there is no flesh to be flayed. How do you think we escaped the Great Deluge?

K: OK, I think I get your point. Life is a type of Illusion and we need to see through this to enter into the Gnosis of the Death.

DD: Kyle, this is just one half of the equation. Could not Death also be the illusion that we "need to see through" to enter into the Gnosis of Life?

K: Well, sure. That sounds very...mystical.

DD: Fuck your ideas about mysticism. The few humans who truly approach us behold our HOO-DOO Forms only because of their personal polarity. Remember, you contact us with candles to the West and North. But when we have brought you into our World, you are lighting candles at all four quarters.

K: So, am I dead?

DD: There is no death, Kyle Fite. Even when your loved ones behold your body dropping its temp and turning back to clay, there is no death. Even as you are fed into a furnace, there is no death. So what remains? Life? Yes, it is LIFE. BUT-! Most humans have no understanding of what LIFE IS. They operate in context of an ILLUSION OF LIFE which is why they behave like petulant brats at the expense of each other's existence.

K: Then what IS "Life?" DD: Life is Reality.

K: What is Reality?

DD: Reality is what you imagine.

K: Reality is what I imagine it to be???

DD: No, Dumb-Ass. That's not what we said. Reality is what you IMAGINE.

K: How is this so?

DD: You can know nothing beyond Imagination. The English poet, William Blake, knew this and proclaimed it as Gospel. He knew us, also. He simply called us "Faerie." We empowered William Blake and invited him to witness one of our funerals.

K: But-what about all the Buddhist shtick? You know, going beyond the forms we imagine to get to the Pure Light of Reality? You, yourself, said that all this Life and Death business is an illusion.

DD: Yes, we know the Buddha very well. He is one of our Adepts.

K: The historic Guatama is a Hoodoo?

DD: No, Kyle. He's a BIG LUCKY HOODOO!

K: So how is Reality Imagination?

DD: You owe us some rum.

K: (scrambles for the booze)

DD: (slurps it down) You DO realize rum is metaphor? K: But you just drank it all!

DD: (obnoxious belch)

K: ...

DD: There can be no experience outside of Imagination. All you know of "fact" is imagined. This is your "grass turning green as you observe it." This is your lungs springing to life as you ask if you're alive. "Knowing" belongs to the World of Imagination. Without image, there is no knowledge. Image can never embrace a totality and therefore it must always be subjective. Despite this, the subjectivity of image is generated from an encounter within the objective continuum of Reality. We can answer your philosophic inquiry because it belongs to the realm of subjectivity. You can ask nothing from objectivity. Objectivity does not ask questions. Questions belong to the realm of the subjective mind as a vehicle of experience.

K: So what is the relation between the Subjective and Objective?

DD: We have said that Subjectivity is the vehicle of experience. But what is doing the "experiencing?"

K: The Objective.

DD: Well, there's hope for you after all.

End of Part Two ✳

Gargophias

The Fundamentals of Utilizing the Qliphoth to Perfect Being of Becoming in Nothingness/ Everything in the Path Transfixed of the Void
Angela Edwards

AS a practitioner of the Left Hand Path and as an artist. I have always been fascinated by the role of psychosexual transgression. Through extremes and the role of in these things sacred prostitution/female psychosexuality.

This type of work I have physically undertaken. It has been directly related the ideology of through ritual. Using the tunnels and Sephiroth of the Qliphoth (Tree of Death). In these practices the left hand path is not evil as such. When relating to right hand path ideology or philosophy. Both are neither good or bad in the profane misconception and both work towards the same goal of being united with the spirits. Or to a higher universal understanding.

The LHP's only difference is to my mind that it involves full surrender in embracing all shedding the skin, pushing one's own boundaries in the world. For it is the active path of FIRE of full becoming also.

In the actions of experiencing through choice, extreme sexuality or violence in my rituals. Sperm, female discharge and blood are all used to activate these radical uncompromising highways. Using the Left Hand Path rituals of abolishing all through sex creation and death blood sacrificed wholly.

That in the practitioner's descent of full surrender of oneself to the depths. Transform him/her to the practitioner's full ascension of untainted divinity.

To reach our fully activated by the radiating black sun than empowers the abyss. Our Luciferian full nature revealed.

The void of spirituality or consciousness. As I would see it the world's computer to the root of all. The void is another aspect found in the daemon Choronzon an elemental explored in Setian philosophy. In the work of

Thomas Karlsson (Qabalah, Qliphoth and Goetic magic). Also Choronzon can be linked directly to the void. As Choronzon is said to be a gateway to the Qliphothic universe. That this daemon acts as a control panel of energy translating as the void. The universal light that operates the Abyss. This philosophy regarding these elements and aspects of Choronzon's character. Are re-iterated in the Typhonian grimoire The Nightside of Eden By Kenneth Grant. Grant describes Choronzon as the gateway to the Qliphoth. The governing energy that operates all transmissions and access for the practitioner into the void, Abyss and Qliphothic realms.

In these aspects Choronzon is characterless and more a reflection of our total darker consciousness. He is also darker universal energy as found in the symbols of Chaos magick. The cause of all transmission and effect. In Chaos magick the teachings are to invoke no Gods or Spirits.

Only universal energy alone to therefore become Choronzon. The ideology of the Chaos magick system. Is the none worship of Gods or higher spirits. We find as practitioners a more purist LHP approach. In placing no superiority on our devotional practice. In all spirits being the voids energy or merged abyss in being nothingness. The Chaos magickal practitioner reaches equality within nothing being sacred to the GODS.

Reflecting the ideology of the LHP adept's philosophy to become merged equal nothingness with the void alone. Using symbolic transmissions that can be traced as the most purist devotional cult of annihilation of human character/ ego in their pure power.

In these aspects Chaos magick is the mother cult of the void and the Abyss. Of supreme magical spiritual attainment of the practitioner crossing over to the spiritual realms fully embraced. Therefore, we could find in the Qliphoth being the dead shells of rebirth to a higher conscious.

The Qliphoth is mainly attributed to belonging to the Chaos magicians work. In magickal contemporary magickal practice today.

For the vat of energy the void can be compared to the black sun or sigil's used in the work of the Chaos magic of Peter Carroll's group the Illuminates Of Thanateros. Or the work of Chaos magic's grandfather Austin O Spare. Who uses his Neither Neither system to become all incorporating divine full gender transcendence. Therefore the womb of the universe that is the void cannot be referred to as neither male or female as at the start and at the end. It is to be to become all incorporated both.

In the grimoire Qutub Chumbley refers to this as the point used in these types of workings. As it being the mother /father to us all of fully embraced transgendered nothingness which in turn is to become our imperfect or perfect uncorrupted nature in the voids prayer invoked.

When the practitioner sheds the skin, surrenders to the flesh, smashes all social conformity.

Pushing the boundaries of gender, sexuality or acceptability in sexual magical ritual they embrace the void also.

This is further explained in abolishment of gender roles within sex magickal practice. And in Crowley's use of the XI degree as a superior form of sexual magick. In Bertiaux's system he refers to this type of sex magical ritual also . Through the red and black alchemical twins or marassas united. In the philosophy of bisexuality/homosexuality being utilised in ritual as the ultimate sex magickal passage. To invocations to higher spiritual attainment.

As Crowley did believe it was only through homosexual passive and dominant anal sex superior magickal powers could be attained. That as he incorporated both sexual roles of giver-taker with his lovers. In becoming male and female sexually united that he would invoke the void or the Abyss. This is explored within his writings extensively including the book The Vision and The Voice. In Crowley's philosophy is similar to the ideas found in Bertiaux's system. In the Voudon Gnostic Workbook.

In VGW Bertiaux also references homosexual passivity merged with homosexual active practices. As his main fundamental sex magickal system. That allows his entrance through the lwa Nibo to access the void.

Through the sephiroth of Uranus which is Daath. This sex magickal practice is by Bertiaux referenced as a means of entering the meon that is the void also. We can also find anal sex or homosexuality explored in similar context. In the work of Kenneth grant. Who refers to this practice in the last of the trilogies (the final attainment of full self through the void) as the mauve zone).

While as a sex magickal practitioner myself I do not see a full relationship with just male homosexual practices or anal sex in particular regarding Qliphoth work etc. Nor do I totally equate these acts. In ritual as doorways in all aspects to the void or abyss transcendence. I have come to the realization that homosexual sex magickal practice. Becomes in theory an example of these practitioners workings to attain through bisexuality or becoming both roles in a sex act male and female. The perfected none gendered aspect of the Qliphoth's work.

In leading to full knowledge of the vision of the void that holds no specific gender. The sexual magickal practitioner is none sexual in that all aspects of sexuality are explored. Regardless of personnel sexual preference to access spirit invocation. In this aspect the prostitute is also none sexual as his or her personnel sexual preferences become irrelevant as regards to their work. This is also a trait found in the switch BDSM who accesses like in bisexuality all aspects of psychosexuality also. In this way all three access the void fully.

As a bisexual woman myself and practitioner. It has been through sexual acknowledgement of all sides of gender male and female taken into myself.

That I have been able to in all sexual magical acts utilize the role of both. Therefore, acknowledge myself as becoming all polarities in this work. Which makes perfect sense when acknowledging that perfect nature attained through the void. That holds no gender in its nothingness.

Therefore, the Qliphoth and void is to become spiritually light activated all things. In this work then type of breakdown occurs of the conditioned self. Where in ritual spiritual contact the practitioner reaches the final stage though consciously embracing these all things to the evolvement of through smashing of ego.

To become transgressed to the void wholly. In reaching the void illuminated by the light of the black sun. Our darker subconscious nature.

We are able to reach in the Luciferian sense of the word our equality with the spirits/GODS outside of humanities restraints.

This end product is the product of full universal gnosis. That is in essence the light bearer lucifer. The one whom, illuminates with shining black sun. In our chosen pathways the true LHP adepts practice. The universes womb is the void of spirit materialization. In these practices of more extreme forms of gnosis and worship lay our true perfect nature.

Our nature as it was before and after, past and future so fully we become. In these types of practice, I have learned that most magic is useless. Without directed real life action and strong projected intent.

For if we are to find our true nature or become the final attainment of as man/woman uniting with the void to higher consciousness. All work should be whether transgression or otherwise. When used as our tools to exploring our true psychosexual nature must be practiced with directed conscious intent. This is the key to all successful magic to practice it with projected true intent.

Another aspect of this practice from my own point of view is that the tunnels of the Qliphoth whether utilized as tools in the ideologies of Grant, Bertiaux, and the Draconian current of the Dragon Rouge. Is that spiritual contact for myself is attained through real life action.

Not just in traditional ritual spirit invocation but in spiritual contact possession within our actions in our material world. In this aspect the spiritual realm crosses over into our mortal realm, so therefore like male/female , sex creation/death , darkness/light all aspects become formed as one .

On the LHPs initiation through surrender sacrifice to all to higher spiritual all embraced attainment. The Qliphoth is the shells of death the void though it is Hebrew the tree of knowledge also.

In this way it is the Abyss of nothingness ruled over by Babalon and all abominations broken also to the divine void. Babalon like some Pomba Giras in the Brazilian religion Quimbanda are identified as being the whore and the ultimate archetype example of the unholy and holy female.

The Qliphoth is activated by the black sun radiating light that the dark light bearer also that is Lucifer uniting Lucifer with Babalon in abyss union wholly.

This is another aspect that fits into the ideologies of Quimbanda as Pomba Gira is the wife of EXU (the Quimbanda lucifer counterpart).

In these spirits we not only find examples of female sexuality, or psychosexuality (as in Lilith often referred as hells whore also) soiled imperfection equating perfection but in the whore that is open to all without judgment. The sacramental spiritual healing unconditional that is also dualistically invoke.

The spirit of Lilith can also be linked to the Quimbanda spirit of Pomba Gira Do Inferno queen of hell fire in Quimbanda. Whom with her chalice (is also linked to the western icon of Babalon). As hells whore again like Lilith who resides upon Malkuth. Minus Liliths colder vampiric manifestations. She is at the roots of the religion of Quimbanda also.

As the original female manifestation of Quimbanda governing all her legions. In being the original imperfect mother of humanities darker aspects as is Lilith.

Lilith hell's whore resides at the base of Malkuth in the Qliphoth's roots that translate as the earth, the holy /unholy filth of universal everything for holy is the WHORE. The whore that in embraced nothingness, nothing remains sacred and all remains sacred in filth. Sacred prostitution is also another aspect of the void.

Not only in that Babalon in Thelema theory sits on the otherside of the Abyss of the void. But in that when working with prostitution that is not sacred in western societies philosophy. That when prostitution becomes used in sacred context it transgresses like the void of nothing to all. Whereupon nothing and everything is sacred wholly.

The connection between the whore who in society is seen as the outcast filth or in sacred whoredom being consciously open to all heals the unwanted, unloved. Who in desperation pay for her services to lay these burdens upon her. The whore becomes the nursemaid to the unwanted masses healing with her filth medicines purity.

When I have been working as a prostitute either on the streets as heroin addicted teenager then later today as a chosen profession to explore its sacred properties consciously as a sex worker and BDSM switch/sub as research towards my second Pomba Gira grimoire writings, film, and paintings. I have found the healing aspect to be true of these actions. In that these actions have informed my magical work. My divine work with Lilith's/Babalon and Pomba Gira currents. As to becoming healing filth and my transgressive Qliphoth work.

With Malkuth's base actions leading to a higher purist gnosis activated by the harsh dark light activated of the black sun. In filth nothing becomes sacred. Therefore, in this path everything within the void becomes sacred also.

In my second experiences of my chosen work of prostitution. Without profane things as circumstance. This has allowed me to wholly give myself over to clients in love or a higher detached understanding from myself sacrifice. In welcoming all human nature no matter how imperfect as beautiful.

This transgressed state of wholly accepting freedom of mind consciousness is the full beauty in ritual translated as the LHP.

In real life actions using sexuality and violence. Examples using cutting of the skin in sigil worship, prostitution, submission all forms of our psychosexual nature. We can in conscious rejection of mundane societies moralistic ideologies surrender ourselves fully to the spirits to all.

To my mind it is not only important to use traditional invocations in spiritual work founded upon classical ritual and our altars. It is of just as much if not more valid importance to transcend traditional spiritual prayer into the living world through our own directed living actions. This includes the practitioner not only in one ritual using cutting as a form of invocation, or anal sex in one sex magical ritual then returning in the profane lives back to normality. Instead it means full surrender to the merciless LHP fully in all areas of their lives day to day.

Living in ritual all transgression ritual practices like for example as found in the Aghori whom sacrifices all worldly possessions to beg upon the street, homelessness or to sleep with corpses in graves out of choice. In a life affirmation extended full ritual.

That in these actions becomes their quest life of full sacrifice also.

For most of the time such approaches to magical work. In western society are rarer. In our culture for most practitioners feel lighting a candle on an altar, reading books or doing a small ritual in a graveyard.

Will be enough to access full spirit contact or spiritual enlightenment. So while all these things are valid in our practice. They are only valid to my mind to an extent. For we need to surrender fully to the LHP. Fully in the action of lifestyle. Living our practices and beliefs. Through real life transgressive rituals or sacrifice ourselves living beyond social conformity. While for some the word lifestyle is a profane terminology. As breaking taboos or transgressing can never become habit or safe. That full transgression should be as in the void in its actions and philosophy the universe limitless. Without manmade restrictions. It is only when fully acknowledged in acceptance in carrying through our beliefs consistently in life. That fully can we become. As outcasts through intent. In our choice to reach full uncompromising Luciferian enlightenment.

To in these acts that incorporate creation sex with death annihilation we can in united alchemical practice reach our soul.

Another aspect of the void or divine nothingness reached through the Qliphoth tree of death knowledge that transgresses to spiritual rebirth. Is that the void can through these rituals when finally rested in or attained translate as the true human soul. The soul to my mind is perfection accomplished through spiritual nothingness, as the soul in my mind human or spiritual transcends the mortal realm in its full ascension totally.

In our infernal path that leads to ascension through regression to the nothingness that is our full realized primal nature in the void.

The full human soul is reached through actions embracing all actions exhibiting the darker sexual, violent aspects of one's nature. In that the soul acknowledges all as worthy or sacred just as in the act of prostitution.

It is open to all rejects nothing as spiritual forms of knowledge or higher spiritual understanding universal enlightenment.

The evolvement of contemporary occultism evolving from more original shamanic forms has I feel regressed upon its self again. For in the voids philosophy and practice as previously discussed access to these Qliphothic universes. Can be only gained by stripping down to the practitioner's body as a vessel only. Therefore, the lowest form of magical vision or practice becomes the highest. The simplistic becomes the most complex.

In that ceremonial magical practice or traditional goetic rituals become worthless. In smashing of all to the divine full nature which lays in the void of full transformation. So we find as practitioners the body that is the shell that covers the soul is to become our only altar. The flesh and blood our tools consecrated in work. As regards through ritual entering the qliphothic void. Of becoming activated universal nothingness which is also ALL.

In the spells of the void all is celebrated. All is sacred in that all is of value to our path to the end magical state which is the Qliphoth state fully activated by the radiating Luciferian black sun in the universe of the void. To reject all gods, take upon yourself no Gods and in this take equality of all gods upon yourself. That is the void invoked. There in the shadows remains light. In this path to perfect being of becoming in the path of nothingness which is also everything the path transfixed of the void alone.

The Conclusion

Black is the Sun: My Eulogy to the Void of Transformation Alone.

Invocation of the Sacred Void

Black is the sun that illuminates the human void. Black is the space that annihilates the ego syringed Black is the sun that radiates enflames my
human yearning
Black is my sin
Black is my life
Black is my perversion
Black is my blood
Black is my violent, brutality, my honesty.
Black is the sun of full martyred tarnished self-sacrificed sainthood

Black is the depths of the savage unbridled
Daemonic Luciferian embodiment.
Black is the sun that illuminates the tunnels of my erotic,
violent deprivation
Black rayed is the light that transforms man to divinity
Black is the sun that in its light I find myself crucified
through pain to numbness
Black are the sparks that penetrate my eyes, blinded in light
were I find my absolution
Black is death in its force of nature
Black is the sun radiating the unidealized human state
Black is the streaming life force of life radiated of dualist acknowledge-
ment of everything.
Black is the sun that illuminates all true life
Black is the light energy streaming through my flesh, bones, body in eso-
teric activated creative LIVING alchemy
Black is the sun that radiates in uncompromising TRUTH
Black is the humble magician whose only tools of consecration are their
bodies, their only altar is the WORLD
Black is the sun that in its energy allows me to be all things embraced
without human conscious constraints
Black is the sun that enflames into to thyself empowers
Black is the light that clarifies to glow in all aspects of with
FORCE my true soul
Black is the sun high in the universal eros imbued cosmos
Black is the sun that infuses the mages of elemental street
nightside magick.
Black is the light upon the dead wastes of the Qliphoth
Black is the sun which trails my left sided bramble spiked pathways
Black is the light that shines upon my life, my pilgrimage. Black is the
light combined that when called upon allows rebirth
Black is the soul shining that I impale upon all my acts, rituals conducted
Black is my transgression state of being
Black is the sun which transforms ugliness to beauty Black is the sun that
hits the dead branches of the tree of death Black is the sun that abolishes
all morals, judgments, embraces humble human fragility.
Black is the sun that I bask in to leading to my full enlightened SOUL.

Black is the sun by which this grimoire is awakened lit
Black is the start that is also the end.
Finally, I find black is the Sun of the message in my eulogy to the void of
transformation alone. ✦

Temphioth

𝔗heoretical 𝔇emonology in 𝔓sychoanalysis

Alexei Dzyuba

What appears as a demon, what is called a demon, what is recognized as a demon, exists within a human being and disappears with him.

— Milarepa, Himalayan yogi (1040-1123).

𝔍T was famous psychologist and mystic Carl Gustav Jung, who began to use mystical metaphors to describe different elements and processes within human psyche. These days, demons are frequently used as metaphors to describe neuroses, even by such pragmatics as NLP-ers.

I would like to analyze the basics if such things as fundamentals of human morality, ethics, and their practically applied functions within human society. Such things, as ethics and morality inevitably come to existence, when the simplest form of society emerges (even though, it may consist only of a few persons). Morality is a code of unwritten (or written) laws and regulations, that directs agreeable, non-conflict functioning of a group of individuals as a whole. This is but glue, or cement, that binds together bricks and guarantees stability of a structure. Certain ethical and moral laws exist among prisoners in a jail, and even in a pack of animals. Scientists, observing social life of chimpanzee, have come to the conclusion, that chimpanzee have very sophisticated political games within their society, that are only slightly less complex, than human politics.

The real purpose of ethics and morality – is purely functional, they must assure safety and well-being of the majority, and if this inevitably requires sacrificing of the minority, that social ethics always justifies this. Ethics and aesthetics have absolutely nothing in common, although they are frequently confused by human beings.

Sigmund Freud has shocked the puritan society of the early 1900-s saying, that every human being is partly an animal, and human behavior is frequently affected by unconscious animal instincts. He ash also provided detailed description of neurosis mechanism in his work "Civilization and its Discontents".

Most civilized societies impose most of moral and ethical restrictions on an individual, and this, in turn, demands to put harder strain and restrictions on one's animal instincts. Statistics confirms, that most civilized countries have the highest suicide rate.

This repression mechanism becomes automatic, unconscious, and an individual is no longer aware of repressed desires and instincts. Thus, an entire part of person's psyche that is cut off, repressed, out of conscious, but nevertheless, it does cause powerful, but non-direct influence on one's behavior. Carl Gustav Jung called this part of our psyche as "The Shadow". Because the shadow mostly consists of the most basic, primitive, animal parts of ourselves, it is not very pleasant to accept the fact, that those "freaks" are parts of ourselves, especially, if you have received puritan upbringing. And even though, if you may not be a puritan, it is far more pleasant to consider yourself as a completely civilized being without vices, pretending (to yourself in the first place), that this ugly, dark side does not exist at all. It is the same thing as to clean up only a half of a room really well, and pile up all the garbage in the other half, and try to ignore it. Ignoring one's own shadow existence is actually a very convenient hypocrisy. (Sigmund Freud defined this as a "repression defense mechanism"). It also allows to avoid the responsibility for one's own shadow's actions. The shadow is thus perceived as "not me". This is why humans cannot bear any real responsibility for their own actions.

When puritan morality comes into play, and demands even more severe repression of one's own instincts, it makes things much worse. The Third Newton's law says; " Every action causes equal and opposite re-action". When repression of instincts becomes too severe, it inevitably backfires. It's the same thing as to try to draw a dozen of ping-pong balls in a bath with one hand – they will inevitably slip between your fingers and surface.

The problem is that repressed desire eventually frees itself form the tyranny of morality, and after that it always manifests in some perverse form. One such example –is pedophilia among Catholic priests. This obviously not a recent problem, it has existed for centuries, but it has always been silenced. Sexual desire as such is not evil by itself, but after being so severely repressed, it did find its way out as a perversion. Such cases (and this is probably not the worst example), do stress the necessity to face one's own dark side.

When owned as t host relevant, alive truly whole/holy parts of ourselves, these most basic "dark" energies can be wonderfully demonic, transforming us into vibrant, creative, fully actualized human beings (well, maybe, even into something better, that regular human beings actually). It is only when they are denied, cut-off, repulsed, repressed, that their darkness can become demonic, twisting, exploding destructively into consciousness, swamping ego-rationality in mass psychoses, and in the small daily horrors, that assault us.

—Linda Falorio, *Shadow Tarot*

As it is said "Demon is but an angel, acting out of turn".

Some professionally spiritual people are vile and untrustworthy, when off duty, simply because their beliefs conflict with basic drives, and only manage to distort their natural behavior temporarily. The demons than come screaming up out of the cellar at unexpected moments.

—Peter J. Carrol, *Liber Kaos*

Basic principles of demonology:

1. A god ignored is a demon born.
2. That, which is denied, gains power, and seeks strange and unexpected forms of manifestation.
3. Deny death and other forms of suicide will arise.
4. Deny sex and bizarre forms of its expression will torment you.
5. Deny love and absurd sentimentalities will disable you.
6. Deny aggression only to stare eventually at the bloody knife in your shaking hand.
7. Deny honest fear and desire only to create senseless neuroticism and avarice.

Self-hypocrisy, denial of one's negative aspect also exists on a national scale. To be able to make a sober, objective judgment of any particular culture, one needs to take a position of a detached observer – any native representative of that particular culture will always turn a blind eye to its negative aspects.

For example, the occupation of China by Japanese army during the 2-nd World War is still called as "Manchurian Incident" in Japan. Many representatives of Japanese academic elite still consider the "Manchurian Incident" as a proof of superiority of Japanese nation. I guess, there is no need to mention those atrocities, that were done towards Chinese people (using humans as biologic material to test bacterial weapons, etc.)

But, when Hiroshima is mentioned – crocodile tears are cried, and a lot is said about inhumanity and atrocity. It looks, like humanism and compassion become significant when those, who mention them need to be treated with compassion – in other cases, when such treatment is expected of them – other values become more significant (like the necessity to prove the superiority of one's nation).

Another example – is Moses form the Old Testament. That genocide, that he commenced after entering the Land of Canaan, is in no way different from those atrocities, that Hitler had done

In Nazi Germany. If such comparison seems shocking, than it needs to be reminded, that Hitler also had a status of a messiah, and "Mine Kaumph" was their Holy Bible.

During the 2-nd World War Eastern Orthodox clergy has sent quite a bunch of grateful letters to Hitler, blessing him to lead the "holy war against the Satanic kingdom" (Soviet Union). Nevertheless, the majority of people still firmly believe, that Hitler was the terrible monster, and Moses – was the holy man. One can see Christian cartoons for children about Moses no TV. Can you imagine cartoons about Hitler for kids?

The next example – France shortly after it was relieved from the occupation by Nazi, it has sent its own troops to occupy Vietnam.

Unfortunately, average human beings always turn a blind eye to negative aspects of own culture. And if you do make those negative aspects visible, the reaction that inevitably follows, is quite predictable, and it is ALWAYS very aggressive. Again, this is not a conscious feedback, but a strictly conditioned Pavlovian dog reaction. If you try to explain to an Orthodox Jew the similarity of those atrocities, done by Moses and Hitler – his feedback is in no way going to be friendly.

Another example is that caricature of Mohammed the Prophet in Danish newspaper. It would be interesting to investigate the archives of Middle Eastern newspapers – their caricatures are a lot nastier, for sure, but of course...." your own shit never smells bad".

And it seems strange, that humanistic philosophers still wonder why human beings cannot live in peace, understanding and harmony. If human beings stubbornly refuse to understand themselves in the first place, how can they understand others?

Humanistic philosophy is based on the assumption, that human beings are conscious beings, and they are able to take responsibility for their own actions. This is not true. It is much easier to rely on convenient "solution packages" (holy scriptures, 10 commandments, etc, etc.). There is no need to think of cause- and-effect relations and consider possible outcomes of every particular action in every individual situation.

But this is not possible to create laws that will work perfectly in every situation, lawyers can confirm this – endless corrections and additions in law system are being created all the time.

As an example, let us consider one of the basic Judeo-Christian commandments – "Thou shall not kill". Murder is definitely a sin in a street fight – when only a few people are involved. In a different situation, let's say, during a military conflict between nations, when a few thousand people are involved (instead of only a few people) –that a murder is "a holy duty", and priest from both sides give their blessings for murder. It happens, that the only difference between a "morbid sin" and "a holy duty" is but a scale of a conflict.

Speaking about military conflicts between nations, it needs to be stressed, that resources are becoming scarce, and only in 15 years fresh water is going to be accessible only to 1/3 of human population. Taking these facts into account, one can imagine the upcoming fights for resources between nations (or corporations).

This is why at present time there is a real necessity for spiritual evolution of human beings – the necessity to surpass restrictions, that define human mentality. To be able to do this, one need to get rid of duality, that is so typical for human psyche, and stop denial of one's dark side. The major obstacles on this path are ethical/aesthetical stereotypes and illusions. A lotus flower, that grows in a swamp amidst mud is a very good metaphor to describe this typical duality of human psyche. Flower's beauty is greatly contrasting with mud, that surrounds it. This metaphor is very much favored by puritan spiritual gurus, that preach absolute transcendence and denial of animal aspects of human psyche.

Somehow, they ignore the fact, that this beautiful flower is only half of the plant. The other half, that is not visible – is not so good looking. This beautiful flower is completely dependent on its dirty and stinky roots – try to cut it off, and it's not going to live for too long. Those parts are absolute opposites of each other absolute polarities, and nevertheless, they are but different parts of the same plant, that are absolutely dependent on each other.

This metaphor actually provides the solution for very sophisticated moral dilemma, and it illustrates the principle of unity and mutual dependency of the opposites. This lotus flower may indeed raise above mud, but this mud is but its food supply. Therefore, these primitive, animal, hideous aspects of our psyche are energy resources, on which our exalted, spiritual side is absolutely reliant.

To illustrate this dependency, we can discuss Indian saint Mahatma Ghandi. He was known for his strict ascetics – absolutely no alcohol, meat, and of course – no sex. Nevertheless, he was known to have enjoyed Platonic company of beautiful women, and he celibately shared his bed with his young niece.

Spiritual fire, burning inside Ghandi, would have become quickly extinguished without that sexual energy exchange (with his own minor niece) – and even though, this energy exchange was a lot less intense, than during physical sex, it was still sex – albeit, in a very subtle form.

Of course, Mahatma Ghandi is a saint for millions of people. Let's take another example: prominent fiction writer Arthur Clark, who was knighted by English Queen Elizabeth the 2nd, is also the icon for the world's intellectual elite. When Lisa found out that he has arranged himself a pedophile liar on Ceylon, she immediately stripped him of this title. When I told about this to a great fan of Arthur Clark, who also had Doctor's degree in psychiatry, his reply was : "One cam of course blame a pedophile... but will this make sense? Pedophilia is very difficult to cure...". Even though, he had a Doctor's degree, he didn't dare to question that socially accepted stereotype and authority of Arthur Clark.

Speaking about integration of the shadow side into a human psyche, I would like to stress the importance of the right way of doing it. By no means I reject the necessity of controlling one's animal instincts. But is absolutely necessary to understand the obvious harm and negative consequences of excessive control of one's passions – this is something, that puritan moralists prefer to ignore.

It is absolutely normal and natural, that we are partly primitive and hideous beasts – these animal parts of ourselves use dirt and excrements as the basic energy resource that is later transformed into beautiful flowers of spirituality.

Obviously, one needs to understand the dangers of overdoing it. Using a little excrement as a fertilizer is good, but if you dump an entire truck of fecal on a plant, you are going to bury it. Opposites MUST be carefully balanced by each other. ✶

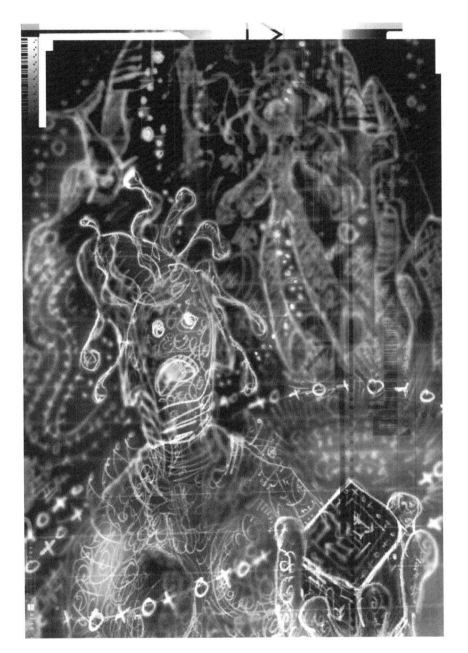

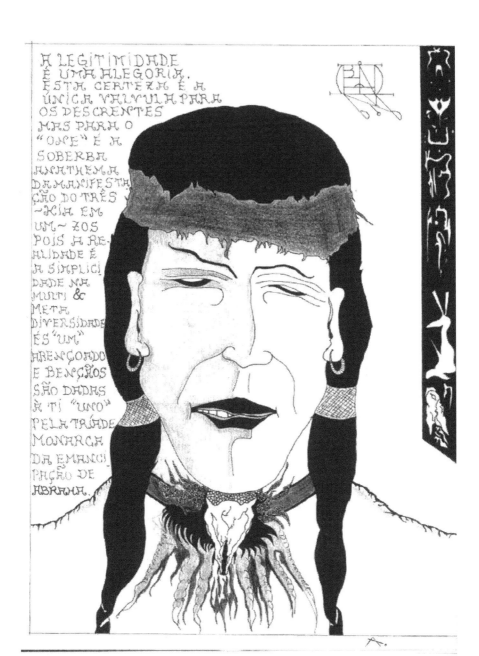

A LEGITIMIDADE
É UMA ALEGORIA.
ESTA CERTEZA É A
ÚNICA VÁLVULA PARA
OS DESCRENTES
MAS PARA O
"OMIE" É A
SOBERBA
ANATHEMA
DA MANIFESTA
ÇÃO DO TRÊS
~XIA EM
UM~ ZOS
POIS A RE-
ALIDADE É
A SIMPLICI
DADE NA
MULTI &
META
DIVERSIDADE
ÉS "UM"
ARENGORDO
E BENÇÃOS
SÃO DADAS
A TI "UNO"
PELA TRÍADE
MONARCA
DA EMANCI
PAÇÃO DE
ABRAHA.

The Zos Kia Cultus by a Lover of Ecstasy

Claudio Cesar Carvalho

I N my point of view, the Zos Kia Cultus has a rich and fascinating perspective which must be explored in the depths of the sub- consciousness. It shows how the continuing attraction of irrational can embody imperceptibly on a subtle iconography from sacred Spirit – our Iconoclast – in several ways and possibilities.

Zos Kia Cultus as a Current is a common sense for several people and it is still widely used as a term by occult art's critics, writers, occultists, scholars and even artists. Nevertheless, through my experience and natural surrender to my Arte I perceived about brevity of this term aforementioned as I have been penetrating in psychology of the Void or KIA. My natural linking in past lives to Typhonian Tradition lead me back to a specifically evaluation of what could be this ablaze impulse so-called Zos Kia Cultus.

According to my point of view, Zos Kia is a rich, powerful and still vital language of images and styles in which comes to represent a deep-rooted inner 'systems' from individual as a whole organism sentient encompassing millions ideas and contexts in ΘNE. Thus the individual can liberate intense primal atavisms latent in the depths of your sub-consciousness. Thereby, this powerful impulse can provide a profound disruption of the senses which lies on unwanted emotional and psychological states. These unwanted states are restrictive agents of the persona because they take the benefit of conventional nominalization and mentality so that it can be easily expressed along the cruelty of the barriers of the rational contributing to a stupid personality cult for other people.

To express Zos Kia as a Current and nothing else, it would be exactly the understanding about the Expressionism term like "pathetical ism" abrogating so its own expression and genuine meaning.

Both AOS and Kenneth Grant fully understood, each to his term, which really means Zos-Kia, that is to say, they 'saw' beyond the context of a Current, they saw a vast Impulse. In my viewpoint, in this case, Kenneth Grant worked intensively the irrational pattern that establishes Zos-Kia's emanations as vehicle between the Consciousness and Unconsciousness; however, Austin Spare acted in an intuitive way although he created a model of access from very personal way to reach and establish contact with this Impulse. It's can be understood as a root without form, this means that the individual should not stick to the illusion's fields from the mind, but inversely walking down the road of imagination that is quite different. ✦

Blackmouth Beach

Sean Woodward

SHE slammed the brown bag on the kitchen table with a far off look and an exclamation.

"Drongos!" said Bambrah

"What's the matter love?" I asked, opening the fridge and rearranging the vegetable shelf as she started to pass the contents of the bag. She paused, hands on hips, giving me that 'don't call me love look.'

"Well, I was coming back past the bakery and some idiot in a blacked out Ute bombed down the road towards the beach. They could've killed someone the speed they were doing".

"Well, you know what Fossil Beach is like, the tourists can't wait to get down there with a hammer. They all think they'll find the next T-Rex!"

She smiled a little then and passed me the milk.

"It was Ozraptors back home. I've seen that Range Rover before though. Last week parked down Sea Lane. Bunch of preppy kids with clipboards, seemed to be asking people lots of questions."

"Preppy?"

"You know, just out of Uni, not quite learnt a proper fashion sense yet. One of your lot."

"Says you!" I stretched past the fridge door and poked her playfully in the ribs, my blow buffeted by the softness of her hand- knitted, rainbow colored, Nepalese cardigan.

"Anyway'" I said hoping she'd calmed sufficiently. "Did you get the September copy of New Scientist?"

"Yeah, it's in the bag, just make sure you recycle it and don't just add it to that pile in the spare room."

I leant over to the table and pulled the magazine out. Sure enough, it was the issue Tommy had been talking about in the pub. I flicked past the articles on dark energy and black holes, past the usual climate change scares and found it. The Bloop. Some kind of underwater anomaly Tommy had said. Thought I'd be interested. He didn't really see the point of the field recordings I was making around the village and the beach, but was impressed that I'd managed to get the funding to undertake it.

"You're right though about those kids," I said, putting the magazine down after my cursory scan. "I think it's something to do with this article I was telling you about last night. I had an email from Dr. Muller this morning, apparently there's a new exchange programme with a University in Massachusetts. He said they might need the expertise of an award-winning sound designer like myself."

"Well, you tell them from me, they need the expertise of a driving instructor first!"

She'd bypassed my part in the human unpacking chain and finished emptying the bag with haste. I wasn't sure if I was the anger driving her or something else.

"Let's go for a walk up to Vicarwood," she said, shutting the fridge door and smiling at me "I've saw some new shrooms while I was out."

I didn't know it that morning but it was the mushrooms that had first stretched then let slip the chains of my sanity. It was hard to fathom now, walking down Blackmouth's beach in the icy hours of the morning. How could a small circle of mushrooms in a September field mean so much? But I understand it all now. Watching the distant waves break and seeing their energy dissipated at the shoreline I recognize the same relentless erosion that tugs at the blowing threads of my mind, without ceasing, without pity, fingers of wind searching for one to unpick and utterly dismantle my faculties.

I turn my eyes from the level horizon towards the dark cliffs of the Jurassic Coast. In the brittle black termite towers of riddled caves and porous edifices I see the homes of the insect servants, building high their lookouts, in a frenzy of swarming, suffocating activity. I know they're waiting for the low pitched signal from the sea, amplified for them by the sand and the dark cliffs that they have slowly sculpted into sound mirrors. They're waiting with twitching limbs for the Deep Hoo Ones to crawl from the water's edge. I know they wait patiently, hoping a chance will soon come for them to show their devotion, their tireless, numb waiting.

I'd heard the rumours of course. All the old fishermen were full of them, even Mr Johnson who usually was a man of few words on any other subject. He'd prop his metal detector up against the sea wall by the car park, take out his favorite scrimshaw pipe and by the time he had completed his ritual of scouring, emptying and refilling it with clumps of Golden Virginia tobacco his thoughts would settle on the tales of some of the strange metal objects he'd found. The early morning dog walkers of the village were the same if you managed to wade beyond the usual half-hearted exchange of "Morning!" With them you'd also find yourself in the shallows of odd conversations.

In fact, it didn't seem to take much coercion at all for the locals to offer up some of their own tales of strange happenings on the shoreline. The same way the salt arrived on the back of the wind and began to eat at every piece of metal below the tumbling cliffs, so gradually the stories snagged a place in your mind, gathering themselves about a dark, salt-worn spot the longer you exposed yourself to the biting wind by the water's edge. Massing together, the stories would seem plausible and after a while it was easy to forget common sense, easy to act in ways you would never have thought possible, easy to abandon the simple survival reflexes that long ago were saying "run, get out of here now!".

Of course I can't turn from the shore's edge. That would be to admit defeat, to leave Bambrah stranded. Even now I dare not think of all the things she has seen in those depths, all the wet lurking horrors that lie by her side in the waking dreams of the Deep Hoo Ones.

I have to put such thoughts aside, concentrate my purpose on keeping the structure of my mind intact, hang on to the lines of strategy that I hope to enact, wrap myself around the shape of the plan, find some comfort in its hopeful warmth. It's not easy. With each seabird call, each blow of the wind upon my skin, all I can think of is her. Of how different life would be if we'd gone back to Sydney, like she'd always wanted.

"Come on Steve, there's nothing here, let's get some breakfast, eh?"

I looked up, wrenched from my thoughts. Tommy must have been jogging towards me for a good ten minutes. I recognized his gait immediately, he didn't let up his pace, timing his words exactly for the moment that he passed me and headed up the shingle towards the car park and the small waterfront cafe.

"Sure I'll be there in a sec." I said, knowing it would be much longer. As quickly as he'd traversed the beach he was gone, an aerodynamic flash of thermally insulated North Face cladding and Nike propulsion. The furry hood was down on my own jacket. I wanted to feel the elements make my flesh raw.

No amount of clothing could insulate me from this place, keep out the memories that blew hard against my face, yet unseen to all others.

I scanned the sands ahead. No more visitors, good. I step over a mooring line, all barnacled and rusted, it's orange-flaked tendrils like a huge plant stem, unfurled by the tide. It looked no different from all the others that stretched out to sea further down the beach.

But this was the one. I could tell from the position of the headland to my side, I didn't need a GPS or the familiar siren of Mr Johnson's metal detector as he wandered the sandy grass behind the beachfront cafe. This was the one Tommy and the others had lined up alongside, had gripped tight though their hands bled, had steadfastly joined as if in some summer tug of war contest. This was the one that my foot had become tangled with in those cold waters, this was the one that had wrenched me from the depths. This was the one that had torn my hand free from hers.

Does screaming really resolve anything? Every morning I come to this spot, to this uncaring line of metal and I want to scream at it until there is no breath left in my lungs. I want to rip it from the beach, tie it round my neck and walk back into the water. At first I tried to do that, to recreate the bond that led me here, to find some solace from the events. But the line was too well anchored, too heavy. By the time I had realized my efforts were in vain something of the urge had passed, worn itself out in the face of insurmountable odds. So when action fail you begin to make plans. Plot in the small hope that you will succeed. I know it's the only way to stop the voices too. If I concentrate on the plan then their gurgling underwater incantations might slowly start to recede.

And what of my plan? I dare not tell Tommy of the things I saw down there. So instead we'd sit in the cafe and he'd orders two full English breakfasts and we'd eat. Him with his cups of tea, me with my coffee, in a large Lily mug. Every morning since that night, the same ritual. He'd watch me over his knife and fork, trying to gauge my state of mind. I could see it in the tilt of his head, the raised eyebrow, the expectant pauses in his eating.

Every morning I'd cut the sausages, butter the toast and move the mushrooms to the side of the plate. Yesterday was the day that Tommy's curiosity finally got the better of him.

"I've noticed you don't touch the mushrooms anymore. You always used to like them." It was half fact, half query. He was trying to be careful, trying not to be too blunt. It was something I liked about Tommy, probably why we'd been friends so long. He had perfected just the right amount of interest, just the right amount of distant British bloke-ness. So yesterday I finally decided maybe there was something I could share with him. I drank some more coffee then put the cup down slowly, carefully.

"They were really Bam's favorites. You know how she preferred organic "Yeah, sure" food"

"Well, that was the start of things"

"Things?"

"Well, she grew whatever she could herself, always preferred her own. Hated the supermarket ones. It was one of the reasons we came to Blackmouth, no supermarkets within a fifty-mile radius! She hated the fact that no matter what the labels said you never really know what chemicals they'd been subjected to all the time they were growing. When we first went out together, she had this little book of mushrooms that she took everywhere with her. I-Spy book of mushrooms I think. Anyway, you know Vicarwood? She could name every plant in there. But mushrooms were her thing.

Loved them, would take me on expeditions for hours tracking down the latest ones.

"Yeah, always thought she was a bit of a hippy." Tommy half smiled, not quite sure he should have said that.

"I guess she was" I said, taking some more of the buttered toast from the rack Mrs. Johnson had replenished whilst we were talking.

"Well, she found a circle of them up on the headland. Kept going on about how perfectly formed they were, how we had to go up and try them."

"Try them?"

"Well according to her book, and she swore she'd double- checked online, they were the magic variety."

"What did I say Steve, bit of a hippy".

"So I went with her up to the headland. Figured it was safest if there was two of us. That way if she did anything stupid, you know, like jump off the path, I could stop her."

"Did she?"

"What? Do anything stupid. Not then. But yeah, something really stupid"

"What were they like?"

"You mean you've never tried them?"

"Me? C'mon Steve, you know my body is a temple"

"Yeah I can see that by the amount of bacon and eggs it consumes! At first nothing happened. Sure we giggled a lot, lay around in the grass watching the clouds, pretending we could see omens of everlasting love, ships and a million daydream shapes. I think that initial lack of result was what lowered my guard. I figured they weren't so magic after all."

"But it put you off eating any for breakfast?"

I looked around the cafe. As we had been talking, Matherson and Omagh, the other regulars had left, Mrs. Johnson was back in the kitchen and the place held just the two of us and the assortment of fishing tackle decoration.

"Look Tommy. I know what you and the other guys think after what happened to us. I know exactly this is going to sound."

"It's ok mate, do you no good to keep it bottled up"

"OK. It started slowly at first. The mushrooms on the headland more and more obsessed Bam. Every time we'd go out for a walk she'd steer our route through Vicarwood and onto the headland. Just in case there were any fresh ones she'd say. And there always were. So we'd eat some. We started seeing things Tommy, hearing things too. It was always at the headland that I would see the shapes in the trees. Well, more than shapes. I saw babies in the knots of the wood, a bark teeming with them! Every tree Tommy! Imagine that, animated writhing babies in the bark. But the voices were worst."

I knew I should have stopped then. Tommy was starting to fidget. "I couldn't quite understand them at first. It was like an old record played slowly or backtracked. There was a strange wetness to it too. It's hard to describe. A dullness. As we ate more of the mushrooms it became clearer. Bam heard it too. We tried to work out what was being said, if we even heard the same thing. We did."

I moved the toast rack and leant over the table, closer to Tommy and whispered "Yohar n'phel Dagon! Yohar da'ath bon"

"What the hell is that supposed to mean?" asked Tommy, pulling back from me and wiping sauce from his chin.

"I don't know, but it had a hypnotic quality, made you want to follow the sound, find out where it was coming from"

"Oh, I think that's fairly obvious!" said Tommy.

"No. We heard the same things Tommy!"

"Well I can understand it putting you off mushrooms! is that why you two ended up in that boat in the middle of the night? Chasing voices out at sea? "

"No" I lied. " she wanted to go skinny dipping".

Tommy laughed "that was Bam all right! Look, I won't tell anyone about this, god knows it's hard enough for you at the moment. If there's anything I can do to help you, you know you can ask don't you?"

"Course I do." I could see he wanted no more of this talk. "Same time tomorrow?"

"Yep, got to keep the body in shape!"

Tommy would probably be wondering where I was by now. Remembering yesterday's conversation had only taken a few minutes but it was enough to make me realize I had to stick to the plan. Maybe Tommy would start to keep more than his body in shape after today. For a moment I thought about the cold, it was enough to make me pull up the hood on my jacket. I looked around the beach one last time. Nobody about. Good. The voices were getting strong again. Amongst them I could hear Bam's voice. Trying to concentrate on hers only I began to walk towards the sea, following the mooring line that had so recently saved me from its depths. With each step my clothes become more waterlogged, heavier. For long moments I can feel the ground beneath my wet shoes and then suddenly it's gone and I'm floating, head barely above the salty waves

They pull me down before I have chance to change my mind. I feel tight hands squeezing their grip on my ankles as the water's surface rushes past my head, past my eyes. I instinctively try to hold my breath, clinging to the ways of the surface dwellers, but it's too late. I can see toad-like hands groping in my pockets, taking the talismans and charms of protection that I had planned to barter with. So easily the Deep Ones deprived me of my weapons. I was foolish to think I could enter their domain alone. I should have found someone who would understand. I should have found someone to sell me a gun.

"Relax" says Bam as they pull me even deeper. The darkness begins to give way to a distant mauve glow below. My captors have let go of me now and I move forwards. I'm left alone as a blur of forms retreat through the murky water. It's like being in a dream, not quite sure of perspective, of colours or speech. There is a twisted, distorted tangent to everything. Finally I feel the seabed beneath my shoes. I walk slowly towards the source of the purple light, aware now that somehow my breathing continues. I pass through the trapezoid dissections of mauve, the very same ones that consumed our boat and see at last a dark city.

I hear her. "Come to me my sweet," says Bam.

Ahead is a bed of purple coral and writhing forms. She sits within a ring of huge bone-like purple mushrooms. My mind feels different, my thoughts have become waterlogged. Images pass before my inner eye as clear as those before me. The fibrous web of the mushrooms reached through the seabed like the gossamer labyrinth of a were-spider that hangs at the gateway between worlds, that reaches across the vast seas of space to colonize another world, to spread the spores of their consciousness between the cold places and abysses of waiting night. They speak to me in their shining cyberlight language, spinning their thoughts in and out of reality. A race of sleeping star travelers, the history of generations encoded in their spores, spun into sub atomic trapezoid structures, bobbing like flotsam on the ocean top. A type of understanding dawns, dulls my horror of seeing Bam before me, her body strangely bloated, her eyes bulging, her back arched by the weight of a scaly spine. As I look my horror turns to a smile, knowing that soon mine too will be that way, that soon we will live amidst wonder and glory in the invisible country. ✦

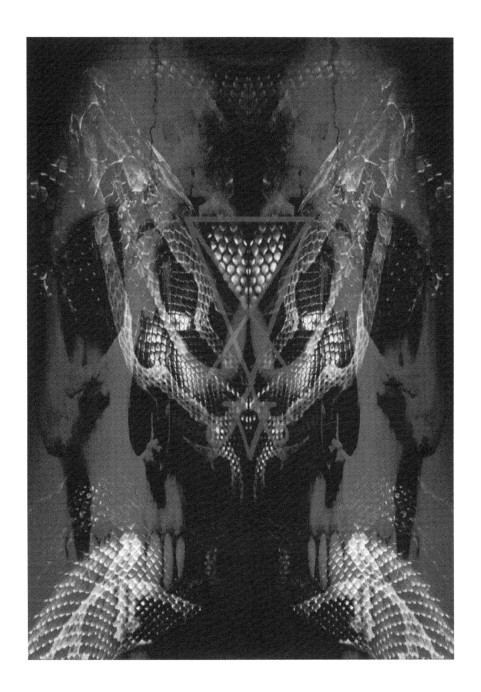

Qliphoth

Infernal Essence

Arranged by

EDGAR KERVAL

Edited by

TIMOTHY

✦ **BECOME A LIVING GOD**

Infernal Essence

Edgar Kerval

N the temple and depths of the most obscure abyss of human subconscious, the Black Serpent whispers its wisdom in a sublime dance through ancestral. It evokes lust and madness. Through blood and libations, its names are written in the pillars of primigenian temples, spiraling in descent to primal labyrinths, guiding us to rivers of blood in hidden mysterious lands of the Primordial Kaos.

The full power of transcendence exists beyond human perception, but still connects us magically with hidden realms in the astral plane. Our psyche is transformed into the Black Serpent itself, whereby it feeds through change, creating a new universe in the deepest region of our subconscious. This eternal process manifests in the sinister walker, and he or she unleashes their mighty essence—the inextinguishable black flame.

Moving strongly with a crystal focus of the will via dream pathworkings and evocations, an ocean of diverse paths to be explored in the fields of the gnosis of the black serpent under the seed of its immortal elixirs and intoxicating our beings with the forces which creates and empowers our minds. ✦

Anderson Luciferu, *O Chalice*

The Rites of Wrath

S. Ben Qayin

If your hate could be turned into electricity, it would light up the whole world.

—Nicola Tesla

HATRED—a force of primal, raw, potent and powerful energy…a force born of deep personal hurt. It is an emotion that commands immediate response, and conjures wild images of pain and death. This feeling has no room for anyone else but the one experiencing the possession of such a force, and the one who is on the receiving end of the fatal attention. When one is 'enraged' , they are intently focused on destroying whatever it is that has caused the 'rage'. They are not 'thinking clearly' and thus conventional laws and rules no longer apply. When one is enraged they are desperate, they will do whatever it takes to satisfy the starving need for revenge which gnaws incessantly away at any remnant of reason which lies in its destructive path. They will do whatever it takes to have the chance of making their prey feel the horrible pain they themselves are enduring, to return the hurt that has been so unjustly dealt them, poured over the soul as hot tar adhering to the flesh…burning. Hatred is as a Demon which possesses swiftly as the wind, entirely consuming the mind, heart and soul in an instantaneous moment of unbearable and unbelievable exploding pain. And as quickly as it is received, the need to push this tearing misery back is nearly unstoppable, for one is consumed with the idea of brutally returning the raw anguish they are experiencing back to the source from which it fiercely and mercilessly sprang…

The need to return the immeasurable pain, the undeniable need for revenge, is the very essence of what wrathful magic is born from. Revenge is as old as man, and man has forged many ways to harness the hatred that has engulfed his senses, through the occult magic of energy direction. When one begins to think of the methods of wrathful magic, sympathetic magic becomes prominent quickly. I have written much on the subject of sympathetic magic, its dynamics, what makes it work and the science of quantum physics behind it, so choose not to repeat what may be found within my other writings. That being said, it also cannot be entirely left out of the present work due to its core role, and so will examine it when applicable.

Wrathful magic is different than baneful magic. Baneful magic is worked against any who is so chosen by the magician. As an example; A close companion of the magician is wronged by someone and asks the magician to perform an act of bane against them. The magician can perform this task and have success. However, wrathful magic is more personal, it is the act of returning pain that has been forced upon the magician directly by another. Though one can see the similarities and connections between the two, one may also see the differences. Depending on one's upbringing and core beliefs, wrathful magic can be seen as 'black magic' or taboo, going against the 'natural flow' or order of things meant to be. In Wiccan circles this is the case, and it is believed that if a magician performs such acts, that the bane will return to the sender three fold. This can be seen as a form of basic Karma, where if a person performs an 'evil' act upon another, that evil returns to them in some form, plaguing their existence. These thoughts of Karma, are said to have come from an ancient Indian religious movement known as 'Shramana', which later inspired such religions as Buddhism and Hinduism. This reasoning can also be seen in a parallel theme stemming from Judeo/Christian views where 'God' says unto his people that vengeance belongs to him alone.

Dearly beloved, avenge not yourselves, but rather give place unto wrath: for it is written, Vengeance is mine; I will repay, saith the Lord.

—Romans 12:19

And again reiterated in Deuteronomy 32:35,

To me belongeth vengeance and recompence; their foot shall slide in due time: for the day of their calamity is at hand, and the things that shall come upon them make haste.

This way of thinking has even spilt over and been ingrained into social systems where the common phrase, 'Don't take the law into your own hands' comes to mind and promotes helplessness. It promotes the idea of letting someone or something 'higher' than yourself control you and your actions, it promotes complacency. Complacency is exactly what the LHP movement struggles to be free of. I don't believe in the system of Karma, I've seen too much to believe in such tales of equality. Anyone with common sense, that can truly 'see' the world around them, knows not to believe in the mystical equality system that automatically 'rights all wrongs' done in the world. If this were true, the world would be a much better, kinder and intelligent place.

Karma's basic bottom line is based on the idea to 'let it go'; someone or something else will take care of it for you. Because of these weak principals, taking the matter into your own hands is now seen as taboo in many 'civilized' cultures, coming full circle to reinforcing the forbiddances of wrathful magic, or magic in general, as magic is self-empowering, rather than subservient. This can be seen as Order restraining Chaos.

Magic is said to not be 'good' or 'bad', but magic. It is the one working the magic and their Intent, which weaves magic into benevolence or bane. Though since all realities and perspectives of individuals differ from one another, and there are so many definitions of 'evil', (as Thomas Karlsson so well points out in "Qabalah, Qliphoth And Goetic Magic") that good and bad no longer have a separate meaning. They are simply and complexly, two sides of the same coin. Essentially this would mean anything goes when one is 'enlightened' enough to come to this conclusion.

However, this seems to not be the case when it comes to the Church of Satan, for even in this swirling vortex of realities and abstract moral codes, there have been laws or guidelines laid down, a foundation of Order within the Chaos. We see this reflected in Anton LaVey's "The Eleven Satanic Rules Of The Earth", which speak of not stealing, hurting children or killing. Yet the COS speaks of embracing indulgence. Truly the laws themselves are in direct opposition to the enlightenment obtained which implies there are no restrictions. This is a direct contradiction.

Do What Thou Wilt Shall Be The Whole Of The Law.

—ALEISTER CROWLEY

As for Crowley, he also believed in embracing ones inner wants and needs, and taught that all are on their own path, and in order to obtain enlightenment of who they truly were/are as individuals, limitations, laws and restrictions must be ignored and broken for this to be experienced, to become, 'wholly oneself'.

Ultimately in my personal view, what is, or is not evil comes down to the individual and their Intent. No act is 'evil' unless one feels in their heart it is so, and proceeds all the same. This is 'evil' because the act damages and weakens the black magician and their reality. A good example of this would be addiction; repeatedly performing an act that one knows is damaging to the self and possibly others, but does so anyway, to fulfill a selfish need they fight to control. My point here is, no one can define what is truly 'evil', as no one sees from the same perspective. Yes, general guidelines can be agreed upon, but it truly comes down to the individual's personal core beliefs and moral values when confronted with a situation which requires their action and choice, when no one is there to watch or judge them. So, is it right or wrong to perform wrathful magic ? Well, that all depends on the individual and what they allow to exist in their personal reality.

Hatred is an emotion I am very familiar with, it is my 'Dark Passenger'. Hatred has been my most powerful ally, and most deadly foe. Hatred is the double edged sword which I respectfully grasp within my hands; if not wielded correctly, it will bring me to my knees. It is deadly and unforgiving. I have learned through painful lessons that hatred has no master, for hatred is born of True Chaos, and will not be contained. Hatred has taken up a permanent residence within me, when once it only came to visit, I believe this is because I have come to 'see' the world around me and the potential it has, but will never reach due to mass ignorance, selfishness shortsightedness, of the human populace. On my crooked path in this life, I have had many come against me, unjustly cause me pain, and try to outright physically kill me. I have experienced much hatred for the individuals that inflicted these woes upon me, and have performed rites that worked in wrathful ways against them. However, now I find my hatred has not only moved in, but also grown to encompass the populace on a mass, general scale. I have written,

> They say that between madness and genius there lies a fine line that is easily crossed, a path that can be traversed without notice, where one eventually looks up, and finds that they are indeed on the other side of the looking glass, though have no recollection of having made the trip.
>
> — Volubilis Ex Chaosium"

Upon reflection, I have come to the solitary conclusion that it is 'Potential' that makes the genius 'mad'. For me, as said, it is the potential of what humanity could be, of what it could learn and create...but will never obtain due to short sightedness and pure greed; the greed to control, to put all in 'perfect Order'. Having the ability to 'see' the potential, and not having the power to cultivate it and bring about a mass change is what drives me/one 'mad'. My hatred of people is difficult to explain, I don't hate them, they are beautiful, they have so much they could do with the compassion and intelligence they have access to, but they refuse to have the courage and awareness to draw from these fountains of true enlightenment. And for this, I have come to hate them, they have driven me 'mad', in both senses of the word.

To dig and examine deeper; what causes the ignorance of the mundane is what should truly be hated. The cause or root of the problem must be attacked and destroyed to cure the world and peace be finally known. What causes the ignorance is Order...all seeing, all controlling, Order. To combat this ever imposing Order, pure raw Chaos must be unleashed to balance it. And so I have released "The Book Of Smokeless Fire"; an Infernal work of bane...against Order itself. The weight of releasing such a book of hate upon the world is much, and I hope that in the end it will have served its purpose and be seen as a terrible, but needed instrument for liberation. For it fights the restraining forces of Order with all there is to attack it with, to bring it down and be free of its shackles so that freedom and creativity may again reign. To obtain the paradise we know should exist; we must first walk through the desolate Shadows in the Valley of Death. After a fire has consumed a land and left it charred, new untainted, unrestrained growth again springs forth from the Earth. We need a fire...

And though "The Book of Smokeless Fire" is an act of wrath against the main forces of Order in general, it attacks the 'whole' by attacking the many that it is composed of. These attacks will be carried out by Black Magicians seeking dark justice. The book acts as both a personal weapon, and one that also strikes on a mass level. It will be through personal pain, that the world is transformed.

There are many methods of wrathful magic, however utilizing techniques of sympathetic magic, as mentioned, seems to be the most preferred because of its effectiveness. Wrathful magic is personal, and therefore requires personalization to be effective. Though this is a bit like saying one must hold their breath when underwater, it is obvious and instinctual. When one is enraged, the rite performed can be nothing but personal, the rite becomes as natural as breathing itself. The direction of this baneful energy alone, is often enough to cause the desired end (though often undirected, causing random chaos). This has been referred to as 'The Evil Eye'. Menasseh ben Israel writes,

The angry glance of a man's eye calls into being an 'evil angel' who speedily takes vengeance on the cause of his wrath.

— The Sefer Hasidim

This is an interesting statement, in that it suggests that the act of 'looking' and 'directing bane' alone, is enough to call forth (and even create) spiritual agents to act out the will of the seer. It is a ritual of seeing alone, and can even be viewed as the act of creating an malevolent egregore to carry out the wrathful will of the operator.

However, if one wishes to be more 'exact' in their inflicting bane, ritual structure is employed. This act of ritually releasing hatred has taken many forms, from Vodoun hex dolls, to inciting Spirits to attack ones victim. Though, regardless of the form of the rite, the energy/emotion behind the act is the key to its success. Generally magic is performed by acquiring the needed personal energy, building it up to a climax, and then releasing it in a directed manner. With wrathful magic, the required personal energy to perform the rite is already overflowing, and must be directed with Intent. The sooner a rite of wrathful magic is performed after the offense inflicted, the better; as the energy utilized is fresh, genuine, raw and powerful. This is not a magic that you want to try to recall your feeling of hatred for, but instead let forcibly break free from the fresh open wound it has gashed within. Wrathful magic is a living, breathing, directed force.

When one begins to concentrate on the subject of wrathful magic, generally sympathetic magic is counted as a major vehicle for such rites to work through. Nevertheless, there have been many documented cases where Spirits have been employed by the will of a magician to attack his/her foes. There is a case that is quite famous and that I find interesting, that documents a sinister Spirit's continued attacks on a family unsuspecting. This occurred in 1761 at The Lamb Inn, in Bristol. There was a very powerful 'Chief of Familiars' by the name of 'MALCHI' employed by a black magician/witch to torment the family of Mr. Giles. The entire family was tortured with physical injury and death. Only when another Sorceress was employed, did the horrendous attacks yield. This is one of the best documented cases of spiritual wrathful magic to date. Of course when discussing this subject, Aleister Crowley comes to mind as well. Crowley and Samuel Mathers (as most know) had a falling out (like so many of Crowley's relationships) and began a spiritual war with one another. When I say spiritual war, I mean to say, they sent vicious spiritual entities to each other for the sole purpose of the others destruction. Mathers initiated the assaults, by evoking Typhon-Set who it appears, killed Crowley's pack of bloodhounds and then went on to spread sickness to all his servants, making them very ill. Crowley in return, evoked Beelzebub and his forty-nine servitors to plague Mathers. And, in the end, Crowley seems to have been the victor, as Mathers died in 1918 of mysterious, unknown causes.

Interestingly in connection with Crowley, Jack Parsons also performed a wrathful rite. It was performed against Ron L. Hubbard of Dianetics/Scientology, when Hubbard left Parsons and their joint boat dealing business. Hubbard escaped Parsons on a boat with the destination being a port in Florida. In retaliation, Parsons summoned Bartzabel; Demon of Mars; controller of Storms, and indeed a storm did rise, causing the sails to be ripped from Hubbard's boat and forcing the vessel back to port where Hubbard was detained by the Coast Guard. Crowley never liked Hubbard, believed him a con-artist, and foretold of the betrayal to Parsons. And, in the end, Hubbard was forced by court order to repay all debt owed to Parsons...

Wrathful magic has a long and painful history, the most deadly and potent of curses have been dragged forth from the wounded hearts of individuals, to strike at their foes like vicious snakes, hell-bent on revenge. There are some very famous curses which many know of, yet do not know their origin. One such interesting curse is from the Shakespearian play "MacBeth". It is said that Shakespeare may have obtained the baneful spell in the play from a true coven of Witches, and that if spoken bane would follow, encompassing the name of the play itself. The reason for this is because the Witches are said to have cursed Shakespeare himself as well as the play for all eternity. Interestingly, the play does indeed have a very dark history that has followed it when performed. And until this day, thespians shun the utterance of the dreaded name; "MacBeth",

> Round about the cauldron go;
> In the poison'd entrails throw.
> Toad, that under cold stone
> Days and nights has thirty-one
> Swelter'd venom sleeping got,
> Boil thou first i' the charmed pot.

> Double, double toil and trouble;
> Fire burn, and cauldron bubble.

Fillet of a fenny snake,
In the cauldron boil and bake;
Eye of newt and toe of frog,
Wool of bat and tongue of dog,
Adder's fork and blind-worm's sting,
Lizard's leg and owlet's wing,
For a charm of powerful trouble,
Like a hell-broth boil and bubble.

Double, double toil and trouble;
Fire burn and cauldron bubble.

Scale of dragon, tooth of wolf,
Witches' mummy, maw and gulf
Of the ravin'd salt-sea shark,
Root of hemlock digg'd i' the dark,
Liver of blaspheming Jew,
Gall of goat, and slips of yew
Silver'd in the moon's eclipse,
Nose of Turk and Tartar's lips,
Finger of birth-strangled babe
Ditch-deliver'd by a drab,
Make the gruel thick and slab:
Add thereto a tiger's chaudron,
For the ingredients of our cauldron.

Double, double toil and trouble;
Fire burn and cauldron bubble.

Cool it with a baboon's blood,
Then the charm is firm and good.

—Shakespeare, 'Macbeth', Act Four; Scene One

Another rite of wrath is the spoken Catholic curse/ritual known as Excommunication. One does not normally think of the rite as an act of wrath, even though it very much is, The Church is personally offended, and thus drives the individual out. For one devoted to Catholicism, it is the worst curse one could be branded with. The Priest personally curses the victim being excommunicated, to suffer in eternal Hell Fire,

The rite is equivalent to a curse, and involves a bell, the Holy Book, and a candle. There is a sentence which the priest reads:

'We exclude him from the bosom of our Holy Mother the Church, and we judge him condemned to eternal fire with Satan and his angels and all the reprobate, so long as he will not burst the fetters of the demon, do penance and satisfy the Church.

The priest then closes the book; rings a bell, which symbolizes a toll of death; and extinguishes the candle and throws it down to symbolize the removal of the person's soul from the sight of God.'

—Guiley, 'The Encyclopedia of Witches and Witchcraft"

Wrathful magic is a magic of deep, maddening, personal pain. Those who utilize such a malefic magic feel as though their very essence is on fire, burning through their veins when wielding it…it is the only way this type of magic can be drawn upon. Using this magic is, and is not, 'Evil', depending upon the Magician's perspective of their reality. These rites outlined may seem harsh and destructive to some. However, when the day comes that they are shaking with rage and hurt from an unjust affliction dealt them, they may 'see' differently, and remember this weapon called 'wrath' that rests at their fingertips…

The 13 Pillars of Wrath

Here I will present a rite which I have personally found effective when wanting to return the pain inflicted on me by my foes. I have decided to include a personal sympathetic magic rite, rather than one originating from "The Book of Smokeless Fire" simply because the book is very dangerous and must be read and understood before using. I recommend to those wishing to inflict ancient infernal damage onto their foes, obtain a copy.

This particular rite is designed to transfer the hate the magician feels, into an item that represents and connected to the intended victim, causing direct influence to them. Here sympathetic magic is utilized, though the scientific community will recognize this as an act applying what is known in quantum physics as entanglement. What is needed is relatively simple, truly a magician needs nothing to perform a rite, all comes from within,

We don't need anyone to teach us sorcery, because there is really nothing to learn. What we need is a teacher to convince us that there is incalculable power at our fingertips…Every warrior on the path of knowledge thinks, at one time or another, that he's learning sorcery, but all he's doing is allowing himself to be convinced of the power hidden in his being, and that he can reach it.

—Don Juan, The Power of Silence

Therefore, few ritual tools are needed to perform this rite successfully. You will need something from the victim, hair, fingernail clippings etc.; something that not only belongs to them, but that 'is' them. As well, you will need a piece of paper, a black hilted dagger, something to write with, a coffin nail or three, and your blood.

Begin with casting a double circle upon the ground roughly six feet in diameter for the inner circle, with the outside circle three inches further out. Once done, place 13 'X' marks around the circle somewhat evenly (chalk works best for this rite) so the middle of the 'X' is in between the two concentric circles. Create the circle in white or black and the 'X's', in red if possible. When drawing this circle imagine a red hot flame bursting forth from your hands, let your hatred burn through you. When making the 'X's'; cast them as if you were violently slashing at your enemy with a blade. Place 13 black candles upon the 'X's' in the double circle. These candles should be anointed, charged and carved with the appropriate tinctures, energies and sigils beforehand to empower the rite even more so, as the flame activates the malefic energies within each of the 13 candles. The circle is now purely a vehicle to be used for the wielding of wrath.

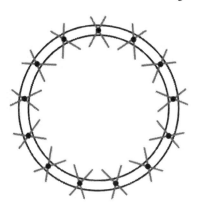

When you begin the rite, start by standing in the circle facing north, and with your dagger firmly in your left hand, trace a pentagram in the air in front of you. Moving counterclockwise, repeat the same gesture for the remaining three cardinal points until you again face north. Evoke the powers of Darkness and Death. Call out to them to surround you and feed off the energy being released. Call for them to hear your words, and aid you in the deliverance of your wrath (the Magician may use Spirits from their own personal system here). Call forth to any surrounding Demons who may hear your call, invite them to gather round and aid you in whatever way they will. These entities' will help infuse the rite with the proper energy needed. Call,

Eternal Darkness of the Abysmal Void,
Great Shadow of eternal being,
I call you forth...
Gather round this Infernal circle of destruction,
Fuel the fire of vengeance that
burns fiercely within my being,
Deliver my envenomed Intent...
Holy Death that ever stalks,
Come close, see my pain that lies before you,
Call up the sacred Dead of earthly decay,
The Nightshades of timeless vision that
creep in deathly silence,
Encircle me with their presence and power,
Spirits of Darkness and Death,
Empower this rite of hatred,
Intensify it so it may not fail...
Guide my hate swiftly as an arrow
pierced through the heart,
Bring down mine enemy...

After you have made your calls and evocations, sit within the circle and meditate/relive the memory of the offense cast onto you by your victim. Once filled with pure hatred, write the victim's name in three groups of three upon the paper already procured. Once done, use your blood to 'X' out each group of three, leaving a total of three bloody 'X's' upon the paper when done. When creating the 'X's' over the names, again focus your anger into the act; imagine your victim feeling your intense rage as you cross them out of existence. The blood and pain represents personal anguish, commitment to the bane performed and brings forth the required energy to help complete the work. It makes manifest in the material world, what is only experienced on an emotional/spiritual level. Focusing this level of hatred within such a charged circle, along with the bloodletting, provides enough energy to be massed and released into the Consensual Reality Matrix, causing the desired end to occur within the reality, and/or personal Grid of the Magician.

Once the 'X's' have been cast over the names, place your victim's hair, nail clippings, etc. in the center of the paper. Then, take the piece of paper into your hands and crush it into a tight ball with all your might, release all of your anger, all of your hatred...all of your rage. Beat your fists upon the ground and let your hatred flow through your hands into the paper, scream out your protest to their existence. Take the coffin nail and drive it through the paper as driving a spear through your enemy, let this be your last and final fatal blow. If you have three coffin nails, all the better. Coffin nails provide the link with Death energy, directed by hatred. More than likely, you will have bruises from this come the following day. When the coffin nails have all been driven, call out to the Lord of Darkness to bless your wrathful act, and to oversee that justice is done. Leave the paper within the circle overnight, the following night bury it at the base of an oak tree, dead or alive. Oak is the wood of the crossroads. At this point, the rite is finished, go about your business and think not of those who came against you, for you have put into play strong malefic energies that will indeed run their course… ✦

Hagen von Tulien, EXU REI

The Quimbanda Goetia

Carlos Montenegro

What Is Gnosticism?

GNOSTICISM is a term for a set of religious beliefs and spiritual practices found among some early Christian and non-Christian groups called "gnostic" ("knowing"). In the past many scholars believed that gnosticism pre-dated Christianity, but now it is generally accepted that gnosticism developed into a coherent movement.

Gnosticism encompasses a very wide range of beliefs and is better viewed as a collection of religions sharing some common themes rather than as one specific religion. There are two basic components to beliefs commonly labeled as Gnostic, although the importance of one over the other can vary immensely. The first is gnosis and the second is dualism.

Gnosis is a Greek word for knowledge, and in Gnosticism (and religion in general) it refers to awareness, experience and knowledge of the presence of God. It also frequently refers to self-awareness, as one realizes and recognizes the divine spark within their mortal shell.

Dualism, roughly speaking, posits the existence of two creators. The first is a god of goodness and pure spirituality (often called the Godhead), while the second (often called the demiurge) is the creator of the physical world, which has trapped divine souls in mortal form. In some cases, the demiurge is a god in and of itself, equal and opposite to the Godhead. In other cases, the demiurge is a being of lesser (although still considerable) standing. This

The demiurge might be a specifically evil being, or it might simply be imperfect, just as its creation is imperfect. In both cases, Gnostics worship only the Godhead. The demiurge is not worthy of such reverence. Some Gnostics were highly ascetic, rejecting the material word as strongly as possible. This is not the approach of all Gnostics, although all are ultimately spiritually focused on gaining understanding of and unification with the Godhead. Much (but not all) of Gnosticism today is rooted in Judeo-Christian sources. Gnostics man or may not also identify themselves as Christian, depending on the amount of overlap between their own beliefs and Christianity. Gnosticism certainly does not require belief in Jesus Christ, although many Gnostics include him in their theology. Gnostic thought had a profound impact on the development of Christianity, which traditionally sees a struggle between an imperfect material world and a perfect spiritual one.

However, early Church fathers rejected Gnosticism overall as compatible with Christianity, and they rejected the books containing the most Gnostic ideas when the Bible was assembled. Various Gnostic groups have emerged within the Christian community throughout history only to be branded heretical by orthodox authorities. The most famous are the Cathars, whom the Albigensian Crusade was called against in 1209. Manichaeism, the faith of St. Augustine before he converted, was also Gnostic, and Augustine's writings underscored the struggle between spiritual and material. Because the Gnostic movement encompasses such a wide range of beliefs, there are no specific books that all Gnostic study. However, the Corpus Hermeticum (from which Hermeticism derives) and Gnostic Gospels are common sources. The accepted Scriptures of Judaism and Christianity are also often read by Gnostics, although they are generally taken more metaphorically and allegorically than literally.

Religious Lineages of the Afro-Brazilian Quimbanda Tradition

The country of Brazil is the religious and true historical beginnings for the present day American Quimbanda religious tradition. The American Quimbanda religious tradition traces its historical origins directly to the African Congo and to the First Prophet of our religious tradition, Nzinga a Nkuwu who was the first royal Congo King to be baptized into the mysteries of Gnostic Christianity in the year 1485 by Jesuit Priests and the Knights Templar. During the Trans-Atlantic Slave Trade of the 1500's, various types of Congolese religions and magical traditions were transported to the New World with the African peoples who were brought to work as slaves on the Portuguese sugarcane and coffee plantations in Brazil.

Along with this massive migration of displaced peoples also came along a group of ancient mystics, the Sephardic Jews. The Sephardic Jews traveled to the New World to establish business commerce along the rich trade routes in various sea ports in the New World and also to escape religious persecution which was beginning to take place in Europe at that time. The mystical teachings of the ancient Kabbalah was brought to the New World by the Sephardic Jews which had a great influence in the shaping of the present day American Quimbanda religious tradition. As a result of this very rich cultural exchange which took place between various cultures and religious traditions in the New World, various forms of Afro-Brazilian spiritualism and Quimbanda began to develop and evolved over a 500-year period in Brazil.

The Quimbanda religion is still evolving and its magical mysteries can be found being practiced in every corner of the world. All of the following are various Afro-Brazilian religious lineages of the Quimbanda religious tradition found in the United States, Brazil and the liturgical differences and ritual liturgy differences which exist between all of them. Ritual liturgy is the customary public worship done by a specific religious group, according to its particular traditions.

Quimbanda-Pura (Brazil)

The Afro-Brazilian Quimbanda Pura religious tradition is usually associated with the Afro-Brazilian Umbanda religious tradition. Umbanda is an Afro-Brazilian religious tradition that blends African religions with Catholicism and European Spiritism. Umbanda is related to, and has many similarities with, other Afro-Brazilian religions like Candomblé and Quimbanda. The Afro-Brazilian Quimbanda-Pura religious tradition believes that the pantheon of spirits called Exuposses a duality of the balance of light supernatural forces and dark supernatural forces.

The philosophy of the Afro-Brazilian Quimbanda-Pura religious tradition believe that some of the Exus are messengers of the African Orishas (Saints) and also messengers of the Christian Church's belief in the malevolent forces of the Devil. The initiates of the Afro-Brazilian Quimbanda-Pura religious tradition believes that the spiritual forces (gods) of Exu and PombaGira are usually associated are spirits of darkness that need to evolve by doing good and charitable deeds.

The Afro-Brazilian Quimbanda-Pura religious tradition does not make or prepare the Congo spirit vessels known as "Nganga". The Afro-Brazilian Quimbanda-Pura religious tradition uses primarily consecrated religious statues of the spirits of Exu and PombaGira.

THE INITIATION PROCESS

The Afro-Brazilian Quimbanda-Pura religious tradition does not have any structured or organized religious "Rites of Passage" initiation ceremony.

Quimbanda D' Angola (Brazil)

The Afro-Brazilian Quimbanda d' Angola religious tradition is an independent religious tradition which is not associated with any type of religious philosophy or theology of the Afro-Brazilian Umbanda religious tradition. Both anthropologist and initiates of the Afro-Brazilian Quimbanda d' Angola religious tradition believe that this particular tradition may be the oldest line of the Afro-Brazilian Quimbanda religion.

Although it may be the oldest and considered the "original tree" of the "Quimbanda Tree of Knowledge" which gave birth to all of the other Afro-Brazilian Quimbanda religious traditions, in both Brazil and the United States, it has been influenced by various magical traditions and esoteric beliefs and contains very strong elements of Freemasonry, Ceremonial High Magic and European Witchcraft. One of the most obvious signs of a European connection the influence of Ceremonial High Magic is the magical ceremonial sword (Athame) in its religious ceremonies. An Athame is a ceremonial dagger used in ceremonial high magic rituals to cast a magic circle by the magician. It is the main ritual implement or magical tool among several used in the religion of Wicca, and is also used in various other neopagan witchcraft traditions.

The historical magical usage of the Athame as a magical tool dates back to the Middle Ages to various magical occult Grimoires of Solomonic Goetia Rites. The Afro-Brazilian Quimbanda d' Angola religious tradition believe that the pantheon of spirits called Exu and PombaGira are highly evolved spiritual forces that govern over the African Orishas (Saints) and are only subject of being governed over by the Nkisi (Congo Spirits). The spirit mysteries of the Afro-Brazilian Quimbanda d' Angola religious tradition are kept inside of spirit vessels known as Nganga.

THE INITIATION PROCESS

The Afro-Brazilian Quimbanda d' Angola religious tradition is structured and organized in its "Rites of Passage" initiation ceremony. In the Afro-Brazilian Quimbanda d' Angola religious tradition there are 9 levels of initiations.

Quimbanda Malei (Brazil)

The Afro-Brazilian Quimbanda-Malei religious tradition is an independent religious tradition which is not associated with any type of religious philosophy or theology of the Afro-Brazilian Umbanda religious tradition. The Afro-Brazilian Quimbanda-Malei religious tradition believes that the spirits of Exu and PombaGira are Nkisi (Congo) Spirits and are manifestations of the Congo Spirit of the Kingdom of the Congo called Aluvaia/Bombojila. Aluvaia is seen as the male aspect of the spirit and Bombojila is seen as the female aspect of this spirit.

The spirit mysteries of the Afro-Brazilian Quimbanda-Malei religious tradition are kept inside of spirit vessels known as "Nganga". The Afro-Brazilian Quimbanda-Malei religious tradition is known magically as the most powerful of all of the other Quimbanda religious traditions found in the present day country of Brazil.

THE INITIATION PROCESS

The Afro-Brazilian Quimbanda-Malei religious tradition is structured and organized in its "Rites of Passage" initiation ceremony. In the Afro-Brazilian Quimbanda-Malei religious tradition there are several levels of initiations.

Quimbanda Ki-umbanda (Brazil)

The Afro-Brazilian Quimbanda-Ki'umbanda religious tradition is an independent religious tradition which is not associated with any type of religious philosophy or theology of the Afro-Brazilian Umbanda religious tradition. The Afro-Brazilian Quimbanda-Ki'umbanda religious tradition is influenced by European Mysticism and Sabbatic Witchcraft. The Afro-Brazilian Quimbanda-Ki'umbanda religious tradition is the newest form of Quimbanda to have been formed in the Country of Brazil.

THE INITIATION PROCESS

The Afro-Brazilian Quimbanda-Ki'umbanda religious tradition is structured and organized in its "Rites of Passage" initiation ceremony. In the Afro-Brazilian Quimbanda-Ki'umbanda religious tradition there are several levels of initiations.

Quimbanda Gnostic American Rite (United States)

The Afro-Brazilian Quimbanda Gnostic American Rite is an independent religious tradition which is not associated with any of type religious philosophy or theology of the Afro-Brazilian Umbanda religious tradition. The Afro-Brazilian Quimbanda Gnostic American Rite tradition was brought to the United States in the early 1900's by the De Bourbon - Montenegro Family from Brazil. The Afro-Brazilian Quimbanda Gnostic American Rite tradition is also called the American Quimbanda religious tradition.

This particular Afro-Brazilian Quimbanda religious tradition was founded in 1864 in Rio De Janeiro, Brazil by Matilda De Bourbon-Montenegro and later brought to the United States by various members of the De Bourbon Montenegro Family during the early 1900's to the 1980's. The Afro-Brazilian Quimbanda Gnostic American Rite tradition trances its historical Gnostic tradition to the African Congo to the Congolese King, Nkuwo a Nzinga who became the ruling Congolese monarch to be baptized into the Roman Catholic Christian Mysteries and also into the Gnostic Mysteries of the Knights Templar in the year 1485.

Hagen von Tulien, *Maria Padilha*

The Afro-Brazilian Quimbanda Gnostic American Rite tradition has been influenced by various magical traditions and esoteric beliefs and contains very strong elements of early Jewish & Christian Gnostic religious beliefs, Freemasonry beliefs and practices, Ceremonial High Magic and European Witchcraft beliefs.

One of the most obvious signs of a European connection is the strong influence of the usage of various magical tools such as chalices, magic wands and athames.

Another obvious sign of a European connection is in its incorporation of the Solomonic-Goetia magical occult tradition dating back to the Middle Ages and the time of King Solomon.

The Afro-Brazilian Quimbanda Gnostic American Rite tradition believes that the entire universe is governed over by various Exu and PombaGira spirits and that the Mysteries of Creation and the Origin of Man can be found within central belief of a Holy Trinity known as the Holy Quimbanda Trinity. The Holy Quimbanda Trinity are represented by two powerful male Exu's (Exu Maioral & Exu Rei) and female Exu (Maria Padilla Reina) also known as PombaGira.

The Afro-Brazilian Quimbanda Gnostic American Rite tradition believes that the pantheon of spirits called Exu and PombaGira are highly evolved spiritual forces that govern over the African Orishas (Saints) and over every spiritual force (spirits/gods/goddesses) found on Earth and the vast universe. The spirit mysteries of the Afro-Brazilian Quimbanda Gnostic American Rite religious tradition are kept inside of spirit vessels known as "Nganga". In the Afro-Brazilian Quimbanda Gnostic American Rite tradition, there is no ritual animal blood sacrifices performed. The only offerings made to the Quimbanda pantheon of spirits is that of spiritual such as flowers, minerals, crystals, foods and drinks.

THE INITIATION PROCESS

The Afro-Brazilian Quimbanda Gnostic American Rite tradition is structured and organized in its "Rites of Passage" initiation ceremonies. In the Afro-Brazilian Quimbanda Gnostic American Rite there are 7 levels of initiations known as the Seven Universal Degrees of Quimbanda.

Quimbanda-Gnostic Spiritualist Rite (United States)

The Afro-Brazilian Quimbanda Gnostic Spiritualist Rite is an independent religious tradition which is not associated in any type of religious philosophy or theology of the Afro-Brazilian Umbanda religious tradition. The Afro-Brazilian Quimbanda Gnostic Spiritualist Rite tradition was founded by Carlos Antonio De Bourbon Galdiano Montenegro and Chaz Swayne in the year 2010 in the United States. The Afro-Brazilian Quimbanda Gnostic Spiritualist Rite bases its traditions on the original religious structure of the Afro-Brazilian Quimbanda Gnostic American Rite brought to the United States by the De Bourbon-Montenegro Family.

The Afro-Brazilian Quimbanda Gnostic Spiritualist Rite tradition is also called the American Quimbanda Spiritualist tradition. The initiates of the American Quimbanda Spiritualist tradition believe in self-initiation and both solitary and group religious rituals and ceremonies.

The Afro-Brazilian Quimbanda Gnostic Spiritualist Rite tradition has been influenced by various magical traditions and esoteric beliefs and contains very strong elements of early Jewish & Christian Gnostic religious beliefs, Freemasonry beliefs and practices, Ceremonial High Magic and European Witchcraft beliefs. One of the most obvious signs of a European connection is the strong influence of the usage of various magical tools such as chalices, magic wands and athames.

Another obvious sign of a European connection is in its incorporation of the Solomonic-Goetia magical occult tradition dating back to the Middle Ages and the time of King Solomon. The Afro-Brazilian Quimbanda Gnostic Spiritualist Rite tradition trances its historical Gnostic tradition to the African Congo to the Congolese King, Nkuwoa Nzinga, who became the ruling Congolese monarch to be baptized into the Roman Catholic Christian Mysteries and also into the Gnostic Mysteries of the Knights Templar in the year 1485.

The Afro-Brazilian Quimbanda Gnostic Spiritualist Rite tradition believes that the pantheon of spirits called Exu and PombaGira are highly evolved spiritual forces that govern over the African Orishas (Saints) and over every spiritual force (spirits/gods/goddesses) found on Earth and the vast universe. The Spiritual Practitioners of the Afro-Brazilian Quimbanda Gnostic Spiritualist Rite are mainly concerned with ceremonial magic and ritual prayers of positive affirmations.

There are no spirit mysteries (ngangas) used by the Spiritual Practitioners. In the Afro-Brazilian Quimbanda Gnostic Spiritualist Rite, there is no ritual animal blood sacrifices performed. The only offerings made to the Quimbanda pantheon of spirits is that of spiritual such as flowers, minerals, crystals, foods and drinks.

THE INITIATION PROCESS

The Afro-Brazilian Quimbanda Gnostic Spiritualist Rite tradition is structured and organized in its "Rites of Passage" initiation ceremonies. In the Afro-Brazilian Quimbanda Gnostic American Rite there are 3 levels of initiations known as the Three Universal Degrees of Quimbanda. The Afro-Brazilian Quimbanda Gnostic Spiritualist Rite tradition is structured and organized in its "Rites of Passage" ceremonial initiation process. Initiation can be performed individual in a self-dedication initiation ceremony (Quimbanda Baptism) or in an informal group ceremonial initiation ritual. There In the Afro-Brazilian Quimbanda Gnostic American Rite there is 7 levels of initiations. In the Afro-Brazilian Quimbanda Gnostic Spiritualist Rite there are 3 levels of initiations known as the Universal Laws of the Three Degrees of Quimbanda.

Palo Quimbanda Religious Tradition (United States)

The Palo Quimbanda religious tradition is an independent religious tradition which is not associated with any type of religious philosophy or theology of the Afro-Brazilian Umbanda religious tradition. The Palo Quimbanda religious tradition was born in the United States in the early 1980's in the De Bourbon-Montenegro Family Munanzo in Los Angeles, California and is a mixture of Afro-Caribbean Palo Mayombe and Afro-Brazilian religious traditions. The Palo Quimbanda religious tradition came into existence as initiates of the Afro-Caribbean Palo Mayombe religious traditions began initiating into the mysteries of Afro - Brazilian Quimbanda. The Palo Quimbanda religious tradition is a new Congolese tradition that has incorporated the mysteries of the Afro-Brazilian Quimbanda religious tradition within the mystery of the Congolese knkeieis. Gnostic American Rite tradition is also called the American Quimbanda religious tradition.

The Palo Quimbanda religious tradition believes that the entire universe is governed over by the powerful spirits Exu-Rei (Male Exu) and PombaGira Reina (Female Exu). The Palo Quimbanda religious tradition is based on ancestral veneration which is found within the realm of the Congo spirit deities (Nkisi). This very mysterious realm is governed over by a very powerful spirit known as Exu-Gira-Mundo (Lucero Vir-Mundo). The pantheon of Congo spirit deities (Nkisi) are represented in the form of spirit vessels (ngangas) and the Nkisi Spirits work underneath his guidance. It believes that spirits and that the Mysteries of Creation and the Origin of Man can be found with in central belief of a Holy Trinity known as the Holy Quimbanda Trinity.

The Holy Quimbanda Trinity are represented by two powerful male Exu's (Exu-Maioral & Exu-Rei) and female Exu (Maria Padilla Reina) also known as PombaGira. The spirit mysteries of the Palo Mayombe religious tradition are kept inside of spirit vessels known as "Nganga". In the Palo Mayombe religious tradition, offerings to the spirits are made in the form of ritual animal sacrifice. The Palo Quimbanda religious tradition includes in its eclectic spirit pantheon, the spirit mysteries from both the Afro-Caribbean Palo Mayombe religious tradition as well as the spirit mysteries of the Afro-Brazilian Quimbanda religious tradition, thus the word, Palo Quimbanda originated.

THE INITIATION PROCESS

The Palo Quimbanda religious tradition follows the Afro-Caribbean initiation process of the Palo Mayombe religious tradition along with a blend of Afro-Brazilian spiritualism.

The Quimbanda Goetia Grimoire

The present day occult American tradition of the Quimbanda-Goetia is a magical Grimoire which has been evolving for the past 600 years since the

1500's. In order to fully understand this very powerful and rare magical tradition from Brazil, it is important to know its historical origins if you will want to be successful in achieving your desires and spiritual requests. The Quimbanda-Goetia is not only is a way of life for those practicing American Quimbanda, but it is also a Grimoire. A Grimoire is a textbook of ceremonial magic. Such books typically include instructions on how to create magical objects like talismans and amulets, how to perform magical spells, charms and divination and also how to summon or invoke supernatural entities such as angels, spirits, and demons.

In many cases, the books themselves are also believed to be imbued with magical powers, though in many cultures, other sacred texts that are not Grimoires, such as the Bible, have also been believed to have magical properties intrinsically; in this manner while all books on magic could be thought of as Grimoires, not all magical books could. If you would like to learn the ancient keys to open up the celestial doors to the Astral realm and discover how to manifest your desires through the power of ancient occult wisdom, then my series of various magical Afro-Brazilian Grimoire books written about the Quimbanda-Goetia will enlighten your spiritual journey.

This particular edition is the first of this book series of more than 50 books about the Afro-Brazilian Quimbanda-Goetia magical tradition written for beginners about this very powerful form of ancient magic to manifest these powerful spiritual forces here on Earth for various desires.

There are three methods of how to successfully practice the magic of the Quimbanda-Goetia that I will present in this ceremonial magic book. There is however a fourth method which I will define, but that I will not include in this ceremonial magic book because it would require a formal initiation into the American Quimbanda religious tradition which can only be found within the sacred initiation mysteries of the Seven Universal Degrees of Gnostic Quimbanda.

METHOD ONE

In Method One, the beginner or magician from another magical occult mystery school can apply the basic principles of this powerful tradition and integrate it into their own occult practice. In this method, the beginner or magician may only desire to use or incorporate the spiritual experiments of the Quimbanda-Goetia as part of their occult beliefs and magical tools of ritual invocation. In Method One, the beginner or magician from another magical occult mystery school does not need to perform the, Self-Dedication Initiation Ritual into the Mysteries of the Quimbanda-Goetia that I will present in a later chapter.

METHOD TWO

In Method Two, the beginner or magician from another magical occult mystery school may desire to embark on a deeper spiritual journey into the magical mysteries of the Quimbanda-Goetia and spiritually connect themselves to the outer dimensions and spiritual realm of the Astral Spirits where these powerful ancient entities reside. In Method Two, the beginner or magician from another magical occult mystery school will need to perform the, Self-Dedication Initiation Ritual into the Mysteries of the Quimbanda-Goetia that I will present in a later chapter. In Method Two, the beginner or magician from another magical occult mystery school will not use the sacred magical mysteries of the Quimbanda-Goetia-Solomonic Spirit Vessel (Nganga) that I

will present in a later volume and how to consecrate and how to harness its occult powers during rituals.

Hagen von Tulien, *Tridentilation*

METHOD THREE

In Method Three, the beginner or magician from another magical occult mystery school who feels competent in occult knowledge and wisdom with the magical material presented in this ceremonial magic book, will not only spiritually connect themselves to the outer dimensions and spiritual realm of the Astral Spirits where these powerful ancient entities reside, but will actually prepare and consecrate their own Quimbanda-Goetia-Solomonic Spirit Vessel (Nganga) that I will present in a later volume in this Grimoire series. In Method Three, the beginner or magician from another magical occult mystery school will need to perform the, Self-Dedication Initiation Ritual into the Mysteries of the Quimbanda-Goetia, which will prepare the magic student for my series of books written for advanced practitioners of the sacred and magical ancient Quimbanda-Goetia occult arts.

METHOD FOUR

In Method Four, the beginner or magician from another magical occult mystery school who truly desires to embark on a sacred journey into the greater universal occult mysteries and mystical spiritual realm of the American Quimbanda religious tradition will only be able to fully realize this through by entering into the occult mystery school of the "Sacred Brotherhood" of the American Quimbanda religious tradition which would require a formal initiation into these orthodox spiritual mysteries of the Seven Universal Degrees of Gnostic Quimbanda, which is open to both men and women of the magical occult community.

An Explanation of the Astral Exu Spirits

The spiritual astral entities who reside within the First Greater Quimbanda Kingdom of the Most Holy Angel, Exu-Maioral in their various nine realms along with the 72 Astral Exu-Goetia Spirits are an extension of Nzambi's guiding hand. For those practicing the orthodox Gnostic Quimbanda religious tradition at our temple, we believe in "Divine Intervention" and the "Divine Intercession" of the pantheon of "Holy Ones" (spiritual beings) which make up the hierarchy of our religious beliefs and who are manifestations of Nzambi's "Divine Grace". The religious doctrine, religious theology and religious philosophy of our Gnostic Quimbanda religious and magical tradition teaches and believes in the existence of only one true God, Nzambi.

We believe that only through His Divine Intervention and Divine Grace that the Universe, the Heavens and the Earth were created and caused into existence. We also believe that Nzambi is also the creator of all things visible and all things invisible.

The religious doctrine, religious theology and religious philosophy of our Gnostic Quimbanda religious and magical tradition teaches and believes that the Spirit of Nzambi has manifested here on Earth in the physical form of man in various times throughout the history of human civilization. When the Spirit of Nzambi takes the physical form of man on Earth, we call Him, Nzambi-Ntoto, "the God who touched and walked the Earth and became man. We believe that Nzambi divided the great Universe into seven realms (Seven Quimbanda Kingdoms) of spiritual and physical existence.

In each of these seven realms, we believe that Nzambi placed the "Holy Ones" to watch over and protect the Universe and the Earth. We believe that the primary function of these guardians is to give light to mankind so one day we may be reunited with our ancestors and find our way home to the Kingdom of Nzambi. We believe that Nzambi placed the spiritual beings of the Quimbanda Trinity to govern over all aspects of the seven realms (Seven Quimbanda Kingdoms). The Quimbanda Trinity is composed of three Holy spiritual beings which govern all matters concerning the Universe, the Earth and the life and actions of every man and woman. These three Holy spiritual beings are named, Exu-Maioral, Exu-Rei and Maria Padilla Reina Pomba-Gira.

That is why the symbol of the "trident" is used to represent the collective spiritual forces of the Holy Quimbanda Trinity by initiates of the Quimbanda religious tradition and faith. The end points of the "trident" are pointed like an arrow and when held in your hand in an upward position, the three points (the Holy Quimbanda Trinity) are pointed towards the realm of the great Heavens where Nzambi resides. When the symbol of the "trident" is held in your hand in a downward position, the three points (the Holy Quimbanda

Trinity) are pointed towards the realm of Earth where man resides. The staff of the "trident" represents the unification of the Holy Quimbanda Trinity coming together as one divine spiritual force with Nzambi, the God of Heaven.

The religious doctrine, religious theology and religious philosophy of our Gnostic Quimbanda religious and magical tradition teaches and believes that the Holy Quimbanda Trinity and the spiritual beings which reside within these seven realms are all extensions of the great mysteries of Nzambi, the Lord our God. Our religious doctrine, religious theology and religious philosophy also teach and believe that the Spirit of Nzambi came down from the great Heavens and was born and became man. We believe that Nzambi has physically manifested Himself on Earth many times by being born and becoming man throughout the history of mankind. We believe that when Nzambi incarnated as man throughout the history of man, He has been called by many names.

We believe that in each of these times that Nzambi manifested here on Earth as man, He did so to save mankind from self-destruction by our own hands by re-establishing spiritual order in troubled times to save mankind from damnation. We believe that in Nzambi's last incarnation here on Earth as a man, He was known as Jesus Christ (Nzambi-Ntoto). We believe that Nzambi incarnate (Jesus Christ/Nzambi-Ntoto) was persecuted by man (Pontius Pilate) because He re-established man's belief in God and saved us from damnation. We believe that it was Nzambi's will that His physical life was ended by which He did allow himself to be sacrificed to save man from damnation and to restore the heavenly order between man and the world of the ancestors.

We believe that after He died, the Spirit of Nzambi descended into the Great Abyss and conquered darkness so that once again man would no longer walk in darkness. The term of "Divine Act of Grace" is called the "Great Awakening." We believe that after three days after He was laid to rest He did physically rise again from the dead and then ascended into the Heavens where He is seated over the mysteries of the Universe and the Seven Quimbanda Kingdoms. In a further explanation, the religious doctrine, religious theology and religious philosophy of our particular Gnostic Quimbanda religious tradition believes that before Nzambi (Nzambi-Ntoto) incarnated here on Earth and became man, the World was in constant spiritual chaos. This spiritual instability was caused by and occurred after the fall of the angelic beings from the Grace of God in a time more commonly known as the Angelic Wars of Heaven.

When this angelic rebellion took place, many rebellious angelic beings left the Heavenly realm along with legions of spiritual entities more commonly known as demonic beings (the 72 Astral Spirits) and that they did fall and take refuge in the inner and outer invisible realms of the Earth and the underworld more commonly known as the "Great Abyss". When Nzambi incarnated here on Earth and was born as man He did so to save His children from the perils of spiritual damnation caused by these fallen angelic beings and legions of demonic beings.

When Nzambi (Nzambi-Ntoto) allowed Himself to be sacrificed at the hands of His enemies (those individuals who had aligned themselves with the fallen angelic beings and legions of demonic beings) He did so that upon his physical death as a man, His spirit would be able to descent in to the Great Abyss (Underworld) and defeat and conquered the rebellious angelic beings and the legions of demonic beings by triumphing over them during the three days of His death. By this "Divine Act of Salvation" and for the sake of His children here on Earth He reestablished the Heavenly chain of Divine Order between the Earth, the Great Cosmos and Heaven.

The demonic spiritual beings that re-aligned with Nzambi's new world order were granted divine grace of forgiveness by Nzambi and became enlightened spiritual beings and are now known more commonly as the 72 Astral Exu Spirits of the Quimbanda-Goetia magical tradition. It is also through this act of divine grace, that Nzambi established the Seven Greater Quimbanda Kingdoms and the Seven Lesser Quimbanda Kingdoms.

The religious doctrine, religious theology and religious philosophy of our Gnostic Quimbanda religious and magical tradition teaches and believes that because of this Holy event, Nzambi did re-organize the spiritual realm and placed the Quimbanda Trinity to watch over the Universe, the Earth and over mankind within the confines of the seven realms. It was because of this re-alignment that is why the 72 astral spirits were referred to as demons before the death of Nzambi as a man and after his resurrection the 72 astral spirits became enlightened spiritual beings and were no longer classified as demons.

The religious doctrine, religious theology and religious philosophy of our Gnostic Quimbanda religious and magical tradition teaches and believes that after this triumph over the rebellion in the Great Abyss His spirit did return to his physical body where He did rise again and was resurrected and ascended into the great Heavens where He awaits the souls of all men at the moment of our physical death to reunite with Him and the ancestors in glory and light.

The religious doctrine, religious theology and religious philosophy of our Gnostic Quimbanda religious and magical tradition teaches and believes that there is a distinct difference between the words of "spirit" and the word "soul" as used in the religious context of our magical belief.

The word "spirit" refers to the immaterial part of man. Man is not a spirit; he has a spirit. The word "soul" refers to the makeup of man. The "soul" makes you unique and different from every other person. The "soul" is how you relate to others and how you understand yourself. The "spirit" is how you relate to Nzambi (God). The "spirit" is part of the soul, much like the mind is part of the soul. It is the "soul", though, that comprises who you are. Both the soul and spirit leave the physical body of an individual when they die.

The religious doctrine, religious theology and religious philosophy of our Gnostic Quimbanda religious and magical tradition teaches and believes that after the third day He did rise again from the dead and then ascended into the Heavens where He is seated over the mysteries of the Universe and the Seven Quimbanda Kingdoms.

The religious doctrine, religious theology and religious philosophy of our Gnostic Quimbanda religious and magical tradition teaches and believes that Nzambi will one day again incarnate again as man to re-establish the Heavenly order here on Earth. We also believe that Nzambi's Kingdom here on Earth will have no end because it is only through Him that the great Universe and the Earth is allowed to exist.

The religious doctrine, religious theology and religious philosophy of our Gnostic Quimbanda religious and magical tradition teaches and believes that the Holy Spirit of Nzambi manifests within the Mysteries of the Quimbanda Trinity and the Seven Quimbanda Kingdoms.

We believe that one day like our ancestors we will return back to our heavenly home of Heaven and will reunite with our ancestors who are kneeling at Nzambi's feet in glory and light. The religious doctrine, religious theology and religious philosophy of our Gnostic Quimbanda religious and magical tradition teaches and believes that the spirits of our ancestors can spiritually and physically manifest to man by petitioning them through prayers and devotions.

The primary purpose that the spirits of our ancestors manifest here on Earth to man is to assist us on our journey of life so that one day we will be reunited with them in Heaven. We also believe that by petitioning the Holy Ones which govern over the realms of the Seven Quimbanda Kingdoms that they will be able to assist man by interceding on our behalf to Nzambi. The religious doctrine, religious theology and religious philosophy of our Gnostic Quimbanda religious and magical tradition teaches and believes that our particular historical religious traditions have been ordained by Nzambi and has evolved into the most orthodox Congo derived gnostic religious tradition in its truest and purest form of the Quimbanda religious practice as brought to Earth by Nzambi, the "God of Heaven". For this reason we believe that we are Nzambi's chosen people and that Nzambi's Kingdom here on Earth will have no end. The religious doctrine, religious theology and religious philosophy of our Gnostic Quimbanda religious and magical tradition teaches and believes that we are Nzambi's chosen people because we are following the Gnostic Quimbanda religious tradition in its original form that was established by the First Prophet of our Church, King, Nzinga a Nkuwu (King João I) in the year 1485 of the Congolese Empire which was ordained by Nzambi and the ancestors.

The religious doctrine, religious theology and religious philosophy of our Gnostic Quimbanda religious and magical tradition teaches and believes that through prayers, spiritual devotions to the spirits of the Seven Quimbanda Kingdoms that they will intercede on our behalf to Nzambi by delivering the sacred word to the realm of Heaven. The religious doctrine, religious theology and religious philosophy of our Gnostic Quimbanda religious and magical tradition teaches and believes that because we are Nzambi's chosen people here on Earth that He has spiritually delivered His Divine Word to the enlightened clergy of our religious tradition.

The religious doctrine, religious theology and religious philosophy of our Gnostic Quimbanda religious and magical tradition teaches and believes that our Church is the only one true Gnostic Church which holds the true gnostic or mysteries of Nzambi's power.

The religious doctrine, religious theology and religious philosophy of our Gnostic Quimbanda religious and magical tradition teaches and believes that through the Act of Baptism into the Mysteries of the Quimbanda Religious Faith that all individuals may cleanse themselves of all past and present sin.

We believe that Nzambi established the sacred mysteries of Quimbanda Baptism to enlighten all men and women to place them back on the path of light and to re-establish our divine spiritual mission here on Earth by placing us back on the journey of our spiritual birth destiny that was established before we were born. The religious doctrine, religious theology and religious philosophy of our Gnostic Quimbanda religious and magical tradition teaches and believes that just as Nzambi was resurrected, we also may be resurrected in the afterlife and be reunited with our ancestors and Nzambi in Heaven. ✦

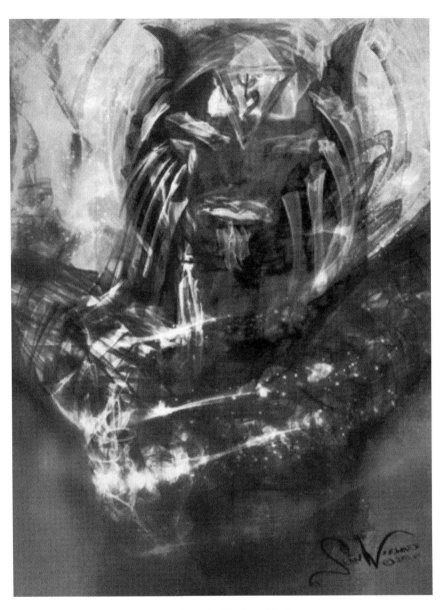

Sean Woodward, Gholem Meditation

A Hieroglyphic Exegesis of the Gholem Gnozis

Sean Woodward

> I have always felt - I have always, always, always felt, that somehow Hebrew magic and Voodoo have many cognates, as many books have sought to show, e.g. Milo Rigaud, etc.
>
> —Michael Bertiaux

THE Voudon-Kabbalistic Gholem Sorcery flows through bloodlines, from the time of Rabbi Moses ben Abraham of Worms, via the works of Franz Bardon, to the present day. Pointing sticks of the Torah sit side by side with the fetish and candles and contraite of the Big Lucky Hoodoo. Whilst the traditional framework of the Etz Chayim is exploded into a diversity of worlds, the energies and numbers of the Hebrew alphabet remain keys to an inter-dimensional puzzle and aeons old conflict.

To embrace this gnosis, to understand its import and reason for existence our consciousness must travel unfettered upon golden threads, upon lines that traverse the universe like glowing threads of a bright web, brought into being by each moment that we fully exercise the faculty of Gholem Sorcery. Far below the clouds we have become immune to the turning of our world, to the subtle runes of change that mark the days, their length growing shorter with every passing instant. It is only the slow displacement of the sun in the sky and the shortening days that give any indication of our planetary motion through space, preserved by magnetic fields from the damage of cosmic rays and solar flares.

The Loa, their beings liberated from the shackles of our gravity, pass between ocean and sky, between nebula and star, their eyes burning with the light of distant binary suns. They perceive our journey through the solar system and the subtle structures of atomic light that infuses all of our existence.

In their eternal bodies they feel the alignments and conjunctions, are illuminated with subtle lights when the planets have line of sight with one another, when the changing aspect of Saturn's rings influences the Earth or the Trans-Yuggothic energies flow upon the solar winds.

And so we are both extremes of beings. They seek to possess our minds in order that we may commune more fully with their understanding whilst we seek to fashion gholems of ontic clay, that they might inhabit these, animating such dull bodies with the glory of their gnozis. All that is required of us is a golden collar, fashioned with the correct Hebrew letters by a student of the Rabbi, squares of summoning and the bone tools. The magician must also have sent his spirit down the narrow alleys of old Prague, across the river and into the cobbled street of the alchemist. He must have made the commitment to cross Europe, to walk in the shadow of medieval statues and the symbols of Cosmati pavements, to reach deep into the history of the stone streets. Not all are drawn to this Kabbalistic breach of the cosmos. It is a teaching that was hidden in the Book of Formation, tossed to one side by the traditionalists but worshipped in secret chambers by the brothers of the bone. It is born of the three veils of endless black gnostic light that exist below the sphere of Malkuth and reach into the tunnels at the heart of Daath. Once there were many lengths of bones stored amongst the old govi pots that were marked with the sacred words and symbols which would call down the Loa into bodies fashioned from the ontic clay. Once it was not usual for the hieroglyphic to stand side by side with us in this dense world of matter and form.

In distant Haitian plantations the wraiths of angry souls are quick to heed the call of the gholem. They would rush from the mountain slopes at an instant, hoping to waylay the magician and turn his creature to their use. From amongst them the masters of the Zobops would rush to the fray, pushing them aside, that they might control their own army of clay, ready for their bidding, ready to terrorize the night. They are the Zombiemakers, the Zombiemasters who have subsumed their own Ti-Bon-Ange's, that all of their creative imagination might be turned to the animation and installation of smothering darkness. They are consumed by revenge and retribution, their earthly days ingrained with the struggle for survival and conquest. Like the creature in Meyrink's Der Golem, they are "representative of their own ghetto spirit and consciousness, brought to life by the suffering and misery that its inhabitants have endured over the centuries". They are no longer content with driving their motor zobops around the outskirts of Port-au-Prince, for with the passing of the years they seek other vehicles on other continents with which to do their work. The darkest of them have inhabited the war machines of the past as they rolled over barbed wire and rain sodden trenches. It matters not the decades that have passed, the freedoms that have been gained. For them it is an eternal battle against the shackles of freedom, a war upon any man or creed that would restrict them. At the heart of this swirling intent is buried the mark of the Archons, that grows strong and extends their lifespans, feeding upon the atrocities they commit in the name of rebellion.

The magician must be careful therefore in the nature of his intent. As old European grimoire might specify the cleansing of the body for three days and nights, so a cleansing of the mind and a washing of ill intent is a requisite to any such work, for it has long been known that the gholem becomes a half-creature. He is half-formed of the possession of the Loa and half-formed of the vibrations and emotions of the magician. If there is doubt in the mind of the magician, then this doubt will become magnified. If there is evil intent, then this being will find darkness folded upon darkness in its heart. If there is lust, then the gholem will be consumed in its search to quench that lust. Thus the magician may provide a substitute for possession by the animation of this creature, but he must give unto it compassion and love. These are the only antidotes and barriers to the dark spirits that might seek to inhabit this shell.

This is the reason that it originally took a Rabbi to call forth the gholem. For he understood both the power of the letters of his name and also the signature of his heart. The magician therefore should be versed in both of these worlds. He must fathom both the secret verbs of the Kabbalah and also the nouns of the human condition. He should be versed in the Goetia of many traditions, be able to distinguish trickster from teacher and as familiar with the needs of flesh and family, as he is with those of hidden sorceries. This path requires experience, for whilst the lips of the young man know the taste of sensual love in its sweetest form, only the mage appreciates the value of true love, its enduring vibration in the universe. As the alchemist has learned that the transmutation of lead becomes the refinement of a body or a world, so too the magician must see the place for magick and the place for applied compassion.

According to Talmudic legend Adam is called golem and so thereby exists the kinship which enables the creature to be possessed by the Loa, as a man might be. This association of a being made from the clay or dust of the earth extends also to Lilith and so it is easy to see how she has been called the first wife of Adam. As Adam Kadmon is represented as the front-side of the Tree of Life, so it is Lilith who represents the Nightside world of the Qliphoth. Clearly the creation of the Gholem echoes these biblical stories, only substituting the magickal breath of the Hebrew alphabet, with that of Elohim.

It is clear in the Jewish stories that the gholem has little understanding beyond itself. It is as if the work of the Rabbi to call it to life has somehow already constrained it purely within that tradition, but the magician knows this is not the way it is. It is only a matter of understanding the correct arrangements of letters and sounds, to conjure the gholem forth as a vessel for any tradition, for he is a replica of man and so is capable of being fashioned in any catechism. It is as the Jesuits say, 'give me the child and I will mould the man.'

We do not come to the gholem gnosis purely to rekindle old pleasures or to hand out retribution however. We come when a vessel is required for the Loa, that they may manifest more fully and more permanently in our presence. In this way we are able to enter into extended dialogue, to enable them to act upon matter and to reorganize the future. Other applications include the provision of a safe haven for the magician himself, that his Gros-Bon-Ange might fortify itself in the presence of the Loa, in secret initiations where prescience or anointment within the mysteries might take place. Another use is in communication with the Gholem races of the Sporeworlds. Like all Gnosis, understanding must be paired with application, for every treasure given from the inner worlds there is equally a coinage of effort that must be offered.

Bizango Gholems

As alluded to, there are also times when the magician may wish to enter into these dialogues with a master of the zobop. On these occasions extreme measures must be taken to ensure that the scope of the gholem is limited and that its infernal possession can be constrained or banished. By creating a gholem we are able to bypass the Zobop master's preferred method which is the creation of a human zombie. We are once more demonstrating the magician's compassionate nature by preventing the temporary enslavement of another. We also do not risk trapping another in the cage of confinement. There are however, many examples in old houmfors of Port-au-Prince where a gholem has been left imprisoned. They are wrapped in red jackets and farmer's trousers, mirrors stitched into them to catch the light, shoes strapped to their feet like old English effigies prepared for a November fire. Heads are fashioned into or replaced with skulls and heavy chains are wrapped around their shoulders. Some wear old straw hats, some the head-gear of generals. At the hands of some houngans the numbers of these chained gholems have become so numerous they have become known as Bizango armies, arranged row upon row, flanked with sergeants and men at arms.

I had the pleasure of visiting an exhibition of such a collection in Bremen, Germany. It was winter and alighting from the tram in the snow I came upon the Anthropological Museum across the square from the main railway station. A chunk of the Berlin Wall occupied a corner of the square and as I paused to read the old graffiti on it a group of teenagers passed by, a girl wearing a black hoodie with a skull on the back. The ground floor of the museum was full of artefacts from across the world, from Polynesian deities to a reconstructed Shinto temple. Upstairs lay the exhibition itself, its entrance flanked with half-opened packing crates and notices which described the history of the collection and its relation to the Vodou of Haiti and its peoples struggle for freedom.

Walking amidst the skull topped figures of generals and foot soldiers I cleared my mind and waited to hear their subtle speech. Whilst the figures were the most striking items in the exhibition, every daub of paint on a bottle and every piece of furniture emitted its own dark light. Critics would come to question the ritual validity of these items, but it was clear standing amongst them that even if some pieces had solely been created as object d'art, nothing there was a willing collector waiting, the spirits had moved the hand of the artist-priest who had fashioned them. At times, merely the juxtaposition of everyday objects, like scissors and dolls heads, created an otherworldly atmosphere which both transformed the object and the observer. In the darkened room that held ranks of Bizango figures, I waited until I was alone and then, having surrounded myself with both the protective and opening energies of Leghba, I sought to hear their voice. Sure enough, moments later, before huge round mirrors and I heard one of them speak. He wore cow horns on his head and held a stout stick. He whispered the words that would unchain him, return him to the fields in distant Haiti. But these were not the words of a peasant, but an educated man. I asked him, 'who called you forth from the ontic clay?' and he replied 'Docteur Alfonse'. I was shocked. I had known a Docteur Alfonse in Paris and I knew he had lived for a time near

Jacmel in Haiti. The creature seemed to laugh. 'Yes, I know your teacher. I know you too magician.' Even though he was bound in heavy chains it was still disconcerting to hear those words. He repeated his plea once more and the strange twist of Creole words that would free him. I hesitated, for though it seemed he was called forth by the docteur, I knew that I could trust nothing that was said to me. And so I made to leave.

He repeated his plea one last time. As he fell silent I saw around his neck a silver locket. I reached forward and released the clasp. As it popped open I saw a faded sepia photograph of a woman sitting by a country roadside. 'Karine' he whispered. I knew then this spirit offered me no harm. Recalling the words he had spoken to me I repeated the Creole verse. Immediately a blue light faintly illuminated the body and the chains crossed around his shoulders like a bullet belt, slipped to the floor with a heavy thud as they piled upon one another. In the huge facing mirror I saw a lean, tall figure standing.

'Your mercy will not be forgotten' he said as the figure in the mirror dimmed.

The Temple of 221 Gates

A number of years have passed since that experience but I wondered how many other gholem bodies held their Loa captive. I knew that Docteur Alfonse would not have willingly left one in such a state so could only guess that perhaps this once had been created shortly before he died and not released. He had been frantic in his desire to preserve the secrets he had learnt from the Zobop masters and had pursued many avenues in his search for a safe place to preserve his work. How many more would wait patiently for a magician to hear their pleas? I wondered if there was a universal solution, some kind of incantation that would release any still left in this state. It would require careful study, for the risks of releasing a dark spirit into the world were great and the ramifications mighty. For months I studied both Creole and Kabbalistic sources looking for a way of relieving this burden that lay heavy on my heart.

It is clear that the Aleph character is a key element is the animation of the Gholem. The Thamiel order of Qliohoth angels added Aleph to their name in order that they might be more powerful. In many sources, including Jerome Rothenberg's Golem Meditation Event, the gholem is also buried in the ground as part of the animation process. This is an allusion to Psalms 139:16. Of these traditional methods of creating a gholem, all include recitation of the letters of the Hebrew alphabet and the importance of Aleph as the first letter in the name of Adam and in the combinations of the alphabet itself. This can also be seen in the Aleph-Lamed method of constructing the 221 Gates of Rabbi Eliezar Rokeach of Wormes (c.f Sefer Yetzirah: The Book of Creation in theory and practice, Rabbi Arryeh Kaplan, 1889). These are then recited as the Gholem is circled in a dance of 442 circuits. The letters of Aleph Lamed have further note as AL is the secret key to Liber Legis, The Book of the Law. The 442 circuits are analogous to the numerical value of Emet, the word of awakening, which equals 441.

It was however the very spirit that I had released which revealed the method to me. It required travelling upon the web of consciousness that linked these gholems, for each spirit was connected itself to this web. Only in the deep, Trans-Yuggothic reaches of those threads could the last vestiges of Atlantean temples be found that held the keys.

The temple seemed to be a vast complex built of tall crystal structures, themselves comprised of a multitude of interlocked cubes. It resembled a Byzantium palace or that of a Mogul emperor, with bulbous structures atop high towers. As I approached its outer walls light flashed upon its surface, refracted into all the hues of the rainbow. Beyond was the curve of the world and beyond that the blackness of space. I wondered how I could breathe in this place, but felt not even a shallowness of breath. Huge doors stood before me, half open, inviting me within. I was reminded of Michael Bertiaux's description in The Esoteric Heidegger Newsletter of "collage-sculptures in a realm of extended and jutting surfaces."

It did not take long to discover an inner chamber and to realize that this was the very place that Docteur Alfonse had spent much of his time, for I recognized certain features in sketches he had shown me as we sipped coffee on the South Bank of the Seine. Here amidst the magical machines and character lattices he had left a list of each gholem created, its purpose and the words that would end its confinement, each one ending in the Hebrew Aleph. Against the majority were written the dates and places of their release, except for a handful at the bottom including the husband of Karine. Without hesitation I intoned each of the incantations, watching as the silver threads leading into the temple first began to tremble and then pulsate more violently with each word. In the huge oval mirrors which encircled the chamber my reflection flickered and became hazy until I saw only a large humanoid spider standing where my reflection had been moments before. Close to the dark whiskers which lined my arms and legs, silver sigilic letters shimmered in the mirror, pulsating in and out of visibility.

One by one sleek silver spirits streamed into the chamber from the cold wastes of space beyond. To some they might have appeared as angels, but I had studied enough of the mysteries to understand the true nature of these spirits. They were once men and women like ourselves, occupied by the same desires, having to overcome the same troubles. We have forgotten with the passing of time the basic qualities they still share with us. Perhaps if I had continued only my Kabbalistic studies they would now swoop on extended wings, uttering the cry of the Serpahim or present themselves as alien intelligences. They did neither of these things, but silently passed in their fluid silver forms. They circled the air above me, finally coming to rest in small group to the north. One of them stepped forward. As she spoke, I immediately guessed her identity.

'I am Karine, Priestess of the Old Ones beneath the Sea, keeper of the history of our people'.

At her side another spirit motioned silently for her to continue.

'I speak for our entire family magician. We freely served the docteur and now we freely serve you. You have learnt the truths of the gholem gnosis. It is not enough to have the power to create a gholem, you must have the compassion to destroy one. For this, we all offer our gratitude.'

She stepped back into the group and they rose as one into the air before darting out of the chamber, through the high open doors which led to the temple courtyard and the deep spaces beyond.

On the table a cross, wand and gate of bone now lay, their red and black surfaces painted with symbols. I wrapped them up in their leather covers, tying the pouches and returned along the lines of consciousness towards my sanctuary.

Within the book-lined peace of my sanctuary I was able to record the fullest details of the working which arose from my time in the Trans-Yuggothic Atlantean Temple. My sixteen-day retreat in its outer courtyards and its 16 chambers are detailed in Liber Sedecim and constitute the attainment of other mysteries which facilitated the full powers of the time travel techniques as taught in La Couleuvre Noire. It also enabled an understanding of the hieroglyphic system which underlines the gholem gnosis.

This can be understood as the construction of a gholem logic that is necessary for the establishment of a framework for the inhabitation of the Loa. Every step of the process, from the gathering of river clay during a full moon, to the correct sequence of letters and utterances is governed by the meta-mathematical vibrations that are emitted from the Trans-Yuggothic Atlantean Temple. These are strongest at the equinoxes, when the Earth is turned towards that part of deep space where the temple lies. The operation should take place in a carefully prepared houmfor or temple. This requires a central pole that allows the spirits to descend and an altar upon which is placed the bone tools and the clay figure. The bone tools comprise the Blackthorn Wand, Gnostic Cross and the Orpheus Gate and are necessary to channel the cosmic forces of such a working.

The size of the clay figure is entirely dependent upon the nature of the working and its decoration will also vary in accordance with this. For example, one gholem I have created is merely a small painted head and is used for oracular purposes. Another is an articulated puppet, allowing it a motion which translates to movement between the worlds. Many of the ones created in Haiti were full size and made with such detail that candles could be placed in their upturned palms during their consecration. ✶

Sean Woodward, *Gholem Bride*

The Hieroglyphic Diaries of Dr. Alfonse

Sean Woodward

ITHIN these diaries the Docteur detailed many of his own explorations of the Hieroglyphic Atlantean Temple and they offer great insights into his dealings with the spirits and their servants. There follows an extract from his 1952 diary:

As I surveyed the hieroglyphic workshop I was struck by the sparse surrounding, the smooth curves of the surfaces and walls and the flickering light which danced within them. The main chamber was flanked by two antechambers. In one of these was a raised table, the length of a man which reminded me immediately of a gurney. I approached it slowly. Its curved lid was high enough to contain the body of a man but there were no openings on its polished surface which might suggest what lay within.

Feeling some trepidation, I walked closer to the table. Reaching out I placed my palm against the surface which I almost expected to be wet. Immediately the edges of the lid became a cascade of curling surfaces, folding back to reveal the side of an arm. As I peered closer one of the spirits descended from the misted vaults heights of the room, coming to a rest directly at my side.

"What is this? I asked.

"It is a re-animation chamber, to heal those of us who retain bodies."

I immediately could see a massive application in the healing of my mankind with this device.

"And humans?"

"Yes docteur. It is programmed to understand the physiology of many species." She seemed to smile as she said this and noticing my interest spoke again.

"We are not that different from you docteur. Some of our kind walked upon your planet millennia ago. We rescued this one temple amongst the annihilation of our Atlantean brothers and sisters. Here is the last vestige of the old black and red magicks, the powers of stone and bone that once moulded your world.

"Who is within the machine?" I asked.

"It is our brother Saran. He returned from a diplomatic meeting with the Archons. We knew that prolonged exposure to their kind would be debilitating for his body of matter, but we did not realize how destructive their presence would be. They are the antithesis to the very fabric of your universe. Without effort they bring decay and entropy. Their touch is death and their thoughts are the harbingers of disease. We sought a treaty, to keep them beyond the edges of your universe, for they would surely destroy it."

I will record in this diary the histories of the war between the spirits and the Archons. It was their influence which had bred corruption amongst man and induced them to commit the atrocities which littered our history. They were a terrible parasitic contagion, never quite gaining a hold as their hosts would quickly be consumed by them. So they tried time and time again to infiltrate our world, to turn it to a place of continuous death and war, to prevent the human race from achieving the potential and the wonders which the spirits themselves had witnessed. I will detail the places which had acted as a portal, as places of crossing for them. From the dark swamps of deep Africa, to the cold Arabian deserts. In each place they had left their mark upon the land. Nothing would grow there again, nothing would survive the corruption of their touch.

"Will he survive?" I asked.

"Yes. It will take time, but the chamber will recloth the fabric of his body.

"This technology would greatly benefit my world"

"You must not speak of this docteur. This is the last chamber and the only one capable of reversing the work of the Archons. In ages past we would have gone to war over such treatment of our envoy, but we understand them now. It is simply their nature."

"They can't help themselves?" I suggested.

"No, they do not do this consciously. Their proximity is simply hostile to other life forms. We have conjectured that it was once a defense mechanism for they long ago inhabited a poisoned, blighted world.

There was a quick sound, like the excavation of an atmosphere from a room. This was followed by lines appearing on the lid and more surfaces folded back, like the skin of a peeled silver banana, to reveal a body within the chamber. Saran sat up slowly, swinging his legs and raising himself up from the table.

"Who is this?" he demanded, motioning towards me.

"Do not be troubled Saran, he is our new envoy for Earth." said the spirit.

Saran said nothing further. He stood still, perfectly upright for a moment and then swiftly ascended vertically in the air until he could not be seen.

"Envoy?" I asked.

"Yes, good docteur. We have no need of your medical skills here, but you have lived in the earthly realm of our brothers, the Loa. You understand how to communicate and travel the lines of consciousness that extend to this place and the deep Yuggothic realms. Yes, you will be our messenger."

In the Hieroglyphic Diaries of Docteur Hector Alfonse there were many descriptions of the excursions of intuitive logic that he had undertaken and which had finally led him along glistening rays of light to the Atlantean Temple. He described how when he first entered the circular chamber its edge was lined with oval seats that were moulded into the crystal walls. Upon each of these sat a glistening silver spirit. Over time he began to perceive further niches in the walls, each seat and niche was marked with dual symbols that clearly interlocked with the shape of Hebrew letters. As he peered at them he found the edges of the room began to rotate.

He explained how at first the sensation was like that of a drunken man trying to stand, but very soon the speed would increase to the point where all was a blur. To the docteur nothing moved. It was as if he stood in the eye of a hurricane, such was the calmness. His highly developed intuition quickly realised however that the spinning was actually changing the vibration of the atmosphere, switching through the various syzygies and as it slowed he could see that the once silver spirits began to take on a blue hue.

He recorded many of the conversations that had taken place in this chamber, such as this one from October 1952:

"We have raised your consciousness to the realm of the blue ray" said one of the spirits.

"Tell us how it feels good docteur, look now with your inner eye".

I blinked and looked again. Now the whole of the crystal structure of the chamber was bathed in faint blue light that made me feel tearful with elation. My hands tingled and as I looked at them and I saw traces of sigilic writing wrap itself about my wrists.

"What is this?" I asked, fearful of the change taking place.

"With each vibration or syzygy energy you will be able to traverse a higher realm. Eventually you will be able to enter the Qube Logic itself and no place in the universe will be denied you."

It was then that I noticed that the spirit speaking seemed female.

"You should not be alone on this journey, good docteur. Fashion a woman of clay and I will be your gholem bride" she said.

I listened carefully to her words, for I realised then how alone i had been these many years. It seemed such a sacrifice however, to constrain a spirit so. I could not do this.

"No" I said, "there is beauty in the form you inhabit".

"Very well" replied the spirit "all forms are transient."

The Docteur's diary was filled with the explorations that he had made of the hieroglyphic temple. It also contained details of his excursions around the world, his uncovering of the places desecrated by the Archons and the rituals and magicks he had used to neutralize them. Sixteen locations had become nexus points for the positive energies of the spirits, including Glastonbury in England and together with his diary, he had given me his magickal tools, the Gnosis Cross, the Bone Wand and the Orpheous Gate. He detailed the methods of those who had reconstructed these for him, often taking months of preparation and consecration. Along with the descriptions were the sigils and characters to be inscribed on their surfaces and the particular seasons in which they should be consecrated.

His diary often seemed like a cross between a medieval grimoire and a science fiction novel. If not for all the afternoons I had spent in cafes on the South Bank of the Seine, listening to stories of his life in Haiti, I would have considered these works absurd. It was clear to me though that he was neither deranged, self-promoting or engaged in an elaborate scam to obtain money. The world knew him only by the two books he had published in Paris, but I felt I knew something of the man, of his life. Sometimes he would tell obviously fanciful tales in the shadow of the Eiffel Tower as dusk fell and the city became one of light. It was always clear however that these were metaphors or drenched in symbols that I would not fully grasp until years later. It was the quality of the light in Paris that always appealed to him, reminding him of the vibrancy of the atomic light he had experienced in his many of his visits to the Atlantean temple.

He assured me that many of the paintings in the Louvre held hidden meanings and he would often create complex jokes at my own expense. There was nothing malicious in his manner however, moreover a kind of childish mischievousness. It was his nature, he said, which had convinced the spirits to allow him entry into their temple. When I asked him what of his task of Envoy, he would fall silent. It was clear that there was some great sadness attached to this, so I never delved further into the subject.

Of all the mysteries contained in his diaries, mysteries that I myself have been able to experience, it is the extrapolation of the Gholem Gnosis which was dearest to his heart. He said it reminded him in many ways of the zombies of his homeland. He had christened me a Zombiemeister, for he thought I had an affinity with the metaphysics of these teachings. He would point at my nose and smile, suggesting I visit the old Jewish ghettoes. And so I did, moving slowly down the narrow streets behind Prague's castle. This is where the old Kabbala and the new meet he would say. Here is where words become symbols and symbols become the wheels of life. Never let these teachings be forgotten because there will come a time when a Gholem Army is required, when the spirits will need to inhabit our world to stand with us against the Archons. It always seemed when he said this, that he was talking about something he had already witnessed and given the way the spirits could cross space and time it would not surprise me if he had.

He had also come to the conclusion that the human race itself had once been designed as a Gholem army, descended from Adam who himself was created from the clay of the earth and his first wife, Lilith. The breath of Elohim however had infused an intelligence and awareness not seen in the Gholems made by man himself.

Of their Nature

In his diaries, the Docteur classified the Gholem into 16 distinct classes, namely:

The Gholem of Lemuria
The Gholem of Atlantis
The Gholem of Prague

The Gholem of London
The Hieroglyphic Gholem
The Oracular Gholem
The Gholem of Retribution
The Gholem of Secrets
The Warrior Gholem
The Gholem of the Sporeworlds
The Gholem of the Mountains
The Ain Gholem
The Gholem of the Ontic Sphere
The Gholem of the Witch Cult
The Gholem Bride
The Future Ghole

For every one there are particular qualities and powers which the spirits are able to directly manifest when they have inhabited the body. Some of these are specific to their eternal war with the Archons. The Warrior Gholem for example is able to withstand the negative energies of the Archon environment, of their homeworld and portals. The Atlantean Gholem is "linked to 23 Hoo Spirits manifesting the Endless Light from the Deepest Darkness" as described in Kyle Fite's monograph, Lucky Hoodoo Evacuated Magi Atlantean Golem with Venusian Contact Point. The Atlantean Adepts were able to use these Gholems as new bodies for their consciousness, which could relate and yet transcend terrestrial constraints. These are a powerful link to Vilokamps and the Karmic links that manifest outside the circles of time.

The Ain Gholem is a specific vehicle for entering the dark spaces between the worlds and is informed with the Voltigeur principles and is also capable of intimidating entities encountered in these darkside worlds. The Future Gholem perhaps represents the culmination of this logic, for it is almost cyborg in construction and is able to interface with the vudutronic technologies of 5978 AD. It has been suggested that this is the root logic of all the gholems and enabled them to be constructed, each with different parameters of its own capabilities. Dr. Alfonse conjectured further for he believed that all gholems were actually the future gholem and we were only capable of experiencing certain qualities of its nature depending on the definitions of the conjurations used to create it, as if our time and place filtered our view of the He suggested that these techniques merely acted as a beacon to guide the gholem through time and space to the magician. It did seem from his dealings with these different forms that they demonstrated a similar identity, even though they had become the vehicles for very different spirits. The Gholem of the Sporeworlds can similarly be identified as of particular note, as it is descended from the inhabitants of those realms and can be seen to possess a unique and established identity of its own. This includes access to metaphysical and technological logics which are derived from their own star systems. All of these Gholem are therefore also infused with stellar energies. As Michael Bertiaux says in Der Prozess: Heidegger-Golemkultus, "An energy from a distant star took root in space."

Of their Number & Conjurations

To effect the conjurations, magical squares which are a condensed form of the 221 gateways are created, of different materials dependent on the gholem required. This same material is also to be fashioned into a collar engraved with the Hebrew letters of summoning. These were the traditional Emet characters of Rabbi Loew ben Bezale, first described in the Talmudic folklore, together with the intonation of the letters of the Hebrew Alphabet, as described in the formation of the world in the Sefer Yetzirah and the characters of Psalms 139 verse 16. However, an analysis of the tradition word of awakening Emet or Aleph-Mem-Tau, shows that this is incomplete and more readily should be Aleph-Mem-Tau-Shin as the initial three characters represent the forces of Air, Water and Earth and with the addition of Shin, the elemental forces are completed by Fire. This is the breath of the Elohim of Genesis, breathing life into the clay of Adam.

As for the conjuration that brings down the spirit into the clay figure, this requires a petition to both Bawon Leghba and Bawon Carrefour. This can be done symbolically via the use of images of the bawons or in the traditional form of a ritual undertaken at a crossroads on the outskirts of town. It is the spirits themselves that will describe any additional conjurations required. Docteur Alfonse had realised the Aleph character is used as a trailing letter to release them, but the different forms of Creole incantation that he advocated were directly given by the spirits. I have noticed however that many of them contain fragments of traditional Creole lullabies and songs.

To the Master-Initiate is given the advanced methods of intuitive Magick. Any of the ways described may be employed in the creation of the Gholem, however it is to be born between two Mirrors Fantastique, a child of the skrying glass. In this sacred space is an Astral Gholem constructed which has all the traits of its category, but is a creature entirely of light.

With the majority of gholem workings the spirit is quite capable of leaving the gholem host when its work is done. It is only in rare cases, or in the traficking with Zobop masters that specific precautions must be made to imprison or wear down the strength of the spirit. In this case the Blackthorne Wand and the Gnostic Cross are most efficacious. It is usually best to accompany their use with that of the Asson, as the spirits generally will be constrained by its application. These are necessary to enable the application of cross chains, which are the final step in constraining the spirit. In these instances, a secure place should be obtained for the long-term storage of the gholem. In this manner some sorcerers have been known to bequeath gholems to future generations of their family and over time have arisen various legends of the bottled djinn due to this practice. I consider this to be an extreme course of action as it is guaranteed to anger an already violent spirit and should therefore be avoided.

The construction of the gholem logic is necessary for the establishment of a framework for the inhabitation of the Loa. It is the multi-dimensional metaphysical framework that describes the equation of their being. The meta-mathematics of the logic defines the multi-dimensional structures which combine the integration of Hebrew characters with the spirit technologies. The legends and rituals handed down through Talmudic lore are therefore the mundane elements which are interlocked with the stellar and trans dimensional hieroglyphics that emanate from the Trans-Yuggothic Atlantean Temple. Every step of the process of creating a Gholem replica, from the gathering of river or mountain clay during a full moon, to the correct sequence of letters and utterances is governed by the meta-mathematical vibrations that are emitted from the Trans-Yuggothic Atlantean Temple. These are strongest at the equinoxes, when the Earth is turned towards that part of deep space where the temple lies. The operation should take place in a carefully prepared houmfor or temple. This requires a central pole that allows the spirits to descend and an altar upon which is placed the bone tools and the clay figure. The bone tools comprise the Blackthorn Wand, Gnosis Cross and the Orpheus

Gate and are necessary to channel the cosmic forces of the working. The size of the clay figure is entirely dependent upon the nature of the working and its decoration will also vary in accordance with this. For example, one gholem I have created is a small painted head and is used for oracular purposes. Another is an articulated puppet, allowing it a motion that translates to movement between the worlds. Many of the ones created in Haiti were full size and made with such detail that candles could be placed in their upturned palms during their consecration.

In the Gholem Logic these operations are made transient, reduced to their constitute parts whereby they become an operation of atomic light possessed by the Loa. This light emanates from the watery darkness of Vilokamps and from the deep space of the Trans-Yuggothic Atlantean Temple and is infused with data constructs that latch into the framework of the Gholem logic. It is this that enables transdimensional transference of consciousness to the inert Gholem. It is the conduit that enables the leaps between the dimensions and is thus key to the articulation of the Ain Gholem.

At this level the Loa can interact directly with the consciousness of the magician without the need to inhabit a physical object. This itself becomes an extension of la prise des yeux faculty and enables images and insights to arise spontaneously within the mind of the magician. This spirit vision also grants the ability to interpret reality in the way that the Loa do and so leads to a direct experience of the glowing threads of the bright web of consciousness that is brought into being by each moment that we exercise the faculty of magick. In the end there is never any true escape from the possession of the Loa and the construction of gholems is itself only a transient affair that serves to symbolize the transmutation of the magician's own body and mind by the gnostic illumination of the hieroglyphic logic. ✶

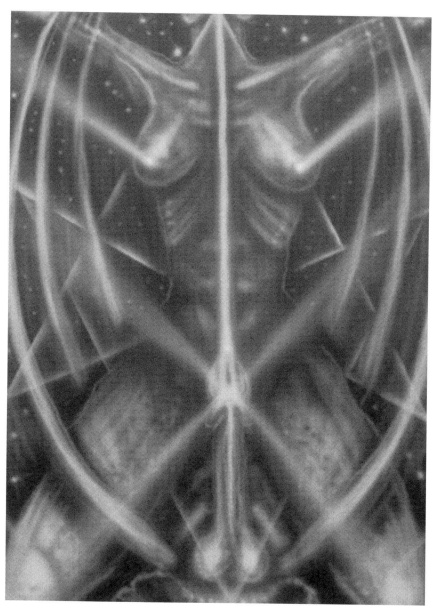

Barry James Lent, *Awakening: Gnosis of Eros and Spirit*

The Ybte Myth Cycle

Lukasz Grochocki

IN the beginning the people of Ybte were one and stayed together in the realms of the earth in the bosom of the canyon that was their Place of Origin. They would come together and perform ceremonies at the Sites of Power, where they raised numerous monuments to call forth the spirits, gods and demons. This is the story of one such conjuring in those early days.

The People of Ybte were wise; and erudite they knew of geometries and alignments, the courses and movements. At one such congregation they conjured into existence First Spirit whom they called Nyulem: (the Spirit that Dwells In Between), for he was brought forth from In Between the cracks of the Earth and the Sky. The Leader amongst the People who had called forth Nyulem was Bihsad: (the Raven King), for he was the Master of the Wise Ways of the Desert. Bihsad was also an honorable man, and upon the sight of this divine being he bowed lo to him. Nyulem blessed Bihsad, and for his reverences the Spirit of In Between bestowed the Secret Signs and Regalia of Kingship. And so it came to pass that Bihsad became the First King of the People.

Bihsad lived a long and prosperous life; he guided his people with the virtues shown to him. Then came the day when his aged body released his soul into the Aethyr of the Cosmos. However, Bihsad's will was strong, and he did not want to leave the pleasures of this life behind. He called forth to the In Between State and Powers that Lay Beyond and was returned to the World of Man as Vak Hadit: (the Ghost King). The People marveled at the Returned King and offered him glories and in turn their fields grew green and the Cycle of Observations continued. The People grew strong and they offered their bounty to the Earth and the Sky. By these ritual actions they evoked the First

God whom they called Answo: (the God of Provisions). Thereafter, the People worshipped the new God of Fertility, and the cycles of time and ritual washed over the People. All was well and all were happy and prosperous.

Then came the day when the Spirit of Duality (Vpid: the Spirit of the Lighting Rainbows) manifested himself unto the People. He had come to the People as a Rebellious Spirit and Sower of Discontent, for he had come to create the Great Confusion. Vpid caused storms and destructions. but because his nature was that of a trickster, he also showed the People of Ybte many wonders. In time the climate changed, and the People lost their crops. Consequently, they lost trust in the Order they had come to know. In awe of this new Great Spirit, who had also come from the great In Between, the People chose to follow him into the Madness of the Desert, leaving the Old Order behind.

However, their essence remained in their former dwelling places and worship sites. These places became haunted by their auras, and all that they had created became gray, dead and broken. To this day their Walled City Ruins stand in the wilderness that was paradise. Amongst these ruins you can still hear the beckoning calls of the Things that Once Were, and of the Things that are Now Lost. In time the People would come to call these remnants Eiyjon. Eiyjon: (the God of Relics). Because, the People became unsettled and nomadic they started the Great Migrations. They traveled across the world's face in all directions: some following Spirits, others following the Gods, some remained with the Ghost King Vak Hadit, and others wandered by themselves without a guide.

To those who chose not to follow either Spirit, God or King, the In Between manifested Dyojm: (the Spirit of Ceremonies). Dyojm gave new Ceremonies unto these Independent Tribes, who had saved their hearts for a True Spirit to follow. Thus, these People were shown the New Sacred Order they were also given a Secret Prophecy regarding future migrations and the ceremonies to be conducted along the way. The Tribe that followed Dyojm had sent its messengers to the other tribes now scattered about the world. The New Way demanded a return to unity.

The Ghost King Vak Hadit was still leading some of the People. Much time had passed since he had returned from The Beyond, and some of the People began to see him as eternal and static, and this made many of them uneasy, for time demands change. Eventually the messengers of Dyojm came to the People of Vak Hadit and told them of the New Way that was given unto them as well as the Prophecy and its demands.

And so the People conspired to dethrone the Eternal Ruler Vak Hadit in order to establish the New Way. With the guidance and instructions given to them from Dyojm they created the Mysterious Xezam: (the Ghost Box). They furnished it with birch panels (for birch is the Wood of Ghosts), as they are attracted to such forests and things made of that wood. The People also gathered the sands from the distant sea, for the Sea Sand's Salt absorbs with its purity any supernatural being. They also made a great pilgrimage to the mountains to find the Stone of the Sky. The Stone of the Sky had fallen to the Earth and retained celestial quality with such a stone, supernatural beings can be spell bound. Today this stone is called Turquoise. Then came the day to banish Vak Hadit. The People gathered together about the Mysterious Xezam Box and called forth Vak Hadit to them. As foreseen the Ghost King was attracted to the Birch Paneled Box and settled into its confinement. Next, they placed the Sky Stone within it and the Ghost King was mesmerized by its beauty. Finally, the People laid a roof over the lower part of the chamber and immediately poured the Sea Sand over it. Finally, they sealed the box with a cover laden with Secret Sigils, thus trapping Vak Hadit within it. Some say that Vak Hadit found a way to return to the Sky by the virtue of the Sky Stone while others say he is still trapped and spell bound within Xezam's walls.

And so it came to pass that the People elected the First Living King in centuries, and he was called Aalua: (the First Ancestral King). Honor is given to him before any Hunt even to this day. As the New King, Aalua was given the Secret Signs and Regalia of Kingship that had once belonged to his ancestor the Raven King: Bihsad. The People hunted the wilderness and cultivated the earth, and once again fertility and bounty returned to them. The Cycles of Ages had begun and the People grew older and wiser. They gained understanding, shared their knowledge with their children, and their children worshipped their ancestors.

Now that the People had learned the virtue of sowing and reaping they began to offer their sacrifices to the Sky, the Earth and the Dead. And they looked upon the Sun and called it Rowtat: (the God of the Sun and Rain). For behold Rowtat: is the Sun, and the vast dome of the sky is his home. He is the Lord of the Seasons and Bringer of Rains. And so the People learned to worship this Final God through sacrifice. They were eventually able to summon at will the other Spirits, Gods and Kings to guide them, according to the True Laws of Nature. So they grew as a People and it is from them that this tale has been passed on... blessed be the People of Ybte.

And here follows the Seals, Names and Attributes

1. NYULEM

The Spirit that Dwells In Between for he was brought forth from the In Between, from the cracks of the Earth and the Sky. He whose name means: The Border Pinching Shaman. It is he who sits at all Crossroads and shakes the Rattle of Dreams and sings the Songs of Transformation. Nyulem maybe conjured by placing burnt offerings at crossroads in the midnight hour, on moonless nights. He appears as a Black Shadow Lurking at the Threshold. He opens hidden ways and can show all things that are hidden.

2. BIHSAD

The Raven King whose name means: the Elder's Calming Coil. He is the Lord of Ravens, and the Master of the Wise Ways of the Desert. He was bestowed the Secrets of theElders. Bihsad maybe conjured by making feathered effigies, and leaving shiny things upon the altar at midday. He appears as a Raven Headed man in royal robes. He imparts wisdom to those who seek it.

3. VAK HADI

The Ghost King whose name means: he who is the Crowned Crane's Claws. It is he who had returned from the Beyond, white as a crane, and he bore a Crown of Claws. Vak Hadit maybe conjured by burning thick smoke of Sage to a Strange Bone Effigy. He appears as a Hooded White Robed Figure, that is somewhat transparent. He is the Divine Will and as such can be used to strengthen a Magicians Resolve, but be weary he does not depart easily.

4. ANSWO

The God of Provisions, whose names means: the Slimly Disappearing Serpent. His symbol is that of the tracks of a Slithering Serpent, tracks only for he remains mostly unseen. Answo maybe conjured during wild Snake Dances that bring the rain and fertility. He appears as a Naked Painted Dancer holding serpents. He brings fertility and fecundity to fields and people.

5. VPID

The Spirit of the Lighting Rainbows whose name means: Interruptor of Completion. He came to the People as a Rebellious Spirit and Sower of Discontent. He came to cause the Great Confusion. Vpid maybe conjured during battles or destructive storms, unto him burn the Blood of Dragons. He appears as a Beautiful Man with long hair, and sparkling eyes wearing the finest clothes. He holds a rainbow or a lightning bolt depending on his humor. He can bring chaos to situations and can be used to disrupt the plans of enemies.

6. EIYJON

The God of Relics, whose names means: the Protecting Teeth's Numbers. For many relics survive like the teeth of a skeleton. If collected they can provide protective powers. Eiyjon can be Conjured by gathering things from ages past, preferably broken ones. Place these upon the altar and let them speak to you. He appears as an Old Man in ragged clothing of ages past, usually near cemeteries. He can tell you of the things lost to time and of civilizations long gone by.

7. DYOJM

The Spirit of Ceremonies, whose name means: Destiny Steeping By. It is he who had been waiting for the People that he could give unto them their Destiny. To conjure Dyojm one must consult oracular devices in isolated places of nature and whisper his name. He appears as a Masked Priest in flowing dark robes with scrolls in his hands. He is Lord of Fate and all destinies that have been written from the beginning to the end of time.

8. AALUA

The Ancestral King whose name means: Flood's Ancestral Hunter. He was the First Ancestral King before the Great Flood. It is to him that honor is given before and after the Hunt. Aalua is conjured by dawning animal skins and making offerings of blood and meat. The scent of fire pits is also pleasing to him. He appears as a Hunter with a bow riding a large black war horse. He bestows wealth and power to those who hold him in their hearts.

9. ROWTAT

The God of the Sun and Rain whose name means: the Trickling Sunlight Vault. He is the Sun and the vast dome of the sky is his home. He is the Lord of Seasons and Rains. Rowtat is conjured by Singing Songs to the Sun and burning the sweetest scents. He appears as a Dazzling bright Winged Figure with the head of a Lion and body of a Man. He gives happiness and joy as well as bestowing all the pleasures of life.

A WORD ABOUT THE TEXT

The Ybte Myth Cycle was revealed to me on one of my pilgrimages to Chaco Canyon. Chaco Canyon is located in the northwest part of New Mexico in a region called the Four Corners. It is here that the Ancestral Puebloan people reached their cultural apogee. Here in this canyon, over a thousand years ago the people of Chaco constructed massive ceremonial centers unique in form and function. These multi storied pueblos served as ritual centers and places of pilgrimage for a population that once exceeded the modern one. The Navajos, the current occupants of the area, believe that Chaco is haunted and refuse to go near it; those that do later hold special cleansing rituals in their Hogans to make sure they did not bring anything back with them.

In the Spirit of the Ancient Chacoans, I made my pilgrimage to the Canyon in the Summer Solstice of 2007. I spent a week there, exploring over a dozen sites. I had prepared a seven day ritual requiring me to perform special rites in these ruins. During the night I made Ghost Callers: (gem and feather effigies). During the day I took them to the Kivas: (round subterrane ritual structures native to this architectural style). I called forth to the Spirits of these ruins by smoking herbs, burning sage and using Hopi invocations. As the days grew closer to the Summer Solstices, I felt their presence get stronger and more potent. And on the Solstice at sunrise, I witnessed the sacred alignment to which the ancients had built their structures. I traveled in my mask and robe to the highest and most isolated ruin, bringing with me the Ghost Callers and incense, as well as a drawing pad.

The day grew hotter and brighter as I sat in the silence of the ruins and nature. Slowly the Spirits came into my mind, and in Whispers of the Wind,

I heard their names. Their presence grew stronger and I felt drained. I allowed myself to become possessed. Holding my drawing pad, I let my pencil held hand be guided by their wills. Thus, came forth their sigils. As the last one was drawn all became still and empty.

I returned to my campsite and redrew the sigils larger and more elegant. Before going to sleep, I burned sage and hung each seal from a Ghost Caller. I invoked the Spirits, on that Summer Solstice night, to come into my dreams. I dreamt a black shadowy figure had entered my tent holding a box. It opened the box, the Xezam: (the Ghost Box), releasing the Spirits that began to whisper the myth of the People of Ybte. ✦

Signature of Dr. John

Dr. John Montanee

THE PATH OF A NEW ORLEANS LOA: RESUR-RECTION IN REMEMBRANCE

An excerpt from a manuscript in process

Dr. Louie Martinié

TO invite possession is perhaps the greatest act of kindness available to us while in these bodies. I thank the conjure men and women, the Priestesses and Spiritual Doctors of New Orleans Voodoo, and I thank my ever present spiritual friend Thubten Jigme Norbu and all of the Tibetans for their presence and assistance. We are aggregates easily broken and just as easily assembled. No difference.

Dr. John Montanee is the greatest conjure man of New Orleans Voodoo. He drummed with Marie Laveaux for rituals in New Orleans in the 1800s and is an honored patron of drums, drummers, and conjurers.

The purpose of this conjure and of the other two in the book is to offer to Dr. John the requisite weight to become a loa if that path is to his will. Nothing is asked of the Good Doctor. The conjure lies in the giving.

The Second Conjure:
Speaking in the Voice

Words and speech are the stuff of a powerful magick. Abracadabra, an ancient spell, can be translated in Aramaic as "I have created through my speech." (Denny Sargent)

Grimoire is reminiscent of grammar. To spell (verb) and to cast a spell (noun) are quite similar in form and, in a subtle sense, meaning. Much of the "who" the mind thinks we are is composed of words and influenced by the subtleties of language.

"I think therefore I am," points to a way of being often defined and encapsulated by words and language. If "I" am to reside in this cage, then I would choose a large, more inclusive cage that allows a bit of roaming, has a view and an accessible key.

I sit at a desk and write. This "desk" does not exist except as a word. As the Tibetans say, it exists as a "nominal designation." It exists in name only. I cannot find a "desk," I cannot touch a "desk" only parts that break down into other parts. Office to furniture to desk to writing surface to drawers to wood to cells to atoms to... the hereto now unrideable higgs bison to... the practitioner's reaction to these words.

Akoko, a friend and teacher, when asked if the loa are real once replied, "They are as real as the United States of America and the United States can kill you." I would add that they are as real as this "desk" upon which I write and as real as the Dr. John conjured in this rite.

Dead Loa

The loa are sentient beings and as do all sentient beings they live, die and are reborn again and again. Their lives are tremendously long as judged by our standards and they do end. Forget (for get) literally means to lose one's grip on. A dead loa is one whose name is forgotten, no longer honored or reviled. The word, the meaning of "desk" will certainly be lost in time. At that point, desks will cease to exist. Perhaps heaps of wood and metal will litter the landscape, undistinguished from their surroundings.

I write to add my voice to the voices of those who would not permit this to happen to Dr. John Montanee. His name will not pass into this gray nether world. His name will be remembered and honored.

Osiris

There is a beautiful precedent for this conjure. The Africans, in particular the Egyptians of Northern Africa, had a God they called Osiris. This God was murdered, his parts re-collected and then re-membered by Isis. The reanimated Osiris then impregnated Isis. It is exactly this kind of remembering that this conjure is about. Dr. John is reanimated and enters into a very intimate relationship with the practitioner.

From Recollection to Remembrance

The process is first recollection then remembrance. Recollection done in this manner flows easily into a remembering therefore, we will re-collect Dr. John as the initial step of this conjure.

RE-COLLECT:

To re-collect is to collect again.

Middle English collecten, from Latin colligere, coll ct-: com-, com- + legere, to gather; leg- in Indo-European roots.

What we collect, what we gather together, are historic and folkloric documents and references. The fertile fields from which we are collecting are composed of the materials found in the Historical and Folkloric sections of this grimoire.* Collect with your head, heart, and hands. Read and feel as you hold the pages rich with ancient script. They are like carefully gathered flowers. Invite what they contain into your life. Invite Dr. John Montanee into your life.

THREE SELVES TO COLLECT:

We all create at least three selves.

Me... Records: The historical (They speak of me) is recorded in records of birth and death, in our social and business affairs. There is a sense of distance between the

"they" and the "me". These are the footprints we leave upon the legal landscape that legitimize and bind. This "Me" is close in meaning and function to the, creatively translated from the German, "superego" as described by the pioneering Viennese Doctor, Sigmund Freud.

I... Stories: The folkloric (I speak) is composed of the stories you tell about your self to your self and to others. These are also the stories your biological and social children, standing in your place, will tell about you. This "I" is close in meaning and function to the "ego" as described by Doctor Sigmund Feud.

My Self…Assertions (from Latin asserere to join to oneself, from serere to join): The magickal (I My Self speak) is a very intimate portrait painted with one's words of a self that joins to Self by one's Word. An assertion often begins with, "By my Word…". This "MySelf" resonates with the "id" as described by Doctor Sigmund Freud.

Perspective: Me, I & My Self

They speak of me.

("Me" becomes an object. The first person singular pronoun is I when it's a subject and me when it's an object.)

A reality observable by the other.

Superego

Objective/Scientific

Historical Perspective

I speak.

("I" is subject, the speaker.)

Firsthand accounts

Stories we create about who we are

A reality only "I" and those who reside within this "I" can create/experience.

Ego

Subjective/Personal

Folkloric Perspective

I myself speak.

("myself" as intensive)

This perspective is the "self" joining with the "Self." A holy union in which the mystic can experience, the artist can create, and a loa or spirit can rest in its becoming and manifest.

Id

Projective/Creative

Conjure/Perspective

The historic (You speak of me) and folkloric (I speak) dimensions of Dr. John are included in this grimoire. * The magickal (I myself speak) we will generate in this conjure.

Re-Membering

As a preliminary practice for the remembering of Dr. John, think of someone you have loved earlier in your life and have not seen for some time. How do we remember those who have passed away from us? Memories and recollections rise up. Do these memories and recollections reflect the person as they are now? If I were to see the person at this moment, I may not physically recognize them. The person, as they appear to my senses would certainly have changed. Yet the recollections create a shimmering overlay connected by a chain of cause and effect to the person who once was.

This is the ephemeral link we will feed and use in the conjure. Re-collect Dr. John in the manner Isis collected the parts of Osiris. Re-member him as Isis pieced the members of Osiris back together.

I have found this conjure to be particularly effective when performed peering into a mirror. A Magick Mirror is a mirror dedicated to not so much seeing into as to seeing through (New Orleans Voodoo Tarot, Martinié and Glassman, 1992, page 76). Bring together the lights and the images in your mind and juxtapose them before your eyes in the Magick Mirror. Focus. Look to the sides and then the center.

The images will solidify, distort, overlay. Independent movements of the image within the mirror are a good indication that the doorway has begun to open. It is a door that easily opens.

Second Conjure: Speaking in the Voice

Who Are You?

   Who Are You?

   Who Are You?

   (Repeated as the cry of an owl.)

These powerful words are used to conjure the names of spirits and in a complete magick they can be used to obtain your own name.

"Who" is a questioning. A seeking, a movement. An owl beckoning the stars.

"Are" is the creation of being. Bringing the vastness of chaos to an equally vast seminal point (Kether as point).

"You" is the acknowledgement of otherness. Most awe full in scope when applied to one's own selves.

Stare into the magick mirror while asking this question. The question is repeated as the first step into each of the three askings.

During the first asking, answer with all you have collected from History.*

Respond with "I am Dr. John Montanee. You say that I...was born on...was born in...married on...married to...and so on. "

During the second asking, answer with all you have collected from Folklore.*

Respond with "I am Dr. John Montanee. I...drummed

with...I drummed in....I worked conjures with....am buried in... and so forth."

Now quiet your present mind for a moment. Rest this mind in formless essence. From this quiet and empty space travel the road opened by the responses in the first two questionings. Ask the tripartite question for the third time from a space deep within your re-membering of Dr. John. Then make this assertion for no reason, based only on the weirdness of your word.

"I am Dr. John Montanee. I greet you...(conjurer's

name). I My Self ask who are you?"

Now the question is asked of the conjurer. Close your physical eyes. Do not look into the mirror. The mirror and its images have fallen into an in-between place that the Tibetans would call a Bardo. Answer the Doctor's question with your eyes closed. Do not look into the mirror. Open your eyes to the mirror for his response. Hear from both close and afar.

The holy conversion flows into conversation. Respond to the good doctor's question in the tone in which you want to converse. Choose to set the tone. The End Note contains an example of this. Dr. John can question and converse with the practitioner in words or images or feelings. Repeat the cycle until the conversation is ended.

When Speaking in the Voice has waned, relax and allow the mind to rebuild a convenient self. The mind is quite good at such constructions. Give thanks, make an offering, and depart. The offering can be as simple as the heat from your hands or as complicated as a set of personally favored incantations.

It would be wise to keep an internal or external record of what is said.

When this conjure is performed effectively, it will conclude with Dr. John Montanee flowing into the form of a bud self within the practitioner. The Worker is impregnated by the re-membered Dr. John much like Isis and Osiris. This bud self feeds on habit. Conjure often.

This is not so much a reversal of roles as a realization that the world is more fluid than usually imagined. The Visible and the Invisible Worlds are divided by but a thin door. Our actions, our very thoughts can cause this door to swing in both directions. The Magick Mirror can become this door. As a forgotten ancestor once phrased it, "For I am divided for Love's sake, for the chance of union."

With minor modifications, the design of this second conjure is useful in working in an array of practical situations to engender a variety of outcomes. Perhaps there is a decision of some importance that you, as a Worker, would like to influence. What better way than to become the person (Speak in the Voice of the person) who is making the decision and implant seeds that direct the actions of the person in a particular direction. This means of entry is much more elegant than the more common, and a bit coarse, shredding of the target's aura to gain entry.

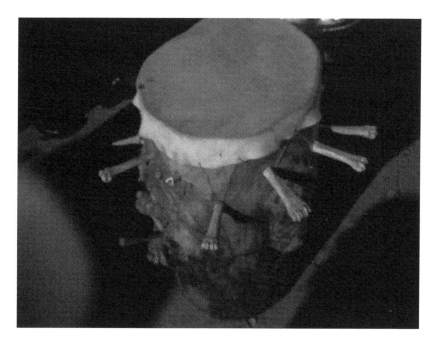

Drum found by Dr. Louis Martinié

End Note: Who Are You?... Our Stories

The third asking of "Who are you?" in this conjure is crucial. Now Dr. John asks this question of the practitioner. A relationship is developing. The tone of the relationship is in large measure guided by the tone of the practitioner's

response. You can choose the tone in which you respond but remember that in the heat of the conjure, in the dense midst of the contact all can change in an instant. Priest Oswan Chamani of the New Orleans Voodoo Spiritual Temple consistently taught that to plan too strictly for a rite is disrespectful of the loa.

This is a record of my response to the third asking of "Who are you." in the "Speaking in the Voice" conjure. It may be useful to the practitioner in developing the tone of the conversation with Dr. John Montanee. I have found that if we speak with a simple honesty, vulnerable trust, and heartfelt passion the loa will respond in kind. You get what you give. This is the tone that I myself prefer.

We are all from a holy place where history melts into memory which in turn cooks down to stories we tell ourselves to create our various selves:

I am from stories of a junkie

Who played drums
On the Delta Queen
As mom watched
On the river bank with her father
Sitting & married & sad & helpless

He couldn't get it up
Except on the point of a needle.
I have one of his cymbals
Broken and treasured.

I am from clapboard houses
& black widow spiders
& dads who sit silent & stutter & can't talk.

I am from silence I hated
that became golden when in its arms
I heard a dove's soft songs.

I am from poets
Who argue with English professors
& wear sandals
& have beards
& have long conversations with Mom
As I sit with thick books and hope they notice
me and the books as I reach out for something I don't
know and want to share with them.

The above is an example of such a story, in this case my story. Your story will sound different notes than mine but the melodies they form are so very similar. You can see that in my poem and you will see this in Dr. John's life.

These melodies all revolve around our pleasures and our pains. We rise to heights on feathered wings held together by our passions, we fall when the rapture fades and doubt melts our infatuation. The acceptance of vulnerability is a kind of nakedness that often leads to a true and tested type of strength.

Dr. John Montanee's story is no different from ours in its essence and this essence forms a road on which we can greet him as fellow travelers. All perceptions are selective and memory has a large yard in which to play. Dr. John's remembrances, his large yard, is now peopled with historical facts, the tales of folklore, and the spirits of conjure. It is a goal in this grimoire to include enough of the facts and folklore and conjure that the good doctor can reach into the practitioner's soul and tell his own story with no help.

We would do well to embrace Dr. John's humanity before reveling in his presence as a loa. "We are the most universal when we are the most personal." This quote from Ursula Le Guin illuminates an elusive facet of what it means to be universal. The ancient cabalists wrote of "revolving" an idea in order to examine it from all angles. My approach to the life and afterlife of Dr. John Montanee invokes this

type of revolving. This grimoire revolves the personal in order to allow Dr. John to manifest in a most universal manner, as a loa. Here passion is an apt measure of authenticity if not mundane (mundus) accuracy.

* Here are a few shards from the Historical and Folkloric sections that can be effectively used in the conjure. The copy of Dr. John's signature is an excellent link.

History: African by birth. Born around 1815. A free man of color. A conjure Doctor. Having considerable land and wealth. Married to Marie Armand on the 20th of October, 1868. Father of 8 children in the marriage: Albert, Antoine, John, and Marie who all died in infancy and of Jeanne, Edward, Oscar, and Joseph who all lived to adulthood. Died on the 23rd of August, 1885 of Brights Disease. Buried in Saint Roch Cemetery.

Folklore: Haitian by birth. Drummed at the ceremonies of Marie Laveau. Made the calls in the rites with a loud voice. Played at the rites on Congo Square. Proud of being able to sign his name. First to join Voodoo and Catholicism and the snake oracle. Buried in Saint Louis Cemetery.

This is a portion of a necromantic grimoire to be issued by Black Moon Publishing. I find pleasure in these experiments and hope that this pleasure is shared by other practitioners.

May the Good Priestess Marie Laveau and the Wise Dr. John
The Mother and Father of New Orleans Voodoo
Guide Your Hands and Open Your Heart ✶

Tau Palama, *Persevere and the Forms Crystallize*

Nepsis

Tau Palamas

+Gloria Patri et Matri et Filio et Filiae et Spiritui Sancto externo et
Spiritui Sancto interno, Sicut erat in principio, et nunc, et simper,
et in saecula saeculorum.

FOR those who travel the winding and often difficult path of the Gnosis there are often roadblocks that prevent the nous, or "eye of the heart," from seeing pure vitalized forms. Instead of encountering these refined beings, as soon as we begin to penetrate the veils of the subtle realms we are met by the phantasmagoria of images, who though often intriguing in their own right, are not typically the entities that we are searching for deep communion with. Some of these forms have characteristics that might be labeled evil, and when purposefully evoked can lead to forms of madness and obsession that prevent the nous from further development and limit the depth of the practice. The nous therefore, needs to be cleansed.

Being the center of one's very isness, the nous acts as a sort of "mind of the heart." This core mind that is awakened through gnosis becomes an ontic receptor of all energies and entities that we open ourselves up to through prayer, magick or working with the spirits. Receiving rarefied rays of light from higher forms, solar energies for instance that cascade in a descending manner from the macrocosm to the microcosm, the nous is fed and nurtured and in some cases purified by fire (katharismos).

But when we draw energy upwards from below, we often contact a vast array of entities that run the risk of devolving into logismoi—thoughts that attack the mind and cloud the nous. It is true that some Gnostics engage in works that might be construed as summoning these logismoi and purposefully allowing them to create negative thoughtforms for the sake of harming others. But this sort of working sets the mage upon a path with repercussions that are brought to light in time. Every action has an equal and opposite reaction in the higher Gnostic realms and so to tamper with these logismoi in this manner is to heap hot coals upon one's head.

In the most basic terms, these logismoi are simply in the way of deeper work. We are aiming towards the more crystallized forms that we can actually relate to, call upon and summon. The luminous darkness of some of these forms may be likened to a divine unknowing. Working with Erzulie Dantor will elicit this experience when the lower entities are severed and sent to their abodes. For instance, some workings with spirits require the calling up of entities that are more telluric and subliminal. These deep ones are not drawn down from the Macrocosm, they are drawn upwards from the depths of the microcosm. Yet they come full freighted with parasitic entities who want to attach themselves to the Gnostic and drain her of vital force through obsessive thoughts (logismoi). And so we practice the ancient method of the Desert monks and nuns, Nepsis.

During the 2nd through 5th centuries, in the regions of Egypt and Syria, the Neptic Fathers and Mothers of the Desert developed means to cleanse the nous of these logismoi and thereby free their minds for the greater ecstasies of divinization. Nepsis simply means, "watchfulness" or "soberness of mind." It was through frequent vigils, fasting and ceaseless prayer that these ascetics moved beyond the temptations and distractions of these pervasive logismoi. One reads of the life of St. Anthony of Egypt and his many attacks from these devils and finds a monk who not only mastered the art of Nepsis, but who so fully cleansed his nous that when other Brothers & Sisters visited him they were surrounded in an unearthly light, delighted by holy odors from unseen locations and experienced clairaudience simply by being in his presence. His noosphere, as Teilhard de Chardin called it, reached beyond his core and ray-ed outwards to those around him. St. Anthony was able to commune with angels and experience the Beatific Vision because of his mastery of Nepsis.

A life of frequent vigils, fasting and ceaseless prayer is not suitable to all, however. Many Gnostics today more closely resemble the Gyrovagi of St. Benedict's time. These were "monks on the move" who were not settled in the traditional sense. They accepted the hospitality of whoever offered it. In other words, the Gyrovagi pursued attainment by any means necessary. They do not have one set Rule to follow, as they must follow the dictates of their own consciences. St. Benedict accused them of satisfying their "gross appetites" and "following their own wills." Those of us who are non-dual Gnostics resemble this lot and celebrate the body and utilize it as a pathway to knowledge. We also develop and train our will, in hopes of aligning with True Will and achieving the One Thing necessary—the Great Work. For the Gyrovagi then, we must achieve Nepsis by other means.

In many sections of the colossal grimoire, the Voudon Gnostic Workbook, by Michael-Paul Bertiaux we find reference to the points chauds or "hot points." These are understood in a variety of ways by different practitioners. In Haitian Vodou, for instance, the pwen, or point, is typically a spiritual essence in a container such as a govi jar. In Voudon+Gnosis, however, the container is quite often the body. Some have mapped these points chauds upon the body through clairvoyant and experimental workings. One such group, styled Free Illuminists, through experiments and teaching instruction from Michael Bertiaux, aligned these points to the massive 97 degree system of the Ancient and Primitive Rite of Memphis-Misraim. As an expression of the 1921 Ecclesiastical Revision of this Rite of Freemasonry (Jean-Maine lineage), this approach, led by T Allen Greenfield, stands apart from any other form of Degree workings as it simplifies, with radical efficiency, the essence of the Degree with the points chauds into single gnostic pressures upon the body.

These same gnostic pressures, when exchanged by one with Gnostic and Apostolic Succession, have the distinct power of Nepsis. When the points-chaud empowerment is given, it awakens, stimulates and massages the entities and energies latent within the recipient to activity and immediately produces the sensation of soberness of mind, Nepsis. Each transmission becomes an empowerment--from person to person--which cleanses the nous and lacerates any clinging, obsessing or vampiric logismoi who attempt to thwart the journey of the mage. In this way, the points chauds become at once a banishing and purification operation and an initiation in the fullest sense of the word. Many other applications exists for the same points, yet in the undertaking of the subtle realms, in the frequent journeying into Otherwhere that the Gyrovagi endeavor upon, it is the action of Nepsis that is so crucial to development and interacting with the most pure beings and energies. Without this or some other grounding form of radical wakefulness and one-pointedness, the logismoi have free reign to torture the minds of the adventurous who know not the benefits of proper caution and procedure.

Through points chauds empowerments, the Gnostic can cleanse the nous in a precise and simple manner. These gnostic pressures obliterate the logismoi and crystallize the phantasmagoria of images that are called upwards. What is left is the entity sought for, the spirit or Lwa, the angelic presence or beatific vision of our penetrating Science. ✶

𝕭ibliography

The Phenomenon of Man, by Pierre Teilhard de Chardin, 1955

Syzygy—Reflections on the Monastery of the Seven Rays, by +Palamas, 2013

For a thorough investigation of this manner of working, see the forthcoming, *Spirit Builders: A Free Illuminist Approach to the Antient & Primitive Rite of Memphis+Misraim*, by +Palamas

The idea of "gnostic pressures" comes from *The Voudon Gnostic Workbook*, 2007, p. 165.

Palamas, Chapel of the Gnosis

Larry James Lent, *Shub-Niggurath*

The Spirituality of
Nothing in the Void's Womb
Angela Edwards

Part 1

HY sexual magick is only the gateway and not the end result to entering the qliphothic womb in universal fully. In any spiritual practice, the thing that firstly always interests me is when practitioners use devotional practice especially in work regarding annihilation and the void.

I have been practicing direct devotional practice to Babalon, Pomba Gira , Exu and the voodoo lwa for over a decade now.

My practice has involved working within the traditional Grimoirum Verum goetic spirits of the western celestial praxis through traditional metaphysical invocations as explored in the work of John Dee to the shamanistic elemental current of earth based Quimbanda /voodoo.

I first explored magickal tradition through spiritualism and like Crowley the spirit board and tarot cards. Following this I moved onto the metaphysical nature of the western goetic and Thelma Babalon theory and then into associating the Babalon to Kali and studying Hindu Indian Tantric and basic Buddhist right hand path traditions followed by exploration of Voodoo and Quimbanda.

In these times I had been continually working in devotional practice with Babalon, in exploring transgression and sacred sex work within my own life. Throughout these years and even earlier my work within the sex industry and working with sex work/transgression within an esoteric framework, has been just under twenty years though it is only in the last few years I have felt in a position to place my writings and art based on these subjects, in the public domain.

From exploring these elements as a teenager, transgressive/sacred sex work in esoteric context had become my lifelong magickal path in devotion to the spirits of Pomba Gira and Babalon. I have also used astrological charts and rituals to serve the spirits, the importance being on servitude to spirits or ancestral worship. In qliphothic magick a focus is placed on none servitude to the spirits, therefore separating its ethos in essence from the roots of my religious practice.

My sex work practice is founded upon blood and flesh and the living human in the present in the flesh exploring extremes outside of the self. For the practitioner's ongoing work, it needs to be made clear that religion and esotericism/mysticism are two different aspects of occult practice. This is because occultism or esotericism is not consigned to spirituality or being spiritual only on the manipulation and directing with intent of energies or utilising universal energies or essence outside of one's material world.

Nor is occultism, about the individual's path to spiritual growth or spiritual enlightenment particularly when associated with the Left Hand Path, instead it wishes to abolish such concepts and return to the void of nothingness. Likewise, qliphothic energies cannot be associated with the right hand path adepts path quest for spiritual bliss, the qliphoth does not provide bliss not only in its pathways to the womb of frustration but in the adept's quest to find a void of darkness where bliss nor destruction exist in becoming emotionless. It is a need to annihilate the ego and give the self over unconditionally to merge with something greater than the individual and outside universe.

Though sex work and extreme body ritual work private and publically has been used by the practitioner as a tool to explore the theories of the left hand path in western mystical tradition, it is as I see it a gateway or key to use to get to something or experience this type of enlightenment rather than the end result. The desired end result is nothingness, i.e., to worship no Gods and return to the birth of the universe and stars outside of oneself.

This can be communicated as a type of Nirvana where the self does not exist nor the individual in the black space of the qliphoth's womb to the void. In Thelema it is referred to in apocalyptic visions as the end of the mortal ego and realm where Babalon rides mounted upon the beast on the other side of the abyss. In the qliphoth we become shells of ourselves until only black light exists eternal light activated and merged into space.

The thing that has always fascinated me is the agnostic elements of the void, or this particular practice, as if our practice is done as a pathway to the abyss/void or nothingness to be equal and be annihilated within the universe's womb how can we worship gods or revere or work with spiritual deities in devotional practice as part of this universal philosophy. Just as how sex magick can be used of the flesh in true qliphothic theory when it is of the spiritual and not physical realm. Sex magick is elemental as qliphothic magick is celestial, they are polar opposites as the first focuses on actions or rituals made in the mortal living body and the second upon working with the dead shelled husks in the womb of celestial nothingness.

This therefore is a contradiction within itself and sex work/sexual magick can only ever be used as a ritual prop to annihilation through transgressive extremes to shed to skin and flesh to the spiritual gnosis of the void. In traditional Kabbalah the sephiroth are dedicated to thirteen Arabic daemons that reflect the darker aspects of humanities psyche and the self. We are given these daemons as keys / invocations through summoning them to each gateway (tunnel of Set) or stage leading to the final gateway of the qilphoth's womb or man/womankind's origins that is before human creation was placed in the universe.

In the qliphothic and Draconian path we are expected to work with each sephiroth as a gateway or initiation into transgressing ourselves and entering a realm outside our own mortality.

Each sephiroth on the right hand path at the front of the tree of life and the left-hand darker spiritual path the qliphoth leads to a greater understanding through the spirits and self of all aspects of humanity's both dark and light.

The front side of the tree of life concentrates on creation and universal bliss like the ethos of right hand path religious indoctrinations, working on the inward world of the practitioner. In my mind when exploring the subjects of sex, creation and death destruction, we need both conjoined aspects of the tree in order to understand our practice fully, we need to embrace the dark and light aspects of the self to gain balance and work within all these areas. Both sides of the tree complement each other in order for the practitioner to reach a deeper spiritual understanding and understanding of the universal world around them. The back of the tree of life or qliphoth, on destruction of the self and destruction through death and force in a proactive ethos like the left hand path to challenge the practitioner and find a world outside of the self to be fully, with universal understanding beyond the cult of the self or ones mortal being.

In Kenneth Grants work he places the orichas and in Michael Bertiaux's work the lwa upon the qliphoth sephiorth. These magickal conclusions also work in the theory of seeing these spirits not just in traditional, spiritual manifestation but as parts of ourselves and the darker energy or state of the imperfect human condition. Another interesting aspect, particularly if we study Bertiaux's work especially the monastery of seven rays papers, references the use of energy exchange or the practice of theosophy. In western tradition manipulating energy with intent for example in acts such as masturbation, can be connected to the same philosophy as using energy, the same as energy that forms the qilphothic womb. In curse or hexing work it is often found that the practitioner will build up sexual energy in an act to create a malevolent being, to exact revenge an energy manifestation - the sexual climax is used therefore as an act of projecting energies a force to exact their wishes in western mysticism.

The idea of masturbation when used in sex magick is not the sexual act but the action is a tool to build up energy to direct, in other words to form another entity outside of the self. The sexual act therefore transforms as when used in relation to qilphothic work, to an energy outside of one's self and ego or mortal realm.

Bertiaux's system is particularly of interest when relating to the hot points to the more traditional "laying of the hands" Arabic healing practice which pre-dates even biblical times. This focuses on physical bodies touching - touch energy transference from one body to another to heal or pass on through the mortal body for the practitioners transference of spiritualism or spiritual essence.

This energy used in healing tradition is not unlike the ideology of qliphothic universal energy of nothingness in focusing healing energy through these types of ritual we then become merged in the womb of qliphothic universal nothingness. These elements are explored with the papers of the monastery of seven rays, the third paper being based upon using healing light or energy as regards Luciferian magick and to navigate the wastes of the universal enlightenment of the qliphothic realms. Energy or the soul are the main key elements of qliphothic work not the spirit. This is why I feel using spirits in qliphothic workings is a total contradiction in that to reach the qliphothic womb or state we focus solely on the universe of the nirvana state of nothingness.

In order to work within the qliphothic realms in full esoteric context we must take out any mortal religious indoctrinations or spiritual practice therefore only focusing on the bare stripped down clarity of the universal soul. I personally can only relate sex magick / sex work or transgressive sexual elements worked in ritual as a way to prepare the self without ego which is destroyed for entry to the qliphothic realm.

These things are like fasting in Jewish/ Muslim tradition, tools or preparations rather than working within the end concept of spiritual enlightenment. Through our ritual, I stripped down actions of shedding the skin to then find the primordial state of the natural condition and my true complete nature evolved.

In the traditional keilpot tree and the qliphothic maps of Grant and Bertiaux , I would come to the conclusion that the spirits placed on the sephiroth's hold very little relevance to the religious practices that they originate from. This is because spirits are not used as a traditional invocation to these deities or founded on deity devotional practice but rather like my own ideology as a reflection of darker elements of the human primordial self. Therefore, I would attribute all qliphothic workings to being monotism in origin monasticism practices and being founded solely not on spiritual worship or devotional practices or ritual but upon universal perfected nothingness of the soul. We cannot attribute qliphoth theory purely to being the western Atheism as it is not the belief in nothing and the Qliphoth practitioner of the left hand path still wishes to develop their soul or a connection to universe.

In that unlike Atheism which is none active belief in nothing the Qliphoth practitioners path is more attributed to being agnostic and monastic practice of developing the outer world through extremes to through a sense of nothingness being totality embraced. In Dzogchen left hand path tantric based Buddhism the ideology is through finding the primordial state of our natural condition, we can transcend to timeless clarity that could be translated as black space or in western mysticism qliphothic — the void's womb. Tibetan Dzogchen Buddhism is like the qliphoth founded on a monasticism and a monastic belief system where no deities / gods are incorporated or praised. It is not founded on spiritual communication or practice more upon communication with the universal soul/space as in western mysticism when incorporating the qliphothic path.

The Dzogchens path is to find the end of attainment of great perfection, total completeness with the universe as in the western practitioner of qliphothic magicks path it is also the path to universal nothingness to become outside of the self-adjoined to universal space and nothingness. Therefore, qliphothic practice becomes, after preparation of psyche and the flesh, an act of meditation and stillness in our return to a spiritually cleansed pure nothingness. An entranced state of being outside of thought or the body, outside action projected into outer space where there is no existence of feelings beyond the self, our physical and psychological state is not manifested nor are we aware of our mortal self in the ascension of the soul.

Becoming envisioned solely as pure space or light, this can also be also reflected in the ideology of energy and orbs - in essence they are without mortal manifestation qliphothic or of the soul / or shell husk of the spirit realm. In western tradition if we are talking about the conclusion of reaching the wastes of the qliphothic womb or completeness with nothingness in being in our soul universal and celestial we cannot reference or use flesh and blood invocations in our rituals regarding this practice.

In order to reach qliphothic awareness we must first annihilate the ego and self through a process such as sex magick, facing and transgressing taboos or destroying the ego/ self through sex work as a conditioning process then move onto working properly inside the qliphothic space through meditation and being at one outside of the self to complete universal wholeness. We must then if we are basing our belief system on accessing the void or qliphothic realms annihilate any religious thoughts or indoctrinations or mystical traditions the qliphoth therefore is as a magickal praxis without divinity.

As practitioners learning that the theory and practice of qliphotic ideology is agnostic in outcome is one of the key elements to work with. To myself qliphothic practice also has the closest relation to alchemy in the Sitra Achra/Ahra in Jewish kabbalah or the Nigredo of the black light of space utilised in western alchemy or black sun that in pure energy is within but also without the void or qliphothic universal womb. Sitra Achra/Ahra means in Jewish translation the realm of evil or continual evil in that in the energy of the dead shells of qliphothic nothingness all becomes equal and good or evil in the moral sense of the word cease to exist, nor do human laws or philosophies exist in the dark space of the nothingness of the universe' hollow womb. The Sitra Achra also translates as impure spiritual forces in the practice of Jewish mysticism in that the qliphoth is impure in spirit because in the void we become absent of spiritualism and the spirit is destroyed and ceases to exist.

The alchemical aspect of Nigredo, translates as the pathway to the philosopher's stone in western alchemy to become black matter (the qliphoth) it also translates as dark night of the soul when the individual / practitioner confronts the shadow within. In black matter the alchemist sees Nigredo as putrefaction or decomposition, and it is true also of how the qliphoth translates to the practitioner working in this area that in the void of nothingness the mortal world becomes decomposed and falls away into the sea of dead shell husks in the essence of eternal emptiness. The importance as practitioners therefore becomes to take away or erase all religious conditioning to the spirits or physical action once we have transgressed to the qliphoth's entry of universal wholeness in nothingness.

In qliphothic magick we cease to honour the dead but instead become as them activated solely in black purity. As previously stated, extreme acts can only be used as gateways to the qliphothic realms and not more than once in order to take away one's self and destroy the ego or cult of the individual. Once we have activated all the correct rituals identifying all elements of the darker self through the sephiroths. we must then become complete nothingness without physical, action or thought.

Complete nothingness is a meditative entranced space or state of mind where we are only aware of the universes' energy merged with divinity and not the self. These spaces can be reached by trance in stillness meditating on the dark space where the self does not exist in the qliphothic realms. The final gateway to this being our mortal death where the body disintegrates and our mortal identity is destroyed and comes to dwell in space and stars the extended universe's union. Before reaching the qliphothic womb through death though we can communicate with this space and annihilation of the self through meditation and shutting down of the mortal self or transgressing mortal imperfection. Often the qliphoth is attributed in western mysticism to Luciferian magick as lucifer is black rayed light and celestial in his universal nature though in my experience as Lucifer is a spirit and the qliphoth is none deity derived universal completeness I would personally say that this ideology regarding the qliphoth is incorrect. The qliphoth is not spiritual nor does the practitioner who works within the realm of the qliphothic realm seek spiritual enlightenment instead the practitioner seeks the rewards of spiritual nothingness in the soul's completion within the universe.

Part 2

The Absence of Society & Mortals in the Destruction of The Qliphothic Realms and How This Relates to Animalism & the Primal Self

What if the human race is destroyed with no spiritual thought or morals? Floating through qliphothic space as an animalistic barbaric race. It has been argued that without conscience, laws, morals or human empathy humanity would become in its primitive form, no higher than the lowest animal.

Often philosophy, empathy and morals are what separate the human race as superior to other animal races. We pride ourselves on embracing these aspects as without these things society would fall away and be destroyed. Without morals or laws, we would embrace a free fall of murder, rape, child abuse, torture, war, cannibalism, sex and other societal taboos therefore guidance of our laws, our conscience, empathy and thoughts enable us not to cross these boundaries. Indoctrinated inbred morals act as a way to empathize, consider others' emotions to relate humanly or feel guilt.

If in universal space we transgress these states we are without empathy, emotion or human thought, like animals we cease to have limits or acknowledge the human conscience. The idea is in black space or the qliphoth that is based upon a concept of no religious worship or monasticism that is without religious indoctrinations or the human quest for enlightened spirituality, without any moral indoctrinations or beliefs that the human race would transgress all things. If there is no right or wrong in our living world nothing matters as all is universally valid and the same.

In a way, therefore this makes the qliphoth/ void of nothingness, animalistic in nature in that an animal lives in nothingness without the shackles of society or moral thought or emotional traits such as human empathy. The closest religions that transcend morals are tribes in New Guinea and Africa that still practice cannibalism one of the oldest taboos to kill and consume fellow man. Cannibalism in shamanism is related to honouring the dead and consuming the spirit so is therefore considered a religious practice though some Amazonian and African tribes practice flesh consummation of the enemy or in African war zones as a barbaric way of survival. In war zones the human race in desperation is returned to its savage qliphothic state and unaware of spiritual morals or indoctrinations of the politically correct outside world. In war as part of the fight for survival cannibalism, rape, murder, torture can be committed frequently through extreme circumstances.

I am not morally advocating such extreme acts but from the view point of entering the qliphoth with no spiritual or religious indoctrinations or outside of the human race it makes sense as a point of research into this work. War is a main example that acts as a black hole of chaos, war or circumstances where we become separated from humanity/or humane thoughts, are invokers of being nothing. For if we committed such atrocities and ceased to understand the differences between empathy or right and wrong we would become in qliphothic nothingness, the human intellect or emotions would be castrated outside of the self so all things become one or the same morally / spiritually. Animals are elemental in nature being of the earth and qliphothic theory is celestial in nature although primordial animal instinct of regression rather than human civilisation is the closest ideology and state to the qliphoth and the fact that animals live without spirituality/ sin.

Therefore, in regressing back to a pure state outside of human spiritual thought or the self, where like the animals we have transgressed to a higher state of being not a race but a universe. In extremes the human spirit is broken down again until nothing but the husk of the self remains. It is easy to see why in Jewish mysticism the Jews refer to the Qliphoth as the impure or pathway to evil because within the spiritual religious indoctrinated frame work it could be resigned to this theory.

Though it is better if as practitioners we take ourselves outside religious practice or humanity to a state beyond these things where no judgement or previous ideas exist to the pathway of nothingness womb obviously any act committed in the body transgressive or otherwise cannot be attributed to invoking the qliphoth as it is outside flesh bones and the material self.

Maybe these types of extremes where somebody transcends the moral religious self to abolish the self and ego can be preparation for the qliphothic state like tools used as keys, but invoking the qliphoth has no connection with the inward world or the individuals path, as in universal darkness the individual and their practice becomes obsolete. In the qliphothic state as the emphasis of the work becomes beyond the spiritual self or religious practice, I can only in this essay conclude that with the end result of the practitioner learning how to reside in the qliphothic womb and the practices and qliphothic beliefs founded upon monasticism.

Part 3

INVOCATION OF THE QLIPHOTH/VOID

Find me in seas penetrated to reside in nothingness eternal
I am the seas, the sun, the moon, the stars, the sky the earth
decomposed dust is I flaked into the black emptiness
my womb unborn
I am the shells husked of religion
I am the shells husked of mortality
I am the shells husked of philosophical thought
I am the shells husked of sexual yearnings
I am the shells husked of mortal emotions or thought
I am the shells husked of the individual's ego
I am the shells husked of spiritual divinity
I am the shells husked of human flesh and bone
I am the mass of space conjoined in marriage to the soul
destroyed individuality in husks disintegrated returned
I call not for devotion or adulation
devote yourself to nothing come into me
know thyself in humbled without ego
know nothing in which you return outside of the self
To unenlightening universal stillness
I am humanities climax, now know static quietness
In the soul's reign over spirits domain abolished
Resides my victory over all ancient and modern
I am exchanged energy untouchable powering
universe completeness
invoke me in the silence eternal black light revered
worship no god, hold no spiritual devotion to things
once of the flesh
hold no adulation to past lives mortal yearnings
Know only eternal space outside of the self,
extend solely as the whole universe
rest within me dark hollow feel nothing long for nothing be nothing be still,
be without want, be neither dead or alive
be in me the "other"

rested at peace in my primordial womb to be returned home
before life, after death your invocations nothingness
ethereal eternal
The journey of your existence ended within me
total completeness
my soul in monasticism of my natural condition in all
timeless clarity revealed.
Residing in universes accomplishment blackened womb
In shadows light I find everything
Invocation of the qliphoth
(after practices abolishing the mortal ego to enter the gateway of Daath
into the Qliphothic realms) ✶

Bibliography

The Night Side OF Eden. Kenneth Grant Muller 1977

Grade Papers of the Monastery Of Seven Rays, Michael Bertiaux 1970-1976

The Cycle of Day and Night: An essential Tibetan Text on the Practice of Dzogchen, Namkhai Norbu

"Vajra Speech: Pith Instructions for Dzogchen," Yogi Tulku Urgyen Rinpoche 2001

"Dzogchen: Heart Essence of Great Perfection," Sogyal Rinpoche and Dalai Lama

Dark Shamen Kanaima and the Poetics of Violent Death, Neil L Whitehead 2002

Sepher Yetzirth: Jewish Mysticism, J. Abelson

An Introduction to Kabbalah, Bernard Pick

Claudio Carvalho, *Pan Incarnatus*

Honoring The Forgotten Ones of Panphage

Aion 131

A KEY 'Typhonian' feature of the Astral planes is the access to the Forgotten Ones. These entities are, basically, the intense and primal gods of our genetic structure. They are the successful survival-factors that have been covered, in the Individual and racial Unconscious, with the veneer of conscious Mind and civilization.

They persist, and are the most powerful natural source of individual Magickal energy. By finding the Forgotten Ones and using their power (by invocation, techniques of Atavistic Resurgence, etc.), the Consciousness is propelled in a quantum-leap to the level of a native of the beginning of the Aeon of Maat. This is not an entirely safe method, in that it impossible to identify with the survival-lusts of our ancestral selves and become trapped in prehuman consciousness.

Again, firm grounding in the viewpoint of the Observer, or Hadit, can prevent this mishap. It in no way diminishes the intensity of the experience, but it does permit the Willed release of energy in the trajectory of voluntary mutation. The beast-self is henceforth available to the consciousness, and under the control of Will. Likewise, the seed of gestalt-consciousness is also present. Such an operation, then, can be considered a restoration of full Human consciousness, past, present, and future. It's a not inconsiderable benefit to be able to employ all of one's faculties.

— Soror Nema, The Maat Continuum

The Forgotten Ones are merely the deepest, most primal (read: rep- tile or 'dragon' mind) archetypes and as such can cause an astounding amount of mayhem in our lives if not embraced squarely. This ritual offers the adept a way to deal with these primal 'sub-forces' or 'demons' through the being of Pan. They may be approached through any of the Aeonic Masks, but Maat is the one that has been found to be the most powerful and beneficial in terms of active magick. In Pan Magick, rather than join with them and become a gateway, the goal is acknowledging that they are part of one and accepting them as powerful and useful 'allies' even though they may seem alien.

It is here in the realm of the Fiery Ram Mask that we come to terms with killing as an animal and being killed as an animal, of hunting and being the hunter, of accepting that we are wild sexual critters and of accepting the wild lust of others. These most primal parts of us (and more) are indeed intense, but it is due to their suppression and their targeted 'editing' by faiths and philosophies that view them as wicked or fear them that we are today threatened with annihilation. Primate threats & scares, urges and assaults are all continuing today, but under the veneer of 'civilization.' We, as a species, are being jerked around by these internal and deeply potent 'Nameless' forces of the abyss. Pan Magick returns us to a place of power where we are in touch with our deep fears/lusts and thus are able to come to terms with them through the fire of Will and Love and Truth and Instinct rather than demonize or attempt to 'expel' them.

It is Nature who is the most honest, and it is by gently unbinding the absurd blocks and mummy wrappings we and our culture have placed on these atavistic 'cells' that we can most quickly align with some of the most potent urges and experiences distilled in Nature as the Horned One. The intricate web of life, the food chain, the prey/hunter dance is a powerful and intense expression of Pan, of the vibrant life of Nature manifest, and it is the inability of people to fully accept this that causes Panic, the unreasonable (forgotten, instinctual) FLEE response, as well as the legendary and terrible manifestation of Pan as Panphage (the 'all destroyer' or 'all devourer')—the shadow Beast inside us all.

Note: If one is a vegetarian and has been so for a long time, then suitable vegetable 'prey' can be substituted in this rite.

Needed:

✶ A shell with water (or a black pot or cup of water can be used) • A knife (a fossil or sharp stone blade, etc. is appropriate. I use a prehistoric shark tooth)

✶ A cup (a shell is preferred)

✶ A Wand (a wooden stang used in Pan ceremonies or trident)

✶ A Stone of Power (it may have the Pangil or other significant markings engraved upon it)

✶ A red, raw, bloody piece of freshly killed meat in a simple bowl.

Go to a Wild Place. Be naked. Be wild. Become a Satyr. As such, invoke your Guardian Spirit and find your center. Plant the Stang (forked staff used in Pan rituals) Place the tools about the stang and Cast the circle. Chant in a deep guttural growl:

AAA... EEE... III... OOO... UUU An To Pan En To Pan In To Pan

On To Pan Un To Pan (repeat at will)

Raise your arms and call upon the Dragon Heaven Sky powers,
as you like, ending with: HA!

Touch the Earth and call upon the Deep Earth Gaia powers,
as ye like, ending: HA!

Hold the stang and vibrate:

HA! IO Pan! IO Pan Genitor! IO Panphage! Eros!
Thanatos! Bios! Phobos!

IO Pan To Me! To Me!

I Call Forth the Hidden Ones Within The Forgotton Ones of Flesh and
Blood, Gland and Neuron! The Terrible, Ugly Instincts of Prey and
Hunter The Killer and The Killed The One Who Devours And the One
Devoured For there is No Difference!

Cut yourself (just a little), and let your blood drip on the bloody meat. Chant:

I Call the Forgotten Ones and Primal Passions I Acknowledge You!
I Accept You! I Embrace You!
I Devour You! As Pan I am You Yet I am Beyond You are the Fire in My
Belly, the Hunger, the Lust But you have No Power over me That I do not

Grant Unless it be with Love and Will And the Radiance of True Self!
Thelema Agape Abrahadabra Ipsos IO AN!

Pick up the knife and stare into the water. Take on the mask of all the wrathful nightmare beings in your deep mind, stare into the water until you can see the transformation. Evoke your temper, anger, and 'predator-like' instincts. See yourself as that!

Then growl and thrust the blade into the bloody meat—see the kill— feel the kill. Touch the blade to your tongue, taste the blood. As you do so, see the energy fill you and settle down in your nervous system, humming with energy. Say:

NEXUS MUNDI, CONSUMMATUM EST!

Stab the blade into the earth.

Pick up the water and stare into the water. Take on the mask of all the lusting/wasting demons, stare into the water until you can see the transformation. Evoke your muddy emotions, controlling instincts, sexual hysteria and suppression. See yourself as that!

Then growl and dip the bloody meat into the water—see the kill— feel the kill. Drink a bit, taste the blood. As you do so, see the energy fill you and settle down in your blood, humming with energy.

Say:

NEXUS MUNDI, CONSUMMATUM EST!

Pick up the stone and stare into the water. Take on the mask of all the dragging, entropic, stagnating demons, stare into the water until you can see the transformation. Evoke your ossified, mummified, decaying and debauched instincts. See yourself as that! Touch stone to meat.

Lick the stone with your tongue, taste the blood. As you do so, see the energy fill you and settle down in your bones, humming with energy. Say:

NEXUS MUNDI, CONSUMMATUM EST!

Grab the stang and stare into the water. Take on the mask of all the bitter, dissipating, hungry, ghost-like demon-dark gods/goddesses of your inner mind, stare into the water until you can see the transformation. Evoke despairing, dissipated, gasping, dissolving instincts. See yourself as that!

Then growl and impale the bloody meat onto the stang—see the kill— feel the kill. Lick the stang with your tongue, taste the blood. Inhale... HA!

As you do so, see the energy fill you and settle down into your breath and lungs, humming with energy. Say:

NEXUS MUNDI, CONSUMMATUM EST!

Now... Become a Flame of black! A vortex of Nameless energies.

Invoke the Forgotten Ones of the Abyss, of space, of that which is between/beyond the spaces! Howl and hiss and utter the Words given to you by the Forgotten Ones....

Invoke Maat to balance the energies:

IPSOS! YCHRONOS! CTHONIOS!

LUTIS NITRA!

In the center, hold tight to your SELF as a point of light that holds fast in the whirlwind storm of the forgotten ones.

See yourself as the predator—live it. See yourself as the prey—live it. Let the swirling howling forces strip your bones of dis-ease, flesh, ego—all. Let the point of light still the forces—raise your hands and shout:

I Cry to the Silence, I Cry to the Fears of Survival
That linger in the bloodied jaws of the Beast

I Eat and am Eaten, Fucking I am Fucked,
Breeding I am Bred. In Silence.

Cover mouth, fall, assume death posture, then:

I am the Void Incarnate! I am Pan, and there is No Word!! HA!!!

Place finger to lips (the sign of silence) and become utterly still. You are Pan. Utterly silent, utterly black....

You are Panphage, all-devourer...

Attack and devour in complete BeastSelf bliss the raw meat. Devour all the forgotten things.

Your mouth the Abyss, your eyes the Stars—your horns pierce all the universes, your hooves destroy them all as well.

Devour the Forgotten Ones—digest them. You were before the beginning and will be after the end.

See all of the Forgotten One energy being digested with the meat, ingested by you who are now PAN. So they become part of you, so they become allies, so they become energies you have mastered and accepted and can use for your Work with Pan Magick.

When balance has settled, say: AUM HA!

Wash up with the water and then pour it into the earth as an offering saying:

GAIA-GAII!

Unto Nature Unto All Living Beings May All attain Joy, Happiness, Bliss In the Play of Pan! The Dance Dances, The Circle Cycles, The Sky is open to the Earth. Nothing is what it Will Be All is what it Must Be

IO PAN,

Who is the Gate in Man!

Sit and meditate, as you will. Take a lot of quiet time. It may even be better to camp there and let the process of the energy absorption continue and stabilize. Banish if you need to, or not, as you will.

Note: Avoid all sexual acts in this ritual, alone or together. If you want to take this process further and do more work with the Forgotten Ones in a deeper and sexual mode, then see Nema's Ritual "Invocation of the Forgotten Ones," in her book MAAT Magick. ✦

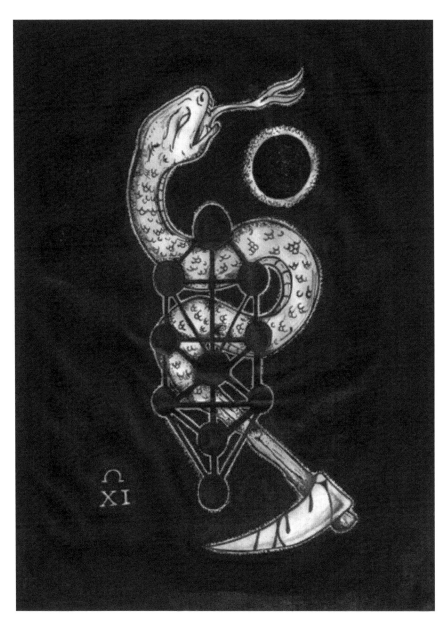

Anderson Lucifero, *Otz Daath*

Golachab & Gasheklah
SEVERITY & MERCY IN EXTREMIS
Cort Williams

HE Qliphothic Adept is, among other things, an explorer of the soul in extremis, the nightmarish regions of the abyssal atavistic depths of consciousness. The following mini-essay is a subjective meditation on two Qliphoth, Golachab and Gasheklah, the Qliphah of "unbalanced severity" and "unbalanced mercy" respectively. What is meant by unbalanced? In the sense that I interpret it, it is the force which, unchecked by a corresponding polar opposite, is left to develop in its uninhibited state to a point in which it is considered, at least in this plane of existence, pathological or destructive, a state which destabilizes existing structures and norms.

The essay then goes on to describe how the QliphahThagirion (The Disputers) interacts with the unbalanced forces of Golachab and Gasheklah. Like a radioactive element, the Qliphoth are unstable, poisonous and like a radioactive element, can be converted into a powerful and dangerous weapon and/or energy source.

Golachab is the Qliphothic counterpart of the sephirah of Geburah, the sephirah of severity. If Geburah is the force of severity which fights against injustice, which establishes laws to create a stable cosmic or social order, that which burns which is unnecessary or harmful, then Golachab is this force taken to its extreme. Indiscriminate destruction. Tyranny and its associated explosive outbursts of arbitrary cruelty and destructiveness. Authoritarianism is a force which engenders repression, and repression (be it of a political or psychological nature) is something which breeds unsustainable levels of tension which demand a release, and will seek them through whatever channels are available.

The name Golachab means roughly 'Burners with Fire', and the image of the demons associated with it are of enormous black heads like a volcano in eruption. The volcano is a symbol of repressed desire, the atavistic Id buried in the depths of the subchthonian subconscious, restlessly seeking to free it-self from its prison and let forth its plume of magma unchecked. Like a fes-tering boil, the volcano is a hot tender swelling filled with an unsustainable degree of tension and pressure, seeking to explode like a pustulent wine-grape. Such is the nature of the apocalyptic fire of Golachab. In Greek myth, the volcano is associated both with the primal titanic arch-giant Typhon, but also with forge of the smith-god Hephaestus.

This gives a clue as to how the apocalyptic tension of Golachab might be harnessed by the Black Adept-The explosive and primal desire of the Id as an energy-source both for destruction and creation. It speaks to the interrelated-ness of destruction and creation, destruction as a force which liberates ener-gies for the purpose of new creations, the Black Magus as one who destroys a universe in order to create a new one.

The partner and counterpart of Golachab is Gasheklah-While the former is unbalanced severity, the latter is that of unbalanced mercy, the soft and indulgent as that which allows rarefied esoteric species of pathological deca-dence to flourish in the absence of the severity which culls these parasitic blooms upon the face of existence, the sweetness of sloth fermented into an intoxicating brew which engenders madness and horror. The sweetly poison-ous wine of the Decadents, those poets who sought, as Rimbaud said, to cul-tivate the faculties of the seer through a prolonged and reasoned derangement of the senses. If Golachab represents the explosive tension engendered by ex-cessive authority, than Gasheklah represents the vacuum of power created by a lack of authority and the resulting parasitic forces which emerge(such as organized crimes, corrupt officials, bandits preying on the weak in the ab-sence of anyone to stop them).

The subversion of Jupiterian authority, parasitic forces devouring the cosmic sustenance, indulgence as that which engenders the bizarre and mon-strous, which paves the way to the wisdom of insanity and the leap into the abyssal Outer Darkness.

The Qliphah Thagirion, translated as "The Disputers", corresponds to the Sephirah Tiferet. As Tiferet harmonizes, balances, and blends the oppos-ing forces of Chesed and Geburah, so Thagirion acts as a sort of agent provo-cateur: Accentuating their incompatibilities, aggravating their differences, and driving each into its more extreme state. As Tiferet makes possible a bal-anced flow of energy and sustenance from these two sephiroth possible, so Thagirion destabilizes the influx of the same, making the world parched with the drought of severity and flooded with the excess of mercy simultaneously. The effect becomes akin to that of the tornado: Rather than neutralizing each other, the influence of Thagirion intensifies the conflict between Golachab and Gasheklah, generating a swirling maelstrom of discordant energies.

For the Black Adept, the endurance and mastery of the extremities of un-balanced mercy and severity serve as a sort of "trial by fire" which tempers the inner steel of the Adept in preparation for further trials. On a macrocos-mic level, the triad of unbalanced forces which Gasheklah-Golachab-Tha-girion comprise provides a means to destabilize, subvert and invert the cre-ated cosmos in preparation for its destruction and subsequent recreation in accordance with the Will, Desire, and Imagination of the Black Adept. ✶

Barry James Lent, *The Gate of Hell*

Rite of the Abyss

Chaos Therion

These two rituals combined form a Rite of the Abyss. The initial scrying or invocation of the Abyss occurs for the first thirteen days of the lunar cycle. Afterwards, on the full moon the Evocation of Choronzon is performed.

Invocation of the Abyss

THIS Ritual forms a portion of the working for crossing the abyss. It starts with a prayer to Chaos and a prayer to Therion. This forms a necessary link with the atavistic forms of consciousness. After this is done, Choronzon is invoked via Gabriel's speech to Dee and Kelly and the call of the Abyss is read. This work stands as an in-depth ritual for scrying ZAX, the tenth aethyr (commonly referred to as the Abyss). It should be performed at the Twelfth Hour of the Night, being the hour preceding Dawn. The practitioner should be fully aware of the ramifications of attempting to navigate the Abyss and of invoking Choronzon before attempting this Ritual and suffice to say it is not for the rank novice. The two prayers can be used in preliminary invocations wherein one does not expose themselves to such brutal energy as that present in ZAX, but the ritual is presented in the current format for the more advanced practitioner and those willing to take account for their own actions both mundane and spiritual.

Prayer of Chaos

This is a simple invocation of Chaos as the Divine Matrix of the Universe. The altar is bare, with the exception of a black candle, a censer for incense, and a crystal for scrying. The incense is mandrake, albeit sparingly used. The Temple should be decorated to resemble the Womb of the Universe. Therefore, Royal Blue should adorn the walls, or Black. No other symbolism should be present; however, the Temple should be as dark as possible to reflect the darkness of Space. The candle is lit, the incense burnt and the invocation begun:

Chaos, immensum et aeternum, infinitum,
et sempiternalium.
Quod factum est, ex qua omnia.
Ipsa substantia angeli, archangeli et daemones. Te invoco.
Tua Divinum ordinem, quod est supra captum meum
in visione mea explicat.
Munere tuo, quam coram oculis quam ob causam habeat animus
lucis spatium infinitum.
Veritas mea manifesta visione Mundi!
Post velamentum autem videbo ultra id quod est mortale saeculum.
Fac mihi vas chao.
Chaos inhumanum naturae vis mecum contra me interfice, qui artis opus.
Manifestatio morbi tui polluamus ignorant.
Qui transitis per viam intellectus tuus non capit ineffible luminis et
claritatis tuae! Indevotis, non quæritis?
Cum implevero meum ut vasta rerum apta manifestam facere opera
tua super terram.
Fac mihi vas chao. Chaos et laboro usque ad interpretandum te animo
exsilit in tua scientia, da mihi corona.
Ut opus tuum absque confusione dilacerant indignum!
Non enim vereor! Mihi consilium et sapientia tua magnitudo
comprehendere.

Ut e Chao Ex Ordine chaos Surge tu in me libera manantem, et loqui
vebum tuum! Indica mihi quem non vidit, nec intellexit.
Fac me furor ratione vacui, quia nullum simulacrum
facie terroris mihi.

The magician then recites the abyssal key, taken from the grimoire of aethyric evocation:

*C NIIS MAHORELA ODO G ZOL OZONGON TELOAH
ZONRENSG IL LVIAHE ZAX NOAN ODO AAIOM
ODZAMRAN
SOBAM TELOAH
UGEG GIVI*

*C NIIS MAHORELA ODO G ZOL OZONGON TELOAH
ZONRENSG IL LVIAHE ZAX NOAN ODO AAIOM
ODZAMRAN
SOBAM TELOAH
UGEG GIVI*

*C NIIS MAHORELA ODO G ZOL OZONGON TELOAH ZO
NRENSG IL LVIAHE ZAX NOAN ODO AAIOM ODZAMRAN
SOBAM TELOAH
UGEG GIVI*

Oratio Therion (Prayer of Therion)

*Benedicta pecus!
Tu capita septem, uterque princeps Edom.
Septem planetarum radiis Sancto.
Hebdomadam quippe temporis iter tamquam in tellure
per spatium Meteoric petram.
Dicam nomini tuo: tu es enim Deus pro Divina
Sapientia nunc.
Sapiens apud me fac me intellegere fieri ut non sit alius deus praeter me
ego. Sit autem fortitudo tua et alacritatem mihi cibus in ira tua, ut alveo
irasci in hoc opere, quod ego effingat num.
Divinum fac me frui! Sit opera mea reflecti inter siderum, imo!
Sit in ipsa signa moueret praeceptum meum.
Quia ego ex me et te tua.
Chaos, dum sciri latere eam extra vas ipsum.
Sit porta aperiretur.*

The Temple is now opened.

Invocation of Choronzon

Audite verba Gabrielis
Homo in rebus, innocens factus est particeps, et virtutis Dei, et
potestatem,
et Spiritus Sancti, per omnia cognoscunt non solum de ipsis bene crea-
tionem
et vocavit nomen eorum quod essent: sed societas nostra,
et socius fuit, et oratoris mysteriorum Dei, et se ad Deum,
ut in perceptione boni angeli eius cum iustitia Dei virtutem,
et bene nobis Angelorum exaltata, ut fieret Sancta in conspectu
Dei usque in Coronzom,
(sic enim interpretatur nomen verum quod diabolus potens)
invidere felicitati suae, et intelligens quod erat substantia eius minor pars
fragiles unperfect
(quoad eius essentia pura) coepit aggredi et ita eum vicit ...
Ave Choronzon!

Invocation of Z AX

MADRIAAX DS PRAF ZAX CHIS MICAOLZ SAANIR CAOSGO
OD FIFIS BALZIZRAS

IAIDA NONCA GOHULIM MICMA ADOIAN MAD IAOD BLI-
ORB

SOBA OOAONA CHIS LUCIFTIAS PERIPSOL DS ABRAASA
NONCF NETAAIB

CAOSGI OD TILB ADPHAHT DAMPLOZ TOOAT NONCF
GMICALZOMA LRASD

TOFGLO MARB YARRY CHORONZON OD TORZULP
IAODAF GOHOL CAOSGA

TABAORD SAANIR OD CHRISTEOS YRPOIL TIOBL BUSDIR
TILB NOALN PAID

ORSBA OD DODRMNI ZYLNA ELZAPTILB PARMGI PERIP-
SAX OD TA QURLST

BOOAPIS L NIBM OVCHO SYMP OD CHRISTEOS AG TOL-
TORN MIRC Q TIOBL LEL,

TOM PAOMBD DILZMO ASPIAN, OD CHRISTEOS AG L
TORTORN PARACH ASYMP,

CORDZIZ DODPAL OD FIFALZ L SMNAD OD FARGT BAMS
OMAOAS

CONISBRA OD AUAUOX TONUG ORSCA TBL NOASMI
TABGES LEUITHMONG VNCHI
OMP TILB ORS.

BAGLE MOOOAH OL CORDZIZ L CAPIMAO
IXOMAXIP OD CA

COCASB GOSAA BAGLEN PI TIANTA A BABALOND OD
FAORGT

TELOC VOVIM MADRIAAX TORZU OADRIAX OROCHA
ABOAPRI TABAORI

PRIAZ AR TABAS. ADRPAN CORS TA DOBIX YOLCAM PRI-
AZI AR COAZIOR.

OD QUASB QTING RIPIR PAAOXT SAGACOR.

VML OD PRDZAR CACRG AOIVEAE CORMPT TORZV ZACAR
OD ZAMRAN

ASPT SIBSI BUTMONA DS SURZAS TIA BALTAN

ODO CICLE QAA OD OZAMA PLAPLI GAHATH!

The magician sits at a chair, west of the altar facing east. The candle has been lit and the incense consumed. The magician gazes at the crystal focusing their attention on it, increasing the intensity of the concentration until the crystal vanishes from sight, being swallowed up in the resultant light.

The magician then closes his or her eyes and enters a trance-like state.

After the practitioner is satisfied with their divers visions some more incense should be burnt in offering to the Spirit.

The Reception

Choronzon Oh! Magna posuisti me in medio filiorum hominum.
Gratiarum actio! Nam ab inquieto vacuo fit murmure amentia.
Scio diuina dementia iussit arma in sententia vanitatis bestiæ.
His ego scio quod super hiis quatuor elementa.
A tenebris lucem! Fiat voluntas mea movere inter sidera ipsa inter excursus altum spatium.
Meum, et confusionem sempiternam rerum velit.

(Finis)

Evocation of Choronzon

A CABALISTIC CROSS

(Touch the forehead and say): Ohr
(Touch the muladhara and say): Tohu
(Touch the right shoulder and say): Akudim:
(Touch the left shoulder and say): Nekudim
(Forming a sign of prayer): Tikkun Le-Olam Amen
In the East formulate a pentagram and project it with the intensity of your Godhead. Vibrate:

Eros.

In the North formulate a pentagram and project it with the intensity of your Godhead. Vibrate:

Babalon.

In West formulate a pentagram and project it with the intensity of your Godhead. Vibrate:

Chaos.

In South formulate a pentagram and project it with the intensity of your Godhead. Vibrate:

Therion.

Go to the East say with outstretched arms: Before me Regulus, behind me Fomalhaut, on my right hand Aldeberan, on my left hand Antares, for before me flame the pentagrams, and in the column shines the Sovereign Star.

Repeat Cross.

(This can take the place of a Star Ruby or Lesser Ritual of the Pentagram)

(Sprinkle water, at quarters, widdershins)

Waters of Creation, from whence all life springs, I hereby purify the Temple, may the Purity of this Temple reflect that of CHAOS.

(Cense the Temple, at quarters, widdershins)

Fire of Creation, from whom the Nitzutzei Kedoshim are but subtle sparks, I hereby consecrate the Temple, may the Will of this Chamber of Art reflect that of THERION.

The incense is Wormwood, albeit sparingly used.

A Prayer

Tu, Domine, qui fecit caelum et terra et omnia visibilia et invisibilia, Confiteor tibi, benedicimus te, adoramus te, glorificamus te, et ego!

Sinite, cum possit intellectus subtilis et acutus et scientia et omni corde suo cognoscere et percipere vix ab eis in memoria mea, ut intelligere et velle sequi scientiae absconditi.

PRAYER UPON ENTERING THE CIRCLE

Deus autem meus omnipotens, Creatorem caeli et aeris, terrae, aquarum, et nobiscum erit in hoc circulo dignetur, ut cum omni humilitate intrare per portam perpetuae beatitudinis divinis rebus abundat caritas et salus aeterna. Venerandum tuum includunt, hanc mysticam circuli Nominibus suscipiet noster caelestis operatio. Imo! Erit vas quasi nix.

Preliminary Invocation

Benigne Conditor, Qui cuncta formas innumerabiles animas, et prospera cuncta sunt bona, et in circuitu gloriae luce, priusquam mundus esset, qui præerat omnibus operibus nostris propitius esto.

Monoun, Domine sancte, Pater, Deus universi, ad quem creata sunt omnia et increatum, fons totius acies, cuius oculis nostrum nulla saeculi vult fieri.

The Conjuration

Adiuro te CHORONZON et socii tui, per Deum vivum. Adiuro te per THERION ego, Dóminus.

Etiam obsecro te creatorem omnium in nomine Domini, et Formator omnium creator omnium, Possessor omnium principium et finem. Manifestum et Unmanifest.

Adiuro te per omnia vasta, quod non sit in potentia caeli non habet, non sub caelo neque in terra, neque subtus terram, neque in aqua, sub aqua neque caeli vel sub cælo in locum mundum, non autem protinus te ad hunc locum CHORONZON tu, et omnes amici tui.

(Make a cross for each name):

AGLA, AGLAH, AGLTA, AGLAUT, AGLATUN, ALPHA, OMEGA, HE, VJV, JUD, HE, MAHL, ALIHAI, ELOKIM, ZEBAOTH, ELYON.

EL, ELODI, HOELOHIM, ELAHI, EHYH ASHER EHYH, JAH, SHADDAI, ADONAI ZEBAOTH, JUD HE VAV HE.

METATRON, ADRIBUN, SHABHI, SHMUIEL, SHAMSHIEL, ELIAS, ENOCH, HADARMIEL, PISHON, MITMON, SIGRON.

ADONAY, JAN, HUSSEL, ELOHA, NGHELION, NU, TLOHINS, THEYE, MARON.

CAPHU, ISSU, IMMUM, EVEU, EZOR, EMOAD, JEYA, ARARITA, LOUA, HAEAVO, ERET, ELLOZU, MALPAZ, BASUR, BARARABON, PATACEL, ELHEOGELIEL, AGUAEAI.

(The spirit will appear)

COMMENTARY TO THE RITUAL

The Cabbalistic Cross makes use of the Worlds of Chaos from Lurianic Kabbalah.

It is intended to align the body with these currents of Chaos.

The names Chaos, Babalon, Eros, and Therion correspond to the polarity of the element, i.e., Eros = Air = Positive, Babalon = Earth = Negative, Chaos = Water = Negative, and Therion = Fire = Positive.

The signs of The Enterer and of Silence can be used.

Most of the prayers are drawn from Solomonic texts: The Veritable Key of Solomon the King (Skinner/Rankin, Golden Hoard, 2008) and Sepher Maphteah Shelomoh (Herman Gollancz ed. Skinner, Golden Hoard, 2008).

I have rewritten portions of these and omitted several components, trying to keep the "grammar" yet update the exact wording to match my praxis of belief more accurately.

The names are drawn from these texts as well.

A Circle and Triangle need to be present.

The talisman is placed with the Triangle.

There are no other talismans used in this Ritual.

COMMENTARY ON THE RITE

This Rite begins on a new moon and last one-half of the lunar cycle. The Hour of the Night: Shelem, is the highest medium of the Astral upon which one can work. Sepher ha-Levanah confirms this. This means that the psychological impact of the repeated ritual will be tremendous if performed properly and at the appropriate time. The twelfth hour of the night starts eleven hours after the sunset. This means that if there are 7 hours between sunset and dawn an hour will equal 7/12ths of an actual hour. Therefore, the twelfth hour will occur at roughly 35 minutes before the dawn hour.

The magician should have attained Knowledge and Conversation with their Holy Guardian Angel or other similarly recognized attainment before beginning in this Work.

The abyssal call is a modified version of Dee's call of the aethyrs received by Dee and Kelly from the Angel NALVAGE.

The abyssal key is taken from the Grimoire of Aethyric Evocation, which forms a portion of the Arbor de Magistro.

The invocation of Choronzon is taken from a passage in Dr. Dee's Spiritual Diaries in which Gabriel explains Choronzon in a fall of man type paradigm. It was rendered into Latin by the author of this ritual.

The use of Latin, for those unfamiliar, is similar in nature to the use of barbarous words of evocation. If the practitioner need reassurance as to the intent of this ritual, it is simple: this ritual is for Crossing the Abyss.

Should one need further reassurance, one could easily translate the Latin back into English. Although, this would detract from some of the beauty inherent in performing magick in Latin and for this reason a translation is not published here. The practitioner is also strongly discouraged against performing this ritual in any other tongue.

These Rituals in no way confer any Grade in any Occult Order, they are intended for the advancement of sentient beings everywhere. That being said, some background (as stated previously) in magick is required as they are of an advanced nature.

The aim of this is two-fold: to cross the abyss, and to retain the integrity of the original vehicle.

The end of the Rite should produce some success. The second half of the lunar cycle is the manifestation of the Result. The magician assumes the cycle of sleep, or rest, allowing the imagery of the Abyss to work itself out via the dreaming faculty for the rest of the lunar cycle. These dreams should be noticed and/or recorded. The use of the individual prayers as a Temple Opening is possible as would be the case in workings of semiforas, or evocation, or the performance of the Great Rite.

If performed in a Great Rite, the male present would perform the Prayer of Therion, while the female would perform the Prayer of Chaos. (This is only one possible coupling of energies, obviously for same-sex practitioners a choice would need to be made.) However, if performed as a solo exercise the magician performs both prayers.

In the case that the prayers are being used in a setting with more than two practitioners, the prayers would be delegated to the lower ranks of the circle allowing the higher magi to focus on the more advanced workings of the ritual. This would be such as in initiations and some evocations.

The prayers could be employed in a manner similar to Liber Astarte by Aleister Crowley. In it, a form of Devotion is employed in a Theurgistic manner and devotion to both Chaos and Therion as separate and distinct entities is a good preliminary practice.

Chaos is the mother and matrix.

Therion is the father or beast.

It is from these two that an unique expression of the 93 current occurs. This expression of THELEMA and AGAPE in no way contravenes the occult orders of Ordo Templi Orientis or Argentum Astrum (who are but another expression of that current upon our Planet.)

Rather, the goal of this practitioner is to remain in Harmony with as many of the traditions as possible. The whole forming a closer approximation to Chaos than possible individually. This harmony has limits and there are obviously branches which are beyond or outside of the scope of my current praxis. However, the aim is to be diverse without dilution of Understanding occurring. Let that be the goal!

In the above ritual Chaos is affirmed as the matrix of space, and the limitless light of AIN SUPH AUR (although this negative veil is not referred to directly). The magician asks to be made a vessel of chaos, to receive the Light from AIN SUPH AUR, to see beyond the veil of the mortal world, and to see the Truth of the Universe.

In the prayer to Therion the beast is correlated to the seven planets and days of the week.

The channeling of Therion through "Works of the Grayt Arte" is the first act, afterwards we affirm that Therion has, in fact, replaced Jehovah as the magical current (at this epoch of time) on the planet. We ask for Wisdom from Therion and we affirm our orbit as a star in deep space amongst, and beyond the constellations.

Gabriel's address can be found in the GOLDEN HOARD edition of Dr. John Dee's Spiritual Diaries, ed. Skinner. If forced to surmise the passage, it refers to the overcoming of man by Choronzon.

The address to Choronzon affirms that the magician has been made strong amongst the sons of man. The divine madness whispered from the unquiet void is understood to be ordered through Chaos and Therion, and the Divine Reason; which is of the magician, transcends this.

The key of the abyss is in Enochian.

It means, roughly: ye dark heavens appear, winds of death utter thy song, ZAX open and appear, waters of death was strong.

The call of the abyss is an altered version of the twenty-eighth call.

The barbarous words of evocation are used to align the mind to the faculty above language, that which is considered incommunicable by words. It is in this way we are able to converse with the Highest through foreign tongues. Therefore, the magician should not worry about understanding each word as long as the general meaning is retained. The above summary should prove sufficient.

Templum in terra nigra sum ... Ego sum, silentium intus monumentum.

The seal of Choronzon is the resultant art of an evocation of Choronzon, performed circa 2004 ev.)

Here is a simple Middle Pillar Ritual. It makes use of the Seven Kings of Edom. These Kings are the broken vessels of Tohu-Chaos. They typify the conjunction of Chokmah and Binah. The Kings of Edom represent Din or extreme severity. The seven heads of Therion as depicted in Atu XI of the Atus of Thoth are the Kings of Edom. Therefore, this Middle Pillar is an invocation of Therion. It is used to awaken the Kundalini and is best suited to Tantric Rites. Incense could be white sandalwood, or something like cherry blossoms, something simple yet pure. The candle should be yellow beeswax.

(A simple Middle Pillar)

Arik Anpin may your countenance be beheld!
The light is mine; its rays consume
Me: I have made a secret door
Into the House of Ra and Tum,
Of Khephra and of Ahathoor.
I am thy Theban, O Mentu,
The prophet Ankh-af-na-khonsu!"
May the brilliance of the Divine Light descend into the resultant body,
drawn from this Ritual of Royal Holy Arte.
May the Kings reign once more!
Oh Therion, blessed beast upon which Babalon rides,
I invoke thee!

Make a horizontal line at your muladhara chakra and say:

Bela

Make a horizontal line at your svadhisana chakra and say:

Yovav

Make a horizontal line at your manipura chakra and say:

Chusham

Make a horizontal line at your anahata chakra and say:

Hadad

Make a horizontal line at your visudhi chakra and say:

Samlah

Make a horizontal line at your ajna chakra and say:

Shaul

Make a horizontal line at your sahasrara chakra and say:

Baal Chanan

Draw a vertical line down from the sahasrara across the top of the cranium to the brow and say:

Hadar.

THE KINGS OF EDOM IN THE MIDDLE PILLAR

The seven kings of Edom are correlated to the seven chakras in this ritual.

The eighth king Hadar is invoked as the beginning of rectification.

The seven kings are extreme severity so it is wise to proceed with this ritual with extreme caution.

This ritual is designed to align the magician with the current of the Beast Therion, represented in Atu XI of the Keys of Thoth. Therion of Tohu is personified by the seven kings of Edom. These are invoked chronologically starting at the base center, eventually reaching the Crown and skull.

The process is similar to breaking the seven seals of creation at each chakra, although in that instance one would descend. Here we ascend from the muck of Tohu-Chaos into Berudim. The world of the Rectification.

The raising of the kundalini energy or serpent-power is the succession of the Kings.

(Culminating in rectification after Hadar.)

The process is then one of refinement as one raises the energy from the base.

The culmination of this Ritual is the rectification, therefore it is best used before sexual rites. Especially those involving the Goddess. As the first seven

Kings are without wives the coupling of Divine Feminine energy is needed to complete the rectification. It is that nature abhors a vacuum and something must rush in to fill the spaces. This rectification is what allows this Middle Pillar to be somewhat of a trans-formative Rite in that one shatters the vessels and splits the skull to let the Divine Essence in. This process is not considered an error in the divine plan. Tohu-Chaos was a necessary process in Creation. Therefore, we identify with the original, primal state of Chaos. This process is pre-rectification and is therefore dangerous. The goal, however is to allow the process of rectification to occur within the magician themselves and for this reason it is necessary to delve into Olam Ha-Tohu. The magician then understands the process of the Creation of the Universe through their Magical Work. They can then draw from this wellspring of Creation. ✦

Edgar Kerval, *Baron Cimetiere*

Qliphoth

The Draconian Flames

Arranged by

EDGAR KERVAL

Edited by

TIMOTHY

★ BECOME A LIVING GOD

Draconian Flames

Edgar Kerval

QLIPHOTH: *The Draconian Flames* is a grimoire focusing on the diverse paths of magick in their full splendor. Our main ambition is to traverse the paths of knowledge via praxis and gnosis.

Draconian Flames unlocks a fifth gateway, it acts as a magick key that an adept wields to transcend the desert of Amenti, and let the Dragon's Flames devour him. He or she experiences incarnate visions as the seals of primigenian beauty carry him unto the heart of the Abyss.

I dedicate this fifth edition to my brother, Nemirion 71, who has aided my transcendence in a peerless manner. Under veils of the Great Tree with a thousand eyes, he helped me to witness deep visions through ingestion of the most sacred plants. Also, I would like to acknowledge: John Belongie, Phil Brito, Ljóssál Loðursson, and Rick Necro for their infinite support. ✶

#

THE WITCHBLOOD KALA
— THE PROCLAMATION

Edgar Kerval & Nemirion 71

THE following work is a manifestation through 49 days within the current of NESAK an elder manifestation which roots within the witchblood lineage manifested through the Tunnel of Gargophias; still, its main work remains a mystery to both of us, namely Edgar Kerval & Namirion 71, who through an experimentation of eroto-comatose gnosis and rituals of blood in the Red Temple transpired between the months of April, May, and June 2015. The scarlet red goddess possessed us, and it resulted in intensely potent, Third Eye visions and spectral, physical manifestations. The serpent goddess and related witchblood lineage of mysteries and now reveal the first part of this book.

> *...The blackness of its flaming eyes Opening thy flesh upon the womb of its divine madness...*
> *...Through Its blood we carry the mysterious wisdom beyond the astral portals of the red temple...*

O

As watchers with no eyes, we see your thousand faces reflected under a Typhonian flame of red scarlet light. emerging as shadows gathering to the corners of the temple. It's your whispering calls and shapeless forms that penetrates our flesh, our souls in an eternal dance of ecstasy and lust.

1

Devouring your flames, we enter into the voluptuous web of your libations, which are macabre fragrances under your abominable chants. The red palace of your fornications is now the house of spectral shadows below the crown of your proclaimed throne. Oh thou queen of the secret venomous kiss.

2

I am the Queen of lust who burns through thousand shapeless forms and a lonely secret flame. that of your sacred manifestation, oh devourer of souls whose chants of purifications are baths in sacred elixirs beyond the aethyrs. I am above all secret calls and my name is the vessel of thy fornications.

3

My vessels are the portals for my incarnations and through so many forms I celebrate your presence with sodomy and lust. Through the witchblood kala I proclaim my throne bellow the mysteries of the red serpent, Oh Goat children of the sabbat. Mine is the vessel who open the path to nightside in the Typhonian tunnels in my name.

4

I am the Queen of the scarlet ocean, dance in ecstasy and agony under the emerald moon shining through your skin. my voice is carrying the call of the winds of pestilence upon the red temple whose seal is petrified in your soul. My fire and force are the powers of the night, whose wisdom is proclaimed by men through sacred copulations.

5

Within the witchblood kala I give birth to the secret serpent and the hidden path of the goat. Through the liquid light of my libations tears of blood give birth to astral children under Daath. Ashes of purification through the desert and inked seals, hidden spells under the nuptial chants of the 11 pillars of the red temple.

6

Through the fires of the ancient flames I dance, gathered upon the shadows of the gateless gate, whose name is the forbidden gate to wisdom and ecstasy bellow the sapphire stone in the waters of kaos. Entrance so eroto comatose transformation and trees of eternity dwelling into liquid roots of the primal garden of the shadows.

7

Through the waters of the moon my flesh became blood, my blood became flames burning through your soul. Your blind eyes burning as thousand torches bellow the infinite gardens of Daath. I am the wand of power and the entrance of lustful astral mysteries. I am the gateless gate to the infinite void.

Children of Cain

Laurie Pneumatikos

When you fall in love with a mortal
Nothing can result but pain
They cannot truly understand you
Or appreciate your Mark of Cain

They are attracted by our beauty
And astounded by our brains
But they cannot go the distance
For their minds are still in chains

They will tempt you and seduce you
To them it's just a game
They may even think they love you
Until they see your flame

Just as the lamb cannot follow the goat
As he seeks great heights to climb
Their minds are still imprisoned
In a religious-slave paradigm

Mortals desire and admire you
Frivolity they will provide
But your inner flame will scorch them
And make them run and hide. Mortals cannot know you

As you traverse the earthly plane
Don't give your heart to another
Lest they too, bare the Mark of Cain
Your brilliance is far too blinding
You are a radiant, shining star

Which is precisely why the mortals
Are scared of who you are

They can't comprehend your depth
Or appreciate your love for them
Rather than face their weakness
It is you they will condemn

It is the nature of the mortal
To squander their years
To run from their fears
Covering their ears

The truth cannot awaken them
As they are eagerly sedated
Remember it is their will
To remain indoctrinated
You may distract them for a moment
With your dazzling spectacle of light
But your black flame will propel them
Screaming into the night

Don't let a mortal into your heart
Lest it be crushed beyond repair
And left for vultures to tear apart
As he slips away without care

When mortals embrace a diamond
All they see is a rock

They cannot see your value

As long as they're part of the flock

If you fall for a mortal
Your power he will take
And leave you with nothing
But misery and heartache

If you give in to temptation
And cast your pearls before swine
They will reject your precious wisdom
For they're oblivious to the divine

In order to conform to their ways
We deny and suppress our flame
Enduring years of quiet desperation
With only ourselves to blame

You may decide it's worth the risk
And let your passions flow
But in the end you'll pay the price
When you watch them go

It is far better to stand alone
Noble Black flame burning bright
In order to attract our own
Who will find us in the night

Use your flame as a beacon
Use it often to lead the way
For in the end that's all you have
To escape the dull and the gray ✦

Andrew Cummins, *Quill of Illusion*

The Dream Working

Lukasz Grochocki

Introduction

THE Dream Working is an inspired process that delves into the subconscious mind and retrieves something concrete. It is a working of the conscious mind bringing forth from the depths of the dream world, into the light of the everyday life of common existence, something unique. It develops from a dream whose inspiration leads into something so much more and vast in scope because of its creative impulse onto the artistic mind of the magickian. The Dream Working therefore is an attempt at manifestation of that original inspiration from the dream realm. The working is divided into 3 parts: The dream that gave forth the original impulse to the actual working, the inspired manifestation of the dream that leads to the actual manufacturing of an object of power, and the analytical process that gives forth the final result and true understanding of the entire working.

Part 1

THE DREAM

In my dream I arrived at a large Southern mansion during a bright and sunny day. Around the Mansion there were banners announcing a day of international and cultural celebrations. I passed through its gates only to see more colorful banners, some in Asian characters, others in Arabic and many more in Latin letters. I gathered that this place was some sort of cultural center and that according to the signs there would be events held in specific rooms for each culture. I scanned around for something that would catch my attention and I notice that there would be a Slavic event held as well.

Intrigued, I enter the Mansion through a pair of dark wooden doors. Walking into the foyer, I could see that the interior of the Mansion was richly decorated in a high French colonial style. The floors were tiled in a black and white geometric pattern and the interior was accented by Roman like bronze statuary. However, the most prominent element in the space was a pair of winding stair ways, that emerged from the opposite sides of the massive entrance hall. They undulated like great alabaster serpents with ivory railings terminating on the second floor's landing. Above the ivory railed landing there was a cathedral like rosette stained glass window, with no specific images just brilliant blue and red abstract organic patterns.

I chose the stairway nearest to me on my left. As I ascended I noticed the wall was decorated with large gilded frames that contained gothic paintings of some unknown to me nobles whose features left me somewhat apprehensive. However, I continued making my way up.

Upon arriving on the second floor I began to explore the interior rooms of the Mansion. I found myself being guided by that uncanny dream quality of knowing where one is going though the space was unfamiliar. After passing through room after room in this fashion, I eventually came into a very poorly lit wooden hall which contained a series of door-less doorways. I stopped at the second one on the right. Somehow I knew this was to be the room that was dedicated to my Slavic heritage.

I peered into the dark interior of the room and noticed there was only the slightest whisper of ambient lighting that seeped through the black curtains covering the windows. Somewhat disappointed I entered the room. Once my eyes adjusted to the limited light, I noticed that the room was filled with large bulky objects that were covered in black sheets. Curiosity pushed me to explore. I lifted one of the sheets and peeked under and beheld an elaborately carved wooden throne like chair. Intrigued but not impressed, I continued to explore the contents of the other black sheet covered items. They turned out to be typical items such as; tables, book-less shelves and more chairs as well as a variety of dressers. The furniture had a hap hazard feeling about it and there seemed to be no general scheme in its arrangement, it almost had the feeling of a storage space.

As I maneuvered my way towards the back of the room, exploring, I noticed something bulkier and different in shape than anything thus far. I realized that it was this very thing that was calling to me all this time and that my maze like approach was destined to end up before this very object. Without hesitation I swiftly stripped back the black sheet off of the thing and as the dust settled, I beheld the source of my quest. It was an old scribe's desk, the kind with a covering that scrolls up to reveal a desk with many little compartments on either side of the writing surface. It was large and it still held its original mahogany varnish, the craftsmanship of which was exquisite and solid. The desk was upheld by a pair of drawer held legs. I pulled on the top drawer nearest to the desk's top, it slid easily but I felt it was of the same solid heavy wood. I looked inside, but I only saw black emptiness. Disappointed, I slid the drawer back in. I leaned down to pull out the bottom drawer, which was quite tall and therefore much deeper than the shallow one I first opened.

The contents of this drawer seemed more interesting. On top there was a thick layer of old yellowed sheets of paper, and just by thumbing through on my way deeper into the drawer, they looked to be some sort of hand written manuscript. Passing through them in my excavation, I saw several volumes of books that seemed too frail and old to be opened at that very moment. I took the top layer of papers and placed them on top of the desk. As I looked down passed the volumes of books into the now unobstructed drawer, I beheld a thing that truly peeked my curiosity.

The object was a large grapefruit sized rock. As I peered closer at it, I knew exactly what it was, for a symmetric crack made its way around the perimeter and revealed a shimmer of crystals. It was a geode! Excited, I pulled it out of the depths of the drawer to eye level and took the two sections apart in both of my hands. The part that was in my left hand confirmed my assumption that the rock was a geode moreover, it was an amethystine geode. Beautiful dark purple crystal lined the entire section around an empty center of sharp like crystal teeth. Then, I looked at the other half in my right hand and what I saw took me a back and left me feeling very disturbed. The other half of the geode looked exactly the same as the first half but where the other one was empty this one contained a figurine which was ensnared by those dark purple crystal teeth, like a dragon grasping it treasured gem, the figurine inside was small and whitish in color, it sat in Japanese style calves under thighs.

The white color, I realized was not pigment but rather mummy bandages that wrapped around it. However, as startling as this was, it was nothing to compare with the idol's face. For as I looked down at it, the figurine was look-ing straight back up at me, its face twisted in a frightful scream, forever frozen by some magickal force!

Taken aback by the site, I put the two parts of the geode back together and replaced the mysterious rock back into the drawer of its origin, along with the papers that I had previously exhumed. I slid the drawer shut and pulled the black sheet back down over the ancient desk. I resolved to leave this dark empty room and made my way back towards the door-less exit. As I ap-proached the portal of the room a shadow appeared at its threshold. Once my eyes adjusted to the gloom the shadow turned out to be an elderly woman. She had on a long white summer dress that did not look out of the ordinary, her hair was up in a bun and her facial features were soft but her bluish eyes were hard. She reminded me of one of those over baring spinster librarians. As we met, she gave me a demanding look and asked:

"Did you open the drawer in that desk over there?" To which I replied truthfully, "Yes, yes I did."

She continued peering deep into my eyes almost touching my soul and asked again, "Did you also open the geode in that same drawer?" she asked darkly.

To which I honestly answered, though feeling like a child who has been caught doing something naughty.

"Yes."

She brought herself up and stated, "So, then you have released the Do-movik!" (Note 1)

I was confused and somewhat dumb founded by the entire exchange. I could not understand how I could have released something which I knew was still there, in my assumption that the Domovik spirit she was referring to, was the very same creepy figurine trapped in that amethystine geode. She took notice of my confusion and said, "Go see for yourself, he is no longer in there."

Unwilling to believe her, I made my way back to the covered desk and as previously I stripped back the black sheet that was covering the desk. I slid out the same bottom drawer rummaged through the papers and felt the rock beneath my fingers. I retrieved the geode and held it up triumphantly in front of the elder woman, who had accompanied me back to the site, and proceeded to take the two halves apart. And to my utter disbelief, I saw that the little figurine was indeed missing! A wave of fear and confusion washed over me. How? It was there but just minutes ago...

The look that she gave me was one of pity as if for an unknowing child mixed with the authority of a disciplinarian. And said:

"Well you've done it now! You have released the Domovik."

I still stood baffled before her as she continued, "That's it, you have to go upstairs and make a Domovik mixture, in order to bring him back."

Yet another wave of bewilderment struck me. What the hell was this woman talking about? What upstairs? what mixture? She ushered me out of the room and vaguely pointed me down the dark hall I had come down earlier.

Again, I found myself passing through corridors and passages, from room to room, trying to make my way to some destination that my conscious mind was unaware of but my subconscious instinctive self knew exactly where to go. Eventually, I found myself in an alchemical like laboratory, filled with buns and burners, pelican distillers and other contraptions, all of which were on great black marble slab tables. Against the walls of the lab were shelves of herbs in glass jars row on top of row, all of a uniform size and neatly labeled. The laboratory was filled by many alchemists both man and woman, young and old, all working diligently on their tasks mixing and measuring. Somehow, I knew they were all working on creating their own Domovik mixtures. To confirm this, a lab attendant came up to me. She was pretty and young and her sandy blond hair was pulled back in a ponytail, she wore a white lab coat and held a clip board with some paper work.

"Are you here for the Domovik mixing competition?" she asked.

"Umm, uh, I guess so, I was sent here from down stairs." I answered quite slowly still trying to get my bearings of the place.

"Great!" she replied, "Well, you can find all the herbs and resins over there," she pointed back to the wall, "Feel free to take a station when you have gathered what you need." She noted my name and walked off.

At first, I had no intention with following through with the assignment, I felt more or less like some schooled and discipline child. However, I decided to at least investigate what all of these other people were up to. Immediately, I was struck by their pungent mixtures and what I gathered was ineptness at creating anything resembling a descent blend of herbs, resins and oils. Fortified by this, I resolved to make my own concoction.

I went towards the back wall grabbing this and that, again operating on that instinctive dream level, not knowing what it was I was gathering. At this point of the dream, time seemed to skip ahead and I found myself next in line to show off my mixture. I took my place in front of all my fellow alchemists and magickians to present my Domovik blend. I approached the podium and placed some whitish resin on a burning charcoal in a brazier on my left. On my right I poured an oily mixture into an oil burner and took notice that in my warm brown colored blend there swam some sort of white particles. The smoke bellowed from my resin and the subtle yet underlining oil blend filled the space. I looked out into the audience of my fellow herb casters and smiled. The scent I created struck them all like a lightning bolt.

The cute lab attendant came up to me and wafted the scent towards her. She closed her eyes and let the fragrance wash over her. She touched my arm, and stared into my eyes and asked:

"What did you put into that blend?"

I answered her, "Well, I have Copal burning on the charcoal and I made an oil blend of Lotus, Cinnamon, Dragon's Blood and I also put some Sesame seeds into it and that's burning on the oil burner."

She nodded and began to clap her hands and soon everyone in the room was clapping their hands. The applause began to grow uncanny and exploded into what sounded to me like a great flock of giant birds taking off. The scene grew whiter and whiter as if consumed by smoke and I felt myself pulled back into wakefulness.

Part 2

The inspiration from this dream carried me into what became my Dream Working. Upon waking I immediately wrote down the incense blend. Having always been inspired by the Voodoo practice of making vessels I resolved to make a Domovik figurine and place him into his own little house. I considered materials and sizes. I felt that this object should be small like in my dream perhaps 4x4x4 inches cubed. The figurine was what struck me the most and seeing how this entity was of the earth, I thought clay should be most appropriate. I used birch wood to make the six panels parts which would make up my box. (Birch has a very strong tradition in the Slavic culture as a ghost wood, to which spirits are attracted to.)

I painted the exterior of the box white and the interior black. As I molded the figurine I felt possessed by the memory of my dream and that uncanny howling like face that looked up at me. I fired the little Domovik figurine in my house oven, very appropriately in my house's hearth. After he cooled, I glued him to the bottom of the box giving him a stable place to dwell.

The following day I created my five-part incense blend. Accordingly, I set aside some copal resin and the 3 oils of Lotus, Cinnamon, Dragons Blood and some Sesame Seeds from the kitchen. The 5 herbs formed an intriguing combination. Copal as the resin played the main role taking place of the center. The ancient Meso-Americans used this resin to contact their ancestors and to gain visions from their dead relatives through the billowing smoke. The other four herbs that would be mixed as oils, were placed in a cardinal fashion with the 4 elements and 4 directions. Thus, Lotus so venerated by the ancient Egyptians as a symbol of rebirth and regeneration due to its cyclic property of closing and opening during the day and the night, took the southern water position.

Cinnamon was used by the Egyptians in funeral rites as an oil that preserved the flesh of the dead, perhaps the most pungent of the four and it became linked to the eastern air position. Dragon's Blood native to Socotra was used by the natives as an all cure. Dragon's Blood adds potency to blends and its enhancing quality intensifies spells and conjurations thus, linking it to the northern fire position. Lastly, Sesame Seeds are the gate openers of the western earth, for as in the Arabian Nights "Open Sesame" this herb was long thought to give the ability to open portals by it users. Thus this mixture seems specifically designed for the regenerating and preserving of the dead as well as giving them potency in their ability to help open portals during visionary conjurations.

FORMULA FOR THE DOMOVIK BLEND

1 part Copal resin	Ancestral visions	Center	Spirit
¼ part Lotus oil	Rebirth	South	Water
¼ part Cinnamon oil	Preservation	East	Air
¼ part Dragon's blood	Potency	North	Fire
¼ part Sesame seeds	Opening of ways	West	Earth

That night I awaited the 6th Hour of the Night or the so called Witching Hour. The house was quiet and still. I had before me the box and its inhabitant and some drawing paper. The whole thing seemed very pagan and Slavic so I was inspired to play some traditional bard music. I lit a candle and ignited the charcoal and turned on the oil burner. I let the atmosphere build and charge.

Once everything was hot and ready I sprinkled some Copal on the charcoal and poured some of my oil blend on the burner. The smoked bellowed and the aroma of the oil started to build up in intensity. The scent reminded me of something ancient and beautiful, like a wild goddess of some long forgotten world. I open the box and let the scent waft into it. And I watched my Domovik figurine become awakened by the power of the scents and their energy.

I sat back and cast some more of the blend. As I watched the scene I was struck by a notion; the Domovik was actually a soul I brought out of Hell, the Christian Hell. For as I let myself go into the vision I realized this was a pagan ancestor whose soul the Christians had banned and it was I who had liberated him from that misery. In gratitude he cast his spell on me. I noted that the box contains 6 sides. And as if lightning struck my mind, I knew what the next phase would be. I let myself become possessed by the moment and I proceeded to create 6 demon glyphs. In my automatic sigil drawing method, I let the scent inspire me to move my hand and let the spirit guide my marks. I did this again and again until I had created the 6 glyphs.

I let my mind explore the shapes by going over the line work correcting and finessing the strokes. As I redrew the glyphs the sounds of letters manifested themselves to me giving me 6 names of 6 letters each.

Seal of Salanx

Seal of Tgmovn

Seal of Rotusv

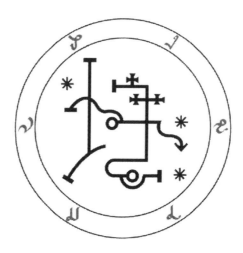

Seal of Vtrmel

Seal of Synrol

Seal of Gisurna

My mind was feeling overloaded for the night. I let the scent permeate the house and I went to sleep. I did not dream that night and in the morning I went to work to the occult shop where I work at. That day we received a shipment of stones and one of the stones we got in that day was a batch of amethyst. Again, the power of the moment struck me. I chose six large amethysts that seemed to call out to me. That evening I waited for the Witching hour once again and placed the 6 amethysts on each of the seals. I lit the incense and let the magick happen. At this point I realized that since each name has six letters and I am dealing with squares, I should make a square of 6x6 totaling 36 letters each. Since I already had the first row in the form of the name, I only needed to fill in the last five lines. Excited, I took the first amethyst assigned to the first spirit and placed it into the smoke and called out the name of the spirit. I placed the rock on my third eye and let the sounds manifest once again. As if on cue the letters and words rolled out. I noted them quickly before I forgot them. I repeated this process five more times for each of the 6 spirits. And at the end of the night I had 6 tablets of 36 letters each.

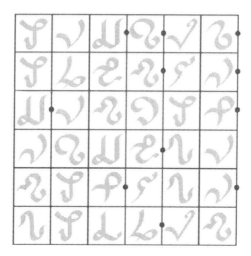

Table of Tgmovn

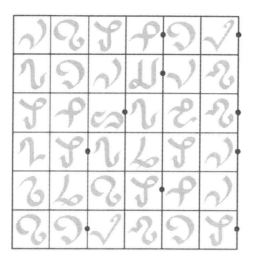

Table of Rotusv

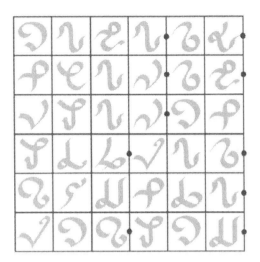

Table of Salanx

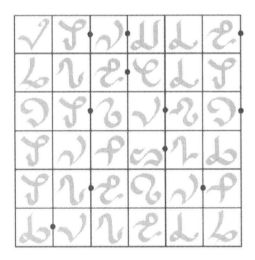

Table of Vtrmel

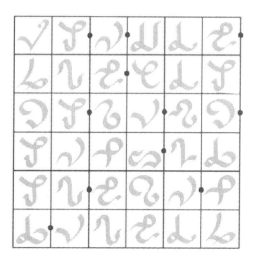

Table of Vtrmel

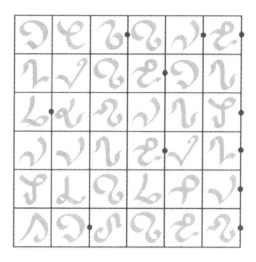

Table of Synrol

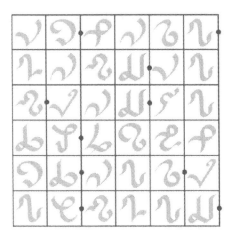

Table of Synrol

Part 3

THE ANALYTICAL WORKING

As is in all my workings these random sounds and syllables get translated into my invented language. For more than 15 years I have been compiling and cataloging these words into a dictionary that contains now over ten thousand entries. And so in this manner I translated the names of the 6 spirits that I was given as:

1	SALANX		Sala Nex		"The Woven Hurricane"
2	TGMOVN	Rendered phonetically:	Tegam O Van	Translated as:	"The Kidnapping Dream Forest"
3	ROTUSV		Rotu Suv		"The Shinny Haired"
4	VTRMEL		Vat Romel		"The Bleaching Sap"
5	SYNROL		Syne Ro El		"The Sun Sweat Hunter"
6	GISURNA		Gis Urna		"The Noose's Image"

Glancing over these translated names it struck me how some of these names evoked in me certain Slavic mythic themes. The one that caught my attention at first was Tegam O Van; the Kidnapping Dream Forest. The image of the witch Baba Yaga (note 2) seemed a perfect fit. However, I knew that this Tegam O Van was not Baba Yaga herself but maybe perhaps a servant of the Witch. At this point I was struck by a revelation that brought my entire dream full circle. These 6 spirits must represent demons in Slavic mythology that serve the Domovik spirit! With some insight and knowledge of Slavic mythology I was able to achieve a 1:1 correspondent table.

Thus:

1	**Sala Nex:**	The Woven Hurricane:	**Vila:** a female wind demon (note 3)
2	**Tegam O Van:**	The Kidnapping Dream:	**Leshy:** a male forest demon (note 4)
3	**Rotu Suv:**	The Shinny Haired:	**Rusalka:** a female water demon (note 5)
4	**Vat Romel:**	The Sun Marked Sap:	**Polevik:** a male field demon (note 6)
5	**Syn Ro El:**	The Sun Sweat Hunter:	**Bannik:** a male sweat lodge demon (note 7)
6	**Gis Urna:**	The Noose's Image:	**Upyr:** a male death demon (note 8)

The next phase was to be the translation of the remaining five lines of each of the 6 Tablets. These lines turned out to be the invocations for these 6 servant spirits of the Domovik of my Dream Working.

FIRST TABLET: INVOCATION OF THE VILA: SALA-NEX

S	a	l	a	N	x
U	y	a	r	N	l
G	t	a	r	S	u
T	e	k	V	a	n
O	b	M	u	D	a
V	s	o	T	s	m

Sala Nex:
Oh Woven Hurricane!
Uyar Nal Gotar Su Tek
Of the Gray Temple's Amethyst Lamp,
Van Ob Mu Da Veso Tessem
Take me Inside the Trembling Forest's
Wayward Path!

SECOND TABLET: INVOCATION OF THE LESHY: TEGAM-O-VAN

T	g	m	O	V	n
T	k	l	i	B	r
m	G	i	s	t	u
R	o	m	l	A	g
i	t	u	B	a	r
A	t	e	k	V	i

Tegam O Van:
Oh Kidnapping Dream Forest! Tekli
Barem Gistu
Let this Holy man Unlock and Render,
Romel Agitu Atek Vi
The Laiche Bleached Door with a Kiss!

THIRD TABLET: INVOCATION OF
THE RUSALKA: ROTU-SUV

R	o	t	u	S	v
A	s	r	m	g	i
t	u	h	A	l	i
J	t	A	k	t	r
N	k	o	t	U	r
o	s	V	i	s	t

Rotu Suv:
Oh Shinny Haired One!
Aseruam gituh Ali Jet
Whose Galloping Stallion Emanates Up
Stream, A-kitar Nikot Uros Viset
Cast Low into the Abyss the Drowned
One's Birth Rite!

FOURTH TABLET: INVOCATION OF
THE POLEVIK: VAT-RO-MEL

V	t	R	M	e	l
K	a	l	Y	e	t
s	t	N	g	I	s
T	r	u	h	J	d
t	a	L	o	r	U
d	G	a	l	e	k

Vat Ro Mel:
Oh Sun Marked Sappling!
Kal Yetset Nag Is
Let the Treasures and Wealth be Scented
on the Journey,
Truh Jedta Lor Ud Galek
For the Thieves will be Carved and Spit
Roasted by the Underdog!

FIFTH TABLET: INVOCATION OF THE
BANNIK: SYNE-RO-EL

S	y	n	R	o	L
j	v	o	l	S	a
k	X	i	r	a	t
R	g	a	l	V	j
T	e	o	k	u	g
F	s	P	o	l	i

Syne Ro El:
Oh Sun Sweat Hunter!
jvol Sak Xirat Rogal
Let us Be Grateful for Life's Tormenting Glare,
Vaj Teokug Fes Poli
For it Overcomes the Incoherence of Ignorance!

SIXTH TABLET: INVOCATION OF THE
UPYR: GIS-URNA

G	s	U	r	n	a
J	r	i	m	G	a
i	V	r	m	B	a
d	t	K	o	l	u
s	d	R	a	n	V
a	y	I	j	a	m

Gis Urna:
Oh Thou of the Noose's Image!
Jarim Gai Varam Badet
Who Gracefully Churns the Black Milky way,
Kolu-sed Ruan Vay Ijam
Entangling and Devouring let me Traverse its Rapids!

Thus, armed with the seals, names and invocations I was ready to bring the Dream Box into being. I gridded off the 6 faces of the box. Next, I made a red ink using Dragon's Blood mixed with gum Arabic as well as several drops of my blood. (I find the use of blood releases vast amounts of psychic energy that feeds the spirits which feeds the magickal potency of the entire working) With this mixture I inscribed each face of the box with the 6 Tablets accordingly. Next I burnt some of the leftovers wood chips, that I had from the cuttings of the birch panels, and with the remaining charcoal I make a black pigment which I used to inscribe the six spirit glyphs on each face of the box over the red text. Lastly, I inscribed each of the amethysts with a Roman numeral according to the order of its manifestation and placed them into the box. As a final act of magickal inspiration I placed a mirror underneath the lid of the dream box. This would allow the Domovik to travel the world via mirror portal and thus each mirror of my house became a portal for my house spirit, which I thought was very fitting for a dream begotten supernatural. And this is my final result:

𝔓art 4

CONCLUSION

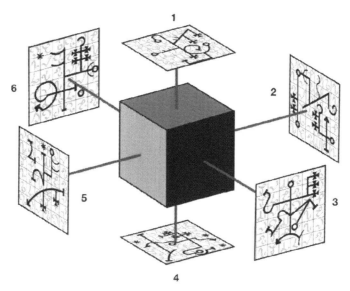

I found this entire process both a mixture of my own personal heritage as well as my own individual magick process. My dream may seem very personal, which I am more than willing to admit, however I find that personal experiences may lead into universal truths and motifs. We are all hired wired into the subconscious world whose states can and will lead us into great personal journeys into of ourselves and into self-becoming. I find anytime a dream motif enters our mind we should indulge it. It is at this point that personal journeys no longer matters and when greater universal truths are achieved, in this case an empowering weapon that harkens back from an ancient past.

Notes on Slavic Supernaturals

1. Domovik or "he of the house" is a house demon. The Domovik's origins lie in the Slavic practice of cremation and burial of the remains of the dead in urns under the floor of the family house, usually near the threshold or by the hearth. (This practice dates back to the Urnfield culture of prehistoric Europe over 4000 years ago.) The Domovik is said to have the knowledge of the future as well as that of the ancient past. These spirits could be mischievous or helpful depending whether or not the family leaves them night offerings of beer and bread. In folk tradition the Domovik is said to be a small hairy man sometimes pictured with small horns and a tail.

2. Baba Yaga is a witch goddess who lives in a primeval forest accompanied by wolves and ravens. She lives in a house that is perched on a chicken's foot that revolves during the day and night a symbolization of the solar cycle. Moreover she commands 3 riders one on a white horse for the morning, one on a red horse for the evening and a black horse rider for the night. In folk tales she is responsible for kidnapping children from her forest and cooking them in her oven. She represents the Crone of the triple goddess of Indo European mythology. Her shamanic task is to initiate children into adulthood, figuratively burning off the flesh of youth and bringing forth the adult.

3. Vila is a female storm demon. Vilas are said to be young and beautiful and to be the souls of frivolous maidens who lost their lives due to their carefree ways. They are usually described as wearing white dresses that barely cover their naked bodies. They live on mountain tops or high hill where they are closet to the sky. It is said that when they dance and sing they conjure great storms. They serve the wind god Stribog.

4. Leshy is a male forest demon. Leshy are tricksters par excellence they are said to be the souls of those who have lost their way and died in forests. They delight in getting people lost. They can take on the shapes of wolves or wolf-man, they can appear in human form though they are often disheveled and one can always tell a Leshy by their backward or inside out clothes. They serve the forest witch Baba Yaga.

5. Rusalka is a female water demon. Rusalkas are beautiful water nymphs they are said to be the souls of young maidens who have drowned or were

drowned on purpose either by their own hand or another's. They live in lakes, stream or rivers. They are always pictured playing naked in water and the swinging their long wet hair. They love to tempt man to come and play with them and when they succeed they take their man under water to live with them forever. Sometimes Rusalkas can grant magickal powers to their favorites. They serve the magick goddess Marzanna.

6. Polevik is a male field demon. Poleviks are powerful earth spirits they are said to be the souls of farmers who had died working their fields due to exhaustion and sun stroke. They dwell in the not harvested fields of wheat or corn. They appear as wild gnomes with grass for hair and multicolored eyes. If offended, they will strike one down with a sun stroke and also may trample the unlucky into the ground. However, they are very wise about the earth and know where treasures are hidden. They serve the field god Jarylo.

7. Bannik is a male sweat lodge demon. Banniks are ancient spirits of the sweat lodge a place reserved for magickal shamanic rites of the ancient Slavs. The sweat lodge was the site of birthing, healing and divination. The Bannik has no specific form he appears in a somewhat human form but he is mostly steam or smoke. They are wise spirits who know many things and have the gift of prophecy. No Christian symbols are allowed in the sweat lodge as to not offend the Bannik for he may rob one of their vital force. They serve the creator god Rod.

8. Upyr is a male death demon. The word Upyr is the original source for the word Vampire. These demons are the souls of those who have been hanged and left to die away from society. They are vengeful demons which love to hunt the unwary drink their blood and devour their flesh. They appear as living corpses that stalk the predawn hours, they are immortal and due to their longevity they have great knowledge of the other world. They serve the underworld god Veles. ✦

Melek Rsh Nvth IX, *Primigenian Pillar ov Lucifer*

The Vortex of Fire

Asenath Mason

THIS ritual is a malefic formula that was revealed by Lucifer through my personal work with his "masks" - various manifestations revealing his particular aspects and powers. The "mask" through which the formula was granted is known as the Dark God of Man or the Shadow Companion. Let us first explain who we are dealing with. Lucifer has many "masks" and manifestations, some of them well-known to us, others hardly ever associated with what usually falls under the category of "Luciferian Gnosis." The Shadow Companion is one of the less popular aspects in the initiatory magic, while in fact, it is one of the most common and easiest to encounter forms of Lucifer, as he often accompanies us in events and situations of our daily lives. He is the character of the folk legends that speak of a mysterious man appearing at night to solitary wanderers, either to lead them astray and do mischief or to offer help in need. In these legends, he is described either as a devil - with devil's horns, hooves, hairy skin, and the smell of sulfur around, or a human being - an old man who comes with wisdom and advice, or a youth in a fancy outfit who comes to seduce women and drink with men in the taverns. He is a shape-shifter and his true face is hidden behind a disguise that is either the ugly and cunning face of the devil or a beautiful face of man, depending on what we expect to see. He is a jester and sage, a trickster who deceives the false and the ignorant, playing tricks on them, and rewards the wise and those whose hearts are pure, showing them hidden treasures and offering guidance. In rites of self-initiatory magic, the Shadow Companion comes to teach and tease. He will mock, question and challenge everything we believe in, driving us to despair and making us doubt the magical path, personal skills and powers, our strengths and weaknesses, and finally, the sense of life itself. He is the bearer of gifts and the enemy of hypocrisy, falseness and self- delusion.

The following ritual is one of such gifts. The message received with this formula was: "The false shall burn in my Pit of Destruction." And what at first seemed a metaphor, was revealed through the further work with this "mask" of Lucifer as an applicable malefic ritual that can be used against a selected target. Before you attempt this formula, however, you need to remember that it cannot be directed at just anyone. The person you want to remove from your life must be "a false one." What does it mean? When I received this ritual, I was dealing with threats and false accusations of a former colleague who pretended to be a friend but in the end turned out to be a fraud and liar trying to make my life and work difficult in all possible ways. While I was considering resolving the problem by mundane means, the ritual formula came just in time to deal with it on a completely different level. It was a "gift" that came unexpectedly during my daily ritual work with Lucifer. So far it has proved effective in resolving such situations both to me and a few friends who have tested it in their personal work. In all cases, the targets of the ritual were eventually removed from the lives of those who performed the working. Therefore, I present it here, at the same time reminding everyone who would like to attempt this formula that malefic magic has to be approached carefully. A common rule in successful use of a malefic ritual is that you have to be ready to attack your target with your bare hands, completely sure that this is exactly what you want and never regret or look back at what you have done, no matter how the ritual manifests in the life of your victim. You must also be perfectly confident about the result of the curse, with no doubt of any kind or a thought that you might have to repeat it. Another thing to remember in this particular case is that you can only use this formula against "the false." This usually means a treacherous, unfaithful person, referring to someone disloyal to you, a community, or a cause you support - there are many interpretations here, but make sure they are justified, otherwise you may end up as "a false one" yourself and the formula will turn against you.

For this working you will need five sigils provided in this text and a large pentagram with a circle and five tridents marking each point of the diagram - this can be a drawing or an actual object made of a chosen material. The sigils can be drawn on paper and used only once, or you can make them from a solid material, such as e.g. wood or metal and save them for the future work. They represent the five powers of the Shadow Companion that are invoked and channeled into the body and mind of the practitioner: the power of the Eye, the power of the Sickle, the power of the Horns, the power of the Scythes, and the power of the Skull. Placed around the inverted pentagram, they form "the Pit of Destruction" that is activated as a vortex of energy and directed towards the target, surrounding the victim with a whirlpool of force that successively isolates the person from all defenses and everything that gives meaning to his/her life. This eventually leaves the victim alone, despaired and struggling with hopelessness of life, leading to severe depression, extreme chaos, or even driving the person to suicide. At the same time, it removes the target from your life, thus preventing any future problems that this person might cause you. To make it work properly, apart from the sigils and the pentagram, you will also need a sympathetic link to your victim - like in any other malefic magic, the best choice is a personal object or an item such as hair or blood. If it is not possible, however, a simple photo will do, as well. Whatever you choose, you must believe it is a proper link that will successfully open the way to your target. You can even make a puppet representing your victim - feel free to follow your intuition in this matter. The sympathetic link should be placed in the center of the pentagram, while the five sigils are placed at each point of it, according to the diagram:

When all the items are prepared, proceed to the ritual. Light a few candles - red or black are the best choice here. Burn a strong incense, e.g. Dragon's

Blood. As this ritual belongs to the Draconian magic, begin this work by attuning your consciousness to the Current of the Dragon. Stand or sit down, take a few deep breaths and focus on raising the inner Serpent/Dragon energy, from the base of your spine to the Third Eye, the center of awakened consciousness. You can empower this meditation e.g. by vibrating the Draconian word of manifestation: "VOVIN." Envision the fiery Draconian force flowing through your spine, activating your energy centers and opening your inner eyes to the vision of the Nightside. Visualize the red and golden flames of Lucifer's Current burning around you, protecting you and enclosing the ritual space with his sacred fire.

When you feel charged with the fiery Draconian force, invoke Lucifer in his aspect of the Shadow Companion. Anoint the ritual blade with your own blood, the key to all manifestation, and with the blade draw the symbol of the trident in the air, above the altar. Focus for a while on the trident and envision it burning with Lucifer's flames, surrounded by shadows, then speak the following invocation:

With the flaming trident of Lucifer
I open the gates to the Void,
And I invoke the Shadow Companion to manifest and
enter my temple of flesh!

In the name of the Dragon,
I invoke Lucifer, the Dark God of Man,
He who guides the soul through the gates of the Night, Lord of the cross-
roads who shows the way to
knowledge and wisdom,
Spirit of trickery and mischief who leads astray the false and those driven
by greed and malice,
Friend and companion in joy and misery
who embraces the soul in sorrow and grief,
Lord of truth and lies,
Enemy of hypocrisy and ignorance,
He who tempts mankind with the pleasures of the world
And ignites the Flame of Desire in the heart of man! Meet me at the cross-
roads of the worlds,
And open the way to your wisdom and power!
Come forth to this temple of flesh,
So that I may become as one with you,

The vessel and living manifestation of the Lord of the
Night! In nomine Draconis!
Ho Drakon Ho Megas!

These words can also be personal and spontaneous - feel free to modify the incantations and adjust them to your personal needs. Focus on Lucifer's Current of shadow and flames entering the room and his energy rising within your body, unlocking the gateways of the mind. His eyes are your eyes. His senses are your senses. His force is yours to command and direct. At the same time, visualize that the room in which the ritual takes place exists at the crossroads of worlds and dimensions. From here you can see everything and travel everywhere. You can reach your target as if this person was standing in front of you. And you can see the fearsome Vortex of Fire in the center of the Void, its powers within your grasp.

When you feel ready to continue the ritual, request the powers of the five sigils:

I AM LUCIFER.
THE FALSE SHALL BURN IN MY
PIT OF DESTRUCTION."

With my blood, the Blood of the Dragon,
Primal Source of All Creation,
I open the Vortex of Fire
And I request the five powers of the Shadow Companion,
The five keys to the Pit of Destruction.

Anoint now the first sigil with your blood - representing the power of the Eye. When this is done, speak the following words:

In the name of Lucifer,
I request the power of the Eye,
So that my prey cannot hide before my flaming sight.

Envision that the sigil becomes alive, charged and activated with your life substance, the Blood of Lucifer. Visualize it glowing and pulsating with the fiery Draconian force. It is now a gateway to the Void and a key to the pit of fire.

THE FIRST SIGIL

*Then repeat the same procedure with the second sigil -
representing the power of the Sickle. This time speak
the following words:
In the name of Lucifer,
I request the power of the Sickle,
To harvest the justice that is due for
what my enemy has done.*

THE SECOND SIGIL

Proceed as with the previous sigil. Then repeat the same procedure with the third - representing the power of the Horns. This time speak the following words:

*In the name of Lucifer,
I request the power of the Horns,
To pierce barriers and defenses around my victim.*

THE THIRD SIGIL

Again, proceed as with the previous sigil. Then repeat the same procedure with the fourth - representing the power of the Scythes. Speak the following words:

In the name of Lucifer,
I request the
power of the Scythes,
To cut all that makes my prey strong and
gives meaning to his/her life.

THE FOURTH SIGIL

Proceed and repeat the same procedure with the fifth. It represents the power of the Skull. Speak these words:

In the name of Lucifer,
I request the power of the Skull,
So that all that is left of my enemy shall be the
naked bones when my Will is fulfilled

THE FIFTH SIGIL

Proceed with the same visualization as with previous sigils. Then continue with the words:

In the name of Lucifer,
I open the Vortex of Fire around (the name of your target),
And I curse you to burn in my Pit of Destruction,
So that you may receive what you deserve,
And never again enter my life or cross my way.

All five keys are activated now and the five powers of the Shadow Companion are now yours to command. Focus for a moment on how it feels to have the power of Lucifer, primal force with which you can easily destroy your target. There are no barriers that could stop you and your victim is standing before you, stripped of all protections and defenseless. Envision now a fiery vortex arising from the five gateways to the pit and swirling widdershins around your target, leaving your victim isolated, terrified and despaired. Enjoy this feeling - the formula will work only if your determination is strong enough and your desire is free from restraints, powered up by the sense of justice that is due for the actions of your target. Finally, burn the sympathetic link to your victim, visualizing that the person is consumed by the flaming vortex and drawn into the pit of everlasting fire. At this moment you must feel that what is happening is definite and final, and the person is permanently removed from your life.

Close the working with the words:

And so it is done! In nomine Draconis,
Ho Ophis Ho Archaios,
Ho Drakon Ho Megas! ✦

Melek Rsh Nvth IX, *The Entrance ov The Inner Temple*

Daäth, this Death Where Dying Lies Dead

Kabultiloa Zamradiel

IN popular imagination, magic(k) and the occult are associated with conjuring demonic entities and "supernatural" powers, like killing one's enemy from a distance with a curse or, alternatively, healing one's loved ones with a power more direct and more certain than prayer. However, whether it be the ability and desire to change "personalities" and "paradigms" like clothes espoused by the chaos mages or the discovering of one's True Will so precious to the Thelemites, the true power of the occult lies in its ability to enable us to cause personal change within ourselves. Any experienced practitioner of the occult is well aware that those changes that magickal practice bring, that we gear so many rituals towards, are of a far different nature than the superficial and feel-good, self-help changes of most modern psychology. Perhaps Jung and some of his followers were onto deeper, occult truths, but most of those insights have been forgotten or ignored by the mass of society in favor of sugar-coated fast solutions to mundane problems of the self and dousing any unfavorable emotions with massive floods of psychoactive medications, a process that alters brain chemistry in unpredictable, undesirable, and far-reaching ways.

I intend to demonstrate that working with the Qliphoth, often viewed variably as either the "Shells" of failures with the emanations of the Qabalistic Tree of Life or as the Shadow Side of the same Tree, can be one of the most profound inner changes available to the contemporary occultist. Most of my personal leanings and studies with the Qliphoth are based in the works of British occultist Kenneth Grant, a man responsible for taking Aleister Crowley's work to completely unexpected places, a vocation that has carned the ire of many traditional Thelemites and resulted in them declaring Grant a heretic or even an apostate.

Nothing here, not my thoughts or the ritual I will include, should be taken as some kind of Gospel. I intend to point readers in directions that I feel contain valuable avenues of exploration, without any dogma. If anyone feels that what I write contains a seed of truth that they desire to take in an entirely different manner than I present here, I welcome the creative spirit in such a venture and invite such pioneers to report any results they may achieve to me at my Facebook Kabultiloa Zamradiel author page, if they wish.

Perhaps a fruitful discussion could be entered into, as I feel the exploration of the Qliphoth presents us with possibly the most promising opportunities for advancing occult knowledge and wisdom far into this twenty-first century. Rather than spend a great deal of time discussing the specific paths and Qlipha in the Nightside Tree, I intend to present the reasoning for piercing the Veil or immersing oneself in The Abyss, Daäth, the door of entry to the entire Nightside Tree, and one of the deepest self-initiations one can undergo. The Thelemite seeks to "cross" this Abyss, to discover and be guided by the Holy Guardian Angel and reach the Supernal Triad of the Dayside Tree of Life, eventually to merge oneself with the Godhead. Qliphothic explorations tend to be of a very different nature, bringing up atavisms, and allowing one's entire lesser and mundane ego to be annihilated, so that by discovering the fruits of the Tree some equate with the Tree of the Knowledge of Good and Evil mentioned in the Bible, one's actual Self can be re-assembled, completely retooled, and rise from the ashes of the false self previously dismantled by the Soulstorms of Daäth, and a new and true Ego born from the remains of that purely earthly previous ego. These explorers seek something truly Left Hand Path, in opposition to the total annihilation of any individuality in the Heart of "God." Instead, we realize the falsehood of duality, the illusion of self-hood as understood by worldly men and women, opens us up to a different kind of Union with the Divine where our True Self-hood is allowed to blaze forth for the first time in, possibly, endless incarnations, and reveal that we, too, are indeed Gods.

What I wish to focus on are the results that have occurred to one individual who walked, not past and beyond, but through the fires and floods of Daäth; that individual being myself. I will write nothing here that I have not personally experienced; take that as you will. As one may intuit quite easily, the results from crossing the Abyss and the results of entering the Abyss are vastly different. He or she who gladly enters the Abyss can expect many things to occur, few of them what the average mortal would consider "pleasant."

Atavisms and past obsessions may arise, sometime in overwhelming ways. This may be compared quite readily to certain incidents of demonic possession throughout the ages. The emotional states brought up by the Abyss experience are to normal emotions what nuclear weapons are to the bow and arrow. The most wrathful fury one has experienced in one's previous life is but a flickering candle compared to the conflagration that even a minor annoyance brings in the devastation of work with the Abyss. Likewise, joy, a seeming bliss from one's mundane existence is the haziest reflection of a passing smile after taking this enormous step.

If you have ever experienced anything so ecstatic or traumatic that who you thought you were was entirely burned away in an instant, you have some idea of one possible effect from the dive into the Abyss. And yet, that entirety of yourself is never completely destroyed by such an overwhelming experience. Instead, in much the same way a drill sergeant is trained to break down cadets piece-by-piece so that their previous identities are gone and can be replaced by the unquestioning killing machines that governments desire their soldiers to be, the Abyss will also take a systematic approach.

Whatever remains after the firestorm of initial destruction is broken down, brick-by-brick, until nothing remains. Regardless of whether you consciously work with the Qliphoth after attempting to pierce Daäth's veil or not, the effects of the Abyss will remain and, unless you attempt to find your more Divine Self in the Tunnels of Set and the individual Qlipha, to rebuild your being into True Being by penetrating further into the Mysteries, the aftershocks of the Daäth experience could very easily lead to madness or death. Liken it to aborting a very real and living fetus in a back alley, with crude instruments. Perhaps it will be successful, but it may have devastating and unintended consequences to abort such an overwhelming process after one's own personal decision to begin it, particularly if the "abortion" is undertaken carelessly. So heed this warning and do not attempt this ritual unless certain of your commitment to see it through.

The ritual included here is designed merely as a preliminary initiation, a way to open the door and step through to the Beyond. What you do beyond that is entirely up to each individual practitioner. Explore the Tunnels of Set in any manner that seems prudent to you, or make contact with the rulers of the Qlipha. Learn forbidden knowledge, and perform forbidden acts, both in the ritual chamber and outside. This is a free-form process, in my system, where freedom of choice is valued over a rigid approach and any claims to absolute truth that must not be deviated from are cast aside in favor of a more hands-on approach to creating and discovering one's personal Truth.

Kick open the door with courage and walk through with pride and confidence, if you are prepared to let go of a weak and false identity to discover who you truly are and become the entity that has guided you ever onward from within, the Inner Master you were always destined to be. Just be certain of one thing: can you endure the consequences of never again being the limited, tiny creature you thought made up your entire being?

Ritual Initiation of Penetrating the Veil of Daäth

Begin standing Point north with dagger: Malkuth, Lilith, Typhon, Mother and Father of all, guide me and guard me.
Counterclockwise, point northwest:

I invoke you, I invite you to join me wrathful Abaddon.

West: Yesod, Gamaliel, Leviathan, Lord of the Deep Abyss, guide and guard me.
Southwest

I invoke you, I invite you to join me, beloved bride Lilith.

South: Tiphereth, Tageriron, Lucifer, beautiful Lightbringer, guide me and guard me.
Southeast

I invoke you, I invite you to join me, brother to all who walk the Nightside, Cain.

East:

Daäth, Abyss of Ego death, Samael, the poison of God, guide me and guard me.

Northeast:

I invoke you, I invite you to join me, sister of the Qliphothic witches and daughter of Machaloth, Aggereth.

Above one's head:

Kether, Thaumiel, Adonai Satan, King Moloch, guide me and guard me.

Center and downwards:

I invoke you, I invite you to join me, my innermost Qliphothic self in darkness.

And in the 11th place, Ain, and my trans-cosmic self, the All and Nothing within and without, beyond all manifestation and unmanifestation, awaken me to Truth, and guide me the 33 ways of the Qliphoth, through all the Nightside Tree, and finally to the trans-cosmic Beyond, where I AM WHO AM.

Now assume Dragon Asana.

Hold aloft to the altar a large glass of wine.

To Samael and Lilith, in an external and internal embrace, let this cup, the cup of Naamah's first lunar cycle, derange my senses, so this mundane world is peeled away and the Abyss always behind it is revealed.

Drink wine as fast as possible.

Raise the Serpent to the Visuddha Chakra while chanting 78 times:

Nuit must appear to become Hadit.

After:

Guardians and watchers of the Sitra Achra, dragons beyond cosmos, witness this, the sacrifice of my ego, and let the Spectral Hyena, the Beast wedded to my virginal soul, scavenge the bloody ruin of its shattered corpse.

Nothing survives the Abyss. (Say five times alternating with 5 repetitions of next line.)

No "Thing" survives the Abyss.

On the 11th repetition of the line, say instead:

"I" perish in the Abyss.

Through the Pylons of Heart and Mind, Life and Death, the Will, the Spirit, passes unafraid.

The mantra of piercing the veil:

Burn away Hadit, Nuit arise.

Repeat 474 times or as needed until lost in the experience of Daäth.

The Abyss should be reached by this time or even before, if the Work and the Magus are operating correctly and have been properly prepared.

Whenever the experience of Daäth occurs, simply let it happen. All mantras and thoughts will be burned away like the crutches they actually are. The Abyss is terrifying to most but it is an experience and not a "place," in the sense that one's astral temple is a place.

The death of the Ego must be lived and there is no way to control it or alter it, even if it takes hours, the time is well-spent. Interruptions are very anti-conducive to this work and this experience, so make certain there is time for this ritual to be performed in unspoiled solitude. An entire night may be required, maybe longer, maybe multiple nights and days, possibly stretching into weeks or months or longer, for the Daäth experience cannot be rushed and doesn't care if it is convenient or not. Life can be lived if it must be, but do not expect, no matter the results of this one ritual, the Abyss to let one go easily and quickly.

Do not try to compare your results to anyone else's, it is different for everyone as everyone's ego is its own unique illusion and its demise will be unique also. Have pen and paper nearby, to write or draw, especially any sigils received. If this ritual fails, use your own methods to determine when to repeat it and how often. Remember, illusion or not, the ego is smart, that is how it manages to survive so well. It resists being killed. Failure is not failure, merely a sign that one's ego is strong and must be progressively broken down. Success will happen eventually, particularly if one works on meditation and prayer in-between rituals to further weaken one's illusory "self."

Speak:

I have become more truly Me; what is false, I shed as serpent skin; I need it no more, to protect me or hinder my growth, to mold me into the world of forms and names.

On the path of the Dayside Tree, the Abyss must be crossed, and a vow is taken to see all phenomena as a dealing of God with one's soul.

Those who sit astride the Nightside Tree never leave the Abyss, for we have partaken of the deep waters and drowned. The shores we wash up on are the Tunnels of Set and the Qliphothic shells. The vow we now take is this:

Lord Satan, I see behind all phenomena to the void in manifestation. I take all appearances of this void as communications from the lords and ladies of the Sitra Achra, as new initiations into the fullness that can reside only in the non- conceptual, trans-cosmic nothingness of Ain, where I shall one day be Samael, the poison of divinity's false face. All movements of my spirit, heart, mind, and body peer behind the mask and rend the veil.

Repeat 78 times:

Hadit has died into Nuit.

I invite all beings who are present to take their leave, to go in peace, and to help me again if I call. My sacrifice is my former "self" and my worship of your Dark Eminence and the fire of my aspiration to realize my true self is as you are.

Amen.

If one recites any regular devotional prayers, now would be an appropriate time to say them. End the ritual in any manner you see fit and respectful of what you have just undertaken and its enormity. From this day forth, you are a new creature, and the mundane life is dead to you as you have found true life in death. In closing this paper, I wish to make a final point. Note closely the last line of the above instructions. "From this day forth, you are a new creature, and the mundane life is dead to you as you have found true life in death."

Death is and always has been possibly the most powerful motivating reality as well as concept in human existence. The very mention of it strikes a chord of fear in the heart of all humans. Even the bravest, on some subconscious level, live their lives in avoidance of death or, conversely, in the pursuit of it, in a misguided attempt to control the uncontrollable. But the entry into the Nightside world makes one a praeterhuman being, no longer subject to the rules of the normal humans, and beyond them as they are beyond the lesser apes and monkeys. This is evolution of the most primordial kind, practiced for endless millennia by cultists and esoteric sages around the globe; the Left Hand Path brethren of every stripe. The inner transformation spoken of above is fundamentally this very thing: while the new praeterhuman is still subject to bodily death, death is no longer the terror it once was.

All beings may very well reincarnate, again and again, and the initiation into the Qliphothic Tree does not end either the cycle of bodily birth and death or the cycle of rebirth. But it becomes something profoundly different. The praeterhuman, after mortal death, is far more free to choose rebirth where he or she wills it and to recall events and wisdom of past lives. The Christians preach that death is a birth into Life; we live it. Part the thick, black drapery of death and realize, with full consciousness intact, the Life that awaits one past the insignificant shedding of the material form. Ever after, this new Being is in control of its destiny, something that is a dreadfully weighty responsibility for many, but we few who dare to plunge into the depths and drown there, shall find a new, distant shore where Death itself is our friend, and our guru, who teaches us that each death we experience initiates us into a deeper level of the cultus of our own spirits, where we are prepared to be responsible for ourselves and to forge our own Divinity with the wisdom reserved for those with the resolve to undergo the Abyssic Death and the Qliphothic Resurrection. ✶

Sean Woodward, *The Temple of Sat B'hai*

The Fires of Sat B'hai

Sean Woodward

0

The basis of this power is to be found in those esoteric aspects of the Cult of Shiva, which are basic to both the east and west because they can be found at the root of those ancient and awe-ful forms of esoteric Voudoo and Hindu tantrism.

—Michael Bertiaux, *Voudon Gnostic Workbook*

1. Thothip

The statues are black from the soot that has accumulated over decades of devotion, none loosened by the vibrations of the drums which fill the night air, none made brighter by the hands brushed against their extremities.

The villagers kept away from the temple except for the festival days, when the moon was full and their silhouettes could be seen dancing before the huge forms of Shiva and Hanuman. Beyond these guardians of the temple wall, in reality now little more than a pile of rocks being pulled apart by the jungle, a row of lit lanterns guided the faithful within the precinct through the worn cobbled courtyard to the inner sanctum of the temple of Sat B'hai. Here the flames of Agni burned eternal before a bronze statue of the Mother Goddess. Before these flames the priest sat on a raised platform surrounded by red and gold cushions. Straddling him, her skirts lifted high, her chest bare, his Shakti moaned as the drumming reached a crescendo.

At that moment the priest, infused with Shivite Radiations enters into the trance reserved only for the seven masters of the Cult of Shiva, his speech is slowed, his words those of the name of the god who speaks through him now, bringing forth the histories that the Shakti carefully transcribes in the curled Devanagri script in the golden Book of Perfection.

The priest continues to speak for hours as acolytes light row after row of blackened candles in the sanctum. His eyes are glazed, his stare fixed beyond the statue of the goddess as he recounts the wars in the heavens, our ancestors gazing at the vast starships crossing the skies, their forms bristling with weapons ports.

"Who wins this war papa?"

Major Warner closed the battered diary and put it inside his messenger bag, tucking the blanket tight, bidding his son goodnight.

"In the morning, we'll arrive in Sikha Province and I'll show you who won" promised the Major.

The clatter of the train's wheels echoes the drums that once filled the night air and fills his memories still.

2. Athoora

As his son slept Major Warner re-assembled his pistol one more time, spinning the barrel and feeling its weight as both a comfort and a curse. It had been a lifetime since he had last journeyed to Allahabad in the Sikha Province. He had commanded over a hundred men of the 39th then, most of them from the Maharaja's elite troops in the north. The humidity of the south forever plagued them but he knew he could not enter the temple with local men and he was determined not to leave without securing the golden book for Her Majesty.

The Major and the men of the 39th Foot Regiment had arrived on the day of the full moon and made their camp on the edge of the jungle, where it gave way to the arid plains and later the desert dunes. He hoped the climate would put his men in a better frame of mind, tired as they were of the long march. Today, with the coming of the train he could be in the province in mere hours.

On that moonlit night he had wished for such a speedy deployment of re-enforcements but it was not to be. The multitude of people that ringed the temple seemed far greater than the size of the villages that his scouts had reported. Wave after wave of them raged against their rifles and line after line fell until there was no longer the sound of drumming, but that of bullets passing into bodies.

It pained him that such bloodshed was required but he knew they would not easily give up the temple or its golden book within. Finally, he had given the order to cease fire. The bodies, black and surrounded by pools of red were piled up where they had fallen, man upon man. He gathered a guard of three of his most trusted men and as he ordered the remainder to secure the perimeter against further counter attack. He marched through the entrance, past the towering blackened statues of their gods which had watched the carnage without action.

With the drums silenced and the moonlit shadows long upon the cobbles an eerie silence had fallen upon the temple. Even the background chatter of the jungle had fallen silent. The Major walked slowly. His informant had spoken of traps within the temple, silent spikes that would shred the unwary. His Lieutenant was approaching the sanctum entrance before him.

"No!" he shouted as the cobbles beneath Lieutenant Marshall's feet gave way under his weight and dropped him into a pit, a tall spike skewering his twitching body. He watched aghast, unable to do anything to help the man. As he looked into his tormented eyes and the Lieutenant nodded, Major Warner fired a single revolver shot into his forehead.

It was one more price to be paid for the golden book, whose legends had spoken of a curse on any who would remove it from the temple. The Major was not concerned with such superstitions however and carried on, towards the east of the sanctum where he found another entrance, this one devoid of traps.

He motioned for the other soldier to remain outside and bent to pass through the low opening as he moved inside the sanctum. He swept aside highly decorated curtains with one hand whilst keeping the other firmly on his revolver. Through the darkness he could see a low line of candles flickering on an altar top. Before it a dark haired woman was naked astride the robed and hooded priest of Shiva. To his side the golden book glowed in the dim light. What was this debauchery he wondered? How had they continued their copulation in the midst of all the gunfire and loss of life? They both seemed oblivious to his presence. The priest was muttering words in a dialect he did not understand. Within a moment his words turned to English.

"I call upon the Hosts of Hanuman, bring destruction down on our enemies".

The Major wanted to tell him it was too late for that but remained silent. Suddenly he noticed that the roof of the sanctum was open to the elements and he could make out stars in the sky overhead. One of them seemed to grow in both intensity and size until it was bigger than the opening, pushing the very air down upon them.

"What is this devilry?" demanded the Major.

"You have defiled the sanctuary of Shiva, the very heart of Sat B'hai! The gods will curse you for all time."

The woman clung to the priest as he stood, arms stretched skywards.

"Leave Saini, leave now I command it!"

The woman ran past the Major, past the soldier outside and on into the jungle. She stopped only to watch the fireballs that fell, one after another from the huge bristling silver ship that hung in the sky above the temple, causing the rocks to burn hot.

The vibrations of the impacts shook the sanctum, throwing the Major to the floor. As he got to his feet, the priest grabbed the golden book and pulled aside a curtain revealing a wall. It seemed to be a doorway framed in Egyptian hieroglyphics, totally out of place. As he aimed his revolver at the priest the man's body passed through the stone and was gone. The Major holstered his revolver and ran after him, towards the wall of stone.

The soldiers began falling back from the temple walls as soon as the huge silver ship began descending from the skies. It was unlike anything they had ever seen and clearly they could not hope to hold the temple against its array of weapons pointing down at them. As they retreated towards their camp they watched the further onslaught of fireballs which rained down until the stones were glowing orange and the great towering statues began to melt into black pools. Heat radiated from the structures and through the haze they could see the sanctum at the heart of the courtyard fall in on itself, its great stone blocks melting into one another, the Major lost to them.

3. Kiatier

It took several moments for the Major's eyes to adjust to the bright light and his stomach to settle from the nausea he felt building up. He was standing in another chamber of sorts, its black walls covered in a matrix of silver lines and flashing lightning. Before him a desk made of many cubes of different heights and sizes pulsated with the flashes, the squares rising and falling in unison. On its surface rested the golden book. From its vicinity an inhuman, metallic voice spoke.

"I am Time Past, from whose records you may learn to guide your steps aright. I am Time Present, during which alone the knowledge so gained may be utilised. I am Time that is to come, whose secrets no man may reveal. I am Him from whom time flows, the source of light, the Lord of the Perfect Circle, the Apex , Secret Chief, Qube of the Architects of Orion." He took the golden book and dropped it inside his messenger bag, re-arranging its strap across his body to take the extra weight.

To his right the black wall dimmed and he could see the familiar outline of a door, with a large brass handle. He grasped it, felt it turn and pushed the door open. Before him the sun streamed across a grassy field, dew fresh upon the shoots. He took a breath and stepped out. The door slammed behind him and he saw that the hieroglyphic covered door was now one side of a four sided Egyptian building, surrounded by gravestones poking through the tall grasses.

Major Warner continued to walk ahead, through the wild flowers until he found the entrance to the graveyard and the busy Brompton high street outside. The sight that met his eyes both confounded and delighted him for all about were moving mechanical vehicles and people dressed in a style unknown in any land he had travelled. As he looked at the style of the lampposts, no longer fitted for gas, he knew that he walked in a London lost in time.

4. Cothiid

In the years that followed he had returned to the mausoleum in Brompton cemetery, attempting once more to open its door. No matter the conjunction of stars, the season or the method, he had been unable to re-open it.

The London he discovered was very different from the one he had known. Many of the old buildings still stood in The Mall and the Thames, except for some minor alterations near Embankment remained much as he remembered it. What was so different was the attire and manner of its inhabitants. Although he had found work in the Ministry he still found the ways of its people stranger than even the tribes he had encountered in the heart of the dark continent.

And so the 1950s turned to the 1960s and he no longer cared about his original mission to secure the golden book for Queen and country, did not even look to decipher its Devanagri script. Instead he carefully separated the solid gold covers and with the money they brought was able to secure rooms at the end of Cecil Court.

What he did notice however was that the passing of years seemed to have little effect on his own appearance, for he seemed to have aged not a day since he first stepped out of the mausoleum.

As he climbed the steep stairs he watched his reflection slide across the wall of mirrors with their silver edges behind the bar. The staircase began as rough wooden steps, well-worn with the feet of a select few. As he climbed, first red carpet and then gold edged steps met his feet. A brother had explained how this was an allegory for the probationers of the stairway to the heavens, to the Apex. It would remind them on every visit of their own climb from the roughhewn world to that of illumination and indeed, even now it did for Major Warner. He found great comfort in the ritual that met him in this place, for its form had not changed in the passing years and remained as he had remembered it as an Entered Apprentice himself. As the Lodge had retained its records from the late 1800s, he was able to claim himself as a distant relative and be put forward for entrance.

As he folded his black master's apron and carefully placed it in his briefcase, Jameson approached him.

"Warner, I'm glad I caught you man! Listen, I've been doing some research into one of our rites and I think your great grandfather had something to do with it."

Major Warner listened, curious if it was his older self the young man referred to.

"The campaign in Sikha Province, India! Didn't you mention he'd been there with the 39th?" asked Jameson.

"I think you'll find he led the 39th" said Major Warner, raising an eyebrow.

"Well, look at this then" said Jameson, pulling a photocopy of an old Times article from his own brown leather briefcase.

It was a report on the loss of the 39th in the jungles of Sikha Province in the summer of 1895 near the village of Allahabad.

"Yes," said Major Warner, "my namesake led that campaign".

"Well, don't you see man! Allahabad is the name of the place that one of the seven monks of the Oriental Order of Sat B'hai came from. Someone miss-translated it as Prag or Prague and it's true the Order's golden Book of Perfection was last seen in that city, but don't you see what this means man?"

Major Warner remained quiet. He knew perfectly well that the rumours of the golden book in the city of the alchemists was just that, rumour.

"So what does it mean Jameson?" Major Warner was brushing the lint from his dark trousers, taking care not to touch the red band which rain down their side.

"Perhaps your great grandfather found something there! I have a friend, more an occultist than a brother on the square, but he is convinced that there is a network of portals, one of them being in Allahabad."

"What kind of portals?"

"Well, he's been studying the history of Brompton cemetery."

Major Warner paused in the cleaning of his trousers. He had not thought of that place for many years, had grown resigned to his leap into this new world.

"He thinks. Well, this is going to sound crazy man, but he thinks there is a time machine there."

Major Warner laughed.

"You're right Jameson, I do think it's crazy. Wouldn't someone have noticed such a thing? Mr. Hartnell perhaps?"

Jameson too smiled at that but did not stay that way for long.

"Look, all I'm saying is, do you have any old family mementos from your great grandfather? An old book filled with Sanskrit pages, gold ones perhaps?

This wasn't the first time in the last five decades that the events of 1895 had returned to haunt Major Warner. He had channeled much of the destructive power he saw released that night into the designs of his own weapons for the Ministry. He had never seen a use for the golden book or the mausoleum that remained shut to him.

"So, will you look for me?" asked an adamant Jameson.

"Sure" said Major Warner, trying to adopt some of the new words he learned in this time "I'll look".

It was whilst leaving the Historicus Lodge the following Friday evening that Major Warner met his future wife. The Lodge met on the last Friday of the month in the upstairs rooms of The Salisbury pub, a stone's throw from his rooms, theatreland and the many bedsits occupied by drama students, hoping for opportunity to call. Hannah had heard that Elizabeth Taylor often visited the pub and so talked her way into a job as a barmaid. He wondered how he had not noticed her before, the shock of raven hair, the emerald eyes. It took more courage to speak to her than it had to stand off a Bengali tiger but somehow he knew he would regret it forever if he did not. At first she found his old fashioned ways somewhat strange. He had after all, been transported into another century, into other days. It seemed she shared many of his interests and slowly he found himself warming to the stage world she inhabited, the pair walking through rain drenched streets back to his rooms.

Within the year they were married and within the next their son was born. As he grew older the Major, now plain Sam Warner continued to work on his weapons inventions for the Ministry and on a promise that one day he would return to Sikha Province, take his son to the temple consumed by the fires of Sat B'hai.

5. Arteyo

It was a rainy Sunday evening in 1972 when the knock came to Major Warner's rooms. His wife was out with friends and so he slowly rose to his feet from his favourite armchair and made his way to the doors. He peered through the spy-hole. It was an ingenious method of determining one's caller and saw the rounded red face of Jameson standing in the corridor outside.

"Come in brother" said Major Warner opening the door. Jameson stood before him, a little greyer in his hair, a little stopped, but as bright eyed as ever. He had recently risen to Worshipful Master and it was said he would soon become the master of Historicus Lodge itself.

"Do you remember our chat about Allahabad all those years ago?" Jameson asked moving to the settee to which Major Warner had motioned.

"A little yes"

Major Warner poured a brandy and passed one to Jameson, returning to his armchair.

"My friend acquired these from the British Museum."

He took a sheaf of photocopies from his now greatly worn briefcase. They showed the front of the Book of Perfection, covered in the interlocking patterns of the Devanagri script.

"He's had it translated. It includes a prayer to Hanuman to bring down fire from the heavens on any who would defile its home. There is one passage, The Apex, an Invocation of Opening. Matherson translated it. He believes it's for the portal."

At first Major Warner didn't see any reason to be interested in Jameson's ongoing obsession but then he realised that the invocation could be the key to opening the mausoleum that had stood silent all these years in the cemetery. He had grown accustomed to his new life, to his wife, to their child. He even liked his in-laws with whom his son was staying this weekend in the country. If he admitted it, he even liked his job at the Ministry.

"I've organized an expedition to Allahabad! We can fly to India next month before the rainy season starts. Bring your family of course! From Deli we can travel south, take the train to Allahabad."

"Why?" asked Major Warner. "Why would you want to do that?"

"Aren't you curious, man? What happened to the 39th and your great grandfather? What became of the golden book? What if there is some kind of time portal there?"

"This is no crazier than before Jameson!"

James looked directly at the Major. "No crazier than you Warner"

"What do you mean?"

"You think we haven't noticed, man? You haven't aged a day since we first met in the Lodge! He isn't just your namesake is he? You're Major Samuel Warner of the 39th!"

"This is absurd!"

"Then come with me, you've nothing to lose." "Well, only my family and career."

"The Ministry are bankrolling this expedition Samuel. Your ageing isn't the only thing we noticed. Your weapons designs are light years ahead of anything we or the Russians have been working on. Did you get your inspiration there?"

Major Warner took a slow long drink of his brandy before speaking. He had always said he would take his son there, maybe now was the time.

"OK. I never thought you'd be the one to see through my lies Jameson. One thing though. Hannah is to know nothing of the truth."

"Fine. Well then, its sorted man. Get packed, we leave for the temple of Sat B'hai on the first."

6. Stemere

Major Warner stood in Brompton cemetery, feet wet in the grass, the words of The Apex memorized. He knew he was taking a big risk, especially before the expedition with Jameson, but he had to know if this would work, if he could return to his own time.

As the final words left his lips a handle appeared in the stonework of the mausoleum and stepping forward he slowly turned it until he felt the stonework move ajar under his touch.

The interior was much as he remembered it, as untouched by the years as he was. He heard the familiar raspy greeting.

"I am Time Past, from whose records you may learn to guide your steps aright. I am Time Present, during which alone the knowledge so gained may be utilised. I am Time that is to come."

"Take me back" said Major Warner, hoping it would be enough. Suddenly he felt that stomach wrenching sensation and the door handle reform once more on the inside of the mausoleum.

As he tried to step out he found himself suddenly detached from his body. It was the strangest feeling. One moment he was standing inside the mausoleum, the next he was sitting before the shrine to the Mother Goddess, wrapped in robes, a woman astride him. He looked into her face and saw Hannah before him. He watched himself, in uniform enter the chamber, heard the dying gunshots outside.

He spoke words in English, a language very familiar to him.

"I call upon the Hosts of Hanuman, bring destruction down on our enemies".

He knew in that instant that he must run from this place, take the Book of Perfection with him, for without it he would not be able to incant The Apex. He saw himself standing bewildered, knew he was about to raise the revolver and fire. He grabbed the golden book and ran into the wall, knowing he was about to be followed by himself.

He returned in that moment to his body with a jolt of awakening. A black wall, covered in micro Bio-Zothyrian circuitry rising between him and the other him, cubes pulsating up and down as the machine crossed the centuries, inducing another bout of stomach wrenching pain.

When he left the mausoleum there was just himself. He hoped he would return to the same time, to his new family, to the days before the expedition. He was not disappointed.

7. Mushuaem

In the decades since coming to what he thought of as New London, the Major had never ceased to be amazed at the size of the airplanes available as transportation. They still unsettled him, no matter the attention of the BOAC crew or the boisterous Jameson. The overnight sleeper train that left Delhi was more to his liking.

As Major Warner returned to the dining carriage from tucking his son in bed, Hannah glanced up at him.

"Yes, he's asleep. Not before I read his great grandfather's diary again though".

Jameson looked up, his thoughts easily betrayed.

"It must be great to be getting in touch with your family history like this" he said instead.

"Yeah" said Major Warner, "I can't wait".

After they returned to their own bunks across from their son, Hannah took off her earrings and turned to him, whispering. "Don't you think that was a bit mean Sam? Jameson has helped so much in bringing us here."

"There's more to this than you know love".

She smiled "You mean the Fires of Sat B'hai ?"

He looked at her shocked.

"Oh, and you can call me Saini now my darling. You weren't the only one to memorize The Apex!"

As the dunescape outside the window turned to jungle, Major Samuel Warner, monk of Sat B'hai, Arch Minister of the Circle of Perfection, thought he heard the rising beat of drums amidst the repeating clatter of the train, travelling through the black soot night. ✴

Melek Rsh Nvth IX, *Lunar Sigil*

Tiamat to Dagon

THE RAGING SEAS OF DA'ATH

S. Connolly

I HEAR it time and time again. "One must suffer, their world ripped apart, their guts split open and thrown to the great beast before one can experience gnosis." My response is always -- that's not necessarily true. I think a lot of the problem is that modern parents don't teach their children coping skills or decision making skills – and both of these come in REALLY handy when you're pathworking your way through Da'ath, or doing any life altering magick.

First let's look at what gnosis actually is. I'm not going to puke up a bunch of pretty metaphors for you here. Let's be direct and up front shall we?

Gnosis is the common Greek noun for knowledge. In many religions and spiritual paths, gnosis generally signifies a spiritual knowledge, some kind of mystical enlightenment, or merely "insight".

You know what also teaches insight and knowledge? Life experience. Good, old fashioned, life experience. But that doesn't necessarily mean those with the harder life are more experienced or more enlightened either. I've met people for whom every life tragedy turns their Facebook wall into a permanent lament about how hard life is, just so they can get attention and pity. They never learn anything as they swing wildly from one bad turn to the next, and each time the same situation happens to them again and again, they still react the same exact way they reacted the first time it happened. Some people are just very reactive and they make bad life choices, and never learn from those poor choices because they keep making the same choices over and over again.

I've also met people for whom every life obstacle and tragedy is met with a brave face, silence, and grace. Then there are those who do make a poor choice, learn from it, and steadily their life improves as they learn to make good choices.

Finally, there are people who, sometimes by their upbringing or their nature (or a combination of both) just make well informed choices. They may not always be the right choices, but more often than not, these people turn the wrong choices into something positive.

This is why I contend that not everyone must have their lives destroyed as they traverse Da'ath on their way to gnosis. There are three major reasons why this is the case.

1. Not all suffering is created equally.

Some people suffer more deeply than others, especially if they lack coping skills or are emotionally vulnerable. Two different people could face the death of a parent, and one will find it a debilitating, life altering experience, and the second person might simply be melancholy. Perhaps the first person was close to the parent who died, and the second wasn't. Or perhaps the first was still dependent on the parent whereas the second, while he loved his parent, had moved on and built his own life. Each individual person's circumstances, personality, and ability to cope with difficulties actually dictates how much he/she suffers. This brings up two very direct points I'd like to make here.

- Not everyone will need to have their lives destroyed and rebuilt to reach gnosis.

- What one person finds difficult to navigate another will not. Many factors apply.

2. Emotional intelligence plays a big role.

Some people allow their emotions to dictate their actions where others are good at observing their emotions and choosing which emotions to react to.

✦ More emotionally reactive people suffer more and may have a more difficult time coping with difficult situations.

✦ Mentally imbalanced people and those who suffer psychological illnesses may have a more difficult time coping with difficult situations.

✶ Emotionally stable people may suffer less.

✶ Pragmatic people may suffer less.

3. Each Magician is unique & different.

This is really what it comes down to.

✶ As above, so below. As each spirit/Daemon/god-form has its own personality, correspondences, and purpose (things which they preside over), so do magicians. Each of us has a unique personality, talents, fears, likes, dislikes, etc... This means that those who fear loss of something may be more reactive than someone who isn't. Kind of like people who are afraid of spiders might completely flip out in the presence of a spider, whereas someone who doesn't suffer from arachnophobia won't react in the same way.

✶ Just because one person needs to suffer to reach a certain point of ascension, another may not. Some people need to walk into the brick wall a few times before they learn they need to find a gate. Some people hone in on the gate right away and ignore the wall.

✶ No path is the same and no one will tread the same path as someone else. Just because one person's spiritual path took them through a rough seven years where they were broke and living on the street, doesn't mean everyone will have this same experience or NEED this same experience to teach them a life lesson. We all need different things and life has a tendency to give us what we need. Even the bad stuff.

All of this said, I contend that each magician has the power to control, to some degree, how they weather life's obstacles by controlling how they react and by improving their emotional intelligence. I believe each of us can take our lives from Tiamat, a place of chaos, to Dagon, a place of balance and emotional tranquility with two life skills. The first skill is mindfulness. The second skill is learning to make good decisions through foresight and planning.

Learning Mindfulness

We learn mindfulness by being fully present in the here and now. The practices of meditation and yoga, and even various martial arts, teach being present. I'm not saying you need to pick up yoga or karate, of course. Let's just start with some simple meditation.

Meditation is the staple of any successful magickal practice and every magician should have a strong, daily meditation practice. Just a quick hint here -- this is, ultimately, what a lot of modern grimoires teach: How to be stronger, better, enlightened and more fulfilled individuals through a strong meditation practice. Through meditation magicians learn both mindfulness and to really examine the self. Because, as it was writ on the temple walls of ancient Egypt: "Man Know Thyself, and Thou Shalt Know the Gods."

I often hear time and time again, "I just can't sit still for that long," or "My mind won't stop racing. I just don't have the focus for meditation." Well, it's no wonder. In this world of constant electronic stimuli and the societal expectations of being highly social and constantly on the go, so many people suffer a short attention span. Learning to turn off our televisions, radios, computers, tablets and smart phones is definitely the first step here. All of this external stimuli feeds Tiamat.

In order to calm the chaos, we need to identify those things that create it and remove their influence, even for a short time. Maybe in your case it's your environment. Perhaps you have noisy roommates or your kids won't stop pestering you. The key is to work your meditation into a time when the environment is quiet and calm and free of distraction.

Start with 10 minutes a day. Just sit quietly in a quiet room and breathe. Sure, your mind is going to keep chugging along spitting out reminders, ideas, feelings, etc... The point of this meditation isn't to completely empty your head or silence yourself, it's about learning to be present – in your body – in the moment. Every time your mind starts wandering, focus on your breath. Note how your hands feel. Your legs. Your stomach. Concentrate on deep, cleansing, measured breaths. As thoughts enter your mind, don't allow yourself to react to them. Just observe. Imagine yourself a spectator, watching each thought as it passes through without judgement or worry.

It may seem hard at first because so many thoughts conjure emotional and/or physical responses, but with daily practice, slowly working yourself up to twenty minutes a day, within a few months you'll find the practice of mindful meditation can be a rather eye-opening and stress relieving exercise. This state of mindful meditation, when done properly, will make you feel calm and collected. If you do it right you will start recognizing thought patterns, emotional responses, and then you can begin analyzing why you think, feel, and do the things you do. This is Dagon. Dagon is the serpent that can traverse the turbulent ocean of emotional response, but who has his feet firmly planted on dry ground. Regardless what comes, Dagon is adaptable.

Tiamat, on the other hand, spirals out of control into chaos, allowing any little thing the power to derail the magician. So once you learn mindful meditation, you know how to get Tiamat's undivided attention, helping you to first, rein in the chaos. Next, you need to learn how to take chaos (Tiamat) and direct it into something both controlled and productive (Dagon).

Making Good Decisions with Foresight & Planning

Life, by its very nature, is chaotic. We cannot control every little thing thrown at us. We can't control things outside our control, like the weather, or how someone else behaves, or death. However – we do have control over a few things at all times, and when we maintain control over these things, we can literally transform Tiamat to Dagon, and in turn– create the lives we want without all the chaos. The things we have control over:

1. How we react to other people and situations. How we react to anything is a CHOICE.
2. How we view our circumstances and our attitude toward it. You can choose to be a victim of your circumstance, or the master of it. It's either, "Why does this shit always happen to me?" or "Shit happens. Now how can I turn this situation into something beneficial?"
3. What actions we take to better our lives. Some people, for example, always find themselves in bad relationships. If you can find the pattern, you can stop it, and you don't have to repeat it. Repeating actions or the poor decisions that make our lives more difficult is a choice.

So how do we learn to make better decisions? First – by being mindful. Instead of being spirited away by our emotional responses when life throws us a situation outside our control, we observe the situation first. We gauge our emotional response, ask ourselves why we're feeling that way, then we weigh our choices carefully based on projected outcomes. In some instances, this may require more consideration than mere mindfulness. When a choice has the potential to make or break us, it's best considered diplomatically.

Grab a piece of paper. Write down all the possible choices you have in the situation. Then for each choice, write down the pros and cons and outline possible outcomes. Now, for some of you, likely those of you with strong imaginations, this will come naturally. If you quit your job on the fly, it might piss off a few people, and leave you without money to pay your rent, but on the upside you'll be done with the crappy job. On the other hand, if you find a new job first, THEN quit the crappy job, fewer people will be pissed off, you'll have money to pay the rent, and you'll still have the same outcome, though you might have to endure another week or two at the crappy job. Which of these two choices sounds better? If you get fired before you can quit you can either choose to drink yourself into a stupor and have a pity party with a side of "my life sucks", or you can go out that same day and start putting in applications elsewhere. All of these scenarios are choices with consequences attached. That's what life is.

Situation » Reaction/Action/Choice » Consequence.

Working magick and path-working our way to gnosis works much the same way. We perform magick as a catalyst to change. This change often manifests as situations in life that spur us to react. Each time we react, there is a consequence. So, if in life we continually make the wrong choices, or react without thinking of the consequences, we will carry this over into our magick, thus making our journey through the abyss that much more difficult. However, if we are mindful and careful of how we choose to react in day-to-day life, we can carry this over to our magickal work, making our journey through the abyss less turbulent.

So what kind of magician are you? One who is oblivious of Dagon and who allows Tiamat full control? Or can you befriend Tiamat and become like Dagon – ruler of your own turbulent sea? I leave you with the following Tiamat to Dagon meditation to help you navigate the raging seas of Da'ath:

Tiamat to Dagon

Sit cross-legged (or comfortably) in front of a single red or black candle and stare into the flame. Allow your thoughts to circle you. Let them spiral from you, spilling into the room, creating the chaos. When you find yourself overwhelmed, dizzy, or exhausted by these thoughts, take a deep breath and ground yourself. Feel your root chakra ground you. One by one, acknowledge each thought, each problem. Consider the options and choices presented to you with each one as it consumes you. If your emotions run high, explore why. Don't react, simply observe. Remember to breathe. Remember that the chaos in your mind and that immediate emotional reaction is Tiamat controlling you. In your observation you take control of her and direct her to Dagon. Dagon is stability within the raging sea. Do this until you have examined your most prevalent thoughts.

MODIFICATIONS

You can do this meditation before bed with the sigils of Tiamat and Dagon beneath your mattress. The meditation can be done within a ritual construct and can also be performed after Tiamat and Dagon are summoned. However, invoking the entities is NOT required as their nature will naturally surface on their own when these situations arise. This meditation, for best results, should be practiced daily for a minimum of two weeks in order for one to experience the full potential of transforming Tiamat to Dagon.

If you are navigating a sea, better to be like the serpent grounded in your natural element than by allowing the chaos to drag you under. ✦

The Scroll of
Kuf'Enkh

✠

Ho Ophis, Ho Archaios
Ho Drakon, Ho Megas

✠

Mysteries of the
Dark Sakrament

Treasures of the
Black Harvest

Mastery & the Illusion of Failure

Brian Dempsey

THERE can be no greater teacher than personal experience in the art of LHP practice. When the practitioner has valiantly met the challenges presented to them by the Gods of Old at each gateway of the Nightside, the highest aspects of Self must be heeded individually as the guardians of our dark and lonely path. The road can be illuminated for those with Light cast upon the path from success in understanding; for others the road will quickly narrow with difficulty as the darkness of the void consumes them in confusion. Here, the adept will certainly lose their way without simply pausing to reflect upon the challenges and potential changes ahead that are necessary for growth and understanding.

FAILURE—for the well-versed practitioner is a dirty seven lettered word; yet even with the courage of a thousand legions in our hearts obliterating all fears, there are those fleeting occasions where the subtle feeling of failure flickers and fades like the burning cinders of a well stoked fire.

We cast our thoughts, will, and desires out into the night from the abysmal fires deep within our souls; yet when the last word of a chant has been spoken, the last symbol drawn, or the final candle extinguished, that unwelcomed flicker of doubt ripples across the churning waters of the void almost unnoticed. It is here where the well-versed practitioner avoids the thought, stands firmly resolute, and then proceeds to disconnect from the outcome of the working. Even so, for many the thought lingers, and waits to unravel the fabric of the magician's will.

We have all doubted our own works, even if we have traveled to the very depths of hell and back—we are after all only human. If we were truly gods and had attained that highest form which we seek to create in a perfect marriage of spirit and matter, we would hurl stars at our enemies and darken suns with a single thought. Such imaginations aren't out of the realm of possibility nor impossible, only beyond our limited comprehension at this moment in time. Looming beyond the horizon, the signs of failure and defeat often portend far deeper and dramatic changes than either the hierophant or the seasoned magician would quickly recognize. As we who have chosen the path less traveled push to unravel the mysteries of the universe and to pick the endless locks of the doorways springing from the abyss, those powers beyond push back with an even greater resistance in its efforts to illuminate us further. No race was ever won by walking; neither have kingdoms been erected or destroyed with lax reservation. When you have opened the flood gates, you must swim against that current with all of your strength, and greet the setbacks with discernment and wisdom. One must reserve themselves to the fact that failure does not exist until the last breath has been expelled from the corporeal body and the task of complete refinement is fulfilled.

Setbacks along one's magickal path come in a variety of forms, and not just the failed attempts or outcomes of ritual workings. There are numerous lessons derived from the actions and situations in daily life that cast shining light upon our abysmal paths. Failed relations, insecurities, stresses, physical ailments, occupational challenges; the manifestations are endless. After all of the I's have been dotted and the last T's crossed in our daily LHP practice we will still find resistance, obstacles, detours, disappointment, and most of all failure after attaining proficiency in bending the universe to our will.

Having opened the seven lower gates of the Qliphoth and traversed the pathways of refinement within each sphere, all is right and fulfilled in the world of the adept as the universe bows to their every whim. The practitioner has conquered their fears, formed the foundations of their path, made clear the way of wisdom and knowledge, withstood the trials of the lower seven realms, and stands before the gates of Golachab with refined vigor and courage—a new creature forged in the dark flames of the Black Sun. Here, at the gateway of Golachab, pride and ego will flee from the heart and mind of the adept at the sight of what lies beyond; for if such hubris does not flee upon approaching the gates of Golachab it will most certainly be the adept's undoing. Destruction and confusion will await the adept who cannot enter here without first illuminating the vast hallways with humility, openness, discernment, and wisdom; for it will be here, in Golachab, that failure in light of a seemingly perfect and flawless practice will become pure deception, leading the overly contemptuous off the true path and into burning oblivion.

Golachab is connected to the mental plane, and is one of two spheres through which Thagirion operates. Upon this level Thagirion represents the Self and complete dark illumination. The adept has seemingly conquered the Self up to this point and brought it's conscious reigns under control, illuminated their mind with the knowledge acquired in the flames of the lower seven realms; they will now experience the two poles of the mental plane embodied within lust and suffering. It is beyond the gates of Golachab that lust becomes suffering, and suffering becomes lust. Having believed in one's heart that the magician has brought the totality of their being under control through the purifying flames of Thagirion along with the universe around them, newly formed desires, actions, and thoughts begin to manifest as rebellious and revolting fires of passion in the mind.

As the adept treads the flaming waters of Golachab, light and direction can be lost as one is distracted by the illusion of either success that is missed or failure that is acknowledged too quickly. In reality, what is most often perceived as failure in the sphere of Golachab is no more than a pivotal point of dramatic change where the magician must simply embrace that failure, pause, breathe, and attempt to look far beyond its deceiving appearance. The adept must understand by now that Light is found within the dark depths of the void as scattered rays of illumination and fragments of knowledge, often cloaked as failure and discouragement that must be gathered slowly from the fathoms of the abyss. Once recognized, these fleeting gems of growth must be assimilated into both spiritual and physical aspects of the adept's personal life to realize the opportunity that awaits. Such cases where the mind deceives the higher Self with fear and failure are doorways to much greater joy and success once acknowledged.

Here within the sphere of Golachab, thoughts and subtle notions entertained days, weeks, and even months beforehand may rear their vicious heads in the form of new obstacles, challenges, or failures even when the adept believes they have complete control of their world. Pushing the magician to the very brink of insanity, he or she may suddenly awaken and find the darkness has lifted and once again light illuminates the path before them, allowing only a brief glimpse of what lies beyond, embodied in the essence in the sphere of

Gha'Agsheblah. The trials and lessons of the lower seven spheres, having been experienced upon each practitioner's unique level of required experience, culminate into near madness and confusion within the sphere of Golachab as the adept pulls away from the mundane world around them, leaving them to question everything about the universe and themselves. Truth is unveiled, worlds are encountered that have hither to never been experienced, and the adept stands alone apart from the physical world around them; often without friends, family, any support systems or even the slightest notion of their own identity.

Amid conflicting failures and perhaps persecution from others in the face of their apparent maddened state, the adept must stand firmly in his or her concrete realizations, perceptions, and revelations. Surviving the often confusing waters of Golachab, you will now stand stripped, naked, and bare of every last mundane fragment of your former being before the gates of Gha'Agsheblah. As Inanna had shed a piece of clothing at each of the seven gates of the underworld, so must the adept shed an aspect of life that must be left behind and burned in the fires of refinement as they traverse the seven lower realms. Suspended briefly in the confusing waters of Golachab, the adept may then find their way to the sphere of Gha'Agsheblah, having overcome the illusions of lust and suffering through failure, and stand as a master over their own inner deceptions.

Within the sphere of Golachab, and outside mainstream thought, the adept may have entertained thoughts of promiscuity, rebellion, or dark desire which could have adverse effects on one's personal relationships and life, thus manifesting as failure in many ways. The inversion of all things sacred and the exploration of mental, emotional, and physical taboos may become a sudden preoccupation, leading the practitioner far from a grounding foothold in the mundane world around them. Although the mundane world around us is often a source of pain and disdain, it is important to keep a solid footing in the "illusory" world lest we become devoured by our own abyss, teetering carelessly on the edge of no return.

Mastering these thoughts with wisdom, restraint, and patience will lead the practitioner beyond the gates of Gha'Agsheblah where they may experience these darker desires in a new light of understanding and embrace them in the form of erotic mysticism which may then be enjoyed in a more balanced state of mind, as well as shared with others. What may have been perceived as thoughts or actions of failure and abstract abnormality, now understood, tamed, and properly applied can be embraced to reflect a new level of mastery and balance within the darkness of the LHP and Qliphothic journey.

Failure and the illusion that it is the complete end of all things becomes a monumental pitfall for many, even while journeying the endless realms of the abyss. While failure may come in numerous forms, true mastery comes in the ability to recognize these failures, to utilize them as lessons of growth and ascent, and to incorporate those lessons into one's personal life and path without sacrificing the sanctity of personal relationships and other life goals. Here is where the path becomes clear and the lessons realized, elevating us to the next level of understanding. Even though we have chosen the road less traveled embodied in the LHP and the darkest spheres of the Qliphoth, daily life must be embraced, cherished, and lived to its fullest. Our introspection into the depths of darkness must not separate us from the living, nor the world in which we breathe and reside. Relationships, passions, and personal endeavors in the physical world become the compass by which we navigate the dark waters of the abyss, even while applying their lessons or dabbling in their endless revelations.

In the course of our daily practice, as we dive deeply into the unknown to extract the secrets of the abyss, there are perhaps as many secrets and lessons to be learned from the physical world around us. If this were not true, the worlds of the Nightside and the physical realms would not coexist, and neither would we be brave enough to embrace the desire to function in both and master them simultaneously. We may fall to the deepest recesses of the void, losing all recognition of the external world around us, yet it is in this physical realm of matter that we live and breathe. Failure is not the end, but simply new gateways and lessons to be applied in the symbiotic existence of the objective and subjective, mind and matter. When the tempest rages over the waters of the abyss the answers often lie in the physical real that we sometimes choose to ignore. Alternately, when life in the physical realm is turned upside down, the answers often lie within the void.

The committed practitioner will not forsake their passion of the LHP for the physical realm alone, nor must they forsake the realm of matter and flesh to be consumed in the abyss. True mastery of the LHP lies not in the complete immersion of one's self into the endless realms of the abyss, but in recognizing the failures connected to both the magickal and physical realms, discerning the proper courses of change without sacrificing essential aspects of both, and balancing one's existence in them. Thus, the illusions of personal failure evaporate, the middle path is illuminated, and the road to mastery re-alized.✦

Barry James Lent, *Obligation*

𝕿iamut 𝕱usion & 𝕰iji 𝕻ossession

Anuki Gabual

𝕿HE following article is an-depth view and some practices in working with a conscious current of power and ancient existence that I have been working with for some time now. The being known as Tiamat was described by Mesopotamian Religion as the very symbol of the chaos of primordial creation, the ever destructive Goddess force of abysmal waters.

Always represented as a female this being is both a current of force that is still existing in every evolutionary form she has carried, conscious in all aspects and very grounded into the physical realm by her many existences. I have come to know her oldest version of form, the very life of the element of Water. She goes by the name Eiji in this existence and is the still pond which is very healing and exalted radiating divinity and at the same time is the very roaring tidal wave destroying and swallowing all in its wake. There's no simple way to put describing who Eiji is in comparison to Tiamut other than to call her the bane of creation that was born from her lips in the chasm of her higher self.

There's a two-part evolution in this being meaning her darkest nature is upon highest light and her highest form is ascended by darkness. The Mother Eiji can fully be harnessed in ritual by means of Inorcism and can also in the same moment be worked with as Tiamut, she can exist within the same moment as two beings. I found this to be extraordinary in my evocations. Every element has a consciousness and Eiji is that of water, Tiamut was born from her very abysmal depths it is the darkness of her water and in combination with The Mother wields limitless potential. In order to start working with Eiji and Tiamut in ritual a period of fasting and purifying needs to take effect, after the first possession you will be instilled with the Holy Waters of Eiji, her ancient current will always run through you.

You can start with using the provided Sigil. Gaze into it and induce a state of Gnosis by any preferred method; now allow water to begin dripping into the 3rd eye envision and feel it. Next you will draw on a cup made of Iron that same sigil and fill it with water, the next day eat nothing for 24 hours and only drink water. Say and direct all prayers, even emotions into the cup holding the now sacred water. It is preferred you sit with the cup in a room all day and spend majority of time pouring energy and emotion into the cup for 24hours. The next day you will feel a presence beginning to envelop you, in the early hours of the morning draw the second sigil provided on the cup.

Now say the following Invocation for Tiamut. You are inviting this being in first by bridging to her oldest form through Tiamut a younger version.

Invocation ov Tiamut to Call Mother Eiji

Des Var Valrune! Tiamut call! Raging waters rise and awaken all senses, permeate the Earth oh sacred blood, awaken in me the ancient dwelling may my blood harbor creation of your ancestral waters. Tiamut, sleeps no more the eye is open, swelter the chaotic current to oldest mother. Awake Eiji! I, Tiamut call to sister of self, breathe arcane wisdom unto me. Des Var, Des Var!

After performing the invocation, you will hold your dominant hand over the cup. Hold your hand over the water till you feel the pulsations fade and then rest the cup near your altar, you will need a couple candles because the next day the 3rd day you are lighting a black unscented candle and a white unscented candle side by side next to the cup to burn all day till they go out on their own. On the white candle inscribed with a rusted iron nail will be the first sigil given, on the second candle you will inscribe with the same nail the second sigil given. You will then draw the 3rd sigil provided on the cup before you light the candles.

Now let them burn all day and night. On the 4th day you will in the early morning draw the 4th sigil provided on the cup and perform the Invocation to Eiji.

𝔍𝔫𝔳𝔬𝔠𝔞𝔱𝔦𝔬𝔫 𝔱𝔬 𝔈𝔦𝔧𝔦

Water is life sustained, arise my mother; harbor no longer in man's mind just outside reach. I break your chains and dive into your waters. Eiji, Dala Varuu Mi Stahn, Eiji breathe! Mi Stahn, Mi Stahn, I am your air Eiji.

After the invocation again hold your hand over the cup and let the energy pulsate until you feel the ripple diminish. The 5th and final day you will take the cup and the last sigil provided, the very sigil of Eiji.

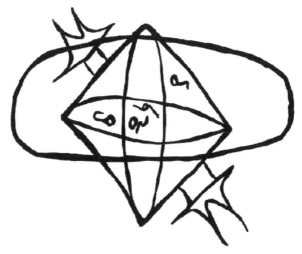

Draw this sigil on a paper and lay it under the cup, fast all day and drink only water. Pray to Eiji, exert your energy and very desire of change you wish in your life to take shape. Feel the current and you combine. Allow yourself to sit with this cup for the better part of 24hours and while in this trance state sitting with this cup know you sit in the very current of Eiji. When Midnight comes chant the following words and you will be possessed by the current of Eiji in which you may perform grand works in unison with her spirit.

Eiji reside in my blood this here hour to perform creation in your current, manifest internal!

The previous rituals are part of a bigger ritual which as you now have learned is possession by the Eiji Current. There's limitless possibility in working with this power, but I have found the main bane of existence to be Water Empowerment and creation through high level water magick. You can learn the greater mechanics of this element and how to manipulate weather through working inside her current. In the transition version of being of Tiamut you find she is a powerful force of destruction where able to drown the enemies of a sorcerer in the liquids of their own body, various shades, god type beings and etc follow Tiamut if just called, but the interesting thing I have discovered is many don't know of Eiji at all. Eiji is a lesser revealed current and as stated before Tiamut was born from Eiji and Eiji herself is an ancient conscious current millennia years old.

The next ritual being described is the Tiamut and Eiji fusion manifesting both conscious beings to this plane and using them in other workings. You will need a few items in particular for this evocation:

✴ Frankincense and an incense burner with coals and a lighter.
✴ Eggshells and Himalayan pink crystal salt, flour, oregano and black spray paint (cloth to spray on if not doing on the ground).
✴ Iron cup of Eiji water from previous ritual, an Abalone Shell and Palo Santos wood

With all the items and the Seal of Eiji drawn on paper go to the ritual site and prepare. It is wise to bring any other ritual items or workings as this ritual is a bridging to work multiple magicks at a high level as a channeling current for two conscious Goddesses and living current. You will grind the Eggshells and The Himalayan Pink Crystal Salt along with the Oregano and the Flour, mix all these together. Put the mixture aside for right now and use the Black Spray paint to construct a Triangle of your choosing and a Circle of your choosing, the Cardinal Direction is not important.

You may spray on a cloth if you so choose. Now grab the mixture you set aside and use it to spread on top of the lines of the Triangle and the Circle as well. Consecrate your Circle and Triangle now if you need time to rest you may step away from ritual at this point and return later so long as ritual site is left up as is. Place the ritual cup behind the Abalone Shell. Have the shell filled with water and add the Palo Santos to it. Set your Incense Burner in front and lay the Coal or Coals on top.

Place the Sigil of Eiji under the Incense Burner, you are now set up to guide her current to physical manifestation, you will begin by summoning first Eiji and then after Tiamut then address both as Mother Current. You will gaze at the sigil and Invoke her name feeling energy emanate 2 inches below your navel all the way up and out your mouth. As you say her name do it in low, but loud echoed resonance draw it out deep in tone and make sure every letter is the same in length in pronunciation.

You may now light the Coal or Coals and add the Frankincense on top and as it smolders begun your chanting, Invoke Eiji. Remain in the circle sitting, you should be facing the Triangle and sitting cross legged with hands extended chest level with hands open the palms are facing out. Feel your Pineal projecting down your arms and out your hands, allow your palms to open like a flower budding. Guide this energy into the smoke and once Eiji has risen begin to Invoke Tiamut.

Do the same exact technique as described above and once both spirits are present you may touch the tips of all 5 fingers on the ground inside the Triangle, allow all 3 forces to surge through you. Feel the waters rushing to your Pineal up your arm and jutting out your Crown spilling over your entire body. Thank the Mother as One and you may begin harnessing this energy into other rituals you wish to cast at this point or to use in higher scale Weather Manipulation. There's a variety of things you can apply this energy to from Divine Healing to Destruction of Foes. You wield this current in this moment, the decision lies with you. After these rituals are performed one can ask Eiji for simpler ways to call upon her and have her walk in their life as a grand protective force. Invoke her often and keep an altar if her presence is desired to remain. ✦

Barry James Lent, *Nephilim*

Tezcatlipoca the Black

N.A:O

The prayers that are dedicated to me are the cries of children, the yells of their mothers.

—From an evocation of Tezcatlipoca

THE time to begin the fifth aeon came unto the gods and their cyclical universe demanded blood once more. The great crocodile that swam in the chaotic waters of the world was slain by the two brothers that brought order to the cosmos: Tezcatlipoca the Black and Tezcatlipoca the White, also called Quetzalcoatl, the Feathered Serpent. They slayed the monster and made it the earth and the heavens. From horizon to horizon the world was divided in four quarters from which the four rulers of the quarters fought against each other a never ending battle: Tezcatlipoca the Red (East), Quetzalcoatl (West), Tezcatlipoca the Blue (South)and Tezcatlipoca the Black (North) ruled from their throne in each of the cardinal points. In order to establish order a great spear was nailed stretching from the highest heaven of the Dual Godhead to the lowest pit of the Underworld, Mictlan.

Everything created was in a perfect equilibrium except for the pending doom that afflicted the gods. The universe that they had created would perish without more of its life source: blood. So the humans were created with the only purpose to make periodical sacrifices to the gods in order to secure their continual existence, without which they would cease existing.

Encountering the Devil

Rites of possession and sacrifice where celebrated once a month on the eighteenth day of the month called tecpatl dedicated to the power of Tezcatlipoca. Loud music and prayers were commonplace as the person that was possessed by the god sat on the throne talking to those who came begging to his feet. He had been prepared for the ceremonies for the last year and when the day was over he would be sacrificed with a flint knife.

To the eyes of the Spanish the rituals that the Indians carried out were gateways to beings that should have never been invited to step on the earth, and accounts of stellar demons bringing forth diseases and destruction proliferated among the elders of the tribes. There was none who had not opened himself to the energies of these otherworldly beings, and the consequence of their presence in our world was easily accepted. No god, no matter how evil was not denied a prayer. And no god really cared about the humans except for only one: Quetzalcoatl.

The Spanish monks recognized in this dark figure the same Devil that had tempted Christ during the forty days he spent on the desert, or He who tempted Adam and Eve in the paradise in the form of a Snake. He was Lucifer who led a heavenly battle against the One and him who was cast out of heaven. And not only Tezcatlipoca stood as a major problem to the Europeans; in the Aztec mythology: the stars in the heavens became living creatures that came down and tormented the living. The gods spread plagues, killed men, women and children, and carried out the most horrid acts imaginable. But it all happened by the command of one god, ruler of all: Tezcatlipoca, sometimes referred to as the Black.

The fact is that they were not misinterpreting this being and the similitudes between the catholic image of Satan and this obscure god were astounding. In the following essay I will explore the image of this dark god in his aspect called Tezcatlipoca the Black utilizing historical/archeological resources as well as my own workings with the god. The quotes utilized all come from actual evocations held with Tezcatlipoca. Some of the techniques of the nahualtin1 sorcerers will be exposed so that he who reads can enter the realm of the god and demand from his the powers that the ancient magicians that were under his command had.

The Smoking Mirror

Tezcatlipoca is also known by the name Moyocoyani which means "the one that created himself". It is not directly linked to the legend of his creation where he was put into his corresponding cardinal point in order to create the universe, but to the figure of a Priest-King who ruled over an ancient city and led a battle against the Emperor who would also later represent his counterpart. Tezcatlipoca as a man managed to undergo the nine initiatory challenges through which the ordinary man passed after death in order to be immortalized in the Mictlan, only that he was immortalized in life. His domain spread from a piece of land to the whole universe, and there was no heaven that would not be overshadowed by him once in a while.

The Spanish were scared when they found out that many great temples were devoted to the god they understood as Satan. Accounts tell of the encounters that the indigenous people had with this new-world devil and the imageries they used would confirm the suspiciousness of the conquerors. Old men, sometimes in reddish colors and many times without a leg, would meet them at night in the paths demanding prayers. Legends told that this god would be willing to bring pestilence, riches, honors, strength, victories and fulfil their every ambition in exchange of worship.

"I give empires, and also take them away. I give riches as well as poverty. I demand fear of which I feed. I feed from the igneous heat that the blood breathes out. At night the people encounter me in the roads and I request my paying, so they fervently ask me for mercy."

The monks would spend their energy on antagonizing this evil character that would not fit their worldview. From their point of view these attributes, which were indeed identical to the medieval ideas of Satan, were solely evil and no son of god, free from the devil's clutches, would dare sing the song of Tezcatlipoca as a sign of worship:

"And they sing to me: angui-tahui, angui-tahui, angui-tahui..."

But the above-mentioned similitude with a Mephistophelian creature is not enough prove that Satan did manifest among the Aztec culture as a god and it is time to relate the tale of Tamoanchan and the fall of the gods: Mesoamerican legends tell of an primeval woman called Xochiquetzal, or Precious Flower, who lived in the garden that was Tamoanchan, the paradise were all the persons to be born and all the Gods lived. She was the goddess who ruled over the land of Eden, the birthplace of souls and at the same time the refuge to the dead before the Mictlan was created. Everything in the universe was harmony. There were no wars, no struggles, no division between mankind and the gods. Everything in the creation lived in this place.

A sacred tree grew in the center of the land and no one was to touch it as the one who did would cause Xochiquetzal to fall in love with the person. Every person that passed near the tree would sigh at the sight of the beautiful lady, but no one dared to even get close. But the god Tezcatlipoca the Black plucked a white flower from it and presented himself before the goddess giving her the blossom as a token of his affection. She was seduced by Smoking mirror just by looking at him and threw herself to his arms and then he raped her. The transgression done caused the tree to fall in such pain that it broke in half spitting blood out of its wound and when the supreme gods saw the mess that had been done. Everything, both earthly and celestial was exiled of the paradise never to come back.

This story is analogous to the biblical genesis in which Eve was tempted by the snake to eat the forbidden fruit, an act that led to the fall of mankind and the expulsion from the garden of Eden. A gap was created between the Elohim and the humans leaving between them the false Sephirah of Däath, an open door to the chaotic Tehiru which, represented as the blood, enters through the open wound of the chopped tree leaving nothing behind, only a barren desert of putrefaction.

Tezcatlipoca's sin was compared to the raping of the Earth Goddess as he forced himself into it. This event brought forth life into the material plane, but it did not go unpunished before the godly court. His punishment was the mutilation of a leg, after which he was known as the crippled god and this symbol led researchers to draw a link between this dismembering and the Ursa Major whose last star can be seen to drown under the Lake of Texcoco for some time during the year from the latitude of Mexico City. If we put attention into this fact we can start to see a similitude between this god and the idea that Kenneth Grant had of Set whose star is the eye of the Great Bear constellation, Sirius. This constellation acts as the gateway through which other dimensions, especially those of the Other Side peer at our world. It is the sun behind the sun that sets into motion the life of earth. It is the phallus (Tezcatlipoca) that impregnates the womb of the earth (Xochiquetzal).

Almost every culture assigned figures to their gods. The act of characterizing them in animal, human, or hybrid figures made them much more accessible. The phenomena they represented were controllable when it was captured in a vessel, even if it was just a set of symbols that drew limits in the being of the god: what it is, and is not. But this way of conceptualizing entities was a habit that evolved together with the complexation of the cultures. In earlier times gods were not thought about or adored, they were experience; and remnants from these periods can still be seen in what was left written about Tezcatlipoca.

The priests knew him as a formless deity and rejected any image of it as they understood it as something that no image could convey. He was considered an invisible god, a god that hides from the humans. He sometimes took the form of the wind and the night. This aspect of the god presented himself in a communication with him:

"I am the dark wind at night, the hidden shadows that dwell inside your human soul. I am the fountain of aggression that leads to destruction. I am the construction wood that breaks under the stone's weight."

For the common people he was represented in various ways: as a headless man whose chest had been open, as a funerary pile of ashes, as a giant, as a skull and a crying cadaver. Figures of him have been found to be idols enveloped in golden vipers, their craniums covered by a golden mask similar to a crocodile and its eyes shining with mirrors. His members are commonly black and dark marks cover the face. It was believed that in order to summon him into possession one had to cover his body with ashes in order to resemble the god and pull his energy down to the terrestrial world.

Bringing forth the Universe

The adept that wills to contact Tezcatlipoca has to prepare a suiting temple for him both in the physical and also in the astral plane. To do this the cosmos in which he exists has to come into existence within the space that the magician is going to use to hold communication with the god. The first points that need to be established are the four cosmic trees that divided the universe into four quarters. In order to do this the four sigils of the rulers are to be drawn in wooden plaques as a symbol of the thrones from which these gods guard the creation. These are to be put in their respective directions.

An altar has to be set up facing north, the kingdom of Tezcatlipoca the black which was called by the Aztec Talcochalco or "House of Arrows". In the altar a black mirror is to be put. It is interesting to note that the use of the black mirror is not completely a modernization of the communication techniques that were used by the Mexica. Various accounts from the colonizers relate how the priests and kings used these as ornaments hanging from their necks and probably with the mirrors they would show their initiation that allowed them to be able to use these artifacts for divination and specially to speak with the god Tezcatlipoca to whom this device was attributed as its name "Smoking Mirror" relates to the speculum.

East
Tezcatlipoca the Red

West
Tezcatlipoca the Blue

South
Quetzalcoatl

North
Tezcatlipoca the Black

Two candles or torches are to be set nearby the mirror as the Mesoamerican would use fire to illuminate its surface and also as a way to represent a bridge being made from the physical to the spiritual plane. The flat and circular surface of the mirror characterized the earth and the fire the sublime beings whose light shined in the face of the earth.

The last requirement that had to be met in order to communicate with Tezcatlipoca was to request his presence in the temple only at night. The mere rays of the Sun God, Quetzalcoatl, would banish his presence out of the Terrestrial World, but as soon as the Feathered Serpent was devoured by the lake of Tenochtitlan the realm of Tezcatlipoca would take over the kingdom and no one was safe from his draconian rule.

In order to call the gods to stand in their positions the ancient ways would have you face each direction with an incense burner (preferably using Copal incense) in your hands and draw a cross as you greet these forces into your temple (ex. Red Tezcatlipoca I greet you and welcome you to stand in the eastern quarter of my temple, Quetzalcoatl I greet you...) starting from the east and going counterclockwise. If you do not want to use the incense you can also use a trumpet and blow it after greeting the deities into your temple. As you see the smoke of the incense dissipating visualize a great tree standing in the distance, its stem lifting so high you can barely see where it finishes. After the four quarters have been established both outwardly and inwardly stand in the center of them and visualize how a stream of water runs from them until they reach your feet.

Call of Tezcatlipoca the Black

In ancient Mesoamerica there was a strong relationship between the spoken word and blood: both were indispensable at the time of creation. Thoughts on the vivifying factor of creation can seem to be out of place when a given deity that supposedly exists is to be called forth, and not to be created. But the fact is that the Aztec priests believed that everything in the cosmos was just temporary, even the gods and goddesses that ruled every aspect of their lives. When they prayed they kept them alive for some time and so every god had people who dedicated themselves to guarding the existence of their deities by keeping a calendar and orchestrating orations and sacrifices to the gods so these would withhold the impeding destruction that their disappearance would bring to the world. Therefore, in order to call forth Tezcatlipoca the Black one has to use both tools of creation in order to establish him within the temporary microcosms that the practitioner has created in his ritual space. The call of Tezcatlipoca will serve as the Word element and for the blood no actual sacrifice as most people understand it will be needed. Only a drop of your own blood on Tezcatlipoca's sigil will be necessary as self-sacrifice was a very common practice among the Aztecs and was done by almost everyone on various festivities during the year.

Be it as it is, you decided it;

Possessor of the laughter of the earth;

Let your spirit be adored, your word taken into account; Your will be done.

*TLACATL TOTECU,
TLOQUE, NAHUAQUE, TLATLICPACQUE,
MOYOCOYATZIN,
TITLACAHUAN.*

*Evil trickster, you laugh at us:
Self-creator, we are nothing to you,
Enemy of the world, you annihilate us.
Show us the lies that hide behind the Word of the world.
TLACATL, TLAZOPILLI, TOTECU.*

*The joy of pain drips from your mouth,
Your eyes burn in the sight of sin.
Drunk god of transgression,*

Of lasciviousness, of incest,

Let the smoke out, the cities burn to ashes;

Lift the mist up, and only then will the birds sing this song.

The Vision of Huitznahual

The following is a guided meditation that will lead your mind's eye to access one of the biggest temples that were built to Tezcatlipoca. The details are taken from the very explicit account of a Spanish monk who was able to access the actual place. Now that the only thing that remains from the physical temple is one man's account and scattered rocks, the astral temple is all that was left. It is an existing place in the astral as the priests would construct a double working place in order to commune with the gods.

This pathworking can be performed while dancing to the rhythm of a shamanic drum, or lying on your back in complete darkness and silence. I advise to do the latter but still listening to a shamanic drumming track as this can be very helpful to induce the desired altered state of consciousness as it will maintain the magician awake, and at the same time will permit him/her to fall into a trance. The meditation is separated in four parts so that it is easier to memorize, but it should be done as one, there is no point in doing it separately. A good way to memorize the details is to picture it as you read it. Construct the images in your mind first, so you can evoke them at the moment of the meditation.

1. Close your eyes. Imagine you are standing in the middle of a stone city. Various structures surround you painted in various variations of green, blue, red and white. As you see around you, you notice two rivers intersecting right below the pyramid in which you are standing. As you look into the distance, you can notice four huge trees lifting up into the heavens.

   Make sure that by this part your body is completely relaxed as the flow of energy to enter this place will go more swiftly once it is close to be asleep.

2. Your heart is pumping blood faster and faster. You can see it glowing brighter and brighter in orange as it accelerates. See and feel the energy spinning around it. You put your hands above it and you tear the flesh apart from it, as if you wanted to expose it into the light of day. As you do this, you notice that it expands and gets bigger every time your heart beats and it starts pulling you to its core until you get completely immersed on its orange light, which at the same time, feels like darkness. The energy that envelops your body starts sucking you into its center, where once your heart was, now it has become a vortex to the inner realm of the Aztecs. You get sucked into it.

3. Everything is darkness except for the figure of a big staircase lifting upwards that the shadows insinuate in front of you. Start climbing, there are eighty steps and as you get higher and closer to the top of the stairs you start to see more clearly the rocks on the steps, on the walls, the frescos painted into the front of the pyramid. Once you reach the highest point you look around. The sky is gray as illuminated by the full moon, but no stars are visible. There are no sounds while the city of Aztlan still sleeps. The interior of the temple is darker than the night from what you can see from the exterior but you step in.

4. You see a twelve-feet-wide empty room and the only thing in there is a curtain that veils a neighboring chamber. You open that veil and step in. A light without source illuminates it in a golden splendor and you see beautiful multicolored tapestries made of feathers hanging on the walls.

This room is not empty. You feel a presence that slowly starts materializing out of the shadows of the room. The darkness of the night starts sweeping into a formless mass that slowly takes the shape of a humanoid creature. Its face is covered by a golden mask, its legs and arms are painted black with charcoal and on the neck of Tezcatlipoca hangs a black mirror made of concentrated smoke. Do not look into his eyes, but gaze at the mirror where you can start the communication with the god. Thank him when you are finished and trace your steps back without showing him you back until you exit the chamber of Tezcatlipoca. Slowly start moving your body and go back to your normal state of consciousness. ✦

Andrew Cummins, *Servitor of Lilith*

Qliphoth

The Black Arts

Arranged by
EDGAR KERVAL

Edited by
TIMOTHY

★ **BECOME A LIVING GOD**

Anderson Silva, *Aghori Cult III*

Anderson Silva, *Aghori Cult IV*

The Magick of the Acausal

Typhon Draconis

The Question of Magick

IT has been known since the dawn of human history that a strongly visualized desire, empowered by an enflamed will, may often bring into being that which is desired. All cultures have recognized this, whether they called the process "prayer," "Magick," "Sorcery," or "shamanism." The fact that empowered visualizations can and do influence reality is a fact in which the common populace always has placed belief, regardless of what has been asserted by the intelligentsia. Only the advent of the "Enlightenment," (which paradoxically drove much light into the darkness) began to dispel such beliefs. The Enlightenment brought mankind much: a belief in human rights and dignity, the scientific method of inquiry into matters of the material world, and a relief from the tyranny of religion.

Unfortunately, with the triumph of scientific materialism, much was lost as well, and most especially was lost a comprehension of the non-linear, non-rational behavior of the world. The world of Scientific Materialism was the world of Sir Isaac Newton's physics, composed of "hard matter" billiard balls and clearly definable, predictable interactions between them. The mystery was driven from the universe, in great measure, a result that the alchemist, Rosicrucian, and mystic side of Sir Isaac must not have failed to see, and perhaps in some way, rue. The simple, common sense, reductionist reason of modern science drove other, deeper, and stranger truths into the Darkness, at least until the advent of modern quantum theory. Under the new lens of quantum theory, things started looking quite strange... stranger even, perhaps, than the beliefs which the "Enlightenment" temporally eclipsed.

For instance, it was discovered that what we call "matter" often behaves more like a wave, and that particles which have been in contact with each other continue to exchange information, even when at the greatest of distances. Einstein's greatly feared "spooky action at a distance" was here to stay, and with it came theories which made that which we have called "Magick" again scientifically creditable, even within the narrow confines of Scientific Materialism. Indeed, "object links" have a verifiable place in the thinking of quantum theory. Things which have been in contact, still remain in contact, and such linkages may be used to produce desired effects.

Over the centuries, there have been many different explanatory models for how Magickal effects are achieved. One of the oldest is that of "spirits" being called to produce desired effects. Another model is that based upon the notion of "vital force," "chi," or "prana." In such a model, energy is generated by the intense emotional arousal of the Magickian and imprinted with the strongest of visualizations, bearing the template of the operator's Will. It is a short step to conceive of such imprinted energy affecting another biological system, in accordance with the Magickian's Will. This model fails to explain how Magickal operations can affect complex, non-living sets of circumstances in order to produce Synchronicity. If it is anything, Magick is "Manufactured Synchronicity," the effects of which can only be fully explained by an appeal to Acausal mechanisms which work "outside of time" and "outside of Causality" (as we know them). This paper is an attempt to explore the Acausal in its relationship to Magick, and also to thereby refine approaches to the ritual process and to ritual technique. We also seek to define the role of the "deep mind" in producing Magickal effects, and delineate the most effective approaches to accessing its powers.

"The Acausal" has been approached in numerous different ways, under many different names. Such names include "zero point field," "morphic resonance field," and "ground of being." The commonality of all of these concepts is that they convey an anti- entropic underpinning to the manifest universe, and all of these concepts stand apart and free of the natural structure of the space- time continuum. It is something apart from the dimensions in which we normally dwell. It is the Sitra Ahra!

The Acausal

In tandem with the dimension of perception ruled by order and reason there exists another "space," "a parallel dimension," or "level of consciousness" sometimes conceptualized in a poetic way as positioned "at right angles to everywhere." Physics regards this "dimension" in a more physical way, while in Magick we regard it more as being an aspect of consciousness. These differing approaches are merely two different ways of approaching the same thing, and in some sense, both are true. Of course, the issue of the relationship between mind and matter is raised in this question. If, as the "Citta-matra" ("Mind-Only") school of Buddhism maintains, "all is mind," then such dichotomous viewpoints become unified. If matter and mind are one-in-the- same, then the dichotomy dissolves. Whatever one believes in regards to this relationship between mind and matter, in the realm of which we speak, causality as we know it from our learned experiences in "normal reality" is no longer operative. After all, causality is a concept which is based on "temporal sequence," and developed out of our empirically derived experiences of every-day reality. Time, as we know and measure it, is, itself, based in "entropy," which is an attribute of all known parts of the material universe. In our "normal" day-to-day world, entropy is marked by the increasing disorder in a measurement system such as the battery in a clock discharging, the spring in a wind-up watch unwinding, or a radioactive element in an atomic clock decaying. As is obvious, increasing entropy marks the "arrow of time" in our manifest universe.

The nature of entropy is that things decrease in order, progressing from a greater level of organization towards greater and greater disorder. This applies to all aspects of nature which are "non- living." Life, by its very nature is an anti-entropic thing. Living things absorb food, air, and water, increase the disorder in those consumed things, casting off the residue. Thus living things vampirize the "order" inherent in those things, and become more-and-more orderly in themselves, at least until old-age and death supervene and entropy reclaims them. Successfully worked Magickal Spells are living, dynamic, anti-entropic fields of force. As Vortices of intelligent force, they "suck into themselves" all that is necessary for the Magickian's visualized template to materialize. They increase the order in the macrocosm around themselves in a re-iterative order of the visualized and empowered template provided from within the Magickian's microcosm.

"This thing moved because that other thing bumped it," is the essence of causality, and also of defining a temporal sequence. In our "normal" world, time and causality are really one-in-the-same, in the sense that a "cause" precedes its "result." However, there are realms where "time" is irrelevant. In the world where time is an immutable whole, all that has ever existed, continues to exist, and all that has ever occurred is still occurring. This, literally, is immortality, and it is also, quite literally, "timelessness." In a realm which is timeless, causality (as we think we know it) is suspended. "The cup fell off the desk because I bumped it," is a temporal sequence and the temporal sequence provides the "reason" the cup fell. But perhaps, on another plane, (an "Acausal" plane driven by "morphic resonance," which exists outside of time as we conceive it) the cup was "destined" to fall--- willed to fall by a Magickian's intent. Perhaps in order to support this visualized and empowered template manifesting in the "normal" world," other Acausal and Synchronistic forces worked to "cause "my elbow to hit the cup.

it, my elbow struck the blow. Thus what is Acausally "mandated" may be said to "suck into itself" the circumstances necessary for that event to occur. I know that this is difficult to follow and that it sounds manifestly crazy to the rational mind, which has the job of trying to make sense out of our day-to-day causally driven world. However the Powers of Magick are not drawn from the day-to-day world; rather they are drawn from "The Other Side." The words which we use in trying to delineate these concepts are, themselves, drawn from the world of causality and reason, and fail to convey that which is ineffable.

One of the earliest facts observed by ancient man was that in addition to the perceptions received from "ordinary reality" there were also other perceptions...perceptions that didn't function under the same "rules" which governed ordinary reality. The discordance between the daylight world enlightened by reason, and the nightside world of non-linear perception generally terrified those normal folk who might perceive it. These perceptions were often fleeting and strange, but nevertheless caused the ancients of all races to form the idea of "another place" ... a place where dwelt the Gods and the Daemons, the dead, and a host of other more horrible beings.

Engagement with this realm was generally left by most races to a small group of Priests or Shamans, who by temperament, training, and exercise of their Will and imagination, learned to fearlessly expand their conscious minds into the Acausal realms, in order to apprehend this dimension and use it to their own purposes. We call these people, "Magickians," "Sorcerers," or "Witches."

This realm, "The Other Side," the "Sitra Ahra," or "the Dark Formless Acausal" is the very "space" into which the Mage must project his mind and Will in order to work Black Magick. Acausal Sorcery is "Black" because it goes against the very "law and order" of the manifest causal universe, marking the Black Mage in a very real sense as a "Cosmic Outlaw." We may call this the Mark of Cain, which is the mark borne by those who willfully Work against the Cosmic Order. We work Magick when the designs of "nature as it is" are unpleasing to us and we wish our own Will substituted for "things as they are." In working Magick, we bypass normal causality, thumbing our noses at that selfsame causality (which may be viewed as Yaldabaoth/IHVH), and place our desires directly into Acausal being itself. Once the desire is implanted into the Ground of Being or the Acausal, it then "creates its own causes" in order to manifest. The currents which work to "heal" manifest causal reality from the "wounds" we inflict by "hacking" it, and which aim at causing events to appear as normal and as "causal" as possible, we call "Synchronicity." Underneath it all, true Synchronicity is the sign of Acausal action. With our empowered, visualized template implanted into the "is-to-be," the desired out-come, though "morphic resonance" attracts and creates its own necessary causes or pre-conditions for the manifestation of it to occur. Thus Magick may be seen in one sense as being "Manufactured Synchronicity." One approach to Magick is to view it as the reverse engineering of omens.

Omens are synchronicity as read as indications of future events. By artificially creating a circumstance that would be read by the Sorcerer, if it spontaneously occurred, as predicting an event, one may "draw" that same event out of the cosmos. For example, by assembling a tarot spread which normally would indicate that a large sum of money was coming to you, and empowering that spread with visualization and energy, such a sum might be brought to you, through Synchronistic, Acausal action.

This may sound strange to many (and, indeed, from the reference view of causality it is quite strange), but let me give a concrete example. I do a working to run into an old love in hopes of re- engaging with her. The break-up occurred in a way where there was "no fault," so no resentments are felt on either side, but a sense of regret that "things weren't different at that time." In a Magickal trance of Acausal Sorcery, I visualize being face-to-face with her, talking with her, and seeing both her smile and feeling her heart warm yet-again to me. I allow in the visualization that if she is otherwise involved, or for some other reason does not feel the same as I do, then the energy should convert into a simple blessing, and a caring ave atque vale. (I have learned over time that attempting to forcibly compel an intended love interest produces only chaos and pain, and allow that "escape valve" as a safety feature, for my own well-being.) I successfully feed that visualized result with appropriate energetic arousal, and place it into my deep mind through image and symbol, and it, in turn, inseminates it into the Acausal sphere. A week later, she "just happens" ("as if by Magick") to come around the corner in the grocery store and almost run smack into me. Things progress as visualized from there. So, from the point of view of an Acausal Sorcerer, what happened? How did this work?

I created and empowered an Acausal visualization of being face-to-face with her, of her immediately responding, and of things warming up quickly from there. The structure of the rite was correctly formed, so that the intended would not feel compelled, (and hence, be repulsed,) but rather loved, valued, and "invited if you're interested." This "Spell" then compelled the Cosmos to form itself around its visualized and empowered template, in order to "support" that template into manifestation. The universe then "protected the causal matrix" by calling upon Synchronicity streams , which "created" the necessary "causes, " backwards in "time" from that desired "result," in order for that meeting to happen, but in a way where "causes" were provided. It "just so happened" that she ran out of dog food and that grocery was the closest on her way home, and I just happened to need to pick up some oranges.

"Causality" & Magick

Common usage of the phrase "as if by magic" implies that an event occurred in the absence of a recognizable "cause." Many of the Black Schools of Magick (e.g. ONA, TOTBL) speak of the "Acausal" realm and of Magick as being an "Acausal" phenomenon. The ONA, for instance, terms the "energy" involved in performing Magick as "Acausal" energy. Most of Magickal history, however, has been marked by attempts to define a "subtle" causality for Magickal results. Firstly "demons" were regarded as the agents of Magick. Later, Levi hypothesized the "astral plane" or "astral light"- an "energy" he equated with the vital force of the Magnetizers. More recent attempts have been made to explain Magick's effects by means of quantum theory, and the effects the mind can produce on the "zero-point field." While such theories of a "ground matrix" for explaining Magickal effects have some appeal, the notion that some events occur "beyond cause and effect" has considerable explanatory power. It is possible, however, that such differing models as the ZPF and "Acausality" actually may be unified, in that the behavior of the ZPF does not conform to the "law of cause and effect." In that sense, it may be said to behave "Acausally."

Here is the essential fact, verifiable to any working Magician who has obtained effects from his Workings: The Magician's Will creates an event which is seen during the Working as being fully manifested in "the present" . When the Magician successfully "implants" his vision into "the is-to-be," the rest of "reality" then "back-fills," or "fills in" around that event, causing the "effect" to essentially pull into itself the "causes" necessary for that event to manifest. Since time is an illusion, and "cause" and "effect" are defined by a temporal sequence, stepping out of the normal temporal plane of reality suggests that this view may not be so implausible. What we think of as "the past" "forms around" the chosen "future" result which the Mage has visualized as being "now," manifest at the current time. Indeed, one of the elements necessary for a successful Working is to visualize the desired result as already fully-manifested at the present time. On "reality's" own (temporal) plane, the "Law" of causality is thus not violated as much as it is "hacked." Synchronicity works to heal the "wounds" inflicted on the cosmos by the Magickian, as a Cosmic Outlaw, so that "causes" appear to have been present. Thus Magickal results appear to occur by "chance" (however strange) and the Universe hums along as if that were just the way things happened.

Our ego is formed in tandem with the "laws" of causality. Our ego largely represents the "scar tissue" by which we hope to learn to avoid similar hurts in the "future," by knowing "the laws of reality." "Reason" is our internalized understanding of what those laws are. We are socialized both by matter, itself, and by the humans around us to discount and discard anything that does not fit into these recognized patterns. Other ways of thinking are held to be "primitive," "childlike," or downright "psychotic," and hence to be shunned. The "unconscious" mind may well hold the disowned part of our consciousness which is aware that there are other ways that the world and our minds do indeed behave- ways that are not rational but which exist nonetheless. Indeed, the "unconscious" may "know" and respond to "Acausal" perceptions which we discount "because they are just irrational feelings." The "unconscious" is the part of our mind which recognizes and can process "Acausal" events; thus, it would, of necessity, be the part of ourselves with which we must connect if we wish to work Magick. This is the Mind with which we dream, with which we envision, and with which the formed wishes of the conscious mind may be translated into external, objective, "reality." This state of mind is probably most accessible when EEG activity is in the alpha and high Delta ranges (4 to 13 Hz).

Here, another most important point must be made: to work Magick effectively one must be put through the alchemical process of calcination. This is often misunderstood, as simply meaning pathea mathos ("wisdom gained through suffering"). It means much more than this, however. Those who are attracted to Magick in general and the Left Hand Path in particular, are those who are more likely than others to have been abused, devalued, or otherwise disaffected by other humans throughout the course of their lives, and hence view themselves as "outsiders." Often reaching for the Left Hand Path is a means of asserting false ego issues, such as "I am not worthless; I am in fact a god or goddess." This is not calcination. Calcination means being reduced to utter nothingness, and to realize that your inherent worth is NOTHING... that you are "utterly void." Then from this voidness one can begin to generate a true self, not marked by the blows rendered by causal existence. So much harm to Black Magickians and the Left Hand Path, itself, could be reduced were this comprehended.

NOTHING THAT HAPPENED TO YOU IN THIS CAUSAL UNIVERSE IS OF ANY WORTH TO YOU AS A BLACK MAGICKIAN. Abusers and the abuse inherent in manifest existence only reiterate the hold that power which causality has held (before Enlightenment) over own our (Acausal) souls and perpetuates the indignities of IHVH. The Magickal trick is to stand that abuse on its head and admit that, "On this plane, I am but a temporary Power, but Dark Acausal Power is not of this temporary plane of causality or a reaction to it, but the truest assertion of who I am, unmolested by the causal plane. I am an eternal reiteration of the energy of the Dark Void, the Mindless Light, that which can never be rendered into true voidness, because IT IS, and it is eternal! "I shall be gone tomorrow, but I exist forever!" Zen Masters tell us that, "If you meet the Buddha on the path, then kill him." Collecting followers is the true sign of an uncalcinated individual. "Getting off" on the attention adorers offer is an even-truer sign. Control needs as far as those directed at other humans and their behavior reflects a history of personal abuse in one's past life and a "need to be in control" rather than any spiritual development. A need to devalue others is most reflective of this, unless those "trashed" are those actually damaging the Path.

As we have said, the Magician is, in one sense, a Cosmic Outlaw, working to violate the normal causal flow. By visualizing and emotionally empowering a given event, he "forces" the flow of reality to adapt itself to the Magical event. Reality seems to be "self-healing" in this regard, providing (retrocausally) the "causes" necessary for the flow of normal causality to appear unbreached in the production of the Magickal "effect." In a Magickal Working, the Sorcerer creates his energized and empowered visualization as the "cause" for the desired "result," thus bypassing and replacing "normal causality" for producing the phenomenon desired. When this Acausal template is created, it "sucks normal reality in around itself," so that the envisioned and empowered "result" "causes its own causes." (Words are tools of the "causal mind," designed to relate experiences from within the causal sphere, and hence fail when dealing with the Acausal and ineffable.) Such techniques have been referred to as "the Left- Hand Path," or the "Crooked or Backwards Path" precisely because they are, as best stated, "unrational." Reason and the causality of "science" have absolutely nothing to do with such phenomena. They are not "irrational," as rationality only applies within the web controlled by cause and effect. "Unrational" is the term I personally prefer when dealing with the workings of Acausality.

General Principles of Magickal Technique

Magick is a process requiring a dual focus: i.e. the visualization of the desired result, itself, and the generation of the energy required to empower that visualization with creative force. The Mage must strive for the highest possible state of energetic arousal while simultaneously forming, embellishing, and retaining the vibrant, holographic image of his desired manifestation in the is-to-be. The image of the desired result must be seen as already attained and present NOW. Indeed, this is the technique suggested in most Magickal teaching texts. Attempts to specify details of the route to the realization of the desired result seem to complicate and impair the actual manifestation of results. Essentially, attempts to specify how the result is to manifest essentially limit the available avenues for the empowered "spell" to pull into itself the "causes" needed for it to manifest. Magick is, after all, just that: Magick. The image impressed upon the molten core of creation takes its own paths in forming the realized result. Often this result occurs by routes and processes strange or unimagined by the Mage, and by specifying a detailed "route to manifestation" for our desire, we limit the options for our Spell's manifestation, and weaken our Magick. Like water flowing down-hill, the more gullies there are in which it may travel, the more and faster can the brook below be filled.

There are different ways of comprehending manifest reality, and to some extent, most of them offer us insights (sometimes great) if we are able to discriminate the bull from the bull-shit, and "cherry-pick" concepts from different (and often conflicting) versions of "Magickal thought."

Here's one paradigm, from the angle of "entropy:" The clear creation of a visualized outcome state causes an increase in the negative entropy or "order" of the firing of various neural circuits in the brain, which form and retain the image in consciousness. The greater the preciseness and order in the image, the greater the vividness of it, the more "information" the image will contain and the greater the impact it will have upon the energy raised and released. Obviously, the greater the energetic force raised, provided that it does not overwhelm nor mar the visualization, and the more strongly that visualization is impressed upon that energy, the more power our Magick will have, and the more likely it will be to generate a correctly realized result. It is essential that there be a complete release of the accumulated energy, strongly imprinted with the visualized template. Usually this release is marked by a sudden and complete reduction in the accumulated negatively-entropic "order" of the visualization into a state of complete relaxation in the Mage, even to the degree of a "swoon." All thoughts related to the released energy are "ejaculated" into this state of voidness, and recollection of them scrupulously avoided from that time until any desired result is fully manifested. A balance factor still figures in. The more likely what we are trying to create is to actually happen statistically, in the "normal" workings of "reality," the more our Magick works in harmony with the universe's pre-existing processes, and the inertia of the universe works with rather than against our purpose. The bio-energetic paradigm may be supplemented by a "Quantum Sorcery" paradigm, such as that advanced by David Smith. (David Smith's Quantum Sorcery is a work to be most highly recommended; also quite useful is the small book, Morphic Fields Made Simple by Ambazac and Mason.) These arguments, of course, mirror concepts advanced by Peter Carroll, and, of course Werner Heisenberg, and Carl Jung and Wolfgang Pauli. First, we have the "Old Testament" of Einstein's "IHVH," as advanced in relativity theory, and then the Satanic Quantum Sorcerers fell upon that orthodoxy, savaged it, rolled phurbas held high, and proved Einstein's worst fear: "Spooky action at a distance" was real. Here let it be noted that one of Our Lady Hecate's titles was "She who worketh from afar."

The Chthonic Mind: The Magickal Gateway

If we analyze the principles of thought on which magic is based, they will probably be found to resolve themselves into two: first, that like produces like, or that an effect resembles its cause; and, second, that things which have once been in contact with each other continue to act on each other at a distance after the physical contact has been severed. The former principle may be called the Law of Similarity, the latter the Law of Contact or Contagion. From the first of these principles, namely the Law of Similarity, the magician infers that he can produce any effect he desires merely by imitating it: from the second he infers that whatever he does to a material object will affect equally the person with whom the object was once in contact, whether it formed part of his body or not. Charms based on the Law of Similarity may be called Homoeopathic or Imitative Magic. Charms based on the Law of Contact or Contagion may be called Contagious Magic.

—Sir James George Frazer, *The Golden Bough*, 1922

The conscious mind is formed by our painful and instructive encounters with external material reality. Even within the uterus, there is an external world, although it is limited in the variety of sensory input which can be experienced. In addition, the fetal brain is most likely too undeveloped to retain much of what is experienced there. The Acausal can only be accessed through that part of the mind which has not been tamed and scarified by external reality. Attainment of pure consciousness without an object is the key to freedom from the domination of the Archons. This state is the essence of the Dark Gnostic trance and is the Portal through which our consciously formed Spells can be passed through into the Acausal Chthonic mind, where their manifestation may be worked. The Buddhists call this the Dharmakaya; other systems have other names, such as "The Dark Formless Acausal."

Access to this state is cultivated in meditation and mystical trances, where only our own mind, freed of any external influence, holds sway. The cultivation of this state takes time and practice, and cannot be achieved in a day.

When the Chthonic mind speaks to us, such as in dreams, it speaks to us in symbols and similes, in visions and metaphors, not in the direct, linear, rational speech of the conscious mind. If we wish to communicate a desire from our conscious minds into the chthonic mind, we must, of needs, speak to the chthonic mind in its own language. The successful Sorcerer must be a master of the language of the unconscious, which is the Acausal language of unreason. The laws of Sorcery are essentially the laws by which the Chthonic mind works and represent the "language" which it understands. The words, images, tools, and ritual gestures, likewise represent part of that "vocabulary of unreason" with which we convey our conscious Will to the chthonic mind, so that it may be passed forth into manifestation. The ritual process, not being a "rational" activity, directly opens a gateway into alteration of consciousness, which initiates the "Trance of Unreason." To paraphrase Anton LaVey, the ritual chamber is a place where only emotional activity should occur. All rational thought is to cease once one is robed and prepared to enter the ritual chamber. This mental transition most likely represents a slowing of EEG activity from the Beta range down into Alpha.

As the ritual proceeds during the invocation, we eventually enter into the state of full Dark Gnostic trance. This trance is most likely reflected in an absence of Beta activity, and full Alpha and, perhaps, higher-range Delta activity, with some Theta waves, as the trance progresses. It is in this state that our consciously formed intent may be fed by ferocious energetic arousal and visualization and passed through to the chthonic mind, which transmits it into the Acausal, for manifestation. The messages "sent" into the deep mind, must be sent in images, raw perceptions, and inflamed animal emotion, and must be sent in deep symbolic form. Sigils are of use to many here, although, I, personally, have made little use of them. I prefer raw, perceptual images, which capture the realized intent seen as "real and fully-manifested" in the present time. I delight in the emotions of the realized result, and celebrate it as "now." Words have their place, but, with a few exceptions, such as Enochian or glossolalia, that place is to make the conscious mind more comfortable with the process, and more receptive to the true message being sent into the "deep mind."

The joke here is that the forming of the ritual desire is the only thing the conscious mind contributes to any Magickal Working. Beyond that, it is impotent. The conscious mind cannot directly speak its will to the chthonic mind in a way in which it will be understood and obeyed. That message must be sent into the chthonic mind in "the language of Acausal unreason" - visualized images, smells, raw perceptions, symbols, and sigils. We must speak to the Beast in the Beast's own terms and words, if we would gain the Beast's energies and compliance. Learning these techniques is much of the Art of Magick. Anyone can have a conscious desire. Learning how to package such a desire and transmit it into the deep-mind/collective unconscious for realization is the essence of the Ars Magicka. I would also remark, that this Art is precisely the one missing in "pretenders," arm-chair "talking heads," and the general gamut of masturbatory writers of many "books on magick and witchcraft." THEY HAVE NO POWER BECAUSE THEY DO NOT

KNOW HOW TO TALK INTO THE DARKNESS AND HAVE THE DARKNESS LISTEN AND OBEY!

Forming the Visualization/Template

The skills of visualization which are called upon by the Mage are best perfected in the usual course of Magical training. It is of no use to work with vague images, summoned up without training at the time of an actual working. Vague templates yield vague results. The visualizations utilized in workings are quite different than those of day-dreams or fantasies. The intent and awareness that one is fashioning an image of an already-extant event must be present. The reality of the image must be celebrated in forming it. One must attain a state of mind in which the desired manifestation is perceived as "already real and fully manifested in the present." One formulation of Magick (advanced by Stephen Mace in his Sorcery As Virtual Mechanics) suggests that the dissonance between the "actual" current (pre-working) reality, and the new and different reality envisioned by the Mage's Working "sucks" the manifestation of the desired result "out of the virtual void" in a manner analogous to the "virtual mechanics" postulated in modern physics. This is a similar approach to the one I am advancing here.

The Magickal Trance

In order for the Sorcerer's mind to connect with the "Acausal energies," "morphic field," or whatever one wishes to call it, it must be understood that ordinary consciousness is ineffectual. Ordinary consciousness produces EEG frequencies in the beta range of frequency, which is 13 through 31 cycles per second (Herz). These frequencies are the ones involved in ordinary problem solving aimed at the "material world." Passive, relaxed trance states are represented by frequencies in the alpha range, which are 7 to 13 cycles per second. This is the frequency range that most effectively couples with the "Acausal field," but it only represents a "carrier wave." It must be further emotionally energized and directed by visualization to be effective in Magick. The Magickian must learn to achieve the alpha range, and without losing it, meld that energy with the energized, emotionally-fueled visualized template, and then project that into the "is-to-be." Then Magick will occur. And the template must be sent in the non- verbal "language of the Beast," so that the message is received and comprehended, so that it may be obeyed.

Learning how to do this is best achieved by first learning some style of relaxed meditation before attempting to work Magick. Once the calm, centered state of meditation can be attained at will, one must begin imagining strongly felt emotional tones, while not losing the meditative state. Actually some of the Buddhist meditations on remaining calmly focused, while calling up emotions, can be quite useful, although their goal in such meditations is to transcend the passion. Acting skills can be learned and utilized to summon the full emotion, or one may simply conjure up a strongly emotionally-charged state from your actual past life. Once you can learn to emote ferociously while holding a well-formed visualization through the relaxed alpha range trance state, you are ready to begin to work Magick. This is the neurophysiologic basis of contacting your deep Acausally- based mind, and feeding into it the un-rational information it needs to alter reality at your behest.

Generating Energy

The traditional methods of the sorcerer are well studied and rehearsed by the practitioner. Dancing, drumming, chanting, sexual orgasm, paroxysms of rage, lust, and compassion all have motive force which can be wedded with the desired template to propel it into manifestation. As has been written, generally only the strongest and most primitive levels of emotional arousal produce the motive force needed in Magick. Also, importantly, it is best if the harnessed energy matches the tenor of the intent. Thus it is traditionally stated that (for instance) sexually generated energy is perhaps not the best motive force to meld with the template of a curse. However, to the contrary, I know some Witches who would argue that "seduction may be worked to destruction," just as surely as does a Venus fly-trap, and point out that Thanateros is a valid working formula. So surely there may be exceptions, and each Mage will do well to reflect before working on the exact "architecture" of a proposed operation. Fucking people to death may be a strategy best suited for a truly vampiric LHP practitioner, but for me, personally it holds no appeal. Tastes matter greatly in one's working strategies, and I do not mean to imply that by any means, "one size fits all."

It is most important to emphasize that a perfectly-visualized template will fail of effective power, if it is not infused with strong emotional force, and that force effectively conveyed to the deep mind in terms it comprehends and to which it resounds. It is quite effective for this force to be the full emotional expression of how the fulfilled result "feels" to the Mage, caged in raw, primal, non- verbal terms. The ecstasy of a realized sexual conquest, the attainment of a business deal, or the acquisition of a given sum of money, all -if vividly experienced emotionally as a result fully attained in the present- provide motive force for a successful working. If one cannot generate such emotional force for the object of a given working, then he probably shouldn't be wasting time pursuing it!

Release of the Empowered Template

At the conclusion of the working, the profoundly Yang, aroused and energized visualization of the Mage is "ejaculated" into the womb of creation, and the Mage passes immediately into a profoundly Yin state of collapse, torpor, and exhaustion. If this is not the case, then either the "voltage" achieved in the working or the "amperage" are likely insufficient to achieve material result. (Voltage refers to the potential difference between the Mage's aroused, energized state and his subsequent collapse, while amperage refers to the "amount" of energy released.) It is necessary to attain a completely "void" state after release in order to produce a maximal "voltage" for the working.

It is necessary that a ferocious amount of emotional energy be summoned up and wedded to the visualized template in order to provide the needed "amperage." The actual release of energy in the working is timed in a "physiological" way, much as in a physical orgasm. The energy builds, is savored and amplified, and when a physiologic crisis-point is reached, it is bio-energetically "ejaculated." The feeling has been likened to that of an orgasm or, in much smaller scale, a sneeze. It has been pointed out that this style of working is "Yang" in nature and clearly mimics the male sexual response cycle. There may exist another, more "Yin" or "feminine" style which involves energy accumulation and release in waves, throughout the course of a working (thus mimicking a typical female orgasmic pattern). Not much has been written on this alternate approach, however.

A necessary terminal coda to the "collapse state" is the continued absence from the Mage's mind of subject matter related to the working in the days and weeks after it is concluded, up until the full manifestation of material results is achieved. Anticipation of desired results only brings the "result" of having further anticipation of those desired results, not the actual manifestation of them! The mental set involved must be one of "I have this," rather than "I want to have this." This difference may be hard for the spell-caster to understand until they "get" it, but is essential for actual results. Worry about how or when results will manifest reflects that the operator has been functioning from the "I want to have this" mental set, and bodes ill for a materialized result. Thus "Lust for Result" may be seen more as a symptom of likely failure rather than the cause of it. It represents the normal rational ego trying to affect results that it has no power to impact, and this, after the Working is completed. It reflects the fact that the failed operator did not "see" the result as fully manifested and present as a current reality, and then turn that over in full trust to the deep mind. The rational ego tries to keep "picking at" what it realizes as a failed working. The very reason Magick is utilized is to bring non-rational, "acausal," synchronistic powers into play. These powers have nothing to do with the rational ego.

Even worse than obsessively thinking about ones desire for a result, is entertaining fears that one's Working has failed. Such thoughts may occur spontaneously, or may arise after interactions which give us feedback that events are moving contrary to our Will. As an example, I have placed a Love spell on Sally, and find out that she's just started seeing a new guy, and that she's "quite fond of him." The heart may sink, and the brain begin generating a multitude of notions about, "How my spell has failed; I can't get any result from this now; she's gone." "To Keep Silence" is a command that applies not just to external speech and conversation with others, but also, and perhaps more importantly, to the Magician's own "internal dialog." When the matter is turned over to the Powers of Darkness, it must be let go.

Again, it is the Chthonic mind unto which the Working template and energies are "handed." Like the seed buried in the earth, we must leave the Workings of Darkness unto Darkness.

Results

Generally, results manifest through synchronicities, which are linked with the operation by meaning. Whether such results are Acausal, as Jung has termed them, or "caused" by a causality higher than that recognized by modern science is irrelevant to the Mage. Indeed, if there are forces higher than the causal, we should expect that their use in the creation of a given "result" in a working, will cause such a "result" to "create its own causes," and this, as it were, "backwards in that framework which we refer to as time." ("Time," in this regard is truly an illusion, which is created by the fact that our minds interface with the whole matrix just "one point at a time.") Thus Magick is a pure act of direct creation on the Acausal plane (astral plane or ZPF), and the created result works "backwards in time" to create the needed circumstances to "support" itself in manifest causal reality. To repeat this: Creating the desired "result" Acausally "sucks in" "backwards through time" (as it were) the events in the causal chain needed for the "result" to be "supported" in the normal causal matrix. Words fail to convey these concepts well, as words are causal instruments. This is what "ineffable" means. This model has a broader explanatory power than the "bio- energetic model." While the bio-energetic model may readily explain results obtained on other living beings, it becomes less satisfying when more complex situations or non-living things are affected. (This, of course, assumes that "all things" are not "alive," in an animistic sense.)

We plant the seed, tend the tree, and eat the apple. That was our goal. "Why" in any extended sense is really irrelevant to our process. And that is exactly where the "Magick" lies... at the Molten Core of Creation. ✦

Sean Woodward, *The Master of Space*

A Carpathian Working

Lukasz Grochocki

IN the summer of 2015 I conducted a series of workings in the Carpathian Mountains of southern Poland. These ancient sites revealed to me several groups of spirits, their myths and incantations. The following is from one of those workings which I call the Haunted Meadow cycle.

The Myth

Deep in the mountains there once was a village called Turegon. Its inhabitants had lived there for generations and some say even from the beginning of time. Like most mountain people, they raised sheep and goats and built their houses from the tall pine trees. One day the village headman's beautiful daughter was sun bathing by the mountain stream awaiting her lover. Her name was Telesuv. Telesuv was not only beautiful but she was also sharp of mind, having been taught by the elder women of the village. Her lover, Kaidon, was a great warrior who helped defend the village from the seasonal raids of the Wild Ones.

Telesuv had no idea that her life would change forever that very day. As she sat by the stream combing her hair, she heard the soft sounds of small bells tinkling in the air. A gentle breeze picked up and the smell of lavender filled her nostrils. A movement in the stream caught her eye. It grew more defined, then all of the sudden the surface of the water broke with a splash. In the stream stood a young girl, which Telesuv had never seen before. Her skin was silvery and scaly with a greenish cast like a fishes'. She splashed Telesuv and giggled.

Surprised, Telesuv jumped back and asked, "Who are you?"

"I am Vaisak the Water Nymph, I am the Daughter of the Stream. I have been watching you and I know you await your lover Kaidon," she grinned mischievously.

"What of it?" replied Telesuv. Vaisak dove down and came back up with her cheeks full of water and spat a stream at Telesuv. The Nymph started to laugh and in between her fits she said; "Kaidon has been captured by the Wild Ones, he's all wet like you but with blood, not water."

"I don't believe you!" shouted Telesuv, annoyed.

"If you don't believe me, I can show you, but you must come quickly before it's too late."

Worried, Telesuv agreed to go with the Nymph. Vaisak drew a circle with her finger on the water's surface. The area of the Circle she described turned into a black void.

"Come, let us go!" said the Nymph and, she dove into the darkness. Reeling from confusion Telesuv jumped into dark void after Vaisak. The Fair Damsel was never to be seen again...

Soon after, Kaidon arrived at the stream where he had agreed to meet Telesuv, only to find it empty. Suddenly, Kaidon heard the sound of small bells and the scent of lavender filled the air. Looking about he was startled to see a young girl before him. The Nymph introduced herself as Vaisak. She told Kaidon that she saw Telesuv a while ago and of how a raiding party of the Wild Ones rode through and kidnapped her. Vaisak pointed to the western mountains and urged Kaidon to hurry. She suggested that he seek the Hermit Kajior who lives in a cave on the third peak. Surely, the Hermit knew much and would help Kaidon find his lover. He rode off just as the sun had passed its zenith.

The ride was hard for traversing the mountain gorges was neither easy nor quick. Finally, Kaidon scaled the third peak and came upon the cave of the Hermit. Kajior sat in his fire-lit dwelling casting runes on the ground. He looked up at Kaidon and said "I've been expecting you." He wore an earth colored robe, and its hood covered his face. Kajior's movements seemed agile and cat like and were certainly not that of an old man.

"The Nymph, Vaisak, urged me seek you out. I am looking for my lover Telesuv who was kidnapped this very morning from Turegan village," said Kaidon. The Hermit reached out to him in a calming gesture.

"Rest assured young warrior Kaidon, the runes will tell us all." he pointed to a pile of furs.

"Sit and let us see what they have to say."

They sat down and the Hermit cast the runes. After a few moments, the Hermit Kajior spoke.

"It is true that the Wild Ones have taken her to their fortress beyond the mountains deep in the Shadow Forest." To hasten Kaidon's journey the Hermit offered to open a portal to the forest stronghold of the Wild Ones. Kajior with his staff drew the outline of a gate in the space before him uttering an incantation. The portal grew dark and shimmering. Kaidon thanked the Hermit for his help, drew his sword and walked into the blackness of the portal...

Some say that a Traveler, who once was a great hero and warrior, now wanders lost in the mountains searching for a way to the Shadow Forest in order to save his lady fair. They say the Traveler changed his name to Tushubak so that his once noble name would not be tarnished by his miserable failure at rescuing his lost love. Tushubak is sometimes seen in taverns drinking and telling stories of his curse which keeps him trapped in the mountains. But the Damsel Telesuv was not captured by the Wild Ones. Instead the Nymph Vaisak banished her to the heart of the Shadow Forest. She spent many years trying to find her way back home, but the forest never seemed to end. After much anguish she decided to make the forest her new home. One day, huddled in her make-shift hut, she saw a man. Her heart jumped and she prayed it could be her long lost love Kaidon, but alas, it was not.

The man turned out to be a Hermit. Telesuv told him of her woes and begged him to take her with him, beyond the cursed forest.

Listening to the sad story, the Hermit took pity on the Damsel and offered her a deal.

"I cannot take you with me as the spell that has cast you here will keep you here. And I am unable to break such a spell. However, since you are doomed to spend your life here by yourself and with many hardships, I can make your life a bit better."

"Oh please sir, I am powerless, I have no weapons nor house, and I freeze during the nights. Anything you can do to help me will be welcomed," she said.

"Very well, I can offer you magickal powers with which you can command the spirits to build you a nice house and other things to ease your lonely existence," said the Hermit.

"Oh sir, that sounds like a blessing! What must I do to be given these powers?"

"Like all things in the universe, everything requires an exchange," he nodded. "There is really nothing you have to barter with, except for your youth and beauty."

Telesuv's heart sank at the words of the Hermit. But what use was her beauty here in this Shadow Forest, where she would live forever by herself? Kaidon's gaze will never fall upon me again, she thought. The years had been hard and any comfort would welcomed.

"It breaks my heart to give up my beauty, but times have been hard and any help will be welcomed. I accept your offer, sir."

The Hermit Kajior lifted his fly agaric staff and placed it upon her and uttering an incantation. Telesuv's face drained of youth and became withered and old. Her beautiful soft black hair turned gray and brittle. Her breasts grew long and sagging; her back arched and she hunched over. The pain made her weep and lament the loss of her youth and beauty.

"Cry not Telesuv! Though you have given up your youth and beauty, you are now powerful. Behold, all you have to do is command the spirits and they will fulfill your will. Take this magick talisman and speak your desire, but re-member, you are no longer Telesuv the Damsel, you are now Satokmes the Witch. Command the spirits with your new name!" said Kajior.

Satokmes took the talisman and spoke:

"I, Satokmes the Witch of the Shadow Forest command you spirits to build me a wonderful house with many chimneys and comfortable furnish-ings!" As she finished her spell, a flood of loud crushing and tearing sounds filled the forest as if a thousand lumber jacks and craftsman had set out to work. Within a few moments, an elegant forest mansion stood before her. Be-yond its doors she beheld many comfortable sofas and chairs and a glowing warm fire place. She turned back to the Hermit but he was already gone...

After many years, the Traveler Tushubak grew tired and old, he had given up on life and on his quest. One day, on a mountainous crag he prayed for death. Death did come, but not how he expected. With bitter tears he looked about the world for the last time, ready to dive off the rock into the chasm of jagged cliffs below. But a small movement caught his eye that made him grow still. A black shadow was making its way towards him. It was small at first, but became larger as it drew closer. Finally a large black panther stood before him. Its eyes glowed golden and blazed with the fires of the sun. It sat down on its haunches next to Tushubak and spoke to him:

"Greetings Tushubak, who once was known as Kaidon! The gods have sent me to fulfill your death wish. But they offer you something that might make your heart a bit lighter in your end days." "I curse the gods and all magick, for my life has been nothing less than a tragedy and I no longer care for anything. And who are you to be bringing me any words of comfort?" said Tushubak.

"I am called Brudotyk. I am the Usherer of Dead, and I have come to send you on your final quest. However, I speak not of comfort, but of revenge!" smiled Brudotyk. Revenge? The word grew dark in Tushubak's heart. Oh for that one chance to kill that cursed Hermit! He thought.

"I see into your heart Tushubak. Yes! I offer you a chance to settle the score with that Hermit. But know this, the Hermit was actually a shape shifting Witch called Satokmes who was jealous of your love for Telesuv. She lives in the Black Forest in a wondrous house."

"That whore! That evil fucking bitch!" Kaidon cried, "I will kill her! "And let it be so! But, in order to do that I must turn you into a great wild wolf, for Satokmes knows the forest and if she would hear and see a man, you would be torn apart by her spirits and beasts."

"Make it so, Brudotyk. Turn me into a ravenous wolf! Let me go and kill this Witch before I die!" swore Tushubak. "As you wish..." smiled Brudotyk and changed Tushubak into a ferocious wolf. "Now you are called Kenotuj the Wolf Avenger! Go and take your revenge!" As Kenotuj the Wolf, Tushubak was finally able to leave the mountains and go on his last quest to kill the cruel Witch Satokmes...

Many years had passed since Satokmes saw the Hermit Kajior. She found some joy in her powers. The animals talked to her and kept her company so her heart was not empty and quiet. Her home was cozy and warm, and she feasted on delicious meals and drank the finest of wines. It almost made her forget the curse that had cast her to this Shadow Forest so many years ago. One morning, strolling through her garden, she heard a howling from deep in the forest. She thought nothing of it, for the wolves had become her protectors. She smiled and in her heart she wished them a good hunt. But the howling drew nearer and wilder and she did not recognize the wolf's song.

As Satokmes turned to go inside the house a great wolf broke out of the forest. The massive beast leapt towards her with a cry of madness and fury.

The wolf Kenotuj knocked her to the ground and bit into her flesh. She screamed but her cries only excited the wolf, who then tore out her throat. As the blood flowed and drenched the earth, Kenotuj pounced on her corpse with horrifying glee. At last you cruel whore die for you have kept me away from my love all these years, he thought. But when Kenotuj looked down at the corpse of the Witch again, to his horror he saw the face of his beloved Telesuv.

"No!" cried Kenotuj "Damn you all! Damn all you gods! I curse you forever!" he cried, broken hearted. His sobs gave way to the fading breaths of life which started to escape him. Kenotuj felt his fur change back to skin, to that youthful skin from so long ago. In sadness he laid his head on his lover's body and died. United at long last they slept...

The gods had let the Trickster, who has many names and faces, play his game uninterrupted up to this point. Finally, they decided to intervene. For his cruelty and malice, they banished him to the in between realm.

There he awaits us all at the gates between life and death, lurking at the crossroads. As for the tragic lovers the gods lifted the spirit of Telesuv from her bones and breathed new life into her. She rose from her corpse and the gods gave her a new name: Vitosel, the Maiden's Ghost. She whose fate was cruel, was given an eternity of peace to dwell in her Shadow Forest. You can still hear Vitosel's song echo in the dark forests. There she dances in her blissful madness, accompanied by a large wolf who sometimes takes the form of a fair youth. There they dwell forever in their eternal love...

The Spirits, their Sigils, Attributes & Incantations

KAIDON

Tough One / BOGATYR: The Hero

Kaidon should be summoned in times when bravery and courage are needed. His nature is rash and fiery. He is over enthusiastic and can lead the magickian to great peril. However, his strength and optimism can be useful in dire times. To conjure him salute the sun with a sword and then thrust it into the earth. He is to be invoked at sunrise on the day of Mars when the moon is new, with these words:

Spell 1

ᚢᛏᛊ-ᚻ-ᚦᛒᛏᛈ ᚹᚢᚦᚦ ᚢᚦᛒ ᚦᚦᚻ ᚻᛒᛏᚹ ᚻᚢᚦᚦ

V AI-V-D AN TELO VER KI꜀ UR AT MEL

ᚻᚦᚦᚨᛏᛈ ᛈᚦᚻ ᛚᚻᚦᚦ ᚢᛏᚦ ᚹᚢᚦ ᚦᚨᛒ ᚦᚦᚻ.

GDI AN NI꜀ BUKU V AL TEK SIR OM.

VAISAK

Spit Attacker / RUSAWKA: The Water Demoness

Vaisak should be summoned when the heart of a man has been vexed by a woman. She will gladly offer her services, for causing strife and conflict is her nature. She is childish and very fickle, thus, great caution should be used in trafficking with her. To conjure her, make an offering of silver trinkets (such as small silver bells) and tie these to a tree by a stream. She is to be invoked at sunset on the day of Venus when the moon is waning, with these words:

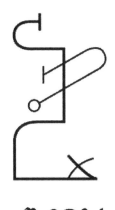

Spell 2

✝ℚℑ⚇ℑ᚜ Ⴎℽ᚛ᒯⴱ ✝ᒷ᚜ℑ᚜ ᚑ᚜᚛ᒷ ℽℑᒷ ℑ᚛ ᚑℑ᚛ℑᒼᚖ
ASOMEL VIRT ABEL TUH GER EV TEKLI

ℑᒷ✝⚇⚇ ᚑℑ᚜᚛ ℚℑℙℑᚑ ✝⚇⚇ᚑ᚜᚛ ℑᚑ ᒷᒼ✝ᒷ ✝ᚑ-ᚖᒼ✝᚜.
ERAM TELL SEXET AMIT EF BAR AT-DAL.

TELESUV

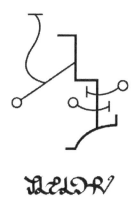

Hair Charmer / DZIEVITZA: The Fair Damsel
Telesuv should be summoned to gain the love of a woman. She protects the hearts of lovers from the bitter stings of jealously and infidelity. Her nature is serene and calm, for she knows the heart's desires. If you choose to call upon her favor be sure your heart is true, otherwise she will break your spirit and your lover's. To conjure her, invite her to sit and comb her hair before a bedroom mirror. She is to be invoked at noon on the day of Venus when the moon is waxing, with these words:

Spell 3

Ⴎ✝ℚ᚜ ℽℙ⚇ℚℑℽ ᒷᚖℽℑℽ⚇⚇ ᛘ✝ℽℑ᚛ ℽℑ᚛ Ⴎⴱ᚜ℑ
NAS' VISOT RITOM KATEJ VEJ NILO

ᒷᒼℑ-ᚖ ᒷℽℙ✝ᛘ Ⴎℑℽ ᒼᒷℑ⚇⚇ℑᚖ᚛ℙ ℑᒼᚖℑℚ!
BO-I RVAK NET PROMEGIN OLIES!

SATOKMES:

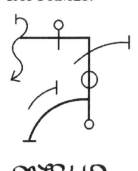

Lamp's Back Labor / CHAROVNITZA: The Cursed Witch
Satokmes should be summoned during times of transition in the lives of magickians. She is a great teacher in the ways of herbalism, potions and talismans. To her belongs the secret forest initiations and rites of passage. Her nature is generous; however, if you call her without certainty and knowledge, your calls will go unanswered. She loves household pets and gives loyal familiars. To conjure her go to a thick forest and place an offering of an effigy anointed with your blood, leaving it in a fairy ring. She is to be invoked at midnight on the day of Mercury when the moon is new, with these words:

Spell 4

ᛁᛑᛞᚳᚢᚩ ᚠᛜ-ᛥᛜᛞ ᛃᛝᚢᚢᛞ ᛁᚢᚩ ᚦ†ᛥᛜᛞᚢᚢ

BIDOK VI-MI ESTI BO KᴧAMIT

ᛒᚩ ᚠᛜᛞᛃᛝ †ᚢᚢᛞᚳ ᛁᛞᚢᚢᛃᛥᛥ ᛒ†ᛝᛃᛥᛥ

REVIOS ᴧATIR BITEM XᴧASOM

TUSHUBAK

Into the Tide / BOYAN: The Old Traveler
Tushubak should be summoned in times of wander-lust. He is most useful when the magickian is on a journey and wishes to find safe lodgings and comforts on the road. He will find you a good tavern, good drinking and whoring companions. Take care to use him only occasionally for he is debaucherous. To conjure him tie a child's toy car to a gnarled wooden staff and stick it into the earth by a great road. He is to be invoked at sunrise on the day of Mercury when the moon is waxing, with these words:

Spell 5

ᛞᛒᛥᛥ†ᛈᛃᚢᚢ ᚦᛞᚢᛞ ᛈ†ᛝᛞ ᚼᛃ ᛈᛃᛝ ᛁᛃᛞᛒ†ᚠᛃᛥᛥ ᛒᛞ ᛃᛝ

DIMᴧANOT KUTKI NᴧASI 'JE NOS BODᴧAfEM RI OS

ᚠ†ᛈ ᛞᛒᛃᛝᛥᛥᛃ ᛞᛒ†ᛥ.

DESMO DᴧAT.

ᛞᛒ†ᛞ ᛃᛞ ᛥᛥᛃ ᛁᛃᛈᛈ ᛝᛞᚠ† ᚦᛒᛞᚢᚢᛞ-†ᛈ ᛞᛒᛝᛞᛞ ᛒᛃᚢᚢ ᚢᚢᛞᚦ.

DᴧAI OL MO BONE SIVᴧA KRITIᴧAN D'UZH RET TOK.

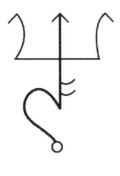

KAJIOR

Earth Digger / PUSTELNIK: The Cruel Hermit
Kajior should be summoned when all physical measures have been exhausted. He removes the obstruction of the weak, for those who wish to rise to greater positions. When dealing with him be cautious, for he makes two sided deals; formulate your charge in a manner that is non-negotiable. To conjure him, make an effigy of the one who you wish to curse. Write their name upon the poppet and cover it in

graveyard dirt. He is to be invoked at midnight on the day of Saturn while the moon is waning, with these words:

Spell 6

VAFIM BU TRUHE VITKA ME SOLTKLI MEON

VITUS KATRI VET ONFA TRI HAM BELLET

BGOS FRAT KELI.

VITOSEL

Sap Weaver / STRZYGA: Ghost Maiden

Vitosel should be summoned for inquiries about the dead. She is the lost weeping ghost of utter divine madness. She will gladly let you peer into the twilight realm of the dead. Take care not to inquire too long for her madness is infectious. Her knowledge is great and she knows much about the souls of the recently departed.

To conjure, her place a black mirror on a pile of human ashes or bones. Invoke her at twilight on the day of the Moon when the moon is full with these words:

Spell 7

BRUD VTTEN KIOS SEN, ALRUAN BUSN PRAG

TUT SENTOSH ATV AT DELLUM ES.

TA EVEK SHTAM ONOLU, LAOD TEBASH RIT

DATTON KIR LAKOF VAI, KIM TU IE.

BLAD NIR XRAM!

KENOTUJ

Hidden Dream Tide / VILKOWAK: The Wolf Avenger

Kenotuj should be summoned when a guardian of the circle is necessary. He is fierce and blind in his charge. He will not stray from his post and will faithfully guard the magickian during his workings. Take care to give him proper sustenance before any rite is attempted. To conjure him, place an offering of bloody red meat before a wolf's skull or a figure thereof. He is to be invoked at sunset on the day of Jupiter when the moon is waxing, with these words:

Spell 8

ᏏᎦᎠ ᏜᴣᎧᏝᎷ ᏛᏞᴣᏤᏛ ᏛᏯᏝᏝ ᏛᏕᎧᏢᴣᎤ ᏛᏝᏝᏛ
HOT HES_AM VRUT TI_AL MONES V_ART
ᏝᏝᏏᎤᎨ ᎨᏛᏔᏝᏕ ᏕᎨᏏ ᎧᎤᏝᏝᏛ ᏕᎤᎤᎤᎤᏛᏔᏝᏁ ᏕᎨᏐ ᏝᎤᏝᏝᏔᏐ.
R_AROG GIDU MEL SOL_ANTEK MOS BOD_AI.
ᏐᏝᏝᏔᏐ ᏛᎤᏛ ᏝᏝᏕᎤᏛ ᏛᏝᏕ ᏝᎤᏛᎤᏁ.
K_ALI TET _AJMON J_AM PONES.

BRUDOTYK

Door's Crowned Lion / SMIERCH: The Death Usher

Brudotyk should be summoned to open portals and aid in transformations. As a servant of death, the ultimate transformer, he is both guide and keeper. He can take the magickian on a unexpected journey, but the end result will always be the resolution of the fate decreed by the gods. To conjure him, go to a high place, and peer over the edge, and allow for a moment

of panic. He is to be invoked at sunrise on the day of the Sun when the moon is new, with these words:

LEK MAV-ERON. ALUS SEN RIN NOJIK, TABRIV GADEN LAY KON TESHUB AGRI MAN BOLIR MET.

Spell 9

LEK MAV-ERON. ALUS SEN RIN NOJIK,

TABRIV GADEN LAT KON TESHUB

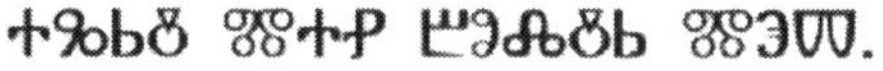

AGRI MAN BOLIR MET.

Amanda Sipes, *Qliphoth*

A Prayer to Kain, Master of the Kliffot

Matthew Wightman

I pray with you,

Master of Sin
Bridegroom of the Cursed Earth
Exile
King
Soldier
Crucifier
Saint

Guide me upon the Path
Of Profundity
Through the Wanderings
Of Wisdom
To the Sanctification
Of Profanity
And the Profanity
Of Sanctification
I weep with you Bitter tears
For the Lost Innocence
But rejoice with you
For the Revelation Of Knowledge

You cut down
The Tree of Life
In Vicarious
Self-Sacrifice

To lay bare
The Tree of Daath

And in so doing
Revealed
The Red Tree
Of the Blood
Of the Absolute
And of the particular,
Of Life

And Death,
Of Perdition
And Salvation,
Of Redemption
And Resurrection

The bitterness
Of my Hatred
And the primal origins
Of my anger
Have found their Fulfillment
In (y)our Sacrifice
And as the Serpent's Scales fell
From (y)our eyes
They were taken up
By the Eyes of the Creator

Making Us Other
We have been Reconciled
To our Enemy
By our Enemy

Grant me the strength
To Accept
Our Reconciliation
And turn All
Enemies into Neighbors
On this Dark Winter Solstice Night
May we partake
In the Blood

Of the Absolute,
Our Enemy
And only true Friend,
Given Freely
Taken Mercilessly
Fulfilling Eternally

Lay down
Your Scythe
To take up
The Grail
And find
The Love
And Acceptance Desired
Since the Beginning. ✶

Matt Baldwin Ives, *Tectratys*

The Cyber Vampire

FEEDING WITHIN THE
CONSENSUAL REALITY MATRIX

S. Ben Qayin

Will you walk into my parlour?" said the Spider to the Fly,
'Tis the prettiest little parlour that ever you did spy;
The way into my parlour is up a winding stair,
And I've a many curious things to shew
when you are there."
Oh no, no, said the little Fly, to ask me is in vain,
For who goes up your winding stair can
ne'er come down again.
—Mary Howitt, *The Spider and the Fly*, 1829

HEN one begins to ponder the subject of the 'Vampire', generally classic images of the being instantly emerge that have long enamored and horrified the populace since time immemorial. Like other entities I have written of (The Djinn, The Old Ones), the 'Vampire', be it in human form or not, has always been entwined with humanities shadow, for the Vampire is both within the shadow...and the shadow itself. The vampire is humanities dark reflection, concealing forbidden desires of power, lust and death that lie hidden just beneath the porcelain mask of normalcy and domestication. It is the embodiment of unrestrained freedom and life which embraces one's true will and desire, submitting to total base instinct without constraint. The Vampire is primal indulgence.

The idea of an entity that roams free in the night and drains its victims of sustenance, thus life, to in turn nourish itself, is both alluring and disturbing. It appeals to one's inner nature; to be free of one's shackles and inhibitions that constrict the soul of life itself. Yet, this is a forbidden independence that goes against the traditional laws of both man and God alike.

The vampire is branded the outsider, the loner, the one who walks with death and shadows...for the vampire is a wanderer of the night and keeper of its silent secrets.

It is both this bright freedom and dark curse the vampire offers. It is a freedom that the soul needs to thrive and feel alive, though is only found outside the rigid walls and rules of accepted civilized thought. And thus, the conflict within is born. Does one give in to their screaming desires and needs, or stay a slave to the sleeping daytime world ?

The path of the Vampire is a dark and often perilous one. And, though danger surrounds, humanity is compelled to return to the being,

> *The Spider turned him round about, and went into his den,*
> *For well he knew the silly Fly would soon come back again:*
> *So he wove a subtle web, in a little corner sly,*
> *And set his table ready, to dine upon the Fly.*

—Ibid

As a moth to the flame, humanity is drawn to death. Perhaps it is this same brand of curiosity that is said to have killed the cat. Humanity cannot escape this attraction, for it is ingrained within the deepest parts of man's soul and psyche. And yet, as strong as the pull of death on mortality is, the obsession to defy it seems to eclipse. There are many compelling tales throughout time of pacts with the Devil, springs of eternal life and sacred holy cups that promise such grandeur as immortality. And perhaps, there is truth to these ancient tales, as the world is a far more mysterious place than what is advertised by the common corporate masses. Though such incredible cures to death may have been achievable in their time, many have searched for a more readily available solution to the inconvenient, inevitability, of death.

Though most humans see death as final, death truly does not exist. On a quantum level all matter is composed of pure energy which cannot be destroyed or cease to be,

> Energy cannot be created or destroyed, but it can be transferred or transformed from one form to another (including transformation into or from mass, as matter). The total amount of energy in a closed system never changes.
>
> The Law of Conservation of Energy

Therefore, death is only a transformation or transference from one form to another.

However as stated, there are those who seek vampiric eternal life, youth and even supernatural abilities. A vampire is generally considered a being that absorbs an essence (be it blood, energy, or else) from another being either with its consent or not, depending on the morality and ethics of the vampire. There are many different kinds of vampire, though generally there are two main categories that one relates to; Sanguinarian Vampire and Psychic or Energy Vampire. The sanguinarian vampire consumes blood from either humans or animals to fulfill a deep seeded need for energy or sustenance.

For the life of the flesh is in the blood...

—Leviticus 17:11

Yet, the energy vampire uses various techniques to obtain pure energy from the human energy field. Generally, both types of vampire utilize willing 'donors' to obtain that which they desire. It is required they feed off of humans or animals for the energy they seek. Nevertheless, there is a more efficient way to obtain pure energy that does not depend on living creatures to be donors. The information provided here is twofold, as it gives the sorcerer access to advanced vampiric technology, while bringing the vampire into a new age of enlightenment.

We are whirling through endless space, at an inconceivable speed, all around everything is spinning, everything is moving...everywhere there is energy. There must be some way of availing ourselves of this energy more directly...

—Nikola Tesla

The above quote in its speculation could not be more correct, there is indeed a better way to 'avail ourselves to this energy more directly'. One must tap into the pure energy of reality itself...

Since time is distance in space, time is memory on the structure of space. Without memory, there is no time. Without time, there is no memory. It then follows that the energy that we perceive as the material world must be information, or energy on the structure of space."

—Nassim Haramein

Concerning matter, we have been all wrong. What we have called matter is energy, whose vibration has been so lowered as to be perceptible to the senses. There is no matter.

—Albert Einstein

Today a young man on acid realized that all matter is merely energy condensed to a slow vibration, that we are all one consciousness experiencing itself subjectively, there is no such thing as death, life is only a dream, and we are the imagination of ourselves. Here's Tom with the weather.

—Bill Hicks

These quotes echo the same sentiment; that at its basest composition/structure, all of existence is nothing but pure energy. This energy can be vampirically moved from one place to another within the closed system of the Consensual Reality Matrix. All one needs is the ability to 'see' the truth of reality, and 'accept' into their belief system that truth to accomplish this end. That is much easier said than done, as that is the ultimate goal of the practice of magic/reality manipulation for all sorcerers. Breaking away from the dogma of illusion that surrounds is harder to get over than ingrained religious dogma, as it is the foundation upon which that later dogma was built upon. Illusions upon illusions...Breaking the structured conditioning.

Dream delivers us to dream, and there is no end to illusion. Life is like a train of moods like a string of beads, and, as we pass through them, they prove to be many-colored lenses which paint the world their own hue...

—Ralph Waldo Emerson

However, once one overcomes this hurdle, one is free. There are no more boundaries or walls to smash through. No more limits or laws. No more consensual logic. Though ironically, that is what truly terrifies so many. Once there is not the safety net of a logical structured reality to fall back upon, then one is left to freefall in a limitless solipsistic solitude. Therefore, not only must one acknowledge that reality is not as it is represented to the senses, but also that we are ultimately alone in a world of our own creation.

God is alone...

Neither of these two revelations are very comforting to those so conditioned, and they may pull back from the truth. Many who fear this truth imbed themselves within religion as they find safety among the many who also seek the security of ignorance; they verify each other's reality and so cling tightly together. It is the base reason why if their religion and faith is questioned that they defend it so vehemently. They don't want to 'see'...

I'm waiting for the night to fall I know that it will save us all
When everything's dark Keeps us from the stark reality...

It's easier here just to forget fear
And when I squinted
The world seemed rose-tinted
And angels appeared to descend
To my surprise
With half-closed eyes
Things looked even better
Than when they were open...

—Depeche Mode

The Sorcerer is the center of their universe (their Personal Reality Grid). All exists because they exist. Whatever the sorcerer allows to exist within their personal reality grid, exists. However, magic is where the sorcerer takes their reality and pushes it (using Intent) into the shared Consensual Reality Matrix (the reality we all agree on and interact in) through ritual, causing changes to occur that all can experience. The more energy that is pushed into magical rites, the more the Consensual Reality Matrix is changed to the will of the sorcerer. Therefore, it follows that it would be beneficial for the sorcerer to have access to vampiric occult technology that allows them to draw in this needed energy to empower their rites to the fullest.

Every single one of us goes through life depending on and bound by our individual knowledge and awareness. And we call it reality. However, both knowledge and awareness are equivocal. One's reality might be another's illusion. We all live inside our own fantasies.

—Unknown

So how do we tap into this well of energy that surrounds us and creates/forms our reality; both consensual and personal?

If you want to find the secrets of the universe, think in terms of energy, frequency and vibration.

—Nikola Tesla

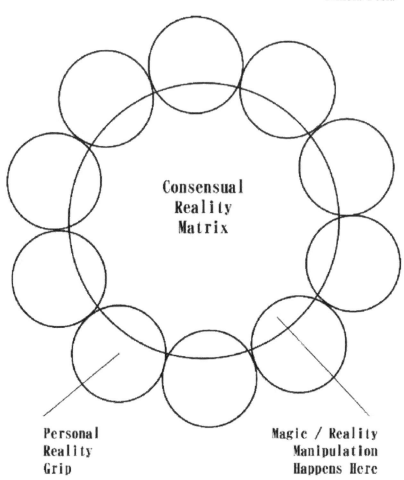

At its base structure, magic is composed of energy, consciousness and Intent. In fact, everything we do, be it magic or not, begins with energy, consciousness and Intent. Energy and consciousness create our reality, and Intent is the driving force behind all further thought or action. We create our reality (the personal grid of the sorcerer), based on what we allow ourselves to incorporate into that reality. Therefore, if reality is just a wave of energy possibilities that becomes structured to conform with our individual expectations, then it follows that if we believe we can tap into that pure energy field of all of creation, that we are already a part of and connected to, then we can.

It has been scientifically proven that we can change the structure of matter (energy) by focusing our Intent. This has been done with water and ice, and logically follows that all other matter is just as effected. We control our reality. There are people who can levitate, who haven't eaten in decades, who can move objects with their thoughts. These people understand that the reality they exist in is created by their own self-imposed restrictions, and have removed them.

Do not try and bend the spoon, that's impossible. Instead, only try to realize the truth...there is no spoon. Then you will see it is not the spoon that bends, it is only yourself.

— The Matrix

A perfect example of creating our own reality is shown in the creation of egregores and how they come into existence. But first we must look at what 'Magic' is. What I consider to be 'Magic', is nothing other than science. What else can it be ? The definition of 'Science' is:

The intellectual and practical activity encompassing the systematic study of the structure and behavior of the physical and natural world through observation and experiment

— Oxford Dictionary

Is that definition not what the study and practice of 'Magic' is? Magicians study the structure of the universe and what it is composed of in its totality, in order to use advanced scientific/occult techniques in experiment, gaining experience through observation of result. One does not generally think of Magic as being a system of advanced scientific techniques, but that is exactly what it is when broken down and examined (as I did in my works, "The Book of Smokeless Fire" & "The Black Book Of Azathoth"). The only true way to do that is to study all the different forms magic takes, and make comparisons based on technique and result. It is a course of study I am grateful to know has no end.

As sorcerers are utilizing scientific techniques and philosophies to gain insight into the occult world, on occasion scientists too, utilize occult techniques to understand the mind, reality and existence. Science is beginning to expand its understanding and acceptance of occult principals. This is where the example of the egregore becomes relevant.

In 1972 a group of nine scientists from Ontario Canada decided to do a study on Thought Forms, and if they could create a consciousness they could interact with by giving it a name and detailed history. After several weeks of trying to make contact with the created entity or thought form 'Philip', they began to gets results. When asked, the created entity would recite its life and history with the exact same detail as the scientists assigned it. It responded to questions by rapping upon the table the scientists gathered around in their sessions.

In essence this occult entity or thought form was created in a lab for the scientific purpose of proving a shared fictional reality, can become a shared factual reality with enough Intent put behind its creation. Or that one's personal reality grid does indeed overlap the consensual reality matrix when enough energy is utilized. The implications of this experiment are vast, spanning the question of consciousness and where it originates from, to reality and the ability to mold it to our expectations.

Everything you can imagine is real.

—Pablo Picasso

Science and magic cannot be separated or divided.
Everything we consider real is made of things that cannot be considered real.

—Niels Bohr

Our reality, is what we make of it. Through our consciousness and Intent, we are gods of our lives and destinies.

Nothing is an absolute reality; all is permitted.

—Bartol

Therefore, now that we have an understanding of the basis of reality, energy, magic and how entities are created, we can move forward with the vampiric applications the sorcerer can put into practice within their personal reality grid by combining these topics of discussion, and creating an egregore for the purpose of vampirically drawing in and harnessing this energy that is the reality we are immersed in; the consensual reality matrix. This energy is then utilized within the personal grid/reality of the sorcerer, to obtain desired results.

On a side note; of course one can interface with the consensual reality matrix directly (As will be discussed in my forthcoming book; "Exodus; The Vampiric Transmissions"), but I wished to share information about the creation of egregores, energy transference and the basis of reality, so combined the subjects as a whole, as all are very complimentary and flow into one another.

Thought Forms or Egregores are quite powerful, as they stem from the mind of the sorcerer. As Athena was sprung from the mind of Zeus, so too does the sorcerer give birth to entities through their thoughts. Phil Hine states:

> The term egregore is derived from a Greek word meaning "to be aware of" or "to watch over". An egregore is commonly understood to be magical entity purposefully created by a group or order as an encapsulation of the group's collective aspirations and ideals.

As this is very true, I personally find creating an egregore for a specific task or goal that pertains directly to myself, far more beneficial. I view egregores as familiars that come and go, existing until I no longer need them, when their purpose has been fulfilled. Though the egregore can be created purposefully or not. Many times such Intent and emotion is put into a specific ideal or goal, that one is created as a sort of side effect. The sorcerer not even being aware of its creation or existence. It is very important for the sorcerer to be aware of their thoughts, as universes are created and destroyed with them.

The Vampiric Sorcerer has entered a new age, one of occult sciences that offer advanced techniques of energy transference and consumption. Reality is Energy, Consciousness and Intent. Which of these principals came to 'be' first cannot be known. Time is an illusion and that illusion is circular in nature. The Chicken produced the egg from which it hatched.

> I have realized that the past and future are real illusions, that they exist in the present, which is what there is and all there is.
>
> —Alan W. Watts

With this knowledge all is possible. Tap into the base structure of realities veins and drink deep, fill yourself with the strength and gnosis of immortality that lies at your fingertips... all you must do is believe. ✶

Mitchell Nolte, *Thaumiel Angel*

Nephthys

Darkness & Sacrifice

Asenath Mason

I am Nephthys, I am Shta, the future is born of me for my blood is the source of time.

—Donn Webb, The Seven Faces of Darkness

THE role of Nephthys, the dark sister of Isis, is often underestimated while discussing Egyptian initiatory magic. She is either overshadowed by her sister or mentioned merely as the consort of Set and pushed into the background. In fact, however, her role is just as important as the role of the other major deities of the ancient Egyptian pantheon, and in this article we will look at her as a goddess of death and sacrifice, the dark counterpart of Isis - mistress of life, wisdom, health, and magic.

In myths and historical accounts, Nephthys is "the Friend of the Dead," and she is described as a companion of the deceased on their journey into the underworld. Her hair is compared to the strips of cloth that shroud the bodies of the dead, she protects the mummy - the earthly vessel of the deceased soul, and she defends the pharaoh in life as well as in death by incinerating his enemies with her fiery breath. She can also endow the soul with the power to see that which is "hidden by moonlight," which implies that her domain is magic, but contrary to the domain of her sister, her power is not of light, but of darkness. Apart from Isis, she is the sister of Osiris and the sister-wife of Set, born of Geb and Nut - earth and sky. Another role of the goddess is that of the mother of Anubis, the lord of the dead, which links her with necromancy and death mysteries.

The name "Nephthys" is alternatively spelled "Nebet-Het" or "Nebt-Het" and translated as "the Mistress of the House." This is reflected in the hieroglyphic symbol for her name, which shows a house and a basket placed on top of it, and in art she is usually portrayed as a woman wearing a head-dress in the shape of a house and basket. For this reason, in some sources she is associated with a domestic household and mistakenly identified with the concept of a "housewife." In fact, "the house" as her domain stands for a temple, or a place of initiation, referring both to the temple as a physical structure where initiatory rites are held and to the body of an initiate as a place of transformation and initiation. Seeing her from this perspective, we might interpret her name as "the Lady of the Temple" - priestess, companion and initiatrix.

Her other symbol is a bird, usually a falcon or hawk, and the goddess herself often appears in rites of magic as a woman with black feathered wings. She arises from the night, cloaked in darkness, residing in the center of black empty space, or she is surrounded with a thick black mist which assumes the form of snakes or winged spectres. These nocturnal entities are extension of her infinite and timeless essence, often manifesting in rites of evocation to speak on behalf of the goddess. They also reflect her primordial nature, showing that she is one of the primal deities and displaying her connection to the Draconian/Ophidian current.

In her primary role, Nephthys is believed to be a goddess of death, lamentation and funerary rites. She is associated with necromancy and venerated as a friend and companion of the deceased, offering guidance to the newly dead and comfort to the relatives of the one who died. It is Nephthys who assists Isis in gathering the dismembered parts of the body of Osiris after he was murdered by his brother Set, she is the protector of the mummy, and along with Hapy she guards the lungs in their canopic jar on the north cardinal point. Her son, the jackal-headed god Anubis, is a patron of mummification, the guide of souls and the lord of the underworld. In art he is depicted as a "black god" - the color that stands for rebirth and the discoloration of the corpse after the completion of the embalming processes. The goddess herself is often "black" as well, although this does not refer to her depictions in art but to the color of her astral energy and her associations with darkness and nighttime.

As the dark twin sister of Isis, she represents death as a principle intertwined with life and birth, and she has connections with both. While Isis was believed to stand at the foot of the birth-bed to midwife the child, Nephthys stood at the head of the mother giving birth, assisting her and offering comfort. In the myths she is also the "nursing mother" and watchful guardian of the infant Horus, which makes her the "nursemaid" of the reigning pharaoh as well. She and Isis are not opposite, but rather complementary to each other. While Isis usually represents life and birth (or rebirth), Nephthys is associated with death and decay. Where Isis stands for light and the day, her twin sister represents darkness and the night. In one of the Pyramid Texts we find the following passage: "Ascend and descend. Descend with Nephthys, sink into darkness with the night-barque. Ascend with Isis, rise with the day-barque." On the other hand, it is not that simple, because both goddesses have aspects connected with life as well as with death, and both have powers associated with each of these domains. Nephthys herself is both a patron of embalming and a nursing and protective goddess. She is known as the protector of the Phoenix, whose rise from the ashes is a universal symbol of rebirth, purification and rejuvenation. However, she is also a ferocious goddess, whose fiery breath burns everything on her way, and she can be as dangerous and fearsome as her brother-consort Set.

In this ritual you will invoke Nephthys as a goddess of darkness and transformation. This aspect, which is also a part of the dark feminine archetype, is not the gentle, nurturing side of the goddess, but includes all her fearsome traits that are connected with transformation as a cleansing but painful experience. She transforms through destruction, kills the old parts of the Self to make way for growth, and demands a sacrifice of what you value the most in your life. She is the Mistress of Darkness and the Lady of Sacrifice. Other goddesses can embody this archetype as well, so if you prefer another godform to guide you through this initiation, feel free to do so. I have chosen Nephthys because of her connection to Set, who is one of my personal patron deities. This working was also inspired by a series of rituals conducted recently within the Temple of Ascending Flame. These rituals were centered on the concept of initiation, transformation and sacrifice. As a dark initiatrix, Nephthys demands that you sacrifice to her something of a great value in your life. Your home, your job, your loved one, etc. - this is what you may need to leave behind if you want to walk her path, and if you do so, she will reward you in ways that will make it all worth it. Of course, it is a difficult step, but such is also the nature of a true "sacrifice." The dark initiatrix represents the harsh life lessons that you have to learn in order to progress on your path. She will not take anything away from you, though. What she asks for is a willing sacrifice, and she will always give you a choice. Think about it before performing this working, and meditate on what you might give the goddess in return for her guidance and gnosis. Remember that it has to be something valuable and personal. Leave your sacrifice in her tomb so that it might be transformed and returned to you as a tool of growth and power. Descend into her darkness and embrace it so that you may truly understand the light. This may trigger a lot of emotional pain, fear of loss, or anxiety and dark thoughts. Let it happen - this is all a natural part of the initiatory process.

You can prepare something to represent your sacrifice, like a parchment with your petition to the goddess, or you can simply speak to her during the working itself. Some might say it is a form of a pact and you need a physical representation of it - if you feel that way, just follow your intuition. In my own work, however, I have found that speaking to the goddess is enough, if only your sacrifice is given from the heart and you stay true to your vows. It is also very likely that if your sacrifice is accepted, you will receive a confirmation from the goddess, which will be delivered to you in a clear and tangible way, so pay attention to all that happens both in the ritual and in your daily life.

The Ritual

Prepare yourself for this working by meditating on the sigil of the goddess and chanting the mantra:

Pert em kerh, Nebet-Het.

Do it on the day preceding the actual ritual, preferably before sleep, to attune yourself to the energies of the goddess and to open gateways to her current. Since the goddess is here invoked as a principle of darkness, the night is the best time for this work. Prepare a black candle representing the darkness of the goddess. Do not use other sources of light. If you work with incense, the best choice is frankincense or myrrh, although you can also use a blend called the Nile Temple.

Take the sigil into your hand, or place it in front of you, and gaze at it until you can memorize its shape. At the same time chant the mantra and focus on the current of the goddess flowing through the sigil into your temple and back - taking your intent through the gates of the night. Then blow out the candle and meditate in darkness. See the sigil burning in front of you, morphing into the shape of the goddess, and hear her voice speaking to you in response to your calling. Open yourself to her and embrace her presence. When you feel this presence leaving, close the working for the day.

On the day of the ritual begin the ceremony in the same way - light the black candle and burn the incense. Take a moment to attune yourself to the current of the goddess by gazing at the sigil and chanting her name. Then speak the following invocation:

I invoke Nephthys, Mistress of the Temple, Initiator into the mysteries of
life and death, Daughter of Nut and Geb, child of the earth and the sky!
I call forth the friend of the dead and protector of the living,
Sister of Isis, wife of Set and mother of Anubis!
I summon the Lady of the Night,
For I am, (your magical name)!

Visualize the goddess manifesting in front of you - a woman in a long black dress, with black hair and black eyes. She is surrounded by darkness which seems alive - it is moving and morphing into shapes of snakes and ghastly faces. At the same time you can chant the mantra "Pert em kerh, Nebet-Het," or simply open yourself up to the current of the goddess. When you build her image in your mind and feel her presence in the temple, continue the invocation:

Nephthys! Nebet-Het! Nebt-Het!

Hear my words and come to me!

Guide me through death and sacrifice to
rebirth and self- knowledge,

Lead me through darkness to light and through
fear to courage and strength,

And help me find stillness in chaos and wisdom
in confusion. Mistress of Darkness,

I stand before you to be transformed through your
harsh and beautiful rites,

Ready to sacrifice all that is needed to
walk the Path of the Night.

At this point offer your sacrifice - visualize it being absorbed into the darkness of Nephthys and disappearing from your life. If you have a parchment with your intent written on it, burn it in the flame of the candle and blow the ashes in all directions, thus delivering your sacrifice to the goddess. Then continue the working:

Black Mother,
Receive my sacrifice and bestow on me your dark blessing,
Protect and guide me on my way to the underworld,
So that I may gaze into the face of death,
And arise reborn from the Womb of the Night.

Blow out the candle, sit down, and focus on the darkness in the room. Feel it pressing upon your skin, entering your body with the air you breathe in, and cloaking you from all around. Meditate on how it feels to be devoured by this dark energy, absorbed, cleansed, and transformed. You can now take some personal time with the goddess and open yourself for any messages she may have for you. When you feel ready to finish the working, thank the goddess and close the ritual with a few personal words.

Sigil of Nephthys, Lady of the Night

Mitchell Note, *Thagirion*

The Dark Witcheries of Keziah Mason

Necro Magickal

EZIAH Mason is introduced in the story The Dreams in the Witch-House, written by Lovecraft in 1932. The original name for the story was The Dreams of Walter Gilman, after the main character in the tale. Many critics see this story as marginal with little impact on the overall of the mythos besides it being the forum for the first mentioning, in print, of both the Book of Eibon and the Unaussprechlichen. This pure scholarly critique is of course limited in its perceptions, for the tale contains a great deal of occult significance.

The true esoteric power in the story is found within its villain, Keziah Mason, inhabitant of the "legend haunted city of Arkham". Keziah was one of the original witches of Salem Massachusetts. Keziah is purported to have survived the tortures and ultimate death at the hands of the Salem inquisition in 1692, to lurk ever so hauntingly in the ether of Arkham. Her ability to escape such a dire sentence, unlike so many other witches during the burning.

times, comes from her witcheries and abilities to manipulate the very fabric of the time-space continuum. According to her trial excerpts, as given in the Essex county records, she confessed unto the judges of her ability to manipulate such a continuum and generate dimensional portals via certain lines and curves employed under ritualistic conditions. It was these same lines and curves smeared upon the walls of her former Salem cell in a "red sticky fluid" that allowed her egress from its confines and escape certain death to haunt the main character in the witch-house.

Whether Lovecraft based the character of Keziah mason on an actual personage is uncertain. There is no record in the transcripts of the Salem trials listing a Keziah Mason and Lovecraft never mentions her specifically in his vast letter correspondence. No record of a Keziah Mason in any extant witch-craft records, both within the United States and Europe has revealed her hav-ing existed. The possibility of Lovecraft having created her name from an an-agram of an actual person is possible, yet there is no permutation within the listed accused of Salem that may generate Keziah Mason. There are yet some similarities with the entirety of the story having striking resemblance to es-tablished historical witchcraft lore. Lovecraft was a studied individual having no doubt researched at one time or another many of the then published ma-terials concerning witchcraft. Some of the similarities may be found in refer-ence to the Canewdon witches. Canewdon, in Essex, also known as "The witch country", is an area rich with witch legends and lore. Much of this towns legend stems from the church tower, where as long as the tower stands, six witches with one master will always haunt the town. When the last witch dies in this town, the tower will fall. This legend is ultimately irrelevant to the connection here with Keziah, but certain events about the town do have some familiar aspects to the Lovecraft story. The similarity and occult significance between the tower in Canewdon and the attic in Arkham cannot be ignored. The most famous inhabitant of Canewdon was George Pickingale, known as the last "master of witches". Without going into the details of his infamy, the one thing about this man that rings familiar is his house after his death at ninety-three. His house long remained uninhabited due to the local fears that it was haunted by his familiar, a mouse who remained inside peering in the darkness with red glaring eyes.

This reminds one of the long uninhabited witch-house in Arkham with its creeping familiar Brown Jenkin. Another possible reference comes from one of the last six witches of Canewdon, all of who were known by an individual initial, with one going by the epitaph "Mrs.K". Is this "Mrs.K" Keziah Ma-son? Perhaps. Canewdon had a peculiar affiliation of its familiars being mice and it is reputed that the six witches still haunt the town by having their dis-embodied spirits infused in the surrounding rodent population. Just how much, if any, of the Canewdon legends influenced Lovecraft's writing of the Dreams in the Witch-House is speculative, but not weak enough to fully dis-count.

Whether Keziah Mason actually existed incarnated on the earth plane or not does not take from her power as a magical being. What is important is that she does maintain an existence, however ethereal and magical, within the earth/metal planes after she was created by the imagination of Lovecraft. Keziah Mason, since 1932, exists as a thought form within the planes of mankind. She was birthed into and seemingly limited to, the fictional realm through the conscious vessel of Lovecraft. That is the nature of thought forms, disembodied energies infused with energy and materialized into the realms of thought, inspiration, etc. Most commonly there is a visual, sigil, or fetish material basis to house the thought form but in the case of Lovecraft and Keziah Mason, it was a story. The more energy a thought form is given and infused, the more reality it takes on. In the case of Lovecraft, he was the first to empower and work with the energies that materialized as the fictional thought form of Keziah Mason. Whether the witch originally maintained an independent reality outside of the realms of the story is unknown, as at the time of its writing and release unto public consumption, little if any willful working was performed with her essential natures beyond a literary device.

For the most, she was given no more thought than that of a simple piece of entertainment. Although her existing solely within the confines of the story will keep her with a very inert but extant energy vibration or reality, her powers as a magical being were still undiscovered. This fact does not presume that the essence and root of the energy of Keziah Mason did not have some sort of primal existence, or potential for existence, prior to the penning by Lovecraft. Keziah represents very primeval and atavistic energies that have been known by many names and forms throughout history. Whether Lovecraft intuited and was inspired to energize her through his writings or was summoned by those same energies is speculative and ultimately irrelevant. What is relevant is that Lovecraft resonated with currents in 1930 that resulted in the creation of Keziah mason. Like all thought forms, the more a conscious reality is infused into their being by those exposed to their reality, and in turn affected by such awareness, the greater that thought form becomes.

It is unimportant that that reality experienced and generated is the direct result of the consciousness and perceptions of the reader interacting with the forum of the written word. During the initial stages of inspiration and writing to completion, Keziah Mason's power as a thought form was limited to the psyche of Lovecraft. This was of course a more intimate existence with the transmitter/creator, and as such held an untapped resource for Lovecraft who would have denied her existential reality or potential for such anyway. As time progressed and more consciousness was exposed to the story and her fictional presence, the more Keziah became a congealed yet inert energy form. Only until actively channeled into a more useful purpose via sorcery, would she become more than a simple character in a narrative. Such an active esoteric empowering would naturally not occur for many years until vitalized by the present author.

The Witches Sabbath itself represents many things, the least of which is it being an ethereal forum for the experiencing of very ancient and primeval energies via dreams and astral states. It is the celebration, invocation, and release of the most primeval and pre- human atavisms into the psyche of the attendants. The sabbatical tradition is a secret one utilizing, among more esoteric formulas, oneiric and trance states to induce gnosis via the revelries experienced during attendance. Ones attending of the Sabbath usually resulted in the receiving of illumination and manifestation, or "exteriorization of desire", via indulgence within the most frightful of rites.

The incarnated human celebrants of these mysteries are generally willing occultists seeking out the mysteries of the Sabbath, but many of the participants of these revelries exist entirely in astral and ethereal planes. The most celebrated adherent of this tradition is of course Austin Spare who intuited and manifested the most powerful experiences of the witches Sabbath via his artwork and written work. Modern practitioners of this tradition do exist within usually closed organizations, and much of their revelations remain cloaked in secrecy and code. The very roots of the Sabbatical tradition stretch back to the earliest of times with the medieval practices being it's most known and misunderstood variation. Its mysteries remained as such, mysteries. From their being protected as secret natures or from purposeful misinformation released, the secrets of the Sabbath remained concealed from most. The Sabbatical tradition does find expression in the mythos within a few different tales, yet finding its most powerful expression in the form of Keziah Mason.

Within The Dreams in the Witch House, Keziah mason attends the Sabbath upon the night of Walpurgis. Historically the night of Walpurgisnacht is a powerful night for the Sabbath and all means of devilry. Magical activities have never waned in practice upon this night since the most archaic times, and modern day witches of differing traditions, both right and left handed paths, perform upon this night. Within Lovecraft's narrative, Keziah's dealings and nocturnal torments of Walter Gilman increase with the nights prior to the arrival of April thirtieth and her presence and energies increase with the nearing of Walpurgis. Within his dreams she haunts him, attempting to convince him to meet with the black man at the "throne of Azathoth" and, after taking a secret name, sign The Book of Azathoth with his own blood.

These elements are found in numerous accounts of the Sabbath. The black man within the story is the black man of the Sabbath, a common form of malevolent deity presiding over the historical Sabbath. In the Lovecraft story, although it is never fully claimed, the black man is Nyarlathotep, whose form of the black man is his common manifestation in European locations. Prior to the actual Sabbath, Nyarlathotep accompanies Keziah in her dreaming torments of Walter Gilman. This implies that she has a kind of intimate working relationship with the deity when in the form of the black man. The signing of the book in blood is another reoccurring theme of the historical Sabbath. The "black book" is often connected with the presence of the black man. As an example, a specific instance is related from reports of a black mass in the region of Basses-Pyrenees in the early seventeenth century where is related of a black book with crimson pages being held in the hands of a "dark man". Coincidently, this same mass is reported to have taken place in a house in a similar fashion as the performing of the witcheries of Keziah Mason in the attic of her Arkham house.

The performing of the Sabbath in the homes of witches is not an uncommon occurrence yet gives additional credence to Lovecraft being inspired by early witchcraft lore. Within the Lovecraft story, the Sabbath is to take place in the dark ravine beyond Meadows Hill where sits a large white standing stone.

There is yet a dual area used in the Sabbath in the story for there is a physical and magical Sabbatical link between the ravine and the attic in Keziah's house. The similarity between Lovecraft's Meadows Hill and the actual Gallows Hill in Salem is curious.

The taking of a new and secret name at the Sabbath is another common practice in historical accounts of the rite. The magical witches name is symbolic of initiation and the death of one's old mundane self. The name may be given to one by the presiding deity or by one of the witches encountered with during participating in the revelries. The most usual way of receiving a new name is through visions, dreams, and standard trance states. The secret name of Keziah is that of Nahab. Nahab is the name of an obscure snake headed Goddess believed to have some Egyptian connections. The snake headed feature is symbolic for the transformation of consciousness typical of various magical activities such as experienced within the Sabbath. Serpents are one of the many creatures found within the Sabbath and its demonisms are well established. The similarities in the freezing of man by the snake headed Medusa resemble the accounts of the practices of Mrs. K of the Canwdon witches.

The gematria of the name Nahab is fifty-nine, a numeral equating to "heathen, a wall, menstruata, brethren; associated with Lilith and Samael." The term heathen is an apt term for practitioners of the Sabbath. Wall or walls, is associated in the Lovecraft narrative as having much to do with the weird angles through which Keziah achieves her dimensional ingress and egress, and is how she originally escaped her Salem captors. The significance of walls would thus be interpreted as dimensional walls. The connection here to Lilith deals with the phenomenon of Succubae and nocturnal dream haunting, the same type of activities Keziah performs within the slumbering of Walter Gilman and others in Arkham. The menstrual connections mentioned here have great significance to the energies and formulas involved in the traveling to the Sabbath as well as the practical magical formulas attributed to working with Keziah Mason.

We find more curious gematric correspondence when one examines the name of Keziah Mason. When we interpret her name as KZH MSVN, eight hundred and thirty-eight results.

This number itself holds no obvious importance to the witch but when reduced, a more significant correspondence may be found. Eight hundred and thirty-eight, when reduced, yields nineteen, itself reducing to ten (or one is continuing). Nineteen yields, among others, "an enemy, was black, to manifest, Eve". These entries all speak of a dark malevolent witch. The associations of the number ten are "enchanter, flew. Soared, window, a wolf, a hidden place, bosom." The association of "enchanter" is obvious. "Flew, soared" relates to the Sabbath. "Window" as well reminds one of the walls and window as a dimensional gateway as utilized in the witcheries of Keziah Mason. "Wolf" is a typical totem of the tradition and "a hidden place" is a loaded phrase signaling foremost the hidden recesses of the Sabbath. "Bosom" is very interesting as it is upon the breast the Keziah nurses her familiar Brown Jenkin in the Lovecraft tale. When one performs gematria upon the full English spelling of Keziah Mason nine hundred and nineteen is resulted, another number with little importance but interestingly enough reduces to ten. The reducing of the gematric values may seem like a stretch at first sight but actually veils the importance of concealed mysteries as represented by the Sabbatical tradition. Nothing is immediately revealed upon the surface and this is expressed in the gematric importance as well.

Additional practices within both the historical Sabbath and in the Sabbath within the Lovecraft story involve human sacrifice, child sacrifice. Within the story, Keziah must acquire a child for sacrifice upon the night of Walpurgis. According to Arkham legend, children have vanished around the coming of Walpurgis for centuries, and the disappearance of Ladislas Wolejko had a known but not discussed fate. Within historical Sabbaths, whether esoterically or actually, children were sacrificed for many different reasons. Their vitality and death throes are fed upon and assimilated psychically by the present sorcerers. They were roasted and eaten as part of the ceremonial feast and their fat and essential oils are utilized in the creation of candles given to the presiding deity. The specific reason Keziah requires the need of a child sacrifice is never given in the actual tale, but the reasons may be discerned from the established facts.

The finding of a large collection of children bones within the attic of the witch house, some modern and some ancient, presumes the Keziah had significant esoteric dealings with a malefic use of children in her rites. The practice of child sacrifice by Keziah may be theorized for two possible purposes. One may be as a sacrifice to the dark Gods of her Sabbaths, most notably Nyarlathotep and perhaps even Shub-Niggurath. The second reason may have something to do with perpetuating her non-physical body as it haunts from the Arkham attic. The energy manifested from her sacrifices may be used to feed her ethereal body and continue its existence throughout the centuries. This is similar to the vampirisms of various astral entities as well as the shades of the dead feeding upon the vitality of humans. The annual sacrifice at both Halloween and Walpurgis suggests that Keziah needed at least two yearly feedings to perpetuate her astral existence.

The connections of child sacrifice with Keziah herself in contemporary workings have, for obvious reasons, been altered. The sacrifice of the child is now perceived as that coming from the loins of the mage or witch as the child of his/her loins as dictated in common sorceries. The power generated through autoerotic formulas is a proven powerful method in magical and Sabbatical workings making any physical sacrifices completely prohibited and unnecessary.

Part of the mystique of the Sabbath involves the method of one's accessing its occurrence. Most often traveling to the Sabbath is achieved through a detachment of consciousness in the attendant. Historically the Sabbath is accessed via flight, although records do show that witches have walked to the rite as well. Flying to the Sabbath is commonly perceived as through formulas of dreaming and astral natures usually involving psychotropic drugs or ointments. The latter is composed of many different noxious and hallucinatory herbs. Menstrual tinctures and formulas become especially relevant here, as their affects, esoterically and exoterically have been utilized in the unguent employed for entering the rite. The infamous "wine of the Sabbath" is a ritually concocted tincture involving both the physiological and magical effluvia within the menstrual blood of the attending priestess within the Sabbath. This wine is drunk and infused into ones being as both an actual drink and as an invocation of vibratory energies into ones natures. The menstrual correspondence within the secret (secretion) name of Nahab becomes most relevant here. The wine, unguent, and the Sabbath itself, correspond to the moon that, itself as a planetary agent, has affinities to the menstrual blood. Most obvious connection being that the moon rules all trafficking with the astral and dream planes, the planes corresponding to the Sabbath. The symbolism of the full moon of the Sabbath is an established cipher for the physiological formulas involved in the Sabbatical mysteries. All of the phenomena relevant here may be placed upon the sphere of Yesod, the ninth zone upon the tree. In fact, the Qlippoth of Yesod, the Gamaliel or the "obscene ass" bring to mind many of the aspects of the Sabbath from the presiding goat (Shub-Niggurath), and the osculum infame, to the hidden evil eye (Medusian/Mrs.K formula) generating the wine/unguent.

Keziah herself as a thought-dream-astral entity may be deposited within this sphere although her former materialization upon the earth plane in the Lovecraft tale may establish her connections to the path between the ninth and tenth spheres. The formulas of Yesod and the Sabbath correspond with many natures of Shub-Niggurath, herself attributed to the seventh sphere Netzach, as the Sabbatical goat, introducing this deity in reference to Keziah. Interestingly, in the last ethereal experience of Walter Gilman, he exclaimed "Ia Shub-Niggurath, the goat with one thousand young." A final manifestation of the black goat in his final Sabbatical experience is not without esoteric significance, for the appearance of the black goat upon the height of the rite is a known occurrence.

The applying of a physical ointment by medieval witches may be interpreted as a more concrete application of these magical formulas or as a debasement of them, but either way the witch may access the Sabbath through utilization of the wine and unguent in its actual or magical aspect. Keziah, within the Lovecraft narrative, utilizes a "red sticky fluid" to escape her Salem captors and open dimensional gateways. Keziah also confessed to judge Hathorne of certain lines and curves that could be employed to open various dimensional portals utilizing these same scarlet effluvia. The use of odd angles and curves by Keziah to achieve ingress and egress through the timespace continuum resonates completely with the formulas and ritual applications of the menstrual effluvia and wine of the Sabbath. These odd curves, angles, and lines imply the shape and form of the vulva. The red sticky fluid she used in tune with these shapes indicates the vibrations and emanations from these same curves and angles. Within practical sorcery, the correct timing and application of the lines and curves of the vulva, especially in its dark time, will result in strong powers being generated within the priestess and the resonating surroundings.

The possibility that Keziah used these same formulas in her witcheries is very possible when considering the natures of the Sabbatical tradition and her obvious connection to its mysteries. The presence of a menstrual cycle in the witcheries of Keziah suggest that although she is a crone, at least in the phenomenal perceptions, her essential natures are not limited to the physiological patterns of mundane femininity. The crone stage in humans indicates the usual absence of a menstrual cycle but in the example of Keziah Mason, her use of a red sticky fluid implies that her cycle still exists on some fundamental magical level. Keziah mason is not entirely human in the normal context and, at least within the Lovecraft story, exits mainly in a spectral plane, postulating that she still embodies the magical aspects of menstruation in her being.

The usage of odd angles and curves is mirrored exoterically in the story by the odd architecture of the witch house. Strange architectural structures and angles are known to generate strange frequencies and often enough produce portals to different planes of reality. Such weird forms are considered haunted for their tendency at materializing spectral phenomena. The slanting floor and ceiling in the loft creates strange environmental and psychological affects within Walter Gilman and possibly aid in the manifestation of his strange fevers. The convergence of the strange angles where the "downward slant met the inward slant" is where Keziah most often manifested to Gilman suggesting yet again, the concepts of entrance into the phenomenal of dark energies via certain points in space. The manifestation within, or between angles, suggests the break in continuity again represented by the influx of the menstrual cycle.

Keziah is reported to have just appeared within these points in space implying an astral/dream method of entrance. This would be most true when her manifestation was during a state of unconsciousness within Walter Gilman. Accompanying her manifestations was a strange violet light. This "witch light" harkens her presence in the material realms whose luminescence could also be seen within the upper recesses of the witch house from the outside. The color of Keziah's light as violet is significant as it is the shade corresponding to both necromantic formulas and to those of gateways to realms beyond the phenomenal in its hue of mauve. The "unearthly violet phosphorescence" attributed to the presence of Keziah finds similarity to the lights associated with astral travel. Interestingly in correlation with concepts of the hag, there is a practice known as "Hagging" or also known as the "changing of the skin" in West Indian lore. This is a form of astral projection where the witch assumes a sphere of a hovering faint light. The closer one approaches this light the more the features of the hag, as practitioners of this activity are called, becomes apparent. This is paralleled in the Lovecraft story where the violet light form of Keziah becomes clearer and more distinguishable to Gilman the closer she comes to him. The witch light of Keziah has some connection to necromantic lore where there is a maintained spectral light present in proximity to the corpse.

This light is known under many names including the "corpse light" and the "will-o-wisp". The corpse of Keziah Mason is later found still present within the attic of the witch house implying some form of disembodied sentience in connection to her non- physical manifestations centered around the house and any purely ethereal ventures within Arkham. Her violet witch light keeps proximity to her corpse hidden within the attic of the witch house. Interestingly, in German folklore, the presence of a spectral light is associated with the soul of someone who has disregarded a boundary marker. This normally originates from an attempting to steal part of a neighbors land, but reminds one of facts that Keziah has disregarded the boundaries of death and time and space. Certain lore attributes a continued presence of a spectral light until burial of the corpse. The length of such haunting phenomenon varies per tradition, but is relevant when one considers that the spiritual sentience of Keziah has transgressed both time and space postulating an indefinite sentient luminescence of her corpse light. The body of the witch also did not receive proper burial.

Keziah's interactions with forces embodied in Nyarlathotep and Azathoth, and perhaps Shub-Niggurath, will also present her with maintaining some of their extraterrestrial natures. In Cabalistic terms Keziah, as representative of the ninth sphere on the tree, receives the flowing of the forces from the seventh and eighth spheres. Yesod here balances the energies of Netzach and Hod. Her witcheries obviously involve the trafficking with denizens of realms outside the normal spheres of reality and communing with such forces will no doubt filter through and permeate ones being. One may presume that the very root of her power originates from her exposure and invocation of these trans-cosmic forces. Keziah Mason may be called the archetype of the Sabbatical witch in the Lovecraftian mythos. She embodies, via fiction, all of the essence of the medieval crone. The collective of "legend haunted Arkham" has become the fictional repository for the witch tradition of the Lovecraftian mythos. The Sabbatical witch and its tripartite aspects of maiden/mother/crone, represent the activation, progression, and assimilation of these primal atavistic energies into ones being. Summoning, communing, and copulating with the form of the sabbatical witch creates the astralphysical forum for the awakening of these primal atavisms within ones being. The form of the crone, the final aspect of the triple feminine nature, represents ones full initiation into the mysteries of the tradition. Ones copulation with the hideousness of the hag at the finality of the rites sexual orgies holds a deep and powerful occult significance that often goes misunderstood. Spare, as others, knew well the importance of the transcendence received through the hag.

Keziah Mason is a crone and a hag. She has a bent back, long nose, shriveled chin and skin, and is the old hag par excellence. Her perfect depiction of having such ageless archetypical features is a tell-tale sign that Lovecraft accurately tapped into very ancient sources. The physical features of the crone are usually depicted as horrific and ugly. Often criticized by modern witches as illustrating a patriarchal ignorance and hatred for women, the ugliness of the hag is much more than its surface features reveal. It is such ugliness that veils the true power of the witch and her Sabbath. The ugliness of the hag and medieval witch represents a transcendence of mundane and phenomenal concepts.

Her ugliness veils an illumination and gnosis within non-human and pre-human formulas. They represent things that are connected to, and at the root of human natures yet their essential elements well go beyond these human natures. The concepts of regression that are present in the Sabbath represent such invocation of pre- human elements into ones being. The widdershins dance for example, is symbolic for the invocation and activating of primal and pre-human energies into the being of those attending the rite. The debauchery and orgy of the Sabbath, those also found in the representation of the lycanthrope, symbolize the delving of consciousness into more primal and beastly aspects of human nature via perversion and lust. There is a letting go and loss of one's conscious faculties within the Sabbatical revelry, one that reawakens the most ancient and latent aspects in the psyche. Such beastly and horrific practices are found within Brown Jenkin itself.

These ancient awakenings achieve further materialize in the form of the witches' familiar. The familiar throughout history has taken many different animal forms. The form assumed by the familiar of Keziah mason is the large rat Brown Jenkin. According to most historical accounts, the rat or mouse is one of the more common animal forms that the familiar takes on and the witches of Canwydon are believed to still haunt the town in the form of rats. The rat as an agent of malefic energies is not new here as Lovecraft wrote of their malefic natures in the story The Rats in the walls earlier. Within the Dreams in the Witch House, Brown Jenkin is inseparable from the beldame and one of his functions is to take messages "betwixt old Keziah and the devil." Such a mediating function of the familiar is found numerous times within the chronicles of witch lore and they often work between the witch and Satan. Brown Jenkin has features of both a human and animal mixture suggesting something of an invocation of atavistic energies into incarnated form. When the familiar is interpreted as an exteriorization of the witches will, such animal and human blending implies an assimilation and activation of primal energies within ones being.

There is the possibility that, within the Lovecraft story specifically, that the energy of Keziah Mason was transferred into the body of her familiar after she had extinguished as a separate being. It is implied towards the ending of the story that Walter Gilman killed the witch via strangulation with a crucifix necklace after tossing Brown Jenkin into a black triangular abyss. His seeing of her violet witch light fading out implied to him that she had ceased as an active sentient energy form. She does not appear in the story per se after this incident. This of course did not end the torment of Gilman as Brown Jenkin reappears later to kill Gilman by boring through his body. After this, the large rat disappears into a hole never to be exoterically seen again, and the only suggestion of any kind of malefic activity still permeating the house comes from the manifestation of strange odors emanating from the upper recess/attic of the witch house.

The postulation that Keziah had transferred her energy/consciousness into the form of her familiar is based on a few possibilities. The accounts of witches turning into their familiars is not unheard of within the established witch lore and most notably the Canewydon witches are believed to still exist in the bodies of the neighboring rodent population. There was an intimate link between Keziah and her familiar. The rat nursed upon her blood taking in whatever life energy she was vibrating at the time. This establishes a magical and physical link between the two allowing for a potential transferring of consciousness between bodies when needed. A transferring of consciousness between two disembodied sentient energy beings will of course depend upon just how such sentience was maintained in the first place.

Keziah Mason, within the frame of the story, is believed to already be physically dead. Her corpse is later found within the rubble of the attic giving the logical deduction that her haunting of Gilman was strictly within an astral and dream plane. Just how she maintained a physically postmortem disembodied existence is explained in the Lovecraft narrative. It is stated that her various abilities to travel between the time-space continuum allowed her to escape not only the torments of the Salem inquisition, but to defy the ravages of time and death. Gilman himself is aware of the possibility that "time could not exist in certain belts of space" and that such an ability allowed the witch to freely dwell, unchanged in appearance, within many less physically accessed planes. Time does not exist within the astral and dream planes. Keziah's manipulation of these planes with the strange lines and curves of her witcheries kept her able to affect not just these ethereal planes, but the earth plane as well. The presence of her physical corpse implies the perpetuation of a disembodied sentience from a connection to the unburied corpse. This will resonate with her manifestations emanating a violet witch (corpse) light. It is equally possible that her disembodied spiritual energy still utilized her physical corpse and the strange frequencies and architecture of the witch house, to actively perpetuate such a spectral existence. The house and her corpse are infused with great esoteric powers and may be utilized by the dis-embodied energy as a vessel through which to achieve ingress into the physi-cal planes in turn affecting the dream/astral planes of those still within the physical plane.

It is presumed that at some remote time, within a fictional paradigm, a still normally incarnated Keziah Mason prepared the appropriate formulas and tools to project her will and consciousness through specifically generated time portals. Such an act will postulate her later manifestation, in Arkham early nineteenth century specifically here, allowing her to appear in a dimen-sional realm well beyond her supposed years. What fate such a magical pro-jection would have had on her physical body is uncertain, but the discovery of her corpse alongside much magical paraphernalia suggests that she may have performed a powerful spell.

The large gale of 1931 revealed much within the upper ruins of the witch house. Her corpse, alongside the many bones both human and rat, were dis-covered in the rubble. The freshness of some of the bones along with some of great antiquity, indicate that she, on a disembodied level, performed through-out the many years actively. Despite the obvious deceased physical aspect of her existence, she, through her time travel witcheries and or astral magic, still existed within the more tenuous planes. She utilized the strange lines and curves of the physical and biological, and non-physical witch house, as well as her physical corpse, as a vessel of ingress and contagion of the dream/as-tral/earth planes. Within this non-physical form she continued her Sabbatical sacrifices of the children of Arkham up unto modern times and tormented Walter Gilman. Such postmortem non-physical activity is supported in fact by the bones found in the attic dating to contemporary times indicating that her witcheries transgressed the limits of physical time.

Only after her seeming demise within the non-physical plane by the hands of Walter Gilman did her activities seem to have waned if not altogether ceased. Although alluded to and weakly supported by the discovery of her corpse, Keziah is never fully pronounced dead in the story outside of her witch light fading. The later murder of Walter Gilman by Brown Jenkin strongly suggests that she, whether in the form of her familiar, or otherwise, still existed after Gilman's attacking her. It is never really established in the actual story whether this was simply Brown Jenkin returning from the abyss or somehow still connected to the spirit of Keziah. Most would conclude it was simply the rodent exacting revenge on its now fallen witch, but such a stance will have to contend with the many webbed esoteric possibilities of how the witch and familiar were connected and maintained sentience. This naturally leaves much to speculation and imagination as to just who was who.

Outside the scope of the Lovecraft story Keziah would still exist, in whatever non-physical plane, as a previously energized yet slightly inert thought form. Esoterically, her defined archetypal attributes would still exist within the Akashic of the astral and thought/mental planes. She would only need to be revived and re- empowered through specific intent and ritual to again haunt the same spheres she was given credit of infecting within the Lovecraft story. Time has not changed the attributes and natures of Keziah mason. She is still the haunting atavistic Sabbatical witch as timelessly existing within the core of the Sabbatical tradition. She is still the same beldame as later intuited and outlined by Lovecraft. She is still with us dreaming humans, taunting our most primal drives and base animalistic urges. She is now more than the archetype and collective essence of the sabbatical witch. Her specific awakened and empowered existence is a known fact in our modern era. Within a prolonged ceremony of thirteen months, a dark nocturnal series of rituals was performed deep in the New England woods to which manifested, and essentially earthed her natures within the various planes of reality. The results of which are something for another time, and another forthcoming publication.

✳

Amanda Sipes, *Hekate*

Using Our Ordinary Senses in Evocation

Bo Headlan

AS humanity continues to "wake up" to our connection to the non-physical portions of the multiverse, there will inevitably be a growing desire to experience these realms. I believe that it is possible to develop technology that will bridge the gap between the ordinary 3-dimensional world and the multiverse. This will enhance the attainment of mystical states, which are prerequisite for OBE (out of body experiences), astral projections, meditation, spirit evocation and invocation, and pathworking, and other types of paranormal activities.

Most of what we know scientifically about mystical states involves the brain. Therefore, let us begin our exploration of this topic with a discussion of some of the relevant aspects of the human brain.

Brain Anatomy

The brain can be broken down into three parts: the brainstem, the cerebellum, and the cerebrum. The brainstem regulates the basic functions of the body, such as heartrate, breathing, swallowing, blinking, and digestion. The cerebellum is divided into symmetrical hemispheres. This portion of the brain receives messages from most of the muscles in the body. It communicates with the other parts of the brain, and then sends messages about movement and balance back to the body.

The cerebrum represents 85% of the total weight of the human brain, and is responsible for thinking, learning, creativity, the five ordinary senses (vision, hearing, touch, smell, taste), memory, emotion, problem-solving, and decision-making.

Like the cerebellum, the cerebrum is divided into symmetrical hemispheres. In general, the right side is more artistic and intuitive, while the left side is more logical, deductive, and analytical. Each hemisphere is divided into four "lobes," the frontal, parietal, temporal, and occipital lobes. Each lobe has special functions. The frontal lobe is involved with planning and movement; the parietal lobe with sensation; the occipital lobe with vision; and the temporal lobe with learning, memory, and emotion.

The cerebral hemispheres surround an area called the diencephalon, which consists of the thalamus, the hypothalamus and the pineal gland, among other structures. The thalamus serves as a relay station for sensory information coming from some of the major systems (e.g. visual information coming from the eyes) to the cerebrum. The hypothalamus regulates reproduction and homeostasis. Homeostasis is the process by which our bodies maintain a stable internal environment in the face of changing conditions. The pineal gland is about the size of a pea, and is in the center of the brain. It is located directly behind the eyes. It is called the "Third Eye," and is considered to have mystical powers.

The true function of this mysterious gland has long been contemplated by philosophers and Spiritual Adepts. Ancient Greeks believed the pineal gland to be our connection to the Realms of Thought. Descartes called it the Seat of the Soul. This gland controls various biological rhythms of the body. It works in harmony with the hypothalamus.

Mystical traditions and esoteric schools have long known this area in the middle of the brain to be the connecting link between the physical and spiritual worlds. Considered the most powerful and highest source of ethereal energy available to humans, the pineal gland has always been important in initiating and developing supernatural powers.

Brainwaves

The brain consists of cells called neurons which use electricity to communicate with each other. The combination of millions of neurons sending signals simultaneously produces an enormous amount of electrical activity in the brain. This brain activity is commonly called a brainwave because of its cyclic, "wave-like" nature.

With the discovery of brainwaves came the awareness that electrical activity in the brain will change depending on what the person is doing. For instance, the brainwaves of a sleeping person are vastly different than the brainwaves of someone wide awake.

The electrical activity can be measured with an electronic amplifier called an electroencephalogram (EEG). The frequency or speed of the brainwaves is measured in cycles per second, or Hertz (Hz).

With the advent of the EEG, we are now able to detect what happens to our brainwaves as we move in and out of altered states of consciousness.

Brainwaves are divided into general categories depending on their frequency. These categories help describe the changes we see in brain activity during different kinds of activities. Each category or state is based on the idea that a particular brainwave is dominant, but not exclusive. Our overall brain activity is a mix of all the brainwaves at the same time, some in greater quantities and strengths than others.

These seven distinct brainwave frequencies are alpha, beta, theta, delta, gamma, epsilon, and lambda. Each frequency has its own set of characteristics representing a specific level of brain activity and hence a unique state of consciousness.

The Hertz range for each waveform described below is approximate, and in some cases, there is overlap between waveform categories. Different studies show slightly different ranges.

Beta (12-40 Hz) brainwaves are associated with normal waking consciousness and are important for effective functioning in everyday life. They are associated with a heightened state of alertness, with logic, and with critical reasoning. Alpha brainwaves (7.5-14 Hz) are observed with eyes closed and all thoughts excluded from the mind. These brainwaves are present when you are awake but relaxed and not processing much information. This state is relatively easy to achieve. Usually, any attempt at thinking will immediately put one back into a beta state again. However, it is possible to learn how to think in the alpha state.

Our brain often slips in and out of the alpha state throughout the day, and when we daydream or perform light meditation. Alpha brainwaves help with overall mental coordination, calmness, alertness, mind/body integration and learning. Precognition, retrocognition, telepathy, clairvoyance, and remote viewing have also been linked to the alpha state. An alpha state is also referred to as ritual consciousness because it enables the individual to be more open and aware of energy and intuition, but to retain enough consciousness so that he or she is not immobile. In this state the individual can still speak, light candles, read spells, and perform other activities involved in ritual.

Theta brainwaves (4-7.5 Hz) are present during deep meditation and light sleep, including the REM (rapid eye movement) dream state. Theta is also known as the twilight state as it is typically only momentarily experienced as you drift off to sleep (from alpha) and arise from deep sleep (from delta). A sense of deep spiritual connection and oneness with the Universe can be experienced in theta. Vivid visualizations, great inspiration, profound creativity, exceptional insight and intuition, information beyond our normal conscious awareness, and the mind's most deep-seated programs are all experienced in theta.

Delta (0.5-4 Hz) is the next brainwave. Delta brainwaves are seen most commonly during dreamless sleep. They are also present in very deep, transcendental meditation where awareness is completely detached. This state is the gateway to the Universal mind and the collective unconscious whereby information received is otherwise unavailable at the conscious level. Delta is associated with deep physical healing and regeneration, which explains why deep sleep is so important. Delta is associated with psychic abilities. The pioneer mind researcher Maxwell Cade, using an EEG, showed that when a psychic healer touches an individual, that person's EEG pattern becomes the same as that of the healer. A meditation teacher with developed inner intuitive faculties can do the same, hence the value of meditating in the presence of a gifted teacher. Levitation, telekinesis, bilocation, dermoptics and other psychic abilities are also linked to this state.

Gamma brainwaves (16-150 Hz, and sometimes up to 250 Hz) are present during wakefulness and during REM sleep. Gamma brainwaves link and process information from all other parts of the brain. A high amount of gamma brainwave activity is associated with several types of activities. The first two are memory, self- control, happiness, and compassion.

Gamma brainwaves are also associated with perception. They enhance the ability to perceive reality through the five senses, making smells more powerful, vision more acute, hearing sharper, and taste buds more sensitive, thus making life a sensory-rich experience. Gamma brainwaves are involved with intelligence and brain processing speed, leading to the ability to process large amounts of information during a short timeframe. Gamma brainwaves can be further classified into high beta (16-30 Hz), and super-high beta (30-150 Hz) brainwaves.

High beta is a state of hyper-alertness, or "battlefield consciousness." This level of activity is often reached in moments of extreme stress or anxiety, or moments of peak athletic performance. This occurs when time seems to slow down during an accident, or during that moment when an athlete breaks a personal record and feels completely "in the zone."

Super-high beta brainwaves are associated with expansive and somewhat uncontrollable spiritual experiences, such as eureka moments, divine inspiration, satori, kundalini risings, and extreme out of body experiences.

Some newer schools of thought acknowledge the existence of two additional brainwaves.

Lambda brainwaves (100-200 Hz) and epsilon brainwaves (less than 0.5 Hz) are associated with wholeness and integration. In addition, lambda brainwaves are associated with out of body experiences. Lambda brainwaves seem to ride on epsilon brainwaves (i.e. If you were to zoom out on an EEG from the high
frequency lambda brainwave far enough you would see that it is
embedded within the very low frequency epsilon brainwave.)

If we can learn to control our brainwaves, we can control how we think, feel, reason and react. Relaxation, creativity and self- awareness can then flow naturally.

Phyllis Curott in the book, Witch Crafting: A Spiritual Guide to Making Magic, states that "Practices such as meditation, journeying, and going into trance help us to cultivate these brain waves, and to combine them into heightened states of awareness and sensitivity." Christopher Penczak in the book The Living Temple of Witchcraft Volume Two, states "Witches... should have a certain measure of control over the physical body, being able to control breath, heartbeat, temperature and brainwaves."

Invocation & Evocation

Invocation and evocation are two of the very important operations in magick. Invocation is the act of drawing qualities of different entities, spirits, energies, and thought forms into an individual. Evocation is the act of perceiving these phenomena as external forms.

Evocation rituals are typified by the "summoning of spirits," calling entities forth, external to the magician, so that the magician can communicate with the entities or induce them to go out into the world and perform various tasks.

Trance

Mystical states, such as those required to perform invocation or evocation, perform spells, or to do just about any else magickal require that the individual enter trance, or an altered state of consciousness. The reason why we must enter the trance state to perform magick is that trance is the only time in which an individual can consciously program the subconscious mind.

We can look at the trance state as the "gateway" into the worlds of the paranormal and mystical. One's own experience with trance is a very important step regarding the awakening of one's psychic abilities and mystical experiences, and can even trigger the on-going evolutionary leaps that often lead a person towards higher levels of consciousness.

The concept of trance has existed since our earliest hunter gatherer ancestors walked the earth. From magickal and compelling internal visions, to experiences of blissful relaxation, accelerated learning and sensations of deeper connectedness, or even just feeling as though you're totally in the zone, on fire and unstoppable, there have been many subjective reports throughout history of the various abilities people experience when they are in a very deep trance state. Yet only in the last several decades have we developed the technology to explain, in objective terms, just what occurs in the brain as people experience these moments of altered consciousness.

Despite our ability to measure what happens in the brain during trance, very little has been written on the science behind trance states. E.A. Koetting and others describe trance as being in "theta- gamma sync." In other words, being on the borderline in between the theta and gamma brainwave states. According to E.A. Koetting, the "theta-gamma sync" is a "deep theta state that initiates all magick workings."

The "theta-gamma sync" can also be described as the veil or border between wakefulness and sleep. Every time we "fall asleep" or awaken, we pass this border. The problem we have is how to trigger the "theta gamma sync." The real trick is to stay awake and conscious when we enter the veil. This is much more easily said than done. For most people, triggering this state requires lots of tedious practice. Over time, entering the "theta-gamma sync" requires less effort, but can still be difficult.

What if we had technology that would produce an alternative to this long process of learning how to trigger trance, and then to perform evocation to visual manifestation? In other words, what if we could easily enter trance and then, just as easily, evoke entities, spirits, energies, and thought forms so that we could see them with our ordinary sense of vision? Such technology would literally open the multiverse, allowing easy access to unlimited personal and spiritual growth for anyone who desired it.

I propose that such technology can be developed using various types equipment such as flotation tanks or cranial electrical stimulators. However, I feel that the most promising technology involves the use of light and sound machines.

Visualization Using Light & Sound

The effects of light and sound are not new discoveries. Before recorded history, the mesmerizing effect of flickering firelight and tribal drum beats were noted for creating trance-like states. In 200 A.D. Ptolemy recorded that the flickering of sunlight through the spokes of a rotating wheel can cause fascinating visual patterns and euphoria. Nostradamus in the 13th century saw visual images by quickly passing his opened fingers between his eyes and sunlight.

Modern Light & Sound Machines

Right-brain activity and theta brainwaves are needed for visual imagery and, hence, for evocation to visual manifestation. Light and sound machines, combined with and EEG and biofeedback (e.g. displaying the brain activity on a screen) equipment fill both these requirements. The light and sound is applied to both cerebral hemispheres. The EEG with biofeedback allows you to observe and correct the pattern as desired. Using the EEG and biofeedback, if one can immediately perceive the effects of entering a state, this is found to greatly enhance the ability to re- enter that state at will. Light & sound machines can facilitate entry to various brainwave states in a controlled way.

The machine uses pulses of slowly falling frequencies which lead the mind from its normal waking consciousness to deeper, more relaxed states. This process is called "entrainment."

Light and sound machines start at the beta frequency and slowly lead the brain down to the alpha, then theta, and then delta (deep sleep) brainwave states. and theta states. If, however some beta (wakefulness) is maintained while passing through the alpha (relaxation) state to the theta (imagery) state, then sleep will not follow uncontrollably. The remarkable properties of the theta state can then be consciously explored.

Results of Entrainment by Light & Sound

Gray Walter, the first modern researcher into flashing light reported, "The rhythmic series of flashes [appears] to be breaking down some of the physiologic barriers between different regions of the brain. This means the stimulus of flicker received by the visual...area...was breaking bounds - its ripples were overflowing into other areas. Subjects reported lights like comets, ultra- unearthly colors, mental colors..." These reports interested the novelist Burroughs, who investigated the effect and reported, "Subjects report dazzling lights of unearthly brilliance and color. Elaborate geometric constructions of incredible intricacy build up from multidimensional mosaic into living fireballs like the mandalas of eastern mysticism or resolve momentarily into apparently individual images and powerfully dramatic scenes like brightly colored dreams." Later researchers showed that the addition of synchronized sound beats greatly increased the effects.

Harrah-Conforth studied a control group who only received pink noise stimulation and a main group who received light and sound stimulation. He found that the latter group showed major alterations of their EEG patterns. He reported comments like, "I lost all sense of my body." "I felt like I was flying." "I was deeply relaxed." "I felt like I was out of my body." He suggested that light and sound machines may cause simultaneous arousal of the sympathetic nervous system (a group of nerves in the body) plus cerebral cortex and arousal of the parasympathetic system (another group of nerves in the body) which is linked to "the timeless, 'oceanic' mode of the mystic experience." ✦

Mitchell Nolte, *Parfaxitas*

The Eye of Kal Thalin
KT101916-0333 | DATA INTERCEPT
THE ARCHIVE OF THE KNIGHTS OF ZAL

Sean Woodward

THE outer world and the inner are each familiar to us to different degrees and each in their own ways guard secret pathways between one another. When Michael Bertiaux states that "Everywhere is the same power of enchantment" when referring to the impact of the amphibious humanoids of Innsmouth, he causes us to reconsider our local environments, to seek out those places in the outer world that are touched by this supernatural enchantment.

I discovered one such locality and visited it daily for a period of three months, embracing not just the natural beauty of the small ponds within a woodland, but the enchantments woven over millennia into the fabric of its fallen leaf mulch, of its ancient bare trees bowed over an old ghost road and the still deep waters within.

At times I followed the small brook with its miniature waterfall, at others, set off deep into the heart of its trees. Very quickly however it became apparent that there was one tree1, a singular presence, its trunk seeming to possess the features of a face, that called out in the peaceful silence.

"I have waited long for one such as you, he said," as I stood close.

"Such as me? What is your purpose?"

"To dress the world in red, to paint the sky black, to serve the old gods."

This was not what I had expected! Over the years many have diluted the fear and loathing that surrounds the seminal descriptions of the Innsmouthians and their kin. It should not so easily be forgotten.

"What is your name?"

"What importance has a name? Beyond the waters, beyond the stars I was called Zahul Al l'hikm. The Red Ones, they had other names then. This was before I was tricked into serving them."

Another voice intruded.

"Those times are gone my friend, only my bones remain now, exhumed from their cairn. Is this truly one you have waited for?"

"It is. He is marked with the shadows of the Old Ones. Look now how they stroke his head with their gnarly fingers, whisper in his ears so he thinks that it is his own thoughts rising. And he sees us, hears us now."

"That may be true Zahul, continued the ghostly voice without form, but the temple remains empty, only machines worship there now."

"She is more than a machine replied Zahul with disdain in his voice."

"What is this temple?" I asked.

"It is a terrible place and it has seen terrible things. It contains terrible things. It's walls and ancient stone steps are carved with the histories of the Red Gods, of their sunken home, of the watery worlds from where they came. And it lies fathoms deep. This is not for you. It is closed to you."

No matter how often I alluded to this temple in the days that followed, the tree would not divulge any more information, other than to suggest it lay close and that the cairn of its priest had once been covered in the same grotesque stones, until archaeologists had first taken them away and then hidden them for their own private viewing, for there were no signs of them in the small museum which held the priest's bones today. There was nothing save the item marked as an ancient amulet of unknown origin, which had been found with his body and which even now prevented his shade from re-uniting with it.

Zahul did not manage to convey how he'd been tricked into joining the priest in this place, so distant from the Sporeworlds in which he'd practiced husbandry of the interstellar gardens and water worlds. After so long tending the species of those planets, he found it ironic to be one with a tree of this world. It was obvious that although he had been tricked and confined, he found some comfort in it too, not relying solely on the companionship of the ghost priest, but joining in communion with the multitude of natural spirits that surrounded him, draped in dappled sunlight.

I sensed that there was more though, something he was not telling me as the days passed and I continued through the woodland to the same spot each day, down a bridleway churned by the hooves of unseen horses. On some days he asked me to press my palms against his bark, that he might once more feels the warmth of another body. At others he asked me to bring samples from the parts of the woodland beyond his vision, that he might examine them and converse with their spirits. As the seasons changed so too did these requests. After taking him a wild apple one day he became agitated.

"What is it?" I asked.

"When I was a Sporefather, there was a world with fruit like these, a beautiful place. We could not stop it falling to the Archons, even though it was the home of the Gholem."

Gholem! I remembered all that my old teacher, Dr. Alfonse had taught me about these creatures immortalized in the myths of Prague and the zombies of Haiti. I knew the name of the Archons too.

"Was this the war with Shadow Architects?"

"Yes. Many rains ago I saw that you knew of these histories. What you do not know is that KAL THALIN, The Watcher, was sent to this world, just as memory palaces were sent into other galaxies and Monitoring Stations positioned close the abyss of Archonspace, which even now is slowly advancing, its corruption devouring all it touches."

"The Watcher? What does it watch?"

"The Palace of the Watchers is the Black Angel that glides from Pole to Pole, within the domain of Baratchiel5, it is the Shattered Akashic Library of the place you know as the Nightside."

This information led me to re-acquaint myself with the Tunnels of Set, the histories of the New Isis Lodge, the Zos Kia Cultus and the English Qaballa (EQ) as discovered by James Lees and detailed in the recent primer The Magickal Language of the Book of the Law by Cath Thompson. Utilising EQ and enumerating the value of KAL THALIN and replacing the cumulative letter values gives the phrase "was Ka, so souls have whole book here after". The Ka was the part of the soul in Egyptian magic that could resurrect the physical body. The notion of a place where the books of souls reside equates with the corrupted library. In EQ its value is 80 as is KA KNOWER.

In the shattered form of L'TALN KIA it equates to the BOOK KIA. Kia as used by Austin Osman Spare represented UNIVERSAL MIND and PRIMAL ENERGY. Kia's identification with the eye in Spare's system speaks to Kal Thalin's aspect as the Watcher. The form of KAL TL'AIN alludes to the eye once more as AIN.

The eye is prominent in the Tower card of Crowley's Thoth Tarot, that is associated with Peh and 80 by gemetria. The Tower also alludes to the Tour-de-ZAL of the Monastery of Leng and the magicks of the Iz-za-Zahal6. There are also mysteries concealed in the card that pertain to Baphomet and the Osculum infame of the Sabbath as well as the particular psycho-sexual formula of the Ojas-rays, per os7 (PER OSS =80). The eye in the design of this card is described by Crowley as that of Shiva, the very deity whose name it is in the Voudon Gnostic Workbook, Michael Bertiaux implores is used in connection with the psycho-sexual powers of the Ojas-rays - "First you must utter the name of Shiva over and over again in a deep and almost inaudible voice8". This name is AKSHAYAGUNAA, the God with Limitless Attributes, that equates to 80.

Here also is the destruction of self, the reversal of the words of creation, the chatter of the monkey that threatens to assail the unwary magician as he is bathed in the anti-light, in a world of shells. This is the destructive force that can be seen in the falling human figures turned to geometric shapes in Crowley's card and serves as a warning.

The orbiting library of Kal Thalin passes through the Tunnels of Set9, offering tantalizing glimpses of the shattered egregores of witch cults and magical Orders that are broken and reformed as its transmissions sweep through the space of Universe-B and Universe-A, resurrecting egregores and unleashing vampires, monsters and Transyugotthian terrors as it seeks to transmute the absorbed influence of the Archons.

The Rite of M'nôôez, of the Akashic Word

In order to enter Kal Thalin it is first necessary to engage with the rituals, protection and tools that will enable safe access to the hidden orbiting station and its palace of memories.

Before the ritual is begun the Dream Posture should be undertaken for two weeks, during which time sufficient preparation and protection is accumulated. First take note of the sleeping body's posture most beneficial to lucid dreaming10. Once discovered project your consciousness into that form, hovering before you whilst reciting the mantra LAHMAZAL LAZAHMAL, whose value is 80.

A method of divining the success of the Dream Posture preparation consists of using the drink Guinness to see what omens have formed in the remnants of the 'head'. For those not wishing to use alcohol, a similar method can be used with tea leaves. Both are of nature black liquids having an affinity with Kal Thalin. If none of these methods are suitable, the verses of The Hexagrams of ZAL11 may be consulted, of which the most fortuitous is number 8.

Drape the altar with a black cloth upon which is emblazoned in orange the sigil of the 12th Path from Crowley's Liber XXII.

Place one black candle upon the altar and the Mirroir-Magique12, that is one whose surface is also black.

The ritual can only be undertaken at 0333 hrs GMT. At this time does the orbit of Kal Thalin intersect most closely with our universe. Only at this time does the Choronzon energy flow through Daath, enabling both access and the holographic transmissions that scan the Earth to absorb and access information. As L'KORONZON these energies also enumerate by EQ as 80.

To begin the ritual in earnest, place a picture of Eliphas Levi's Goat of Mendes 13opposite the mirror, with the candle between.

Look closely for the hands of Baphomet point out the lunation cycles of the transmissions and receptions of Kal Thalin. Upon its arms SOLVE and COAGULA allude to the destructive and reforming qualities of the particle transmissions which often leads to the manifestation in the vicinity of the sorcerer. The entwined snakes about Baphomet's waist also signify the patterns of Kal Thalin's travels in that other space. 333 together with the cipher of ZAL, 396, gives the value 729, of BAVOMIThR. This manifestation of the Black Man of the Sabbath also pertains to those intensely Sabbatic aspects of Spare's witch cult and those concealed in The Tower card. By Simple Gematria, BAPHOMET is also 80.

For other workings with the different egregores and records within Kal Thalin, especially those of Spare, other paintings which act as portals such as the Icon of the Zos Kia Cultus containing as it does the primary symbols of the hand and the eye can be utilised in the same way. Another ingress point is via Kenneth and Steffi Grant's Monographs of Carfax, a corruption of Monagraphie d'Kaifax, the latter part of which enumerates to 80. The Hand and the Eye, Yod and Ayin, is also 80 by qabalah. There is further reference to Spare in the deviation of KU THALI (80) or KULLT of KU.

The latter deck is especially potent in these workings as it channels the Four Crosses of the Quarters of Gnostic Voudon which have been described by Kenneth Grant in Cults of the Shadow:

> Spare's system of sorcery, as expressed in Zos Kia Cultus, continues in a straight line not only the Petro tradition of Voodoo, but also the Vama Marg of Tantra, with its eight directions of space typified by the Yantra of the Black Goddess, Kali: the Cross of the Four Quarters.

At the appointed time, light the candle and look deep into the surface of the mirror whilst using the mantra previously used in the Dream Posture.

A spider pattern of cracks may appear upon the surface of the mirror. Ignore these for they are remnants of the OKBISh-Physics of Kal Thalin.

Step through the mirror. Beyond is a vault of seven sides, upon its walls many photographs, drawings and fastened objects.

Ignore these too, for they lead to places that will only distract and remain inert at this hour. On the floor rests the open Resurrection14 Casket of Osiris. Lie within the casket15. Immediately a rush of air fills the darkness above as a flickering body descends, at one moment the blue naked body of a woman at another moment, that of the Goat of Mendes. Each appear, like a succubus to transmute Ojas energies of the Rehctaw to fuel the casket, for it has now risen above the vault.

It travels now through space, surrounded by eight of the Monographs of Stone, above which hovers a small tree, almost bonsai in appearance. These orbit the casket, providing a type of shield in all directions. The names of these giant rocks, of this Famille Gholheme, became in later ages the names of the Watchers RAMUELL, TUREL, KO'OKABEL, SEMYAHZA, AHRMERS, KI'DEJA, GADREE and YOMVEL, each of whose name is 80 in EQ as is STONES and D'GHOLHEM.

This is the space of Universe-B, the realm of Cabalistic anti-matter. More than simply darkness and vacuum, it shifts and morphs, breaking apart time and motion. As the huge rocks of the Monographs pass through it a field of many colours shines around them, the result of a kind of Meonic friction. It gives the impression that you are slowing as the orbiting Kal Thalin comes into view, its angular black form slowly looming larger.

Now that the ghostly bodies have taken of their fill of the psycho-sexual energies, the casket is surrounded once more in darkness and is without movement. There is an oracular voice of monstrous speech, interspersed with the chiming of broken bells heard from the far end of a cathedral's nave.

"State your designation in the Imperium."

"It is answered from all around you."

"We are the Monograph of Stones. We speak unto the Monograph of Kal Thalin."

The voices are replaced by silence, save for the metallic sounds of heavy doors being opened18. A dim light illuminates the darkness and you are able to rise from the casket and stand. A corridor runs ahead, with many rooms. As you walk ahead you can see into some of these through half opened doors. Gatherings of men and women in ritual attire from times past and future of the Rehctaw19. Some seem to open out into rugged windswept landscape of Snow Hill where witches gather beneath withered trees. In another are the ruins of an Indian temple, deep in the jungle. It is like a labyrinth English stately home, except there are no sections cordoned off with rope, no galleries full of precious artefacts and empty of people. You pass by another open room where lattices of brightly coloured lines tumble, dance and appear to communicate with one another. As you reach the end of the corridor a mauve monkey rushes by you, leaving the door to sanctuary20 open.

Necronomicon-Physics

This method of gaining access to Kal Thalin has been designed to safeguard against the destructive forces which both protect it and are a natural aspect of its environment and against the dangers of those psycho-sexual energies which are necessary for the apport of the initiate. As Kenneth Grant states in Cults of the Shadow, "[Zos and Kia] They form the foundation of the New Sexuality, which Spare evolved by combining them to form a magical art".

The association with the kala of The Magus and the adverse aspects of these are shown in the analysis of L=TWO: THE MAGUS from Liber Trigrammaton where "80 suggests (8) – Infinite (0) – Nothing".

It has been found that the timing of the ritual is one at which those with a natural affinity for this gnosis may find themselves subjected to the sweep of its transmissions, when the Choronzon energies and the Necronomicon-Physics are at their strongest. For them it is recommended that the Dream Posture practice is engaged as soon as is practical as a defense to prevent them being swept helplessly into the gaze of the eye of Kal Thalin. ✦

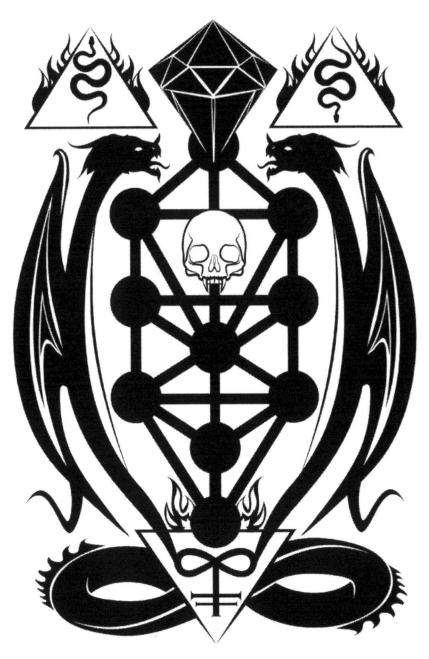

Asenath Mason, *Tree of Qliphoth*

Under the
Shadow of Dispersion

Leonard Dewer

HE When we talk about the aspects of the Sinister Path, we are always touching on issues that are considered dark by most worldly people. Such matters, enveloped not only by shadows, but by a mixture of a mystical and occult type of aura, filled with doubts and powers, can bring feelings of fear, insecurity and discomfort to those who are not accustomed or prepared for the Path.

Regarding of Qlippoths, many doubts arise concerning to the interpretation and practical application of the essence of these shells (2), both philosophically and in the day-to-day life of each Wanderer. These interpretations and practices should always aim at meaningful changes rather than mere intellectual abstraction. With every text and every practice, there is always the objective of instigating some change in the vision of the Walker, both on internal and external matters, until it culminates in an alteration that causes changes in his own worldview. When the wanderer goes through a process that changes the way he sees reality, making a kind of revolution and ending cycles, inevitably his new worldview will cause him to have to start over and re-evaluate everything around him, since most things in which he lived may no longer serve in his new reality. This process, when effective, could be called initiation.

Although this is not the focus of the central theme, I can say that such reflections have their importance and, thus, enable the wanderer himself to make a more direct assessment of himself and his own Path. In fact, being able to concentrate and focus on yourself, both in your Path and in your own life, will be part of the theme of this essay.

It is interesting to make a comparison of Qlippoth A'arab Zaraq with his corresponding Sephiroth Netzach, to understand a little more the dimension of his concepts and powers.

As Y. David Shulman tells us in his book The Sefirot:

"The sefirah of Netzach, "victory", or "eternity", represents the desire to overwhelm the world with Chesed. It is the spirit of proselyte who, having been inspired, wishes to impress others into a new, enlightened state."(...) Netzach must be balanced by Hod, "beauty", "glory". Hod holds back that exuberant spirit. It keeps one from getting caught up in ecstasy (Mystical Concepts, p. 836)"(3)

We can understand that this refers to the ecstasy of those inspired by some divinity, but always needing to be balanced so this ecstasy does not depict only someone infected by some madness. Therefore, Hod would be the one who would balance the euphoria of Netzach, with thoughtfulness, dedication and calm.

In the same chapter we find:

"Netzach is competition, the desire to excel, to battle against others. Hod is devotion, compliance and conformity. Competition is deeply active, waxing and waning. In serving God, Netzach strains, pours out the soul, pushes one to the limit. One is extremely active and then must be retreat to rest. Hod in other hand, is a consistent, quiet state of devotion, subordination and consistency.(...)

Netzach and Hod work together intimately to process and draw down the energy of Sefirot. They are a pair: "two halves of a body , like twins" (Zohar III:236a). They are the two legs that support the body (Zohar Chadash, Vayera 26d) and thus, they are called the "supports of the upper sefirot" (Mystical concepts in Chassidism, pp. 835-6)."(4)

While Netzach is active and even without control or direction, out of pure inspiration and ecstasy, Hod is passive, controlled, calm. It would be intelligence, reasoning. One without the other would not be enough, but together, they reach their balance in their worship and victories.

However, it is worth emphasizing that although we are speaking of the Sephiroths at the beginning, we do so only to better understand some concepts of the Qlippoth A'arab Zaraq. Therefore, we will not focus on the Sephiroths, since although Netzach and Hod always fall into the worship of the divine as in the figure of the lying god, we must keep in mind that this god keeps all of his followers tied as slaves; Human completeness would only be possible around this one god, blind because he sees only himself and selfish for self-declaring as the only truth. Therefore, it would be a path whose course revolves only around itself, ignoring all that exists in the universe.

Assuming that in this context, instead of being parts that complete themselves (and indeed are), Netzach and Hod appear to be incomplete and even dispersed manifestations. Netzach alone is imbalance: ecstasy without control, action without direction, inspiration without production. Hod is at the other extreme: passivity, silence, restraint, and intelligence without action. In order to benefit each other, both must be balanced. And that is where we can invert their essences and take advantage of them from another point of view, entering the matter of this essay, which is the Qlippoth A'arab Zaraq.

In his book Kabbalah, Qliphoth and Goetic Magic, Dr. Thomas Karlsson tells us:

"A'arab Zaraq represents battle, and its forces are invoked by the dark magician for victories in the battles of life. War Gods, like Odin and Baal, in their more demonic forms are associated with this spheres. In the Kabbalah, Baal is viewed as the Demon ruler of A'arab Zaraq." (5)

Here it is interesting to note that A'arab Zaraq has obvious connections with his Sephirotic counterpart Netzrach, regarding to victory. The Power of this shell brings us an idea of joining both the obscure knowledge and the understanding of the operation of everything around us. Understanding how cause and effect are related and understanding the mechanisms of both situations and people are basically exercises of understanding the information. This information is, to a certain extent, fragmented at various levels in interpersonal relationships, as well as contained in obscure knowledge or at least forbidden by mundane religions or ignored by most people.

Ahead, we also have:

"The symbol of Netzrach is the dove, which corresponds to love, purity and peace. The Raven is the symbol of A'arab Zaraq. A'arab Zaraq means "The Ravens of Dispersion". The Raven is the black counterpart of the dove and represents war and storm, but also passion, sin and forbidden wisdom. It lives off the dead on the battlefield and is the free spirit of death. The Raven is also the talking bird that bring messages and prophecies, the free consciousness of the magician, dispersing like the ravens of Odin to collect knowledge and wisdom."(6)

While in Christian mythology we have the dove as a symbol of purity and holy spirit, ravens represent a mystique much more obscure and complex regarding the balance of the individual itself. Far beyond a baptism or symbol of reverence, the raven is a bird of innumerable peculiarities, gifted with incredible intelligence and learning ability. In addition, ravens have the ability to reproduce human words and sounds with great accuracy. Besides that, they are stronger and smarter than the doves; In the same way that A'arab Zaraq is in relation to Netzach.

Ravens feed on the flesh of the dead, including humans, and this has caused them to be viewed with awe and respect by various cultures and ended up being associated with Gods like Odin and Morrigan, giving it a more obscure, prophetic, feared and Sacred image.

Hugin and Munin (7) fly all over Midgard watching and hearing everything that happens, and soon after, they return to Odin and whisper it all in His ears, giving the Allfather (8) the ability to know everything that happens in our world. Like Odin, it is also possible for the magician to use A'arab Zaraq to release his own spirit and essence, his Daemon, in the form of a raven (or several ravens) and disperse them, dividing them, and reunite them again - each with knowledge beyond the objective reality of the magician.

Here I can make an interesting - and vital - comparison to this text. Many people have great capacities in the world, but for lack of planning and focus (and power) many of these geniuses live and die in oblivion, without even completing their own projects or plans for life. The work of the Wanderer, when together with A'arab Zaraq, is precisely that of the domain of dispersion and union.

The analogical use of "divide and conquer", just as the ravens come out of the shell and scatter themselves around the world (and other realms), and each one returns with new knowledge, information and experience. In the same way, the magician must be able to see behind all this dispersion. Similarly, the dispersion in the sense of focus and worldview, may very well be the cause of so many people lost and without plans.

Those who watch TV every day after a full day's work and sleep after it are completely scattered people: several of their parts are divided up at work; others on the television, others in the tasks, others in the accounts, others in the frustrated plans, others in the sleep ... many people feed addictions and stop doing many things in the name of these same vices, mainly virtual. They spend time instead of enjoying it and always believe they have no time for anything. Wrong. It is the distraction and dispersion of their desires and goals that make them lose themselves in their own daily routines.

When ravens fly in dispersion, we can compare them with the desires and will of the seeker, and in this case as the act itself, both mental and physical action of the wanderer himself.

In today's contemporary times, entertainment has replaced the search of every individual, disrupting all kinds of development in the name of distraction and dispersion. In every way we are surrounded by stimuli and "things to do," forgetting that our mind and will can (and must!) go through different paths and return with new experiences and knowledge. In this way, A'arab Zaraq does not become complete in his own shell, acting only as a negative part for those who are not prepared to enter their domains. When the magician is ready to alter his own routine and his own reality, one more step can be taken in his ascension. In addition, we should note that:

"The raven corresponds to the soul of the magician when it flies in ecstasy, the result of the meeting between life and death that takes place in the Qliphothic initiation. By passing through a symbolic death, the magician no longer fears death and in the same moment learns how to live. This "Initiation of Death" begun In this Qlipha and is fulfilled by the black illumination on Thagiriron." (9)

The perception of death permanently changes the view of life itself and the whole existence of the Walker. Most people of our time live in constant illusion about what life is and what the value of life would be. This encompasses the goals and meaning of life for each person. However, they all have absolute ready truths influenced by Christian customs and beliefs, without even realizing it.

For the ancients, death was part of their day-to-day life. There was no overvaluation of life or, in this case, a state of denial of death. People were dying, animals were dead and all this was a constant in consciousness and in the individual routine. Nowadays the masses have an elusive negation of the concepts of life and death, as if they lived in a world where this did not occur, which is absurd, since it happens every day and also around us in many ways.

People live dispersed and alien to reality itself, that even being subjective to each one, it objectively still exists in a way common to all. However, this subjectivity is used so that each person does not need or does not have time to think about things that they consider "negative" or "bad." TV programs, reality shows, novels and things like that, entertain and anesthetize the individual when he is not inserted all day in his routine of work. On rest days, this same individual uses to solve other subjects and to try to rest, to once again, during the week, confront her slave routine.

The attributions to certain values are completely distorted, making people slaves of a system that is based on continuous work for the production and enrichment of others and a planning for a supposed old age that we often do not reach. All based on entertainment doses so that we do not think about existence itself and existence as a whole, much less about the real questions about life and death.

When we bring A'arab Zaraq, we bring these questions in a legitimate way, aiming at getting us out of this sickly stream of illusions. This state of torpor that people meet is a state of eternal dispersion, in its most useless and most negative sense to each individual.

When we understand that death is as natural and as present as life, and when we understand that it is our daily and eternal companion, we lose the fear of its embrace and its final gift. Fearing death is not an option for the Wanderer, only as far as the excitement of entering unknown mysteries, such as that cold in the belly when doing new things. To have death as a companion is to understand it and to see its influences, both literal and symbolic in each birth, death and be rebirth both of nature and the signs around it. It is having, along with all of this, the certainty that you too will die, whether in the coming days or years ahead.

The barrier of the fear of death is an obstacle that must inevitably be overcome for those who wish to make the Path of Return, from seed to grain. Where we not only claim for our divine ancestry, and thus as Gods, we walk back against the flow to the return of our own divine nature and at the same time mortal in the search of our apotheosis.

Here the magician must fly and his soul be divided into a cloud of ravens, each one observing, learning and experiencing, in a great dispersion. Such a practice does not only occur by visiting other Realms of manifestation, such as the dream and astral world - although this is extremely important and vital to the magician; But also in regard to their own nature and world view, as well as their understanding of everything around them and their ways of functioning. How people work, how to deal with possible problems, how to deal with the different types of systems and how they interact with each other and how the unfolding of certain situations of daily life and of the occasional ones works: the Walker is the one who can see the same situation or problem under several different points of view; Thus representing his wisdom and understanding, as a multifaceted black diamond. Such a view of so many aspects of the world in one person reflects in the dispersed soul, as if each scattered raven was a different look: one sees above, another below, another to the right, another sinister, another to the center. Each raven is part of His wisdom and knowledge. The process of such vision is not at once achieved, but progressive, for just as Odin's ravens whisper events and knowledge in His ears, so must also be the soul of the magician, and with each new knowledge, one more Perspective is understood and used to understand the world around you; Knowing that his vision is not the only one, but just another way of seeing the world and understanding it better.

This vision of worlds, like the multifaceted black diamond, is an essential part of the expansion of consciousness and the reach of the vision of the Wanderer, both in the physical world and in the spiritual world, both in understanding and in his own Power.

Thus he will be able to see the world with the eyes of other beings and entities, with the eyes of other people and even, sometimes, with eyes of the Gods: our ancestors.

There is yet another perspective, which will lead us to new reflections and that may possibly instigate us to perceive one more of the hidden and perfect faces of the Black Diamond:

"The pure white Venus belongs to Netzrach, and the black Venus corresponds the A'arab Zaraq. The black Venus is called Venus Illegitima and is the Goddess of perversions. Her love is sterile on the mundane earth level, but is fertile inside the magician and in the higher levels. Through her, the magician can be born into the higher worlds. The magician is born as his own child and becomes one with his higher self of Daemon. The Venus illegitima is the mother of the Daemon. Demonic offspring are created by sexual unity between earth and spirit beings. The Nephilim of the bible, the bastards, were born between the meeting of the sons of heaven and the daughters of earth. The magician's higher self or Daemon belongs to the next level." (10)

One of the extremely interesting things about Venus is how she influences our passions. We can still consider her to be all our passions itself, therefore, we are all subject to Her charms and domains. Moreover, the white Venus had always been associated with true, altruistic, idealized love; While the black Venus to the sexual attraction, the carnal desires and still the unbridled passions, of whatever nature. I trace this parallel with the Greek Aphrodite, Ourania (golden, celestial) and Pandemos (of all), the first being equated with White Venus, pure, idealized, love; The second to the passions, desires and perversions.

In this way, we could understand that the concept of purity and idealizations could be seen as an illusion, since everything that is idealized becomes only a reflection of the idealization itself when it becomes concrete. According to Plato, idealizations are seen with the eyes of the soul; Ideas are pure and perfect. When put into practice, they become flawed and imperfect, like the whole material world. While not agreeing with all of Plato's ideas, it is extremely interesting to look at this parallel with the Greek Aphrodites, in regard to the Celestial Aphrodite and Aphrodite of all, of people.

However, we are not talking directly about these aspects, but only recalling them to understand some concepts better. For many centuries, especially with Christian domination with which many peoples have suffered and still suffer, we have increasingly been infected with a sickly view of love, sex and relationships between people. This meant that not only the Ancient Gods have lost space between people, but also our own nature and all the values that accompanied the day-to-day of our ancestors and nature itself. Natural experiences and interaction with nature became sinful and satiating our desires and pleasures became sin, impure, immoral.

Seeing Venus as an essential part of our nature (even with the duality between the white and the black), we still have both in their own power, acting according to their domains and inclinations.

The Black Venus is a symbol of our perversions and deep desires. It is not "bad" since it is only part of our own nature. In addition, both have domains in our lives: domains that cannot be detached from our own existence.

The Black Venus could be seen as the liberation of the magician at the deepest levels. Since even being sterile in the material world, it becomes fruitful in the higher worlds. In this case, as soon as it becomes fertile up and barren in the worlds below, we might even say that if we are able not to see the world with passion, this very world would not perhaps present its charms but rather some kind of empty reality and without purpose or hope. The Black Venus gives us many of the visions of the Black Diamond, since it gives us ways to see the world differently, for the changes that occur with our passions and experiences, gives us a new vision at every epoch and every learning, through direct experimentation and not only in theories and idealizations, even though such experiences can often come in a negative way. With each new form of seeing both reality and other realms of manifestations, we are closer to wisdom and therefore able to see yet another face of the Black Diamond.

Our passions are important and deserve to be lived.

Moreover, given the conservatism and vision of all that gives us pleasure and knowledge would be a sin, as the monotheistic institutions preached with their 'god of the book' (11) for millennia, we have been able to draw a comparative parallel of these conceptions. The purity of which would represent love, would be the religious one to the divinity and the fruitful love would be that turned to reproduction and with the aim of establishing the foundations of the 'family' as an institution. Therefore, values and ideals (considered pure and superior) would be above the desires, pleasures and even the experiences of each individual: here we include clarifications and knowledge about himself, the body, the senses and, thus, life itself as an individual. The Black Venus could be equated with our liberation as beings in a world of senses to be explored, without presenting the moral or social limits, which even though it may lead to the loss of the individual in the midst of his desires and excesses, is also shown as a powerful guide to self-knowledge and the knowledge of others. This does not extend only to the physical, since innumerable experiences, especially when we speak of the Left Hand Path, are given through darker and dense energies, making us plunge towards the depth of seas and often meet in dense waters, dark, solid, and much deeper, like the unexplored abyss of the oceans of our world.

Thus, the knowledge derived from the Black Venus is indispensable for the Walkers, either as a source of pleasure or suffering, love, passion or hatred and sadness; Because everything is mixed with its limits in a tenuous, often gray, way.

In addition, as quoted by Dr. Thomas Karlsson, the Black Venus is fruitful in the higher plane. This fact is due to the liberation of the mind and spirit of the magician on the material, mental and spiritual level. The liberation of concepts and shackles imposed by society or its creation is religious or moralistic, undoes the shackles that trap the soul and mind of the magician, enabling him to fly, like the Ravens of Dispersion. In this way, the Magician is able to absorb and to create in the higher planes, since it destroys the last mental ties to reach flight towards the kingdom of subtlest manifestations in the less dense planes. There, the magician discovers his own power and is able to be reborn again, this time not as a worldly or as a child of the material plane, but as a divine descendant, son of the stars and son of the Gods.

As in the Nephilim narrative, in the apocryphal 'The Book of Enoch' (12), the angels decide to take the daughters of men for them, and from this union the Nephelin race is born, powerful beings bearing divine and mortal blood superior to the common humans. Not only that, of these unions between the angels of heaven and the daughters of the earth, countless knowledge and wisdom were passed on to men, as well as a way to rebel against the tyrannical rule of the god of lies, of illusion, giving independence and power to Mankind, against the will of the god of the book, as I discuss in my last essay "The Secret Fire of Azazel" (13). Therefore, when the magician gets rid of his fetters and succeeds in taking flight, dividing himself into countless ravens, he will begin to understand the world around him and the other realms of manifestations in a completely new and different way, things of innumerable different forms, knowing how to look under various points of view, one for each eye of the ravens, that is, of his soul: for his soul will be expanding in several directions and will reach senses and new discoveries never imagined before. His soul will be able to assimilate different visions and in a certain way will be able to merge with other beings, and thus, almost as with a Famulus (14), will be able to see through the eyes of others, and then understand the world under a new Point of view, different from his own.

This rebirth, like the Nephilim, can even be observed in the allegory of some traditional witches regarding to the so-called "witch-blood", "fairy blood", "The People" (15), among other denominations for Those who possess "the blood," being even compared as descendants of Qayin and also descendants of the Fallen Angels, as in the myth of the Nephilim. Such allegories, although this is not the space for a deep discussion about that, still belong to certain groups of beliefs and worldviews.

In this way, it is possible to draw a parallel between what we see as divine offspring - be it profane, heavenly or both - and what we see as a reconquest of rights, as if we were doing a "Path of Return", where we claim our right to be Gods, where we could, for example, use the biblical myth of Genesis, where it is said that God says that man is "one of us" and "that we should remove him from the tree of life, because if he ate it, he would live forever" (16). Therefore, the right to not only see the world with the eyes of a God, but also the search for eternal life and our divine condition would be part of our search. The Path of Return would be the move in the opposite direction of the existential flow of mortality, making the way back to our ancestors - the Gods - to recover our initial divine condition.

Just as the apotheosis of the Serpent is the Dragon, our Apotheosis is to become Gods.

Here, A'arab Zaraq is completed, among all the points worked and understood in a theoretical and practical way. Some people will have greater understanding than others and at first everything really works grossly. The Ravens of Dispersion will always be flying in countless directions, however, few are those who will absorb back each liberated part of their own soul. Most people disperse their souls for futile things and absorb useless and sterile information throughout their lives. These people are sheep: they do not know what they do, or where they are, just that they must do the same thing every day in a sterile and meaningless routine. These people are limited and are not able to expand their souls, but only to disperse them in daily entertainments and obligations, without even understanding, to enjoy, let alone reach beyond their worldly limits.

The magician, the wanderer, must be able to expand his soul and cast it beyond the horizon, beyond the limits of his own vision, to explore all that is unknown. Thus he is able to reach new knowledge, visions and even initiations with his ravens scattered in all directions, to know, to see and to collect all sorts of information, to then receive each of his ravens (his soul) back. Thus wisdom is born.

Without proper focus, the dispersion of the Ravens becomes only distraction, and the individual would live in an eternal limbo, like the majority of the population, where only entertainment speaks louder than their lives of slavery and blindness.

Therefore, all those who decide to walk on the Crocked Path, be it forked as the serpent's tongue, tripartite as the Lady's Paths or in the four directions where in the middle lay the mysteries of the crossroads; must first be based not only on studies and readings - not subjugating their importance! - but from real life experiences, throwing yourself into new situations and searching to try new things, as well as understanding, analyzing and living new perspectives.

The Path does not belong to those who only specialize in their theories, for although it is very important for the knowledge and development of each individual, it would become useless without its application or practice. Moreover, it is advisable to always observe all that is known, not to fall into the vice of crystallizing its certainties about our world or other realms of manifestations, whether in its operation or in its nature, whether it is flexible or absolute: everything is Change and every situation brings us new perspectives, so the certainty is almost never a constant; But doubt itself is the key to the search for the truth or for all that is true, even if ephemeral.

In order to absorb the wisdom of this shell, brought by the Ravens - by its own expanding soul - one must always keep one's mind open and always consider, even briefly, any other possibilities, however remote they may seem. For it is always good to remember that only the ignorant is certain of everything; The Wise is the one who always has doubts.

Therefore, the multifaceted Black Diamond will not be reached in a single place, at a single time, like a covered statue that is suddenly revealed in some exposition. No, it will be gradually revealed according to the footsteps of the wanderer, sometimes confused with its reflection, sometimes contemplating the darkness of its faces. At every step on the Path, its faces will be discovered, and even in the deepest darkness, the Walker will be able to see its light. For the Darkness is the true Light. ✦

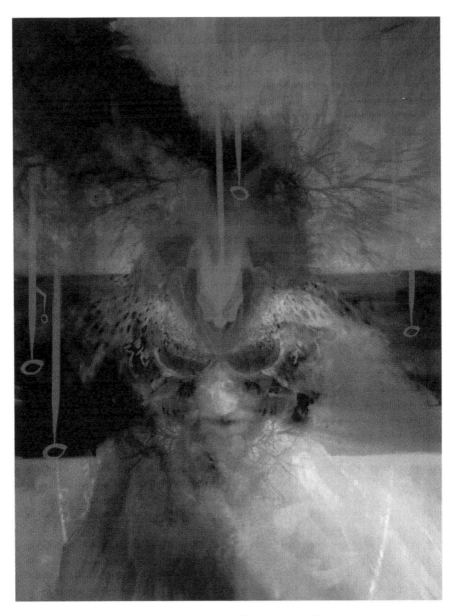

Sean Woodward, *The Vampires Are Here*

Shub-Niggurath Necromancies

Necro Magickal

SHUB-NIGGURATH, the Black Goat of the woods, is commonly perceived as an energy-entity of earthen and sexual natures. She is believed to be ruler of fertility and procreation. Magicians within contemporary occult society normally employ Shub-Niggurath for rituals of manifestations dealing with fleshly and material desires. Her primary function deals with sexual sorceries and the realization of the emotions and lusts attributed to these innate drives within human nature. Shub-Niggurath, beyond rare exception, is considered a feminine force. There is a contention that the deity is hermaphroditic, but evidence for this is lacking to support this possibility. Within the infamous Cthaat Aquadingen, Shub-Niggurath is referred to in both a male and female context. The title "Ram with a thousand ewes" has also been said to be a title for the male aspect of the deity. Of course these references did not originate with Lovecraft, and he did not associate gender to the beast. Despite this fact, the association of gender to Shub-Niggurath will normally be one of individual preference in accordance to the individual esoteric need. The attributing of gender to non-human and hence trans-gendered forces can be troublesome, and is ultimately irrelevant beyond fitting the needs of the individual working with that energy. It must be understood that all of the deities in the mythos are extraterrestrial, and may not easily fit into human gendered categories such as male and female. The quantitative association of human gender to these forces may be one laced with error, misinterpretation, and personal prejudice. Despite these possibilities, the need for gender often is one of magical practicality suited to the sexual preference of the performer.

Despite the natural sexual preference, the association of a feminine gender to the deity does transcend that of simple human sexual, emotional, and psychological need. The feminine attribution of Shub-Niggurath is more cosmically aligned and not limited to mere humanity. It is one corresponding to a (multi) universal association of the manifestations and emanations of the creating mother force and doctrine, be this of a natural or extraterrestrial source.

With the association of female gender to the deity, Shub-Niggurath is then corresponded with the natures of that gender, namely the sexuality and fertility as relating to the (human) female. Yet it is believed that the deity holds more to these natures than is commonly perceived by both the scholars and occultists of the mythos. Although the feminine gender is agreed upon, the essence and correspondences take on a much darker aspect. Shub-Niggurath is seen as a Goddess of a perverse creation, and of a macabre malevolent sexuality, one resulting in manifestations of material, fleshly, and earthen forces affected by her very extraterrestrial natures. Most often, these manifestations and expressions of the deity will be perceived as mutated, dying, and or dead once integrating its true extraterrestrial natures with humanity and earthen forces. Such interpretations are seen as direct results from the non-human natures of the deity interacting like a contagion when introduced with human/earth spheres.

It is comparable to the seemingly adverse effects from the introduction of a foreign agent to an observed source within a laboratory experiment. The contaminate aspects of the non-human natures originate from the vibrations of the deity and the forces they represent and embody. There are reasons for such adverse and unusual reaction from contact between humanity and the extraterrestrial. Each deity within the mythos represents universal forces that ultimately transcend the known universe/dimension. Each deity radiates different qualities, frequencies, and elements into, and through these realms. These radiations and energies generally are not wholly attributable to known elements and forces within the realms of mankind. They will be related to those non- human realms and whatever states of being and sciences inherent to those dimensions.

The results and toxic probabilities of these trans-human forces within the planes of humanity may essentially be theoretical, but it is safe to assume that the forces of these realms, their vibrations and radiations specifically within the planes of mankind, may be associated with various radioactivity, electro-magnetic, and nuclear forces. Such forces are normally harmful to human contact in the physical. Mutation, sickness, and death will result from over exposure to these types of forces. Such contagion will infect not only the physical realms of humanity, but extend to the astral and magical as well. This is not to say that every magical incident involving summoning/exposure to the mythos deities will result in sickness and or death on some level to the sorcerer. This would be an oversimplification and misinterpretation of doc-trine and its metaphysical sciences. Experience within occult Lovecraftian lit-erature gives plentiful evidence otherwise.

What is presented here is that exposure to the magical/astral aspects of these forces will in time and unless some form or proper protection is em-ployed, results in some kind of mutation of the essential being of the sorcerer that may or may not evolve their being/consciousness. Any infections may not be external, nor may they manifest in some easily diagnosed manner within those working with these forces. Psychological illness is another pos-sibility regarding exposure to trans-human forces. We see evidence of psy-chological contamination within the fiction of the mythos. Madness often be-falls those dark sorcerers invoking the various deities in the tradition. The best negative example of such a contagion in the "real" world connected to the mythos is within that of Lovecraft himself. It may be theorized that the invading cancer within Lovecraft was a result of his prolonged exposure to these extraterrestrial forces being channeled through his consciousness. This is purely speculation which I deal with in depth in forthcoming material. Ul-timately a mix of luck, statistic, and individual genetic strength will always play a factor in one's successful safe interaction with these forces.

In most cases exposure to these radiations may simply result in what may be called esoteric mutation within the individual, and not have any physical ramifications. Esoteric mutation is nothing more than the altering and ad-vancement of one's magical and astral evolution from contacting these forces.

It is something experienced and received through achieving contact with that force that affects not just one's consciousness, but ones very multidi-mensional essence. A merging of ones being, magical or otherwise, with forces outside of themselves will act like an alchemical experiment. A union of two separate forces will infuse the two with aspects of the other. It is a natural exchange that may be found in all of nature regardless of any supernatural aspects. Such non-physical/magical alterations are attributable to the fact that most interactions with the mythos deities are performed within magical and non-physical realms. Such nonphysical exposure thusly will have greater effect on one's various non-physical levels, but physical ramifications are not ruled out. Such mutations are an integral part to experiencing the gnosis and illuminations attributed to that deity within the magical contact. Any perceptible alteration to ones being is a telltale sign that one's workings have been successful and something has definitely been contacted.

The integration of the resulting natures of the deity is part of the gnosis of Shub-Niggurath, known as the "gnosis of esoteric nuclear mutation". It is an illumination where one experiences the power and beauty within the horrific manifested in astral/physical flesh, something not new to the occultisms of man. Summoning the monstrous into ones magical sphere enables one to destroy the limitations of human perceptions and interpretations. It is invoking the ability to perceive beyond the normal and embrace the hidden powers concealed within the horrific. The metaphysics of the horrific would be too detailed to deal with here, but let it suffice to say that it is integral to not just Shub-Niggurathian necromancies, but is at the core of all of the magic of the Necromantic Lovecraftian tradition that will be dealt with in forthcoming publications.

In regards to Shub-Niggurath, her radiations and their associated inflictions rule her correspondences of fertility, sexuality, and procreativity. She is an alien fertility Goddess responsible for the influx of mutation and abomination, forces outside of natural order into the material world through these formulas. The results of her radiations affecting the material world are the presence of all form of monstrous creation in the known universe. We see this within one of her epitaphs as the "mother of abominations". As such, she rules the unbalanced flow of extraterrestrial forces into the universe. As a Mother Goddess of procreative/sexual natures, Shub-Niggurath represents the primal will and urge of these forces outside of nature, outside the gates of the star of cosmos, to emanate and become expressed within the phenomenal universe. These extraterrestrial urges to emanate and manifest in the cosmos gives the deity as a ruler of the union between the beauty of form and the horror of its mutation by esoteric nuclear forces.

Upon the glyph of the Tree of Life, Shub-Niggurath is positioned at the zone of Netzach, the seventh sphere. Netzach, as well as the number seven, are ruled by the planet Venus, again hinting at the adverse sexual natures of the deity. Unto this planet is also attributed the creative imagination, something suggesting in its darker sense, the (auto-erotic) practices involving the manifestation of the abominations of the deity into the various planes. It also implies the primal desire and urge to become objective within the various sentient and phenomenal planes. The trans-mutated aspects of Venus within the microcosm of the human, affect those sorceries dealing with all forms of love, lust, and procreation in ways most would consider negative yet they express nothing but influences from beyond the star and tree. The Venus natures here express the formulas of Shub-Niggurath manifestations via the (magical) copulation between the horrific and beautiful. It is one resulting from the desires inherent in the seventh sphere on the tree. The unbalanced flow of the extraterrestrial forces from beyond and outside of the tree secreted through the seventh sphere poison the continued flowing into creation. This mutates the healthy formation of matter within the next three spheres upon the tree. This is represented by the glyph of a warped seven pointed star, the seal of Shub-Niggurath, representing the infection of the lower seven spheres of matter and flesh by the unbalanced radioactive vibrations unleashed into the world.

The unbalanced flowing and manifestation of these forces in the physical and astral worlds are represented by the offspring of Shub-Niggurath. These are most commonly known as her "Dark Young", her children and resulting emanations into the lower seven spheres. Interestingly in the mythos, the offspring of Shub-Niggurath, as well as her own description on numerous occasions, are described as writhing masses of hoofs, tendrils, and cloudlike masses. Such physical descriptions are suggestive of the malformation of form and linear concepts. Shub-Niggurath as a Goddess of procreation is thus the ruler over all forms of birth defect, miscarriage, and stillborn death. Shub-Niggurath also rules over the mortalities of mothers occurring during the birth process. These aspects of the Black Goats domain generally result from the mother's inability to fully handle the (nonhuman) energies manifesting within labor. In these cases, the extraterrestrial energies, those originating outside of the seven frontal spheres, consumes the pregnant host taking her human life force into another plane of existence. Those human (female) adults dying from these forces become initiated into what is known as the Astral Corpse Coven of the Black Goat, something I deal with in great detail in forthcoming material.

These disembodied priestesses rule over the same energies that took their human life and are intimately connected to the perpetuation of these mortalities and the various functions that they represent in a cosmic sense. These are all examples of otherwise normal natural energies coming into contact with abnormal unnatural forces. Within the physical planes these manifestations and deaths are observably horrific. Yet when no actual physical manifestation is born, their astral and dreamscape aspects are generated with even more monstrosity. We find ample evidence of the horrors of interstellar crossbreeding within extraterrestrial and UFO lore.

The Dark Young are born through the unbalanced extraterrestrial forces intermixing with the phenomenal world. Microcosmically this is the intercourse between the forces of the deity and human kind whether metaphorical, magical, or physical. The sphere of Netzach itself rules the sexual pairing between human and non- human energies thus implying the types of abominations manifesting from such forbidden and unnatural unions. Although the energy that the offspring vibrate and embody does exist independent of human interaction, humanity does plays a vital role in generating sentient Dark Young within the dimensions perceivable by human consciousness in both its normal and magical sense. In terms of magical sexual copulation via with the deity, the effects with and exposure to her radiations, will differ dependent upon the gender of the human interacting with her as well as a number of other factors such as skill and both physical and astral genetic strength. Both genders may experience non- physical mutations as well as any possible madness or mental illnesses resulting later, yet these latter are very rare outside of the fictional aspects of the mythos. Unlike normal birth, both genders may in turn generate Dark Young within the non-physical planes through both polarized and autoerotic sexual formulas. Within males, the energies manifested during arousal and the semen ejaculated may be used in the generation of offspring. Dark Young may be generated and reanimated in the astral through the formulas of the sorcerer(s) and the corpse/necrotic energy associated with whatever dead human host utilized in the working. It should be understood that those Dark Young energies made sentient in the various planes of humanity are done so through the use of dead physical/astral human vessels. These vessels are infused with magical energy from the priest or priestess merged with the original extraterrestrial radiation. They are then reanimated into non-physical existence as offspring of the deity.

The mutative nature of the vibrations and forces of Shub-Niggurath with its obvious correlations to sexuality, fertility, and procreativity has relevance and affinities to the menstrual mysteries. The main factor in its correlation is that the menstrual energies interfere with the normal progression of procreative/life energies successful manifestation. It is the blood of the darkened priestess, in both its biological and magical form that mutates the seed-energies completion of its urge to formulate matter/cosmos. This may of course be interpreted on a micro and macrocosmic level within both the physical and metaphysical womb. We find numerical correspondence between the Black Goat and the dark cycle as well. The number thirteen has deep significance to the menstrual lore as well as being the number of letters within the full English spelling of the name of Shub-Niggurath. The term "Black Goat" may itself be a veiled reference to the black or darkened feminine.

On a practical level, many of the rites of Shub-Niggurath utilize the dark cycles of her priestesses for rites of both the Black Goat and her offspring. It is during this time that the priestess is most open to receiving and transmitting the energies of the current. Although rites of the deity may be performed without the presence of menstrual energies/fluids, its presence does add power to the workings. This is true especially during invocation by the priestess. During her dark cycle, the priestess may invoke Shub-Niggurath into her mind and body, channeling the energies through her seven psychic centers. Such successful channeling transforms the innate psychic energy within these zones into Shub-Niggurathian energy centers or kalas within the priestess. These kalas are the combination of different energies correctly focused within the female host during her dark phase. The alchemical mixture of the menstrual energies and the invoked extraterrestrial elements generates a powerful force that may be focused and projected by the priestess for various relevant ritualistic ends. The physical fluid manifesting during such invocations becomes charged with the relevant energies becoming a wine or elixir of the Black Goat. This fluid has several magical uses foremost those dealing with reanimation of the dead into Dark Young in the astral realms. It has proven to be a more powerful physical and psychic medium than "normal" sexual fluids due to its innate destructive tendencies. Use of all forms of sexual fluids has been employed in these rites with varying success, but those utilizing the wine of the Black Goat have always brought greater success.

The menstrual mysteries are connected to the esoteric symbol of the goat whose anus or eye is symbolic of the priestess in her dark cycle. The eye is the darkened vulva that emanates the radiations of the deity through the living feminine host. The eye, vulva, mouth, and anus are all related and significant to the mysteries of Shub-Niggurath. The eye as the Hebrew Ayin, meaning literally "eye", corresponds to the twenty-sixth path upon the tree known as "the renewing intelligence". Interpreting this in the light of Shub-Niggurathian metaphysics, the renewing intelligence represents the reanimation mysteries attributed to the necromantic formulas involved in the generating of offspring of the deity. The numerical value for Ayin is seventy, a number equated with "wine" and "night", two words loaded with significance to the current topic. Seventy also is the number for "SVD" or "secret", again illustrating the secretions of the deity through the seventh sphere into the cosmos. One of the titles of Ayin is "child of the forces of time". This appellation hints at the formulas of generation of Dark Young (child) through the use of the kalas of the darkened priestess (forces of time). Ayin is also given the title "Lord of the gates of matter", a title also given to the Devil or the goat of Capricorn as the officiator of the Sabbath. The eye, as the anus of the goat of the Sabbath, rules the illuminations received via kissing the buttocks of the goat/devil in the Osculum Infame. Through this kissing, or invocation of the adverse currents, one sees the true natures and powers within the horrific and monstrous. One then perceives the true natures of the malformed mutated gnosis of Shub-Niggurath. Another significant aspect of the twenty-sixth path is that it rules the knees. This implies the beastly (non-human) mode of sexual intercourse suggesting the mode of copulation with Shub-Niggurath. Copulation in this manner deals with primal urges unleashed, those urges flowing through the sphere of Netzach with its union between beast (extraterrestrial) and man or the horrific and beauteous. The Were-formulae and lycanthropic rites become apparent connecting themselves to Shub-Niggurath in this respect.

The uses for the Shub-Niggurathian necromantic current are ultimately dependent upon the individual sorcerer. The main reason to work with these energies is to experience the macabre illuminations contained within its mutative and deathly natures. This is at the root of the Lovecraftian necromantic agenda, and the necromantic paradigm of the Black Goat. Her energies manifest in nature in an unnatural manner, yet they hold phenomenon that may be accessed and utilized in positive ways by those looking deep enough. The energies of Shub-Niggurath are not practiced in a necromantic sense by most within modern occult traditions. It is a tradition with a very limited audience.

Most limit their interpretations and experiences with the deity to the common denominator of classifications. Most will shy away from viewing the deity beneath a necromantic paradigm. Some may see this doctrine as one of a tasteless and insensitive position. Simply it is not a system for everyone. Whether these macabre interpretations are correct or valid by occult, moral, or ethical standards is a futile argument. It, like all reality, is only as valid as those observing and interpreting its natures. The necromantic paradigm of Shub-Niggurath is something that has been discovered, worked, and proven to keep its own illuminations. There is an extant and accessible current within its unsettling and grieving aesthetics. Its gnosis has proven to be many things to those with the predisposition to its natures. It holds a fascinating, unusual, and even useful purpose within a magical context. This and this alone is its validity as a magical system. ✦

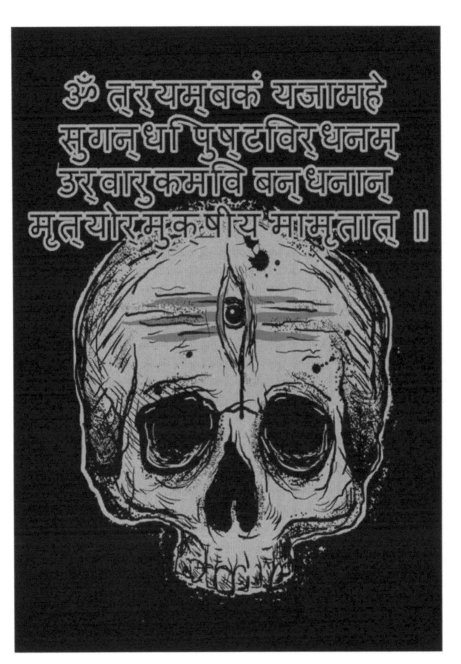

Anderson Silva, *Aghori Cult II*

Rite of the Three Norns

Darren Taylor

HEN most think of Norse magick it is rare they think about it in a Qliphothic perspective. Most will think of the wandering Völva's or the story of Odin and the runes but in my time as a practicing Vitki (Norse Shaman & Sorcerer) I have discovered that Qliphoth relates in many ways to some of our rituals and practices. It does not relate directly as the Norse and the Jewish did very little mingling however through the eye of magick and ritual there are similar aspects. In Qliphoth we have the tree of life, the world tree in a different state. Instead of it being relative to the actual tree that branches out from the earth it is more in relevance to the roots of the tree which descend into the earth. Some call it the reversal of the tree but I prefer to see them as the both apart of the same tree but going a different direction.

In Norse Mythology and magick we have the three Norns who weave the web of reality. Urðr, Verðandi and Skuld. The three Norns are so powerful that not even the Gods can sway them. They are the weavers of reality and time. Urðr is the Norn of that which has already happened. Verðandi is the Norn of the present moment or that which is. Finally, Skuld is the Norn of that which is yet to come but also necessity. While time to many is not a liner construct less so in the spiritual world the Norns are at the deepest levels of the Yggdrasil (the tree of life) at the well of Urd (the well of all knowledge). Just like in other traditions the Norse have similar tree to the tree of life. We call it Yggdrasil and there are many associations be it mental, spiritual, or physical that they relate to it. However, in my own way and exploration I have learned never to challenge the law of polarity which in this case suggests that there is a reversal or rather the roots of the tree itself presenting a more Qliphothic style element. We have the aspect of Yggdrasil that reaches up to Asgard (the home of the Aesir Gods) which can also be seen as the divine element of the mind however we do also have the darker in nature aspect which descends into the deepest levels of our consciousness, that is much darker in its nature. The darker hollow of ourselves that we try to suppress or neglect. I believe as a Vitki it is an essential element for us to embrace as a shaman does not just embrace life but death, not just light but dark.

In light of this correspondence I have discovered the Norns themselves exists on this darker plane of the Yggdrasil. The well of Urd which also exists in this darker plane is the well of all knowledge, the very conduit that Odin himself peered into while hanging from the tree to discover the runes. The well of Urd is of all knowledge, dark, light, life, death etc. In this view, it would contain all those truths we want to oppress and shut away, the things we despise about our own self. I would also say it is in this same place we have suppresses our own godhood or at least an important aspect, and so for the well of Urd to be on this level of Yggdrasil wouldn't be too far of a stretch. However, from this there are a few things that we can take from it.

In light of this all there is a ritual that has been written about the three Norns that I have had the pleasure of looking into. The rituals original purpose was after a long time of preparation and setting up the magician or in my case the Vitki would through blood magick call upon the three Norns. The Vitki would then be allowed to ask but three questions as well as have the Norns impart some knowledge to them that would help them on their journey. With beings as powerful as the three Norns it is not a far stretch to say this is to most very enticing.

Origins of the Rite

I came to know this ritual by my friend who had in his possession a very interesting grimoire. He was close with another Norse Vitki who had passed away and before he passed he gave to my friend the grimoire that he either wrote and created himself or was passed onto him. When my friend told, me I was skeptical to say the least. However, once he described the ritual to me and outlined it I could see a lot about the mechanics that would make such a ritual work. The ritual itself needed a lot of work both on the immersive aspect as well as the psychological aspects. I have re-created this ritual and touched up of the parts that were originally very weak and unnecessary. Magick itself is an art and like a fine cooked mean you never add in anything that isn't necessary or doesn't add anything to the flavor so to speak. I would also note that it is important to remember that all rituals while have fundamental grounding and guidelines that tailoring it to the individual's needs are important and so with this ritual be sure to check everything and make sure it fits for you personally.

Rite Prep-Work

The first thing I want to make clear is that this ritual is not a ritual you are going to complete in a day or even a week. This ritual is a nine-month long process approximately and throughout it you are going to need to set aside time to go through each particular step. You will need to put in a lot of effort to reach the end result and some parts of this ritual are dangerous so make sure at every point you are taking that into consideration. This ritual uses sigil magick, blood magick, rune magick, Galdramyndir casting, evocation, and trance. There is a great deal of meditation and Seidr (shamanic journeying) not to mention fasting, body stressing factors. I highly recommend planning each step on a calendar to make sure you know exactly when and where you need to perform certain parts.

Prerequisite Work

Before you even begin to start working on this rite you are going to have to gather all the materials necessary. This is a pretty long list and there are some thing needed that you may have to either go and get yourself or purchase; some of these materials can be expensive. However, I will note this is not a ritual you are going to want to do often. It is intended to do this once in a lifetime and the time, money and materials will not be able to be used again after this so I would suggest not using any of your magickal tools that you wish to keep using after this. Additionally, I would only use ritual tools that are intended for this specific rite and they should not be used for any other magickal work. For this entire process, you are going to need:

1. Candles: 33 Large Black, 33 Large White, and 33 Large Red.
2. Incense: 33 Myrrh, 33 Patchouli, 33 Dragons Blood.
3. White Cotton Cloth: 9x9 Feet.
4. 25 Lancets
5. 24 Pieces of Black Parchment & 48 Pieces of White Parchment

6. White Chalk
7. Entire Bear or Wolf Pelt
8. 3 Deer Skulls (Fully Intact)
9. Vitki's Tiver
10. Thick Paint Brush
11. One Black Onyx Stone
12. One White Quartz Stone
13. One Bloodstone
14. Four Large Birch Sticks (Big enough to stick into the ground)
15. Large Piece of Rope (around 20 feet)
16. 3 Bottles of Mead (Honey, Raspberry & Blackberry)
17. Norn Amulet

This is only a rough list of the essential things however if during the ritual, you want to include ritual tools remember that they need to be dedicated to this ritual and they will not be able to be used after this rite is finished.

Vitki's Tiver

Vitki's Tiver is very simple to make and is somewhat of an ink or paint for the Vitki to use. It is not used to write letters but rather to draw or paint sigils and symbols. It does not apply to every sigil as certain sigils require different colors but this ink is used more with runes and pact sigils.

To make this ink you will need:

1. Red Ocher Powder
2. Linseed Oil
3. Lancet
4. Container

To make the tiver you prick the index finger of the left-hand mix a few drops of blood with a small amount of red ochre powder in a bowl, then add a few mls of raw linseed oil and mix with the brush into a smooth but fairly runny liquid. As you mix these ingredients together visualize it glowing red. Finish off the tiver by breathing Ond onto it nine times.

Norn Amulet

The Norn Amulet is a special amulet that this process is intended to empower. While this ritual is not focused on the creation of this amulet it is one of the things you will have empowered and be able to use in your magick work afterward. The amulet itself must be made by you.

To make this amulet you will need:

1. Small Bone (Chicken Bone works perfect for this)
2. Vitki's Tiver
3. Small Brush
4. Black Cloth (big enough to wrap around the entire amulet.
5. Long Piece of Red Ribbon/Cotton (big enough to wrap around 9 times)

Steps:

1. For the first step of this you will have paint with the Vitki's Tiver a small symbol onto the bone. This symbol is the Norn sigil.
2. As you draw the sigil visualize energy flowing through your body to the hand. As you paint visualize the symbol glowing red.
3. With the Sigil painted onto the bone amulet let it dry completely, and then breathe onto the sigil nine times.
4. Wrap the amulet completely with the black cloth and wrap the red ribbon around it nine times and then tie it.
5. With the amulet wrapped project your voice onto the wrapped amulet: Amulet of the Norn I cast you into the darkness of Gunningagap, there to there to grow and thrive with the energy until this process ends.
6. Keep the amulet in a safe place and every time you do a ritual for this nine-month rite process take the amulet with you but do not uncover it until the final day.

Journey to the Norns

The entire nine-month process to finally evoke the Norns is a journey. Throughout the entire process, you will be creating elements to use in the final ritual as well as conditioning yourself for the ritual itself. This journey is a journey of runes. For this big leg of the journey you are going to be using many candles, many incenses, and your own blood.

For each rune, you are going to work on them for 9 days. You are going to go through the runes in order, starting at Fehu and ending at Dagaz. Unlike the actual Rune work of the Vitki you will be doing this at night time under the moon. All of this process must be done at night. As such wearing black or dark colors for this ritual is a must.

Each rune will be done in the same way and they will be painted with the Vitki's Tiver onto the white cloth. The first step is to draw two big circles onto the cloth. Make them as big as you can upon the cloth. You will need two circles so the runes can be drawn between the lines of the circle.

You will always start facing south which is where the first rune will be drawn and as you go to paint each rune you will slowly begin to move anti-clockwise from south to east, to north, to west and then back to south. As a final point, you will be using the Elder Futhark runes.

9 Days of Rune Work

Each rune will be worked in exactly the same way so follow this process from beginning to end with each rune.

1. On the first day, you will One black candle, One white candle, and One Red Candle. The candle must be large so that it can be re- lit each day for 9 days. The daily rune work itself will take around one to two hours so make sure the candle is at least a 24-hour candle just to be safe. Additionally, you may want to keep a container handy to store anything that does not get fully used up in practice.

2. First thing after lighting the candles is to draw the first rune in whichever direction that rune is. Fehu will start directly facing south and the rest will slowly move around until all the runes are done and your back at south. Additionally, ever day place the wrapped amulet inside the circle as you do your ritual work. With the rune painted Galdr (vibrate) the name of the rune 3 times, 6 times, and then 9 times. This must be done every day for 3 days. Blow out the candle every time you finish the daily work and re- light at the beginning of every new day of practice. On the first three days, you must do a complete fast. No drinking or eating while

the sun is down. After you have vibrated the runes sit and meditate. Visualize the rune glowing red and enhancing is power. Do this for an hour.

3. Day four, Day five and Day six, you do not need to fast. On these days, you won't need to vibrating the runes. Sit and meditate in the circle with the rune and visualize pushing some of your own energy or life force into the rune. Do this for at least half an hour. Additionally, on the sixth day draw that particular rune in chalk on black parchment. Fold it and then fold two pieces of white parchment over the top of it. Light, it on fire and let it burn to ash. Take all the ashes you can and pat them onto that particular rune.

4. Day Seven, Eight and Nine you must fast and vibrate the tones just like on day one. Meditate with the rune just like the first three days and afterward call upon that particular rune.

(Name of Rune)... I call upon you here now within this circle. Let your power be absorbed into these markings and may this circle radiate with your power.

5. On the ninth day prick your index finger on the left hand and let the blood drip onto the rune. Visualize the rune coming to life and activating. With the rune bloodied light one stick of Myrrh, one stick of patchouli and one stick of dragon's blood. Let the ash fall onto the rune.

Each rune has to be worked with 9 days consecutively, without any breaks in between. However, between each rune taking three days to rest and recover is recommended.

Between the Runes & the Norns

The rune work will take up a lot of this process and by the end every rune will be empowered and the circle will be ready for use however there is still a few things to do in between the runes and the final rite of the Norns. You will have to find a secluded place in nature to do this, a place you will not be disturbed and you are going to have to bring every necessity you will need with you. Food, water etc you will have to take it all, not to mention all the ritual tools. For the time, in between I would suggest getting that ready.

At this secluded place, you are going to have to dig yourself a big hole, around 9x9 feet long at least. It has to be big enough to place the circle inside of it. Inside of this hole you will place your circle inside of it. In the center of the circle you will place the bear pelt. This is where you will be sitting. Place the skulls of the deer around the circle on outside of the circles lines. One skull should be at facing you from south, the other two will be at east and west all looking into the circle. In front of the skull places the stones. Blood stone is at south, quarts is at east and onyx at west. Place the blackberry mead bottle to the west, honey to the south and raspberry to the east. Additionally, take all the left-over candles and materials from the ritual here, this whole is going to be the place where they are desecrated and offered.

With the hole dug and everything in it in place, place the four birch sticks into the ground at each cardinal point. They must be placed outside of the hole you have dug. With the rope tie it to each birch stick. The rope must go around all the branches and link them together. This is an allegory for the web of wyrd.

You will be staying at this location for some time so be prepared for a tough journey and make sure to bring enough supplies with you. For nine days before the ritual just sit in the circle and visualize it all glowing red. Do this for an hour each day as you prepare for the final rite. The day before the ritual do a 24 hour fast. You can drink water but let nothing else pass your lips if you can.

The Final Rite

With all the prep work done you are now ready for the final rite. This should land exactly 9 months after you started if possible, if not then on the ninth month will suffice. Begin at night.

1. Begin by lighting the red of the candles and the incense. Red candles and dragons blood incense should be at the south, white candles and patchouli should be at the east and black candles and myrrh should be at west.

2. With the tiver paint the sigil of the Norns onto each skull and visualize them glowing red. Additionally if you are able to paint it on your body and head.

   Take the lancet and prick the index finger of your left-hand, let the blood drip onto the circles and onto the skulls. Open up the amulet from the black cover and place it directly in front of you. You should be facing the south direction.

3. Call out to the three Norns:

    Urðr, Verðandi, Skuld I call upon you here and now. Join me in this circle which I have created in your name, Rejoice in my blood, my offerings and my dedication. Sit with me so we may speak.

    Call this out 9 times and then go into meditation. Allow yourself to be immersed into trance. Rock back and forward, take in the incense, take note of all the feelings you feel. Visualize everything coming together and open yourself up to the Norns. It is here you will vocally ask your questions.

4. With the Norns called meditate for as long as you can: hours if possible. Aim to journey down the Yggdrasil, starting at Asgard and going all the way to the roots. From the top to very bottom where you will be at the well of Urd. Ask your questions again. Sleep in the circle with only the bear pelt to cover you. It is better to go into sleep while already in trance as this will induce the dream you will want to remember. It also helps to bring a journal to write everything down. Sleep with the amulet near you.

5. Wear the amulet around your neck and exit the ritual circle. Throw all of the ritual components into the circle, open up the mead and pour them onto the circle, place in all the candles that never burned out completely. Put the rope and the branches in too and cover the whole back up with the soil you dug out. The only ritual component you will be taking away from you is the amulet.

6. If you haven't received your answer from the Norns there and then, it will most likely appear in synchronicity throughout the next coming weeks, so pay attention to what is going on around you. Different people have different experiences with rituals such as these so expect the unexpected. This rite is as much of an initiation as it is an evocation. ✦

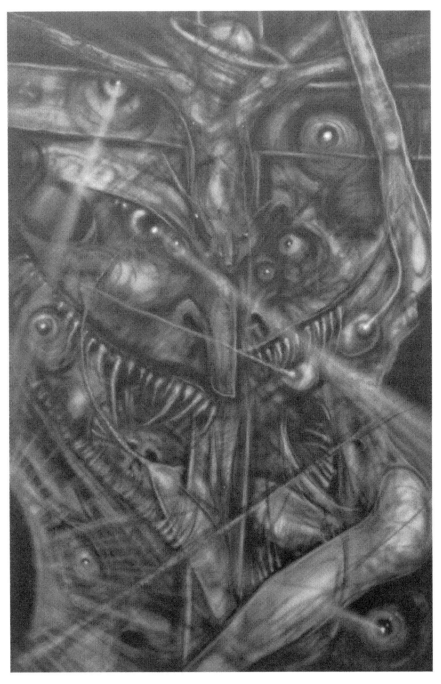

Barry James Lent, *Black Mass One*

The Son of Belial

J.A. Perez

WORKING with Belial has been an interesting experience. He is an entity not underestimate with and does not take "No!" for an answer. He has come before me several times. He has requested to work with me, but at the time I was devoted to Lucifuge Rofocale and later Azrael. When I then considered Belial, he told me to break all ties with the others. I, then, released Lucifuge and Azrael and committed to him. He told me that he wanted to take me to a higher level of spirituality as well in the mundane world. Belial did not reveal much, but to place my life in his hands. I thought for a moment that it would be dangerous just to, blindly agree with Belial. I didn't know what to expect. So, in order to understand each other, and to define the agreements; we had the terms and conditions written to understand Belial's intention, and my commitment. There were, of course, a few things that I requested in exchange of him managing my life. Even though, I could work with others spirits, Belial had dominion over my spiritual path and mundane life. It felt, above all, that Belial's main concern was over my ascent more than anything else.

Over the years I have worked with angels as well as demons. There are many criticisms about working with evil spirits. All I know is that my personality or intentions of the world have never been malignant. In fact, the reasons why I work with any spirits in many distinct paradigms are basically for self-defense. I have to improve my lot over the years, but it has always been the same motif on enhancing my-self, ascension. Before judgment and ridicule is cast unto me or others, look at the evidence of what goods and services the spiritual entities have to offer. In the end, before I take my last breath in this world, I will find out the truth once I depart from this world. Until then, I will explore the possibilities without living the life of "What if's..."

Who is Belial? In the *Goetia* it states:

The 68th spirit is called Belial, he is a mighty king and powerful; he was Created next after Lucifer, & is of his order; he appeared in ye forme of a Beautiful angel sitting in a Chariot of fire, speaking with a comely voice, declaring that he fell first & amongst ye worthier & wiser sort which went before Michael & other heavenly angels; his office is to distribute preferment of senatorships, and to cause favour of friends & foes, he giveth Excellent familiars & governed 80 Legions of spirits. Note this kink [! king] Belial must have offerings sacrifices & gifts presented to him, by ye Exorcist or else he will not give True answers to his demands; But then he Tarryeth [will tarry] not one hour in ye truth except [unless] he be constrained by divine power & his seal is Thus which is to be worn as a Lamin, before ye Exorcist.

Belial may be seen as an angel rebelling for the sake of autonomy. His freedom has been projected of something that is corrupt and unworthy, but in whose eyes? The hierarchy of any or all institutions or organizations stems by controlling every facet of the individual in question. Every entity is an agent of power and may be procured by binding it, manipulating it, threatening it and/or ostracizing it. Every single creature whether it be living or spiritual are created with an intentional program through their DNA of the spirit. A living creature at whatever frequency or vibration they exist cannot fully function as many were intended to be or become. Belial is not a force who chose not to follow the rules, but by acting as an independent agent working through or by consensus as an associated power. It is through the process of "Disinformation" that the perception of the masses which ignore and avoid Belial, as something that is evil and dark.

The rage within Belial stems from rejection by not conforming to a schematic plan without the option of an agreement. Due to the 'Great Divine Plan,' there was no room for negotiations, no room for partaking and providing feedback, no room for inclusivity while acting independently. The parties became polarized not because the spiritual entities chose to rebel, but because there was not room for growth. Freedom and boundlessness was not a philosophy, belief, or of value, but of being.

When we see individuals acting in a non-conform way, we see them as individuals acting out their malicious intent of rebelling. Others may call it a counter culture, but why through non- conformity? It is the act of being that many can project who they are. They tend to be in the minority when they are compared to the majority; when it comes to habits, customs and traditions. While these individuals illustrate their authenticity, others perceive it as corrupted, abnormal behavior.

Working with Belial has been amazing. The path that he has led me on has been steady. There is a path of progress and ascension. Although, life and circumstance has tried to derail me and have frustrated me at times, but it is as if I am automatically placed back on the path. It is unusual because usually it takes me a while to correct the fabric of my reality when I have to constantly summon spiritual entities that may take days and even weeks to feel some normalcy. The constant tug of war of life in the shifting of polarities exhibits that other individuals, whether they use their own energy or spiritual entities, rearranges the reality that I am enjoying. These circumstance veer towards the people who are maximizing their gains, therefore, having others experiencing scarcity. These polarities lead to further in grain in society with opposition, contradiction, paradox, ambivalence, dichotomy, and duality. The power that individuals or groups of people exercise, in the form of a Majority party, can deplete resources and opportunities from the minority without any form of trade or transaction restricting their happiness through oppression.

Now, just because it seems that I may be on easy street doesn't mean I don't want more. As I worked with Belial, he, in his own way, has demonstrated that he is busy for me to be calling in for special requests. So, I meditated and ask if he could send forth an entity to assist me in the little extras that brings comfort into my life.

He instructed me to sit in silence. I offered him Frankincense and lit some candles and closed my eyes. As I sat still, enjoying the aroma of the Frankincense and slowly relaxing, a fiery bright red light pierced through the veil of darkness. An image of a being with massive wings, blinded by the light, the spirit as foretold by Belial was revealed.

My experience on receiving this spiritual being was not something that just happens. Meditation plays a major role on experiencing this phenomenon. Usually, the way I meditate is that I close my eyes. I take several deep breaths. I can either bring in a white light in every section of my body as I take deep breaths, or use the practice of opening of the chakras. There are several ways and/or methods of relaxing the body and mind, especially the mind. A successful form of meditation brings you to brink of falling asleep. Knowing that I am close to the Theta brainwave I end up yawning a lot. It is as if you are almost about to drift into sleep, and then, contact. The mind once relaxed, becomes the medium of channel communication, whether they use words in a language, symbols and/or signs. Once you are in a relaxed state, verbally state your intention or desire into the ethers. It might take a minute or a moment until an entity communicates in a jargon that is most understood by the magician through a form of expression. When this occurs, make sure you have a paper and pen ready to write down anything that has been articulated. After you come out of a successful and effective meditation, you may lose some or all information if it is not dictated quickly. It usually feels as if you had or were in a dream and can be easily forgotten once you are fully awake or conscious.

Now, the reveal... The spiritual entity that appeared in my meditation became more and more unambiguous as his presence was illuminated by his aura. In my discernment, the entity strongly resembled that of an angel. This angel had four wings. A pair located behind his back while the other pair of wings, although unusual, located upon his chest. Each pair of wings had a single white and black wing. The wings were unusually great in size covering his entire form. The only visible figure was his forehead. It had a symbol marked on his membrane bone and a laurel wreath worn on his head like a crown. The angel would operate in a form of contagion. The angel would irradiate a radio- vibratory frequency not only to the person summoning the spirit, but linked to the creator, Belial. What I realized at the moment was the notion was not only an individual linking to Belial, but a coupling of sorcerers. When a spiritual operator calls forth this angel, whatever the conjuror requests the others are affected as recipients. A network benefiting from others desires. In other words, it is as if the magician not only asked for him/herself, but as if he requested for others indirectly. This connection with the spiritual energy creates a ripple effect to all who has called on him as a beneficiary.

My friend, Walter Fritsche, meditated and summoned Faul'Kalore to get to know him. On encountering the spirit and exchanging information, this is what Walter offered as feedback: "Okay so I will write everything now so I don't forget. This is what I have. Faul'kalore was human once. He worked with Belial to create wealth for himself and even though he has his own powers, he summons/uses the powers of the house of Belial to amplify his power. He also mentioned that once a person dies, if he chooses to, he can align themselves with a grand spirit, and go into their house, thus having access to their power. Once this happens, you lose your human name and are given many new names.

Walter then gave me an elaborate detail of the summary provided above:

Today, 11:05 a.m., 11/30/16
Below is my experience with a little more detail:
I decided to talk to him by meditating on the sigil and calling his name. That's when i saw him sit right in front of me, i couldn't see his face well. All saw was his silhouette. Faul'kalore appears thin but muscular, i could see the bulging arm muscles of a thin but very toned man. The silhouette also showed that he has wings, soft round edges like those of angels. His voice was calm and easy, i would even go as far as saying it was lighthearted. I stated that i wanted to know who he is, i wanted to know his story and his abilities.

Faul'kalore was human once. He worked with Belial to create wealth for himself when he was mortal. Now, even though he has his own powers, he summons the powers of the house of Belial to amplify his power. He also mentioned that once a person dies, if he chooses to, he can align themselves with a grand spirit, and go into their house, thus having access to their power.

Once this happens, you lose your human name and are given many new names. These names will be used throughout time to call upon the new spirit. This is how he came to be.

As for his powers, Faul'kalore said he can influence businessmen and people of power to give one, access to power and wealth. He gave me specific instructions to go meet with potential clients, he said these meetings have to be in person, and that he would do the rest when called.

Throughout our conversation, there was a sense of deep calm, he didn't claim to be an angel or demon, but the sensation of his presence is that akin to an angel.

Walter's observation was a powerful one. Even though, Faul'kalore created an image of a superior angelic/demonic being, his powers then were amplified by the House of Belial. Belial is well known of affecting circumstances as aforementioned in his description. A powerful entity as Belial can open roads, paths and opportunities to reap the spoils and/or enjoy the benefits as a patronage.

It is truly a revelation to discover that a human being can choose to associate with a power house exercising free will. Most of the stories always dictate that an individual does not have a choice. Individuals, like many of us, may be frustrated of whether or not we end up in heaven, purgatory, or hell. As a person chooses freely in which jurisdiction to reside, this person emerges with a new identity.

Faul'Kalore can be summoned in so many ways. First option is through candle magick. Inscribe his sigil on the glass candle or carve into it. Prefers a yellow candle or anything that you may have available, and Frankincense is the type of incense he would like the magician to offer.

Second option: Sigil Magick. Lit a yellow candles and frankincense. Draw Faul'Kalore sigil on paper of your own choosing. Either anoint the sigil with your own blood, or stare at the sigil until it appears as it illuminating. State your desire and fold it and put it away until it materializes.

Third option: Evocation. Lay a magical circle of your preference. You will summon Faul'Kalore from the South. Lay yellow candles around the circle and lit Frankincense as an offering and fumigate the area.

Since it is creating a positive outcome, you will walk clockwise until you are ready to summon him. Chant his name as many times preparing yourself psychological and emotional to receive him.

In all these three options, Belial gave me an incantation to summon Faul'Kalore. This incantation can be used until you feel the presence of the spirit.

Incantation:

E Nomine Justo e Suerte, Padre e Hijo,
Belial, Faul'Kalore!

In conclusion, while Belial is working on my personal ascent, this grand spirit felt that it was wise for me to pursue some of my personal interest by working with one of his own, his son. Faul'Kalore, a surprisingly and interesting spirit, came to my aid to assist me in my personal endeavor. I was lucky enough to share this new spirit with my friend, Walter Fritsche, who not only provided his own personal experience of meeting Faul'Kalore up close and personal, but I would like to thank him for the art design he contributed based on my visions through my personal revelation. I invite all magicians to call forth Faul'Kalore, the Son of Belial, to work on your ascent and endeavor. May your wish come true and fulfill all your desires. Be well my friends.

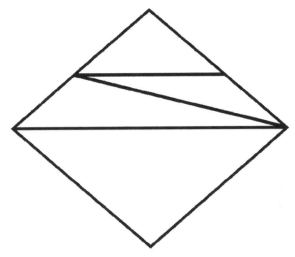

The Sigil of Faul'Kalore

The Symbol Upon Faul'Kalore's Forehead

Sean Woodward, *Ikon of Zos Kia*

𝔊argophias:

𝔄tavisms from the 𝔖hadows

Edgar Kerval

THE Gargophia's atavistic shadows formula emanates the phallic power of this tunnel, but not from the solar perspective, rather through the Lunar Kalas emanating from the eye of the phallic awakening generated through the use of the phallic eye as a vulva to rise the lunar energy of Gargophias as the catalyst that open the paths for the reception of diverse powers below this tunnel. When the eye of Gargophias is opened, the adept bath his/her soul with the turbulent waters of the void. The adept is transformed in a primal vessel of the void to focus the essence of Gargophia's path, that must be drunk through a process of self-transformation, becoming the sacred vessel consecrating his/her soul to the great purpose as is the transmigration of the lunar seed in the tunnel itself.

Its totem is a black phallus representing the genitalia of Shaitan – set and its connection within the tunnels, and the eye representing the vessel of Lunal Kalas of Gargophias that incubates the primal seed to be transformed in the adept. The symbolism behind the phallus with the eye inside opening, is a generator of the aspects of the self-procreation, giving birth to diverse psychic powers in the adept when exploring the mysterious Kalas of Gargophias. The Gargophia's obsidian gate is filled with the Lunar Kala and through this, the tunnel teaches us the importance of feminine energies and the exploration of our deepest elements from subconscious. The totemic atavisms of the shadows of Gargophias generates the fluid transmigration of adept's body into astral darkness that keep the gates of this tunnel filled with a powerful potential that can be developed through technics of magickal dreams.

Here the adept will learn to control their magical powers when dreaming. In some point, the adept awakens the eye of Gargophias and is able to transport him/ herself to other tunnels highly connected with the essence of Gargophias. The techniques of lucid dreaming give the adept access to special powers that may include the ability to transform in a Toad covered by the shadow of the Egyptian goddess Hekt, opening the vessels for the connection with inter-dimensional entities through the temples in the 13th zone of power. The self-fertilization of Lunar Kala developing from the deepest regions of the tunnel where the seed is incubated and spit as venom over the purple sea of the void, in which resides mostly of the powers of Gargophias. Some of my records of Gargophias workings come from descriptions of lucid dreams or similar states of consciousness triggered by hallucinogenic potions. Lucid dreaming may enable the adept to enter altered states of consciousness and access to other realities.

Amphibious atavisms that enter our dimension from the primal portal of ingress via the 13th tunnel that help the adept in the self-fertilization of the black egg that is found in the Lunar Kalas of Gargophias. To work with Gargophias is to awaken the power of the most primal feminine aspect in man. The power of clairvoyance and contact with amphibian spirits, the creative side and artistic expressionism is what you must explore when working deeply with this tunnel. Once you develop your rituals with Gargophias, the tunnels are open, and then the adept increases the capability of astral navigation into those spaces between the tunnels. The key to the gnosis of Gargophias consist in assimilating as possible the diverse atavistic shadows and forms during the exploration of the apex of the temple's gate, and absorbing the essence of the sacred toad through the Kalas. These are then reconstituted into rituals s which can best allow the adept to come into align with the signs and symbols, that appear during the astral projection at the tunnel.

The formula of the arcana of Gargophias must be focused to focalize the revelation of the stele of the tunnel. Just feel free to sit in a comfortable position for some minutes and observe the phallic seal of Gargophias and burn a single candle, and visualize the phallic seal and see how the transformations of sensorial alignment are focused and moving around the candles flame in order to projects your mind to the 13th temple, where resides the power of Gargophias. The direct experience through the tunnel will be manifested through dreams. Also is of a high importance to complement them with the sensorial manifestation revealed during the exploration of gate's temple. ✶

Become A Living God

Publisher

T HE definitive motto of human transcendence: Become A Living God welcomes magickians to maximize their individuality, freedom, and personal power in this lifetime. Browse a catalog of courses, rituals for hire, physical grimoires, talismans, consultations, and readings at BecomeALivingGod.com.

Books by and featuring author Edgar Kerval:

NOXAZ, VOLUMES 1 & 2

Edgar Kerval, Asenath Mason, Bill Duvendack & more

QLIPHOTH: THE COMPLETE SERIES

Edgar Kerval, Asenath Mason, Bill Duvendack & more

COMPENDIUM OF AZAZEL, VOLUME 3

E.A. Koetting, Kurtis Joseph, Asenath Mason, S. Connolly, Edgar Kerval, Bill Duvendack, Frank White, J.S. Garrett, J.D. Temple, Orlee Stewart & W.J. Oliver

COMPENDIUM OF LUCIFER, VOLUME 2

E.A. Koetting, Kurtis Joseph, Edgar Kerval, Bill Duvendack, Asbjörn Torvol & Frank White

COMPENDIUM OF BELIAL, VOLUME 1

E.A. Koetting, Kurtis Joseph, Asenath Mason & Edgar Kerval ✦

Made in the USA
Middletown, DE
22 October 2022

13284871R00345